High Performance SQL Server

Consistent Response for Mission-Critical Applications

Second Edition

Benjamin Nevarez

Apress®

High Performance SQL Server: Consistent Response for Mission-Critical Applications

Benjamin Nevarez
Santa Clarita, CA, USA

ISBN-13 (pbk): 978-1-4842-6490-4
https://doi.org/10.1007/978-1-4842-6491-1

ISBN-13 (electronic): 978-1-4842-6491-1

Managing Director, Apress Media LLC: Welmoed Spahr
Acquisitions Editor: Jonathan Gennick
Development Editor: Laura Berendson
Coordinating Editor: Jill Balzano

Cover image designed by Freepik (www.freepik.com)

Distributed to the book trade worldwide by Springer Science+Business Media LLC, 1 New York Plaza, Suite 4600, New York, NY 10004. Phone 1-800-SPRINGER, fax (201) 348-4505, e-mail orders-ny @springer-sbm.com, or visit www.springeronline.com. Apress Media, LLC is a California LLC and the sole member (owner) is Springer Science + Business Media Finance Inc (SSBM Finance Inc). SSBM Finance Inc is a **Delaware** corporation.

For information on translations, please e-mail booktranslations@springernature.com; for reprint, paperback, or audio rights, please e-mail bookpermissions@springernature.com.

Apress titles may be purchased in bulk for academic, corporate, or promotional use. eBook versions and licenses are also available for most titles. For more information, reference our Print and eBook Bulk Sales web page at http://www.apress.com/bulk-sales.

Any source code or other supplementary material referenced by the author in this book is available to readers on GitHub via the book's product page, located at www.apress.com/9781484264904. For more detailed information, please visit http://www.apress.com/source-code.

Printed on acid-free paper

This book is dedicated to my mother,
Guadalupe Chavez

Table of Contents

About the Author

Benjamin Nevarez is a database professional based in Los Angeles, California, who specializes in SQL Server query tuning and optimization. He is the author of four books, *Microsoft SQL Server 2017 on Linux, High Performance SQL Server, Microsoft SQL Server 2014 Query Tuning & Optimization*, and *Inside the SQL Server Query Optimizer*, and has also coauthored other books including *SQL Server 2012 Internals*. Benjamin has also been a speaker at many SQL Server conferences and events around the world including the PASS Summit, SQL Server Connections, and SQLBits. His blog can be found at `www.benjaminnevarez.com`, and he can also be reached on Twitter at @BenjaminNevarez and Facebook at `www.facebook.com/ BenjaminNevarez`.

About the Technical Reviewer

Mark Broadbent is a Microsoft Data Platform MVP and Microsoft Certified Master in SQL Server with more than 30 years of IT experience and over 20 years of experience working with SQL Server. He is an expert in transaction processing and concurrency control and a lover of Linux, Development, and Cloud Computing. In between annoying his long suffering wife Lorraine and being beaten at video games by his children Max and Lucy, he can be found blogging at `https://tenbulls.co.uk` and lurking on Twitter as @retracement.

Acknowledgments

First of all, I would like to thank the people who directly helped me write this book, starting with everyone on the Apress team. Thanks to Jonathan Gennick, for giving me the opportunity to originally write this book and for encouraging me to write a second edition, especially on the difficult and uncertain times when we all were involved in a global pandemic. Thanks to Jill Balzano, coordinating editor, with whom I worked almost on a daily basis. I would also like to thank my amazing technical reviewer, Mark Broadbent, who did an incredible job providing feedback about every chapter of the book.

I always also like to thank the people who indirectly helped me in this and all my previous books—the people who I learned this technology from by reading their books and academic papers, including Kalen Delaney, Michael Stonebraker, Goetz Graefe, Ken Henderson, and Sunil Agarwal, just to name a few. Thanks go out as well to the people in the SQL Server community from whom I also learned a lot. The long list of names would be impossible to include here.

Finally, thanks to my family, my sons Diego, Benjamin, and David, and my wife Rocio. Thanks again all for your support and patience for the many evenings and weekends I spent on yet another book-writing adventure.

Introduction

I've been blogging and presenting about query tuning and optimization for years. I even wrote a couple of books about this topic: *Inside the SQL Server Query Optimizer* and *Microsoft SQL Server 2014 Query Tuning & Optimization*. Query tuning and optimization are extremely important for the performance of your databases and applications.

Equally important is having a well-designed and configured system in the first place. SQL Server default configuration can work fine for some applications, but mission-critical and high performance applications demand a thoughtful design and configuration. Well-written and tuned queries will not shine if a system is not properly configured. For example, queries will not use processor resources in an optimal way if a maximum degree of parallelism setting is not configured correctly. Database performance will suffer if a database is using the default file autogrowth settings or if the storage is not properly configured. A misconfigured tempdb database may show contention on many busy systems. Even the query optimizer will struggle with a bad database design or badly written queries. These are just some common configuration problems out there in real production systems.

In addition, even when a well-designed application goes to production, performance tuning does not end there. Monitoring and troubleshooting are an extremely important part of an application and database life cycle since performance problems eventually will arise. Workloads may change, hopefully for the better (e.g., an application having to deal with an unexpected increase on business transactions). Sometimes, those changes will require a redesign, changes, and perhaps new configurations.

So this is, in fact, an iterative process, consisting of design and configuration, followed by implementation, monitoring, and troubleshooting, which again may lead to new designs or configurations, monitoring, and so on. In addition, collecting performance data, creating a baseline, and performing trend analysis are an important part of a production implementation, not only to troubleshoot problems but also to anticipate issues or understand future growth and additional requirements. It is essential to estimate and trend those changes proactively instead of waking up to a system suddenly having trouble in handling changing workloads or, even worse, to face a downtime that could have been avoided. There are several tools to help with this process, including the Query Store, a tool which was introduced with SQL Server 2016.

I spend a good part of my daily job working on all these items, so I decided to write a book about them. I wanted to cover everything you need to know about performance in SQL Server that does not require you to know about query tuning, work with execution plans, or "fight" the query optimizer. There are so many areas to cover, and more are being added as new features and technologies appear on SQL Server such as In-Memory OLTP, columnstore indexes, and the aforementioned Query Store.

This book covers all currently supported versions of SQL Server with a major focus on SQL Server 2019. Although this is a performance book from the practical point of view, understanding SQL Server internals is very important too. The best way to troubleshoot something is to know how it works and why things happen. Consequently, I focus on database engine internals when required.

Finally, this book complements my query tuning and optimization books. If you are a database developer or a SQL Server professional who cares about query performance, you could benefit from reading both these books as well. If you are a database administrator, a database architect, or a system administrator, and you want to improve the performance of your system without query tuning, you can read only this book.

Since I mentioned that implementing a high performance database server is an iterative process, consisting of design and configuration, followed by implementation, monitoring, and performance troubleshooting, I have decided to separate the chapters of the book in four parts: SQL Server Internals, Design and Configuration, Monitoring, and Performance Tuning and Troubleshooting. I tried to separate the chapters on these areas, but I am sure some chapters may overlap with more than one of those categories.

As mentioned earlier, understanding SQL Server internals is important to better optimize a system and troubleshoot database problems, so this book starts explaining how the SQL Server database engine works and covers everything happening in the system from the moment a connection is made to a database until a query is executed and the results are returned to the client. Chapter 1 includes topics such as the Tabular Data Stream (TDS) and network protocols used by SQL Server, SQLOS, and the work performed by the SQL Server relational engine, focusing on query processing and the most common query operators. A new chapter on this second edition, Chapter 2, covers SQL Server on Linux. Starting with SQL Server 2017, SQL Server is now available on Linux and can also be run on Docker containers. This chapter covers the SQL Server on Linux architecture and how the database engine works on this operating system.

Part 2, Design and Configuration, includes Chapters 3 and 4. Chapter 3 explains a number of instance-level configuration settings that can greatly impact the performance of your SQL Server implementation. As an interesting fact, it shows how some trace flags originally introduced to solve a particular problem are now implemented as SQL Server configuration defaults.

Chapter 4 covers tempdb configuration, which is especially important as such a database is shared between all the user and system databases on a SQL Server instance. Focus in the chapter is given to tempdb latch contention of allocation pages and tempdb disk spilling, a performance issue that occurs when not enough memory is available for some query processor operations.

Part 3, which focuses on monitoring SQL Server, covers analyzing wait statistics and the Query Store. Waits happen in a SQL Server instance all the time. Chapter 5 introduces the waits performance methodology, which can be used to troubleshoot performance problems, especially when other methods are not able to pinpoint a performance issue.

Chapter 6 covers the Query Store, a very promising query performance feature introduced with SQL Server 2016. The Query Store can help you to collect query and plan information along with their runtime statistics, which you can use to easily identify query performance–related problems and even force an existing execution plan. The chapter closes by mentioning some related new features such as the Live Query Statistics and the SQL Server Management Studio plan comparison tool.

Part 4, Performance Tuning and Troubleshooting, includes the five remaining chapters of the book and covers topics such as in-memory technologies, indexing, intelligent query processing, and disk and storage.

In-memory technologies are introduced in Chapter 7 and include In-Memory OLTP and columnstore indexes. Both features suffered severe limitations with their original releases, so this chapter covers how these technologies work and what their current improvements are. The chapter ends with operational analytics, which combines both technologies to allow analytical queries to be executed in real time in an OLTP system. In-memory technologies promise to be the future in relational database technologies.

Chapter 8 shows how proactively collecting and persisting performance information could be extremely beneficial to understand how a specific system works, to create a baseline, and to understand when performance is deviating from a desirable or expected behavior. The chapter also covers the most critical performance counters, dynamic management objects, and events, along with some of the tools used to display and collect such data. This chapter surely overlaps with Part 3, Monitoring.

Indexing, a required topic for database performance, is covered in Chapter 9, which explains how indexes work and why they are important on both OLTP and Data Warehouse environments. The chapter provides emphasis on using SQL Server tools to help create indexes such as the missing indexes feature and the more sophisticated Database Engine Tuning Advisor.

Another new chapter in this second edition of the book, Chapter 10, provides an overview to intelligent query processing, a collection of features introduced with SQL Server 2017 designed to improve the performance of your queries. The intelligent query processing features provide performance enhancements with no application changes needed and little or no effort required.

Finally, SQL Server storage is explained in Chapter 11. Disk has traditionally been the slowest part of a database system, but newer technologies such as flash-based storage offer great performance improvements and are becoming a de facto enterprise standard as their cost continues to decline. The chapter also indicates that storage optimization is not only about using the fastest disk possible but also minimizing its usage by implementing the methods covered in several chapters of the book, such as proper indexing or some query-tuning techniques.

PART I

SQL Server Internals

CHAPTER 1

How SQL Server Works

SQL Server default configuration allows you to run noncritical applications with little knowledge or administrative effort. This is especially true for applications running the lower Stock Keeping Units (SKUs) of the product such as SQL Server Express edition. However, for most production applications, you need to follow a database implementation cycle consisting of four steps: design, configuring, monitoring, and troubleshooting. This is extremely important for mission-critical applications where areas such as performance, availability, or security are an essential requirement. I want to emphasize that this is a cycle as well. Once these four steps are successfully completed and the application goes live, it does not end there. Monitoring is vitally important. As the workload, database, or application changes—or even during regular activity—problems will arise that may require a new thinking, design, and configuration, going back to the aforementioned cycle again. This book focuses on performance and will guide you through all the four areas, giving you the tools and knowledge required to get the best performance out of your databases.

Before getting into the four areas, this introductory chapter explains how the SQL Server database engine works and covers everything that happens in the system from the moment a client makes a connection using the Tabular Data Stream (TDS) protocol over a network protocol until a query is executed and the results are returned to the client. Although so many things could happen in the middle and may require an entire book to cover it, I focus on the work performed by SQLOS, the relational engine, which consists of the query optimizer and the execution engine, and other important performance-related factors like memory grants, lock, and latches. The content of this chapter is the foundation for the rest of the book.

This book does not explicitly cover query tuning and optimization, so you don't have to be an advanced query writer or understand execution plans to use it. This book can help database administrators, architects, and database developers to better understand how SQL Server works and what to do to fix performance problems. For information on query tuning and optimization, you can refer to my book *Microsoft SQL Server 2014 Query Tuning & Optimization* (McGraw-Hill Education, 2015).

© Benjamin Nevarez 2021
B. Nevarez, *High Performance SQL Server*, https://doi.org/10.1007/978-1-4842-6491-1_1

TDS/Network Protocols

SQL Server is a client-server platform in which a client usually establishes a long-lived connection with the database server using the Tabular Data Stream (TDS) protocol over a network protocol. TDS is an application-level protocol that facilitates the interaction between clients and SQL Server. Sybase Inc. initially designed and developed it for their Sybase SQL Server relational database engine in 1984, which later became a Microsoft product. Although the TDS specification does not define a specific network transport protocol, the current version of TDS has been implemented over the TCP/IP and Named Pipes network transport protocols. The Virtual Interface Architecture (VIA) network protocol was deprecated but still available on older versions of SQL Server. It was finally removed with SQL Server 2016.

Note   You can also use the Shared Memory protocol to connect to an instance of SQL Server, but it can only be used to connect from the same computer where the database engine is running; it cannot be used for access from other computers on the network.

TDS provides several functions including authentication and identification, channel encryption negotiation, specification of requests in SQL and bulk insert operations, invocation of a stored procedure or user-defined function, and the return of data. Open Database Connectivity (ODBC), Java Database Connectivity (JDBC), and Object Linking and Embedding Database (OLE DB) are libraries that use TDS to transfer data between the client and SQL Server. TDS requests and responses between a client and SQL Server can be inspected by using different network protocol analyzer tools such as Wireshark. Another popular tool, Microsoft Message Analyzer (MMA), was retired as of November of 2019.

A SQL Server client can use TDS to execute the following request types when communicating with the database server:

- SQL Batch: To send a SQL statement or a batch of SQL statements

- Remote procedure call: To send a remote procedure call containing the stored procedure or user-defined function name, options, and parameters

- Bulk load: To send a SQL statement for a bulk insert/bulk load operation

Note that a stored procedure or user-defined function name can be requested through either a remote procedure call or a SQL batch. For more details about TDS, you can find the TDS specification at `https://msdn.microsoft.com/en-us/library/dd304523.aspx`.

TCP/IP is by far the most common protocol used by SQL Server implementations. The default TCP/IP port used by the database engine is 1433, although other ports can be configured and are in some cases required, for example, when running multiple instances on the same server. Some other services may use a different port. For example, the SQL Server Browser starts and claims UDP port 1434. When the SQL Server database engine uses a TCP/IP port different from the default, the port number has to either be specified in the connection string at the client or it can be resolved by the SQL Server Browser service, if enabled. The default pipe, `\sql\query`, is used when Named Pipes protocol is configured.

A client can use the following application programming interfaces (APIs) or libraries to connect to a SQL Server instance:

> ODBC: ODBC (Open Database Connectivity) is an open standard API based on the Call-Level Interface (CLI) specifications originally developed by Microsoft during the early 1990s. ODBC has become the de facto standard for data access in both relational and nonrelational database management systems.

> OLE DB: OLE DB (Object Linking and Embedding Database) is an API designed by Microsoft for accessing not only SQL-based databases but also some other different data sources in a uniform matter. Even though OLE DB was originally intended as a higher-level replacement for and successor to ODBC, ODBC remains the most widely used standard for database access.

> JDBC: JDBC (Java Database Connectivity) is an API developed by Sun Microsystems that defines how a client can access a relational database from the Java programming language. JDBC is part of the Java standard edition platform, which has since been acquired by Oracle Corporation.

> ADO.NET: ADO.NET (ActiveX Data Objects for .NET) is a set of classes that expose data access services and is an integral part of the Microsoft .NET framework. ADO.NET is commonly used to access data stored in relational database systems though it can access nonrelational sources as well.

How Work Is Performed

Now that we have seen how a client connects to the database server, we can review what happens next and see how the work requested by the client is performed. In SQL Server, each user request is an operating system thread, and when a client connects, it is assigned to a specific scheduler. Schedulers are handled at the SQLOS level, which also handles tasks and workers, among other functions. Moving a level higher, we have connections, sessions, and requests. Let's review schedulers, tasks, and workers by first introducing SQLOS.

SQLOS

SQLOS is the SQL Server application layer responsible for managing all operating system resources which includes managing nonpreemptive scheduling, memory and buffer management, I/O functions, resource governance, exception handling, and extended events. SQLOS performs these functions by making calls to the operating system on behalf of other database engine layers or, like in the cases of scheduling, by providing services optimized for the specific needs of SQL Server.

SQL Server schedulers were introduced with SQL Server 7 since before that version it relied on the Windows scheduling facilities. The main question here is why there is the need for SQLOS or a database engine to replace available operating system services. Operating system services are general-purpose services and sometimes inappropriate for database engine needs as they do not scale well. Instead of using generic scheduling facilities for any process, scheduling can be optimized and tailored to the specific needs of SQL Server. The main difference between the two is that a Windows scheduler is a preemptive scheduler, while SQL Server is a cooperative scheduler or nonpreemptive one. This improves scalability as having threads voluntarily yield is more efficient than involving the Windows kernel to prevent a single thread from monopolizing a processor.

Note   In *Operating System Support for Database Management*, Michael Stonebraker examines whether several operating system services are appropriate for support of database management functions like scheduling, process management, and interprocess communication, buffer pool management, consistency control, and file system services. You can find this publication online at `www.csd.uoc.gr/~hy460/pdf/stonebreaker222.pdf`.

Schedulers

Schedulers schedule tasks and are mapped to an individual logical processor in the system. They manage thread scheduling by allowing threads to be exposed to individual processors, accepting new tasks, and handing them off to workers to execute them (workers are described in more detail shortly). Only one worker at a time can be exposed to an individual logical processor, and, because of this, only one task on such processor can execute at any given time.

Schedulers that execute user requests have an ID number less than 1048576, and you can use the sys.dm_os_schedulers DMV (Dynamic Management View) to display runtime information about them. When SQL Server starts, it will have as many schedulers as the number of available logical processors to the instance. For example, if in your system SQL Server has 16 logical processors assigned, sys.dm_os_schedulers can show scheduler_id values going from 0 to 15. Schedulers with IDs greater than or equal to 1048576 are used internally by SQL Server, such as the dedicated administrator connection scheduler, which is always 1048576. (It was 255 on versions of SQL Server 2008 and older.) These are normally referred to as hidden schedulers and, as suggested, are used for processing internal work. Schedulers do not run on a particular processor unless the processor affinity mask is configured to do so.

The column max_workers_count on the sys.dm_os_sys_info DMV shows the maximum number of workers that can be created, and the active_worker_count column from sys.dm_os_schedulers shows the number of workers that are active at any given time. If you monitor this value, you can find out the maximum numbers of workers that are really used by your SQL Server instance. For example, running the following on my test system with 16 logical processors shows 512 maximum workers but only 32 active when the query was executed:

```
SELECT max_workers_count FROM sys.dm_os_sys_info
SELECT SUM(active_workers_count) FROM sys.dm_os_schedulers
```

A task is an execution request and represents the work that needs to be performed while a worker maps to an operating system thread (when the thread mode, the default, is used) or to a Windows fiber if Windows fiber (lightweight pooling) configuration option is used. Figure 1-1 shows the task execution process.

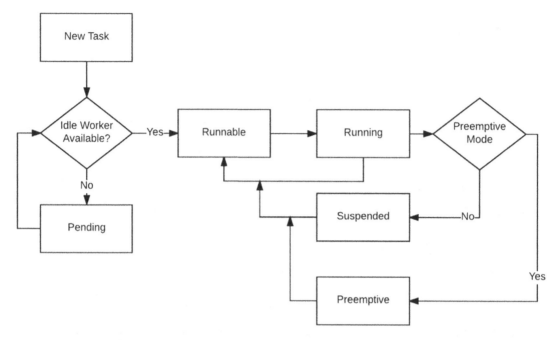

Figure 1-1. *Task execution process*

As mentioned earlier, in SQL Server, a scheduler runs in a nonpreemptive mode, meaning that a task voluntarily releases control periodically and will run as long as its quantum allows it or until it gets suspended on a synchronization object (a quantum or time slice is the period of time for which a process is allowed to run). Under this model, threads must voluntarily yield to another thread at common points instead of being randomly context-switched out by the Windows operating system. The SQL Server code was written so that it yields as often as necessary and in the appropriate places to provide better system scalability.

Figure 1-1 shows that a task can also run in preemptive mode, but this will only happen when the task is running code outside the SQL Server domain, for example, when executing an extended stored procedure, a distributed query, or some other external code. In this case, since the code is not under SQL Server control, the worker is switched to preemptive mode, and the task will run in this mode as it is not controlled by the scheduler. You can identify if a worker is running in preemptive mode by looking at the is_preemptive column of the sys.dm_os_workers DMV.

As indicated earlier, SQL Server by default will run in thread mode. An alternate choice is running in a Windows fiber mode. Running SQL Server in a Windows fiber mode is rarely recommended as it is only helpful for certain situations in which the context switching of the workers are the critical bottleneck in performance. In addition, Common Language Runtime (CLR) execution is not supported under lightweight pooling. The lightweight pooling server configuration option, which defaults to 0, can be used to enable Windows fiber mode, for example, by running the following statement:

```
EXEC sp_configure 'lightweight pooling', 1
```

The lightweight pooling option is an advanced configuration option. If you are using the sp_configure system stored procedure to update the setting, you can change lightweight pooling only when show advanced options is set to 1. The setting takes effect after the server is restarted. Of course, if you try this in your test environment, don't forget to set it back to 0 before continuing. Looking at the is_fiber column on the sys. dm_os_workers DMV will show if the worker is running using lightweight pooling.

Workers

A request can also use more than one worker or thread if parallelism is used. The task_ state column of the sys.dm_os_tasks DMV shows the state of a task, which has the following documented definitions:

> PENDING: Waiting for a worker thread
>
> RUNNABLE: Runnable, but waiting to receive a quantum
>
> RUNNING: Currently running on the scheduler
>
> SUSPENDED: Has a worker, but is waiting for an event
>
> DONE: Completed
>
> SPINLOOP: Stuck in a spinlock

Similarly, you can find additional information about tasks waiting on some resource by using sys.dm_os_waiting_tasks. We will cover waits in great detail in Chapter 5.

The default value for the "max worker threads" configuration option is 0, which enables SQL Server to automatically configure the number of worker threads at startup, and it depends on the number of CPUs and whether SQL Server is running on a 32-bit or 64-bit architecture, as shown in Table 1-1.

Table 1-1. *Max Worker Threads Default Configuration*

Number of CPUs	32-Bit Architecture (Up to SQL Server 2014)	64-Bit Architecture (Up to SQL Server 2016 SP1)	64-Bit Architecture (Starting with SQL Server 2016 SP2)
4 or fewer processors	256	512	512
8 processors	288	576	576
16 processors	352	704	704
32 processors	480	960	960
64 processors	736	1472	2432
128 processors	1248	2496	4480
256 processors	2272	4544	8576

Note   Starting with SQL Server 2016, the database engine is no longer available on a 32-bit architecture.

Workers are created in an on-demand fashion until the "max worker threads" configured value is reached (according to the value shown in Table 1-1 for a default configuration), although this value does not take into account threads that are required for system tasks. As shown earlier, the max_workers_count column on the sys.dm_os_ sys_info DMV will show the maximum number of workers that can be created.

The scheduler will trim the worker pool to a minimum size when workers have remained idle for more than 15 minutes or when there is memory pressure. For load-balancing purposes, the scheduler has an associated load factor that indicates its perceived load and that is used to determine the best scheduler to put this task on. When a task is assigned to a scheduler, the load factor is increased. When a task is completed, the load factor is decreased. This value can be seen on the load_factor column of the sys.dm_os_schedulers DMV.

Finally, SQLOS also has a scheduler monitor, which is a task that runs continuously whose function is to monitor the scheduler's health. It includes several functions like making sure that tasks yield at regular intervals, seeing that new queries assigned to a process get picked up by a worker thread, ensuring that I/O completions get processed in a reasonable time, and ascertaining that workers are balanced equally among all the schedulers. A problem with any of these may return SQL Server errors 17883, 17884, and 17887. The scheduler monitor also maintains a health record using a ring buffer that contains process and memory utilization information and can be inspected from the sys.dm_os_ring_buffers DMV as shown next.

```
SELECT timestamp, CONVERT(xml, record) AS record
FROM sys.dm_os_ring_buffers
WHERE ring_buffer_type = 'RING_BUFFER_SCHEDULER_MONITOR'
```

Note   A ring buffer is a circular data structure of a fixed size.

An example returned:

```
<Record id="6720" type="RING_BUFFER_SCHEDULER_MONITOR" time="1010852139">
  <SchedulerMonitorEvent>
    <SystemHealth>
      <ProcessUtilization>0</ProcessUtilization>
      <SystemIdle>99</SystemIdle>
      <UserModeTime>0</UserModeTime>
      <KernelModeTime>0</KernelModeTime>
      <PageFaults>0</PageFaults>
      <WorkingSetDelta>0</WorkingSetDelta>
      <MemoryUtilization>100</MemoryUtilization>
    </SystemHealth>
  </SchedulerMonitorEvent>
</Record>
```

Having reviewed schedulers, tasks, and workers, let's move to a level higher and discuss connections, sessions, and requests.

You can use the sys.dm_exec_connections DMV to see the physical connections to the database server. Some of the interesting information is found in the net_transport column, which shows the physical transport protocol used by this connection such as TCP, Shared Memory, or Session (when a connection has multiple active result sets, or MARS, enabled); protocol_type, which is self-explanatory and could have values like TSQL; Service Broker or SOAP; and some other important information like network address of the client connecting to the database server and the port number on the client computer for TCP/IP connections. There is a one-to-one mapping between a connection and a session, as shown in Figure 1-2.

Note   Schedulers, workers, and tasks are objects at the SQLOS level and as such are included in the SQL Server operating system–related DMVs, as compared to connections, sessions, and requests, which are included in the execution-related DMV group.

Session information is shown using the sys.dm_exec_sessions, which includes some important information that is helpful in troubleshooting performance problems like status of the session, the session values for some SET options, or the transaction isolation level used by the session. The possible documented values of status are as follows:

Running: Currently running one or more requests.

Sleeping: Currently connected but running no requests.

Dormant: The session has been reset because of connection pooling and is now in pre-login state.

Preconnect: The session is in the Resource Governor classifier.

Finally, sys.dm_exec_requests is a logical representation of a query request made by the client at the execution engine level. It provides a great deal of rich information including status of the request (which can be Background, Running, Runnable, Sleeping, or Suspended), hash map of the SQL text and execution plan (sql_handle and plan_handle, respectively), wait information, and memory allocated to the execution of a query on the request. It also provides a lot of rich performance information like CPU time in milliseconds, total time elapsed in milliseconds since the request arrived, number of reads, number of writes, number of logical reads, and number of rows that have been returned to the client by this request.

Note   The sys.dm_exec_session_wait_stats DMV, available since SQL Server 2016, can allow you to collect wait information at the session level. More details of this DMV will be provided in Chapter 5.

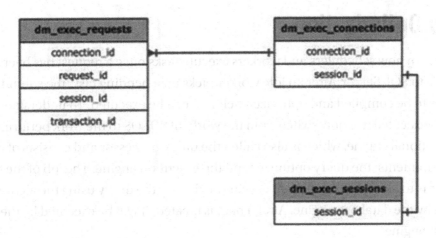

Figure 1-2. Execution-related DMV mapping

SQL Server on Linux

As you may probably know, starting with the 2017 version, SQL Server now runs on Linux, more specifically on Red Hat Enterprise Linux, SUSE Linux Enterprise Server, and Ubuntu. In addition, SQL Server can run on Docker. Docker itself runs on multiple platforms, which means it is possible to run a SQL Server Docker image on Linux, Mac, or Windows.

Although SQLOS was created to remove or abstract away operating system differences, it was never originally intended to provide platform independence or portability or to help porting the database engine to other platforms. But even when SQLOS did not provide the abstraction functionality to move SQL Server to another operating system, it would still play a very important role on the Linux release.

SQL Server on Linux is not a native Linux application but instead uses the Drawbridge application sandboxing technology. This means Drawbridge provided the abstraction functionality that was needed. SQL Server on Linux was born from marrying these two technologies, SQLOS and Drawbridge, and was the birth of a new platform abstraction layer later known as SQLPAL. How SQL Server on Linux works is explained in more detail in Chapter 2.

Query Optimization

We have seen how schedulers and workers execute tasks once a request has been submitted to SQL Server. After an idle worker picks up a pending task, the submitted query has to be compiled and optimized before it can be executed. To understand how a query is executed, we now switch from the world of SQLOS to the work performed by the relational engine, which is also called the query processor and consists of two main components: the query optimizer and the execution engine. The job of the query optimizer is to assemble an efficient execution plan for the query using the algorithms provided by the database engine. After a plan is created, it will be executed by the execution engine.

The first operations the query processor needs to perform on a query are parsing and binding, which are performed by a component called the algebrizer. The next step the query processor performs is the query optimization process. As shown in Figure 1-3, the query optimization process is basically the enumeration of candidate execution plans and the selection of the best of these plans according to their cost, using both cardinality and cost estimations. The SQL Server query optimizer is a cost-based optimizer, and although it uses rules to explore the search space plan, it relies on a cost estimation model to estimate the cost of each of the candidate plans and select the most efficient one.

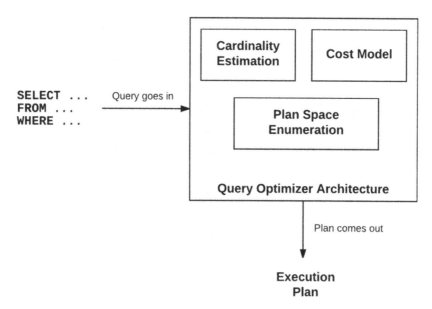

Figure 1-3. *Query optimizer architecture*

The relational engine implements a number of physical operations that are selected by the query optimizer to assemble an execution plan. So, in a simplistic way, query optimization could be seen as the process of mapping the original logical operations expressed in the initial tree representation to the physical operations implemented by the execution engine. Obviously, this is not a one-to-one operator matching and instead follows a more complicated process. Both logical and physical operations can be seen on each operator in an execution plan. For example, a logical aggregate operation has to either be mapped to a physical stream aggregate or a hash aggregate. On the other hand, a logical join could be mapped to a nested loops join, a merge join, or a hash join physical operator.

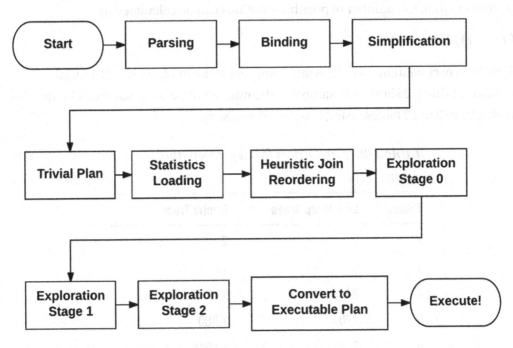

Figure 1-4. *SQL Server query processing process*

The query processing process follows several steps, as shown in Figure 1-4, although the main optimization process is performed by up to three exploration stages at the end. This is the part where transformation rules are used to produce candidate plans and cardinalities and costs are estimated. The optimization process does not have to execute all three exploration phases and could stop at any of them as soon as a good execution plan is found.

In addition to the query text, which at this moment has been translated into a tree of logical operations and the metadata related to the objects directly related to the query, the query optimizer will collect additional information from other objects like constraints, indexes, and so on, along with optimizer statistics.

As shown earlier in Figure 1-4, theoretically, in order to find the optimum execution plan for a query, a cost-based query optimizer should have to generate all possible execution plans that exist in that search space and correctly estimate the cost of each plan. Each of these operations is very complex, which is why query optimization is considered, using algorithm terminology, an NP-hard problem. So, it would be impossible for a query optimizer to perform an exhaustive search of all the possible plans as some complex queries may have thousands, or even millions, of possible solutions. For example, just considering the order of the joins in a query, depending on the tables to join, the number of possible solutions can be calculated as

```
(2n - 2)!/(n - 1)!
```

where both exclamation mark (!) symbols represent the mathematical factorial operation. Table 1-2 shows an example of the number of possible solutions for queries ranging from 2 to 12 tables, using two typical join shapes.

Table 1-2. *Join Orders for Left-Deep and Bushy Trees*

Tables	Left-Deep Trees	Bushy Trees
2	2	2
3	6	12
4	24	120
5	120	1,680
6	720	30,240
7	5,040	665,280
8	40,320	17,297,280
9	362,880	518,918,400
10	3,628,800	17,643,225,600
11	39,916,800	670,442,572,800
12	479,001,600	28,158,588,057,600

Note   Names like left-deep, right-deep, and bushy trees are commonly used to identify the shapes of the order of joins in logical trees. Left-deep trees are also called linear trees or linear processing trees. The set of bushy trees includes the sets of both left-deep and right-deep trees. For more details, you can look at my post at `www.benjaminnevarez.com/2010/06/optimizing-join-orders/`.

In order to explore the search space, a plan enumeration algorithm is required to explore semantically equivalent plans. The generation of equivalent candidate solutions is performed by the query optimizer by using transformation rules. Heuristics are also used by the query optimizer to limit the number of choices considered in order to keep the optimization time reasonable. The set of alternative plans considered by the query optimizer is referred to as the search space and is stored in memory during the optimization process in a component called the memo.

After enumerating candidate plans, the query optimizer needs to estimate the cost of these plans so it can choose the optimal one, the one with the lowest cost. The query optimizer estimates the cost of each physical operator in the memo structure, using costing formulas considering the use of resources such as I/O, CPU, and memory, although only the CPU and I/O costs are reported in the operators as can be seen later on the query plan. The cost of all the operators in the plan will be the cost of the query. The cost estimation is by operator and will depend on the algorithm used by the physical operator and the estimated number of records that will need to be processed. This estimate of the number of records is known as the cardinality estimation.

Cardinality estimation uses a mathematical model that relies on statistical information and calculations based on simplifying assumptions like uniformity, independence, containment, and inclusion (which still holds true for the new cardinality estimator introduced with SQL Server 2014). Statistics contain information describing the distribution of values in one or more columns of a table that consists of histograms, a global calculated density information, and optionally special string statistics (also called tries). Cardinality for the base table can be obtained directly using statistics, but estimation of most other cardinalities—for example, for filters or intermediate results for joins—has to be calculated using predefined models and formulas. However, the model does not account for all the possible cases, and sometimes, as mentioned earlier, assumptions are used. Statistics are, by default, created and updated automatically by SQL Server, and administrators have multiple choices to manage them as well.

Note   Most of the internal information about what the SQL Server query optimizer does can be inspected using undocumented statements and trace flags, although these are not supported by Microsoft and are not intended to be used in a production system. We will cover some of them in the rest of the chapter.

Since our interest in this chapter is to understand how SQL Server works, after this introduction, let us now review the query optimization process in more detail, starting with parsing and binding.

Parsing and Binding

As mentioned earlier, parsing and binding are the first operations performed when a query is submitted for execution. Parsing checks the query for correct syntax, including the correct use of keywords and spelling, and translates its information into a relational algebra tree representing the logical operators of the query.

The binding process checks whether tables, columns, and any other element referenced in the query exist, associating every object on the logical tree with its corresponding object in the system catalog. This process is also called name resolution. Binding also validates that the requested operations between the query objects are valid and that the objects are visible to the user running the query (i.e., the user has the required permissions). The resulting tree after the binding operation is then sent to the query optimizer. For example, the following query will have the tree representation as shown in Figure 1-5, which shows data access, join, filter, and aggregation operations:

```
SELECT ProductID, COUNT(*)
FROM Sales.SalesOrderHeader so JOIN Sales.SalesOrderDetail sod
ON so.SalesOrderID = sod.SalesOrderID
WHERE SalesPersonID = 275
GROUP BY ProductID
```

Note   Most of the examples in this book use the AdventureWorks databases, which you can download from `https://docs.microsoft.com/en-us/ sql/samples/adventureworks-install-configure`. Download both `AdventureWorks2017.bak` and `AdventureWorksDW2017.bak` backup files, which are the OLTP (Online Transaction Processing) and data warehouse databases, and restore them in SQL Server as `AdventureWorks2017` and `AdventureWorksDW2017`. All the code in this book has been tested in SQL Server 2019 so you also want to make sure to change these databases' compatibility level to 150.

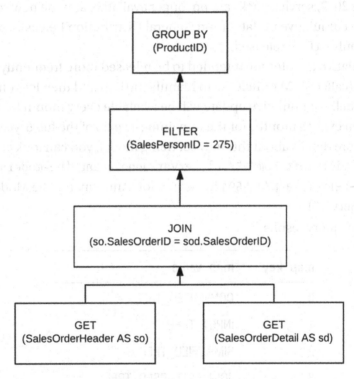

Figure 1-5. *Query tree representation*

Name resolution for views also includes the process of view substitution in which a view reference is expanded to include the actual view definition. The query tree representation, as shown in Figure 1-5, represents the logical operations performed by the query and is closely related to the original syntax of the query. These logical operations include things like "get data from the Sales table," "perform an inner join," "perform an aggregation," and so on. The query processor will use different tree representations during the entire optimization process, and these trees will have different names.

Although these logical trees are not defined anywhere in the documentation, the following query will return the names of those tree representations:

```
SELECT * FROM sys.dm_xe_map_values
WHERE name = 'query_optimizer_tree_id'
```

The following is the output of such query on SQL Server 2019 Cumulative Update 4. The @@VERSION function in my system in addition returns Microsoft SQL Server 2019 (RTM-CU4) (KB4548597) - 15.0.4033.1 (X64) where KB4548597 is the knowledge base article describing the cumulative update and 15.0.4033.1 is the product version. Starting with SQL Server 2017, service packs are no longer available, and the new servicing model will be based on cumulative updates (and General Distribution Releases, or GDRs, when required), and only CU are released.

Note: Cumulative updates are intended to be released more frequently after the original release (called RTM or Release to Manufacturing) and then less often in this new service model. A cumulative update will be available every month for the first 12 months and then every 2 months for the remaining 4 years of the full 5-year mainstream life cycle. For more details about this new servicing model, you can look at https:// techcommunity.microsoft.com/t5/sql-server/announcing-the-modern-servicing-model-for-sql-server/ba-p/385594 (or search for "Announcing the Modern Servicing Model for SQL Server").

These are the query results.

map_key	map_value
0	CONVERTED_TREE
1	INPUT_TREE
2	SIMPLIFIED_TREE
3	JOIN_COLLAPSED_TREE
4	TREE_BEFORE_PROJECT_NORM
5	TREE_AFTER_PROJECT_NORM
6	OUTPUT_TREE
7	TREE_COPIED_OUT

There are several undocumented trace flags (8605, 8606, and 8607) which can allow you to inspect the contents of those internal trees, although the information will be printed as text and not as visually appealing as a graphical execution plan. In addition, the tree will show relational algebra operations which may not be very similar to the logical and physical operations we see on query plans. Next is one example using trace flag 8605 to display a query initial tree representation created by SQL Server.

```
DBCC TRACEON(3604)
SELECT DatabaseLogID
FROM dbo.DatabaseLog
WHERE DatabaseLogID = 1
OPTION (RECOMPILE, QUERYTRACEON 8605)
```

In this case, QUERYTRACEON is a query hint that lets you enable a plan-affecting trace flag at the query level. As we know, a trace flag is a well-known mechanism used to set specific server characteristics or to alter a particular behavior in SQL Server.

Note: The QUERYTRACEON query hint was undocumented and unsupported for many years and only recently has been supported but only with a limited number of the available trace flags. You can get more information about the trace flags supported by QUERYTRACEON by looking at the documentation at https://docs.microsoft.com/ en-us/sql/t-sql/queries/hints-transact-sql-query.

RECOMPILE is not strictly required in this query, but it allows you to force an optimization in case you decide to run the query more than once. DBCC TRACEON and trace flag 3604 are required in order to redirect the trace output to the client executing the statement, in this case SQL Server Management Studio. The output will be shown on the Messages tab. The output for this example is

```
*** Converted Tree: ***
    LogOp_Project QCOL: [AdventureWorks2017].[dbo].[DatabaseLog].DatabaseLogID
        LogOp_Select
            LogOp_Get TBL: dbo.DatabaseLog dbo.DatabaseLog TableID=901578250
            TableReferenceID=0 IsRow: COL: IsBaseRow1001
            ScaOp_Comp x_cmpEq
                ScaOp_Identifier QCOL: [AdventureWorks2017].[dbo].
                [DatabaseLog].DatabaseLogID
                ScaOp_Const TI(int,ML=4) XVAR(int,Not Owned,Value=1)
        AncOp_PrjList
```

Finally, a reminder that this book, especially this chapter, includes many undocumented and unsupported features and statements. As such, you can use them in a test environment for learning or troubleshooting purposes, but they are not meant to be used in a production environment. Using them in your production environment could make it unsupported by Microsoft. I will identify when a statement, feature, or trace flag is undocumented and unsupported.

Although the listed relational algebra operations are not documented in any way and may be even hard to read in such a cryptic text format, we could identify that the three main operations of the query, which are the SELECT, FROM, and WHERE clauses, correspond to the relational algebra operations Project or LogOp_Project, Get or LogOp_Get, and Select or LogOp_Select, respectively. To make things even more complicated, the LogOp_Select operation is not related to the SELECT clause but has to do more with the filter operation or WHERE clause. LogOp_Project is used to specify the columns required in the result. Finally, LogOp_Get specifies the table used in the query.

In summary, trace flag 8605 can be used to display the query initial tree representation created by SQL Server, trace flag 8606 will display additional logical trees used during the optimization process (e.g., the input tree, simplified tree, join-collapsed tree, tree before project normalization, or tree after project normalization), and trace flag 8607 will show the optimization output tree. For more details about these trace flags, you can look at the following post at my blog at www.benjaminnevarez.com/2012/04/more-undocumented-query-optimizer-trace-flags.

After parsing and binding are completed, the real query optimization process starts. The query optimizer will obtain the generated logical tree and will start with the simplification process.

Simplification

Simplification is the next step on the query optimization process and, in fact, the first step of the query optimization per se and performed by the query optimizer. Once the query optimizer gets the final logical tree for a specific query, as indicated in the previous section, it will try to simplify it before going to the full optimization process. Some of these simplification operations include

A)   Predicate pushdown: In this simplification optimization, filters in
     WHERE clauses may be pushed down in the logical query tree in
     order to enable early data filtering. This process can also help on
     better matching of indexes and computed columns later in the full
     optimization process.

B)   Contradiction detection: Contradictions are detected and
     removed on this step. Contradictions can be related to check
     constraints or how the query is written. By removing redundant
     operations on a query, query execution is improved, as there is no
     need to spend resources on unnecessary operations. For example,
     removing access to a non-needed table can save I/O resources.

C)   Simplification of subqueries: Subqueries are converted into joins.
     However, since subqueries do not always translate directly to an
     inner join, group by and outer join operations may be added as
     necessary.

D)   Redundant joins removal: Redundant inner and outer joins could
     be removed. Foreign key join elimination is an example of this
     simplification. When foreign key constraints are available and
     only columns of the referencing table are requested, a join can
     potentially be removed.

Contradiction detection is one of my favorite topics to show on my presentations at
conferences, so I thought I would like to show at least one example here. Let us start with
a check constraint. AdventureWorks has the following check constraint (no need to run
the code, it is already there):

```
ALTER TABLE [HumanResources].[Employee] WITH CHECK ADD CONSTRAINT
[CK_Employee_VacationHours]
CHECK (([VacationHours]>=(-40) AND [VacationHours]<=(240)))
```

This means that no values outside –40 and 240 will be accepted for the
VacationHours column. If you run the following query, for example, you will get the plan
shown in Figure 1-6, a pretty much normal expected plan:

```
SELECT * FROM HumanResources.Employee
WHERE VacationHours < 300
```

Figure 1-6. *Plan for a VacationHours predicate*

However, it is interesting to see the query optimizer behavior if you run the following query:

```
SELECT * FROM HumanResources.Employee
WHERE VacationHours > 300
```

Instead of getting the same or a similar plan to the one shown in Figure 1-6, we now get the plan in Figure 1-7.

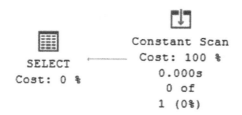

Figure 1-7. *Contradiction detection*

This very simple plan with a single constant scan operation basically means that the query optimizer decided not to create a plan at all. Because of the check constraint, the query optimizer knows there is no way the query can return any records at all and create a constant scan operator which is not really performing any work at all.

You could validate that the check constraint is in fact helping on the optimization by disabling it, running the following statement:

```
ALTER TABLE HumanResources.Employee NOCHECK CONSTRAINT CK_Employee_
VacationHours
```

After disabling the check constraint, if you run the last query again (using the VacationHours > 300 predicate), you should see again the execution plan shown in Figure 1-6 where a clustered index scan is needed. Without the check constraint, SQL Server has no other choice but to scan the table and perform the filter to validate if any records with the requested predicate exist at all.

Before ending this exercise, don't forget to reenable back the check constraint:

```
ALTER TABLE HumanResources.Employee WITH CHECK CHECK CONSTRAINT
CK_Employee_VacationHours
```

Finally, what if someone writes a query like this?

```
SELECT * FROM HumanResources.Employee
WHERE VacationHours > 240 AND VacationHours < 100
```

Once again, this query represents an obvious contradiction, since those two predicate conditions could never exist at the same time. The query will return no data, but more importantly it would not take any time at all for the query processor to figure it out, and the plan created will be just another constant scan as shown in Figure 1-7. You may still argue that nobody would ever write such a query, but this is a very simple example just to show the concept. The query optimizer would still find the problem in very complicated queries with multiple tables and predicates or even if one predicate is in one query and the contradicting predicate is on a view.

After the simplification part is completed, we could finally move to the full optimization process. But first, what about a check to validate if an optimization is required after all?

Trivial Plan Optimization

There may be cases in which a full optimization is not required. This could be the case for very simple queries in which the plan choice may be very simple or obvious. The query optimizer has an optimization called trivial plan which can be used to avoid the expensive optimization process. As mentioned earlier, the optimization process may be expensive to initialize and run.

One of our last executed queries may be a good example of a trivial plan:

```
SELECT DatabaseLogID
FROM dbo.DatabaseLog
WHERE DatabaseLogID = 1
```

When you run such query, you can request an execution plan to confirm it is a trivial plan.

Note: There are several ways to request an estimated or actual execution plan. To request an actual graphical execution plan, select "Include Actual Execution Plan" (or Ctrl-M) on the SQL Server Management Studio toolbar. Once you have a graphical execution plan, you can right-click it and select "Show Execution Plan XML …". For more details about execution plans, see the documentation at `https://docs.microsoft.com/en-us/sql/relational-databases/performance/execution-plans`.

Once you have an execution plan, there are a few ways to verify it is a trivial plan optimization. For example, you may look at the plan properties by selecting the plan and choosing View ➤ Properties Window. Then you can look for the "Optimization level" property. If you look at the XML plan, you would see something like this:

```
<Statements>
    <StmtSimple StatementCompId="1" StatementEstRows="1" StatementId="1"
    StatementOptmLevel="TRIVIAL" ... >
</Statements>
```

If a plan does not qualify for a trivial optimization, StatementOptmLevel would show the value FULL which means that a full optimization was instead required.

Finally, if the query did not qualify for a trivial plan, the query optimizer will perform a full optimization. We will cover that next in this section. But first, as mentioned earlier, a query could potentially have millions of possible candidate execution plans. So, we need choices to create alternate plans and to purge plans most likely not needed. Transformation rules create alternate plans. Some defined heuristics purge or limit the number of plans considered. Transformation rules are the fundamental algorithm for these kinds of optimizers. In fact, some optimizers are even called rule-based optimizers. However, even when the SQL Server optimizer uses rules to search for alternate plans, it is actually called a cost-based optimizer, as the final decision about selecting a plan will be a cost-based decision. So, let us talk about transformation rules next.

Transformation Rules

As mentioned previously, the SQL Server query optimizer uses transformation rules to produce alternate execution plans. A final execution plan would be later chosen after cardinalities and costs are estimated. Transformation rules are based on relational algebra operations. The query optimizer will apply transformation rules to the previously generated logical tree of operators and by doing that would create additional equivalent logical and physical alternatives. In other words, it will take a relational operator tree and would generate equivalent relational trees.

At the beginning of the optimization process, as we saw earlier, a query tree contains only logical expressions. Once transformation rules are applied, they could generate additional logical and physical expressions. A logical expression could be, for example, the definition of a join, as in the SQL language, and the physical expression would be when the query optimizer selects one of the physical operators like nested loops join, merge join, or hash join. In a similar way, a logical aggregate operation could be implemented with two physical algorithms, stream aggregate and hash aggregate.

Transformation rules could be categorized in three types, simplification, exploration, and implementation rules. Simplification rules are mostly used in the simplification phase, which we covered earlier, and their purpose is to simplify the current logical tree of operations. Exploration rules, which are also called logical transformation rules, are used to generate equivalent logical alternatives. On the other side, implementation rules, which are also called physical transformation rules, are used to generate equivalent physical alternatives.

All the logical and physical alternatives generated during the query optimization process are stored in a memory structure called the memo. But keep in mind that finding alternatives is just solving one part of the problem. There is still the need to select the best choice. A cost estimation component will estimate the cost of the physical operations (there is no need to estimate the cost of logical operations). Even when all the alternate plans are equivalent and would produce the same query results, their costs could be dramatically different. Obviously, a bigger cost means using more resources such as CPU, I/O, or memory, impacting the query performance, hence the responsibility to select the best or lower cost.

Finally, keep in mind that the query optimization process is extremely complicated, and by that it is not perfect. For example, it could be possible that an optimal plan may not be generated at all as a specific query could produce millions and millions of plans, and many of those may be discarded or not considered at all. Or perhaps it could be possible that the perfect plan may be generated and stored in the memo structure but not selected at all because of an incorrect cost estimation which instead selects another plan.

Transformation rules work in a very simple way. They take a logical tree of operations and produce an equivalent tree of operations which, if executed, will return exactly the same query results. Since the performance of each tree or plan may be different, we strive to find the best possible plan we can. The transformation

rules available to the query optimizer can be listed using the sys.dm_exec_query_
transformation_stats DMV, which, although somehow undocumented, displays the
names of the available rules. Running the following query will return 420 rules on SQL
Server 2019 CU4:

```
SELECT * FROM sys.dm_exec_query_transformation_stats
```

A sample of the first few rows, related to join optimizations, is next.

name	promise_total
JNtoNL	721299
LOJNtoNL	841440
LSJNtoNL	32803
LASJNtoNL	26609
JNtoSM	1254182
FOJNtoSM	5448
LOJNtoSM	318398
ROJNtoSM	316128
LSJNtoSM	9414
RSJNtoSM	9414
LASJNtoSM	10896
RASJNtoSM	10896

There is not much about transformation rules or how they work in the SQL Server
documentation. But there are also some undocumented statements which could allow
you to inspect and learn more about transformation rules and the optimization process
in general.

To show you how transformation rules work, I will show you a complete example
of a popular optimization. One well-known optimization I regularly show on my
demos at conferences is when the query optimizer decides to push down a group by
aggregate before a join. The transformation rule performing this optimization is called
GbAggBeforeJoin (group by aggregate before join).

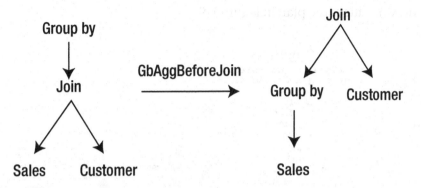

Figure 1-8. *Group by aggregate before join optimization*

As shown in Figure 1-8, assuming we originally have the logical tree on the left, after applying the GbAggBeforeJoin rule, the query optimizer is able to generate the logical tree on the right. The traditional query optimization for this kind of query would be to perform the join on both tables first and then perform the aggregation using the join results. In some cases, however, performing the aggregation before the join could be more efficient.

Both trees in Figure 1-8 are equivalent and, if executed, would produce exactly the same results. But, as mentioned more than once so far, one tree or execution plan could be more efficient than the other, and that is the reason we are optimizing this (and the reason query optimizers exist in the first place).

Now let me show you how that optimization process works on SQL Server. Let us get an execution plan for the following query:

```
SELECT c.CustomerID, COUNT(*)
FROM Sales.Customer c JOIN Sales.SalesOrderHeader o
ON c.CustomerID = o.CustomerID
GROUP BY c.CustomerID
```

This query produces the plan in Figure 1-9.

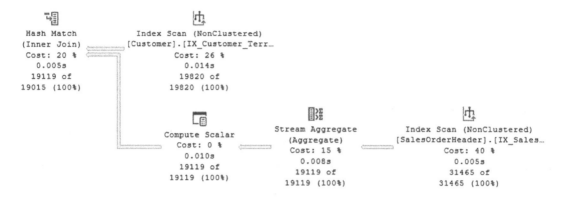

Figure 1-9. *Plan with group by aggregate before join optimization*

There are a few undocumented ways to know which transformation rules were considered for the generation of this execution plan. One of them, although very verbose, is using the undocumented trace flag 2373 as in the following example:

```
DBCC TRACEON(3604)
SELECT c.CustomerID, COUNT(*)
FROM Sales.Customer c JOIN Sales.SalesOrderHeader o
ON c.CustomerID = o.CustomerID
GROUP BY c.CustomerID
OPTION (RECOMPILE, QUERYTRACEON 2373)
```

Although the purpose of the flag is to provide memory information about the optimization process, we will use it to learn which transformation rules are being considered during this process. Running the previous query would create a very large output on the Messages tab of SQL Server Management Studio (notice we are using trace flag 3604 to get this output). I am removing most of the output and including only the information related to the transformation rules used by the optimization.

```
Memory after rule NormalizeGbAgg: 28
Memory after rule IJtoIJSEL: 29
Memory after rule MatchGet: 29
Memory after rule JoinToIndexOnTheFly: 29
Memory after rule JoinCommute: 29
Memory after rule JoinToIndexOnTheFly: 29
```

```
Memory after rule GbAggBeforeJoin: 29
Memory after rule IJtoIJSEL: 33
Memory after rule NormalizeGbAgg: 34
Memory after rule GenLGAgg: 35
Memory after rule NormalizeGbAgg: 36
Memory after rule ReduceForDistinctAggs: 36
Memory after rule JoinOnGbAgg: 37
Memory after rule GbAggAfterJoin: 37
Memory after rule JoinCommute: 37
Memory after rule JoinToIndexOnTheFly: 37
Memory after rule GenLGAgg: 38
Memory after rule NormalizeGbAgg: 39
Memory after rule LocalAggBelowJoin: 39
Memory after rule ReduceForDistinctAggs: 39
Memory after rule GbAggToHS: 40
Memory after rule JNtoIdxLookup: 41
Memory after rule SelIdxToRng: 41
Memory after rule GetToIdxScan: 41
Memory after rule SelIdxToRng: 41
Memory after rule GetToScan: 41
Memory after rule GetToIdxScan: 41
Memory after rule JNtoSM: 41
Memory after rule GetToIdxScan: 41
Memory after rule JNtoHS: 42
Memory after rule JNtoIdxLookup: 42
Memory after rule SelIdxToRng: 43
Memory after rule ImplRestrRemap: 43
Memory after rule JNtoIdxLookup: 43
Memory after rule SelIdxToRng: 43
Memory after rule SelIdxToRng: 43
Memory after rule JNtoSM: 43
Memory after rule ImplRestrRemap: 43
Memory after rule ProjectToComputeScalar: 43
Memory after rule GbAggToStrm: 44
Memory after rule EnforceSort: 44
Memory after rule GetToIdxScan: 44
```

Memory after rule EnforceSort: 44

Memory after rule JNtoSM: 44

Memory after rule JNtoHS: 44

Memory after rule GbAggToStrm: 44

Memory after rule JNtoIdxLookup: 45

Memory after rule ImplRestrRemap: 45

Memory after rule ProjectToComputeScalar: 45

Memory after rule GbAggToStrm: 45

Memory after rule EnforceSort: 45

We have another undocumented way to play with these rules which can help us better understand how they work. But be careful, these are undocumented statements and, as such, should never be used in a production environment. I would not even recommend using them in any other shared environment even if it is nonproduction. But feel free to use them in your personal installation of SQL Server for learning or troubleshooting purposes.

We could use the undocumented DBCC RULEOFF statement to disable the GbAggBeforeJoin rule only for the current session. Disabling means the query optimizer will not be able to use it at all.

DBCC RULEOFF('GbAggBeforeJoin')

Running our previous query again would now show the execution plan in Figure 1-10.

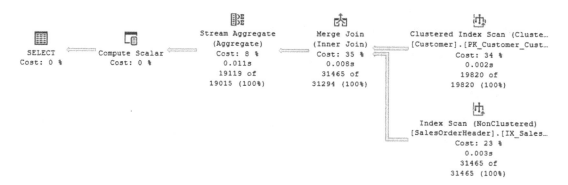

Figure 1-10. *Plan with GbAggBeforeJoin rule disabled*

In this plan, we can see that the GbAggBeforeJoin optimization has been disabled, and the best plan found shows that the aggregation is now after the join. If you wonder why one plan was chosen against the other, you may want to check at the cost of the plan.

The cost of the original plan is 0.309581, while the cost of the plan without the GbAggBeforeJoin optimization is 0.336582, so clearly the original is the winner. In cost, lower values are better, obviously. Although the numbers may not show a big difference, keep in mind these are very small tables and the difference would be bigger on real production databases.

We could play with some other optimizations or rules shown previously. For example, we see that the final plan is using a merge join. Wonder what the query optimizer would do without a merge join? Run the following to disable the "Join to Sort Merge Join" rule:

```
DBCC RULEOFF('JNtoSM')
```

Running the same query will now produce the plan in Figure 1-11.

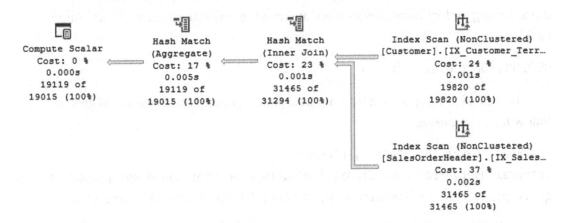

Figure 1-11. *Plan without the Join to Sort Merge Join optimization*

Finally, I mentioned earlier that the query optimizer implements two physical algorithms for optimizing aggregations, hash and stream aggregation. Currently, the plan in Figure 1-11 is using a hash aggregation (or Hash Match Aggregate). Let us disable hash aggregations as well.

```
DBCC RULEOFF('GbAggToHS')
```

The new plan is shown in Figure 1-12. At this point, you won't be surprised that instead of using a hash aggregation, it is now using a stream aggregation.

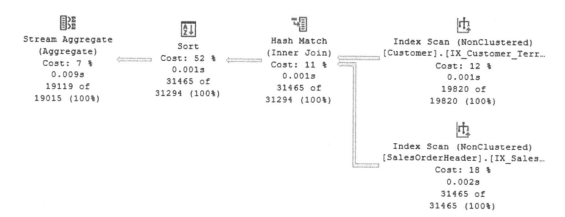

Figure 1-12. *Plan without hash aggregations*

Do you wonder what would happen if you disable stream aggregations as well? Try the following undocumented statement and run the original AdventureWorks query again:

```
DBCC RULEOFF('GbAggToStrm')
```

This time, it is not possible to generate a plan at all, and instead you will get the following error message:

```
Msg 8624, Level 16, State 1, Line 60
Internal Query Processor Error: The query processor could not produce a
query plan. For more information, contact Customer Support Services.
```

Finally, before ending this exercise, you should either enable the disabled rules again or close the session. RULEOFF and RULEON statements operate at the session level. You may get a very strange behavior if you continue working in the same session as you, in fact, have changed the behavior of the query optimizer. You may remember which rules you have disabled, or you can take benefit of the undocumented statement DBCC SHOWOFFRULES to display this list for you. Run the following:

```
DBCC TRACEON(3604)
DBCC SHOWOFFRULES
```

You will see an output similar to this:

```
DBCC execution completed. If DBCC printed error messages, contact your
system administrator.
Rules that are off globally:
JNtoSM
GbAggToStrm
GbAggToHS
GbAggBeforeJoin
DBCC execution completed. If DBCC printed error messages, contact your
system administrator.
```

In the same way, you can use the undocumented statement DBCC SHOWONRULES to list all the rules which are still enabled, which in our case would be the remaining 416 rules available for the query optimizer. To enable the disabled rules, run the undocumented statement DBCC RULEON as shown next:

```
DBCC RULEON('JNtoSM')
DBCC RULEON('GbAggBeforeJoin')
DBCC RULEON('GbAggToStrm')
DBCC RULEON('GbAggToHS')
```

After enabling the listed transformation rules, you can run the query again and verify that everything goes back to normal. You can also run DBCC SHOWOFFRULES to verify that no rules are listed as disabled at all.

There is an alternate, and also undocumented, method to disable rules at the query level only. Try the following query using the undocumented hint QUERYRULEOFF, which will disable the GbAggBeforeJoin rule but only for that particular query execution:

```
SELECT c.CustomerID, COUNT(*)
FROM Sales.Customer c JOIN Sales.SalesOrderHeader o
ON c.CustomerID = o.CustomerID
GROUP BY c.CustomerID
OPTION (RECOMPILE, QUERYRULEOFF GbAggBeforeJoin)
```

You can include more than one rule if you specify a list separated by commas like in the following case:

```
SELECT c.CustomerID, COUNT(*)
FROM Sales.Customer c JOIN Sales.SalesOrderHeader o
ON c.CustomerID = o.CustomerID
GROUP BY c.CustomerID
OPTION (RECOMPILE, QUERYRULEOFF GbAggBeforeJoin, QUERYRULEOFF GbAggToHS)
```

Run one last example:

```
SELECT c.CustomerID, COUNT(*)
FROM Sales.Customer c JOIN Sales.SalesOrderHeader o
ON c.CustomerID = o.CustomerID
GROUP BY c.CustomerID
OPTION (RECOMPILE, QUERYRULEOFF GbAggToStrm, QUERYRULEOFF GbAggToHS)
```

As explained earlier, the following query would not create a plan either because again we are disabling rules for both stream and hash aggregations. But this time you will get a different error message as the query optimizer detected you are using a hint.

```
Msg 8622, Level 16, State 1, Line 119
Query processor could not produce a query plan because of the hints defined
in this query. Resubmit the query without specifying any hints and without
using SET FORCEPLAN.
```

It is interesting and ironic in this example that the query optimizer complains about a hint. These trace flags are undocumented and, as mentioned, should not be used for any reason on a production environment. Ironically, there is a documented and supported method to change the optimizer behavior in a similar way: using hints. This is one reason hints should only be used in extreme cases where no other solution is available. If you want to have a similar behavior to our previous text using a hint, which is documented and perfectly allowed, you could use the following:

```
SELECT c.CustomerID, COUNT(*)
FROM Sales.Customer c JOIN Sales.SalesOrderHeader o
ON c.CustomerID = o.CustomerID
GROUP BY c.CustomerID
OPTION (FORCE ORDER)
```

You will get the same plan as using the undocumented and unsupported version of the query disabling GbAggBeforeJoin as shown next:

```
SELECT c.CustomerID, COUNT(*)
FROM Sales.Customer c JOIN Sales.SalesOrderHeader o
ON c.CustomerID = o.CustomerID
GROUP BY c.CustomerID
OPTION (RECOMPILE, QUERYRULEOFF GbAggBeforeJoin)
```

Using hints may have the same or very similar behavior, but this time it is allowed and documented; however, it is not recommended unless you have really good reasons to do so. By the way, the FORCE ORDER hint specifies that the join order and aggregation placement indicated by the query syntax is preserved during query optimization.

The Memo

As indicated earlier, the memo is a memory structure used to store the alternatives generated and analyzed by the query optimizer. A new memo structure is created for each optimization, and it is only kept during the optimization process. Initially, the original logical tree created during parsing and binding will be stored in the memo. As transformation rules are applied during the optimization process, the new logical and physical operations will be stored here.

As expected, the memo will store all the logical and physical operations created while applying transformation rules, as discussed before. The cost estimation component will estimate the cost of the physical operations stored here. There is no need to estimate the cost of logical operations.

You could potentially see the contents of the memo structure using the undocumented trace flag 8608, to display the initial memo structure, and trace flag 8615, to display its final structure. Let us just try a quick example just for academic purposes. Let us work with the following query:

```
DBCC TRACEON(3604)
SELECT ProductID, ListPrice FROM Production.Product
WHERE ListPrice > 90
OPTION (RECOMPILE, QUERYTRACEON 8606)
```

By using undocumented trace flag 8606, we could see that we have the following final logical tree (this is the tree representation as we showed earlier, and we are not inspecting the memo structure yet):

```
LogOp_Select
    LogOp_Get TBL: Production.Product Production.Product TableID=482100758
    TableReferenceID=0 IsRow: COL: IsBaseRow1000
    ScaOp_Comp x_cmpGt
        ScaOp_Identifier QCOL: [AdventureWorks2017].[Production].[Product].
        ListPrice
        ScaOp_Const TI(money,ML=8) XVAR(money,Not Owned,Value=(
        10000units)=(900000))
```

In the same way, we could see how each of these initial operators was stored in the memo, by using undocumented trace flag 8608. Run the following query:

```
DBCC TRACEON(3604)
SELECT ProductID, ListPrice FROM Production.Product
WHERE ListPrice > 90
OPTION (RECOMPILE, QUERYTRACEON 8608)
```

You will get the following output, which shows each operation from the original logical tree, for example, LogOp_Select or LogOp_Get, is now stored in the memo structure:

```
DBCC execution completed. If DBCC printed error messages, contact your
system administrator.
--- Initial Memo Structure ---
Root Group 4: Card=216 (Max=10000, Min=0)
    0 LogOp_Select 3 2 (Distance = 0)
Group 3: Card=504 (Max=10000, Min=0)
    0 LogOp_Get (Distance = 0)
Group 2:
    0 ScaOp_Comp  0 1 (Distance = 0)
Group 1:
    0 ScaOp_Const  (Distance = 0)
Group 0:
    0 ScaOp_Identifier  (Distance = 0)
```

You can also try at your own risk the same query with undocumented trace flag 8615 to display the final memo structure.

Full Optimization

We just reviewed how transformation rules work. Now let us define how the full optimization process works. As defined earlier, query optimization uses transformation rules to produce alternate equivalent plans and operations and heuristics to purge or limit the number of plans considered. A cost estimation component is also required to select the best plan. Remember, in our previous example, just a simple optimization such as moving a group by aggregate before the join changed the cost of the plan from 0.336582 to 0.309581 (more on cost estimation and the meaning of this cost value later).

We also saw that the sys.dm_exec_query_transformation_stats DMV lists all the possible transformation rules which can be used by the query optimizer. Obviously, the query optimizer does not run all the transformation for every single query; it runs the transformations required depending on the query features. It will apply transformation related to joins to queries performing joins, transformation rules about aggregations only if the query uses aggregations, and so on. There will never be a need to apply rules for star join queries, columnstore indexes, or windowing functions to our previous example as they are not used by the query at all.

Even further, it will not execute all applicable rules at the same time either. Not all the transformation rules are applied at the same time, and rather the query optimization process is performed in up to three steps or phases, and there is no need to execute all of them. This means that the query processor can find a good execution plan on the first phase and finish the optimization process. If there is not a good plan on this first phase, it will go to the second phase to once again try to find what the optimizer considers a good execution plan. If no plan is found, there will still be a third phase, where the best plan found would be returned. These phases are as follows:

> Search 0 or transaction processing phase: This phase will try to find a plan as quickly as possible without trying sophisticated transformations. This phase is optimal for small queries typically found on transaction processing systems, and it is used for queries with at least three tables.

> Search 1 or quick plan: Search 1 uses additional transformation rules, limited join reordering, and it is more appropriate for complex queries.

Search 2 or full optimization: Search 2 is used for queries ranging from complex to very complex. A larger set of potential transformation rules, parallel operators, and other advanced optimization strategies are considered in this phase.

There are a few ways, some documented and some undocumented, to see which phases are executed during a specific query optimization. Let us start with the documented way, or rather partially documented, which is using the sys.dm_exec_query_optimizer_info DMV.

Note   The sys.dm_exec_query_optimizer_info DMV is very interesting in many other ways, so I will discuss a few of them later in this section too.

Run the following statement:

```
SELECT * from sys.dm_exec_query_optimizer_info
```

This is the current output from one production system I have access to.

counter	occurrence	value
optimizations	105870900	1
elapsed time	105866079	0.006560191
final cost	105866079	74.81881849
trivial plan	39557103	1
tasks	66308976	1277.59664
no plan	0	NULL
search 0	13235719	1
search 0 time	17859731	0.006893007
search 0 tasks	17859731	1188.208326
search 1	52398882	1
search 1 time	55005619	0.002452487
search 1 tasks	55005619	578.9377145
search 2	674375	1

counter	occurrence	value
search 2 time	1577353	0.09600762
search 2 tasks	1577353	20065.39848
gain stage 0 to stage 1	4621326	0.252522572
gain stage 1 to stage 2	673774	0.032957197
timeout	3071016	1
memory limit exceeded	0	NULL
insert stmt	36405807	1
delete stmt	3331067	1
update stmt	7395325	1
merge stmt	72030	1
contains subquery	3791101	1
unnest failed	9177321	1
tables	105870900	2.094998408
hints	1528603	1
order hint	1493599	1
join hint	717606	1
view reference	10142222	1
remote query	779911	1
maximum DOP	105870900	7.888350765
maximum recursion level	229	0
indexed views loaded	63	1
indexed views matched	147	1
indexed views used	0	NULL
indexed views updated	0	NULL
dynamic cursor request	4151	1
fast forward cursor request	361	1

Don't be intimidated by the long output; there is a lot of rich information here. This DMV provides insight about the optimizations and work performed by the query optimizer on the current instance. It is worth noticing that the DMV provides cumulative statistics collected since the SQL Server instance was started. Sadly, this DMV used to be fully documented (up to SQL Server 2005), but later versions of the documentation omit descriptions of nearly half of the listed counters and only label them as "Internal only." For example, the entry "trivial plan" used to have the description "Total number of trivial plans (used as final plan)" where now it shows "Internal only." You can find this DMV documentation at `https://docs.microsoft.com/en-us/sql/relational-databases/system-dynamic-management-views/sys-dm-exec-query-optimizer-info-transact-sql`.

As an example, the previous output shows that there have been 105,870,900 optimizations since the SQL Server instance started, that the average elapsed time for each optimization was 0.006560191 seconds, and that the average estimated cost of each optimization, in internal cost units, was about 74.81881849. Most of the optimizations in this system went through search 0 and 1 phases.

A lot of other useful information about optimizations could be found here, for example, it would be important to know the number of optimizations on your system involving hints, order hints, join hints, trivial plans, timeouts, subqueries, maximum DOP, and so on.

Although this DMV includes cumulative statistics, we could use it to provide the same information about a particular query optimization. One convoluted way to get this information is to use a script that saves the information of the DMV before and after and then shows the delta or differences. Since this procedure may lack some precision, it may only be accurate when there is no other activity on the system. I have a version of such script next:

```
SELECT *
INTO after_query_optimizer_info
FROM sys.dm_exec_query_optimizer_info
GO
SELECT *
INTO before_query_optimizer_info
FROM sys.dm_exec_query_optimizer_info
GO
DROP TABLE before_query_optimizer_info
DROP TABLE after_query_optimizer_info
GO
```

```
-- real execution starts
GO
SELECT *
INTO before_query_optimizer_info
FROM sys.dm_exec_query_optimizer_info
GO
-- insert your query here
SELECT RTRIM(p.FirstName) + ' ' + LTRIM(p.LastName) AS Name, d.City
FROM Person.Person AS p
INNER JOIN HumanResources.Employee e ON p.BusinessEntityID =
e.BusinessEntityID
INNER JOIN
   (SELECT bea.BusinessEntityID, a.City
    FROM Person.Address AS a
    INNER JOIN Person.BusinessEntityAddress AS bea
    ON a.AddressID = bea.AddressID) AS d
ON p.BusinessEntityID = d.BusinessEntityID
ORDER BY p.LastName, p.FirstName
-- keep this to force a new optimization
OPTION (RECOMPILE)
GO
SELECT *
INTO after_query_optimizer_info
FROM sys.dm_exec_query_optimizer_info
GO
SELECT a.counter,
(a.occurrence - b.occurrence) AS occurrence,
(a.occurrence * a.value - b.occurrence *
b.value) AS value
FROM before_query_optimizer_info b
JOIN after_query_optimizer_info a
ON b.counter = a.counter
WHERE b.occurrence <> a.occurrence
DROP TABLE before_query_optimizer_info
DROP TABLE after_query_optimizer_info
```

You will have to insert the query you want the optimization information from at the specified place. For example, running the previous query shows the following results:

counter	occurrence	value
elapsed time	2	0
final cost	2	0.708588242
insert stmt	1	1
maximum DOP	2	16
optimizations	2	2
search 0	1	1
search 0 tasks	1	383
search 0 time	1	0.001
search 1	1	1
search 1 tasks	2	341
search 1 time	2	0
tables	2	5
tasks	2	724
timeout	1	1
view reference	1	1

An alternate way, but undocumented, to achieve the same results is to use the 8675 and 2372 trace flags. Let us do both examples:

```
DBCC TRACEON(3604)
GO
SELECT RTRIM(p.FirstName) + ' ' + LTRIM(p.LastName) AS Name, d.City
FROM Person.Person AS p
INNER JOIN HumanResources.Employee e ON p.BusinessEntityID =
e.BusinessEntityID
INNER JOIN
   (SELECT bea.BusinessEntityID, a.City
    FROM Person.Address AS a
```

```
    INNER JOIN Person.BusinessEntityAddress AS bea
    ON a.AddressID = bea.AddressID) AS d
ON p.BusinessEntityID = d.BusinessEntityID
ORDER BY p.LastName, p.FirstName
OPTION (RECOMPILE, QUERYTRACEON 8675)
```

The output is

```
DBCC execution completed. If DBCC printed error messages, contact your
system administrator.
End of simplification, time: 0 net: 0 total: 0 net: 0
end exploration, tasks: 145 no total cost time: 0 net: 0 total: 0 net: 0.001
end exploration, tasks: 317 no total cost time: 0.001 net: 0.001 total: 0
net: 0.002
end search(0),  cost: 0.57573 tasks: 383 time: 0 net: 0 total: 0 net: 0.002
*** Optimizer time out abort at task 707 ***
end search(1),  cost: 0.57573 tasks: 707 time: 0.001 net: 0.001 total: 0
net: 0.004
End of post optimization rewrite, time: 0 net: 0 total: 0 net: 0.004
End of query plan compilation, time: 0 net: 0 total: 0 net: 0.004
```

Finally, if we use the same query but with undocumented trace flag 2372 which seems to be again related to troubleshooting memory issues. This is the output

```
DBCC execution completed. If DBCC printed error messages, contact your
system administrator.
Memory before NNFConvert: 14
Memory after NNFConvert: 14
Memory before project removal: 16
Memory after project removal: 17
Memory before simplification: 17
Memory after simplification: 29
Memory before heuristic join reordering: 29
Memory after heuristic join reordering: 34
Memory before project normalization: 34
Memory after project normalization: 37
Memory before stage TP: 40
```

```
Memory after stage TP: 55
Memory before stage QuickPlan: 55
Memory after stage QuickPlan: 67
Memory before copy out: 67
Memory after copy out: 68
```

All three methods show that this particular query went through two phases of the query optimization process, transaction processing and quick plan.

Cost Estimation

As mentioned earlier, the quality of the execution plans the query optimizer generates is directly related to the quality of the equivalent plans produced and the accuracy of their cost estimates. This means that even when the query optimizer is able to produce a perfect execution plan for a query (and have it stored in the memo), an incorrect cost estimation may lead to the query optimizer choosing another less efficient plan.

The query optimizer uses costing formulas considering the use of resources such as I/O, CPU, and memory, and the resulting values may look like a mystery for many. For example, you may be surprised that cost estimation does not consider if your query has to read data from disk or if the data is already in memory. It does not consider either if you are using a very old-style magnetic hard drive or the fastest SSD volumes. But despite not taking these considerations into account, cost estimation works very well for the purpose of selecting a good enough execution plan.

Finally, if you ever wondered how a cost number like 2.65143 was calculated, I will include a basic introduction here so at least you know the basic concept of how it works. Cost estimation is performed for each operator, and the plan cost is the sum of the cost of all the operators in such a plan. The cost of each operator depends on its algorithm and the estimated number of rows the operator will return. Some operators, like sort and hash join, will consider memory available in the system as well.

As you can see in every execution plan, every operator includes a cost associated with it. Some operators may have both CPU and I/O costs. Some others may have only CPU cost. Usually, operators at the beginning of the execution plan data flow (meaning starting from the right in the plan shape) will have I/O costs. Some examples are table scans, clustered index scans, or index seeks. An example can be seen in Figure 1-13. Once again, notice that this is an estimated cost. Although plans show both estimated and actual values for some properties (like number of rows), there is no such thing as an actual CPU or I/O cost (but there are multiple tools to find out the real performance information of a query; many of those, like the Query Store, are covered in this book).

Clustered Index Scan (Clustered)
Scanning a clustered index, entirely or only a range.

Physical Operation	Clustered Index Scan
Logical Operation	Clustered Index Scan
Actual Execution Mode	Row
Estimated Execution Mode	Row
Storage	RowStore
Number of Rows Read	121317
Actual Number of Rows	121317
Actual Number of Batches	0
Estimated Operator Cost	1.05377 (93%)
Estimated I/O Cost	0.920162
Estimated CPU Cost	0.133606
Estimated Subtree Cost	1.05377
Number of Executions	1
Estimated Number of Executions	1
Estimated Number of Rows to be Read	121317
Estimated Number of Rows	121317
Estimated Row Size	95 B
Actual Rebinds	0
Actual Rewinds	0
Ordered	False
Node ID	3

Figure 1-13. *Operator showing both CPU and I/O costs*

Note: I am saying data flows from right to left in an execution plan. By definition, execution goes on the opposite direction, that is, from left to right, which means the top-level operators request rows from the operators on the right.

Now let me show you a cost estimation example for the following query:

```
SELECT * FROM Sales.SalesOrderDetail
WHERE LineTotal = 35
```

Run the query, request a plan, and show the properties of the clustered index scan operator. For this specific example of the clustered index scan, I noticed that the CPU cost for the first record is 0.0001581 and 0.0000011 for any additional record after that.

Since we have an estimated number of 121,317 records, we can calculate the total cost as 0.0001581 + 0.0000011 * (121317 – 1), which comes to 0.133606, and it is the value shown for the estimated CPU cost in Figure 1-13.

In the same way, I noticed that the minimum I/O cost is 0.003125 for the first database page which then grows in increments of 0.00074074 for every additional page. Since the clustered index scan operator scans the entire table, I can use the following query to find the number of database pages, which in this case returns 1239:

```
SELECT in_row_data_page_count, row_count
 FROM sys.dm_db_partition_stats
 WHERE object_id = object_id('Sales.SalesOrderDetail')
 AND index_id = 1
```

Because the operator scans the entire table, which has 1239 pages, I can now estimate the I/O cost which is 0.003125 + 0.00074074 * (1239 – 1) or a total of 0.92016112 or 0.920162 as rounded and shown on the plan in Figure 1-13.

So the total cost of the operator is both the CPU cost, 0.133606, and the I/O cost, 0.920162, for a total of 1.05377 as shown in Figure 1-13. Following the same process, the cost of the entire plan is the sum of the cost of every operator on the plan. In this case, we add the cost of two computer scalar operators, 0.01213, and finally the cost of a filter operator, 0.05823, which goes to a total of 1.13626, which is the cost shown in the execution plan in Figure 1-14 (again, sometimes the numbers are rounded).

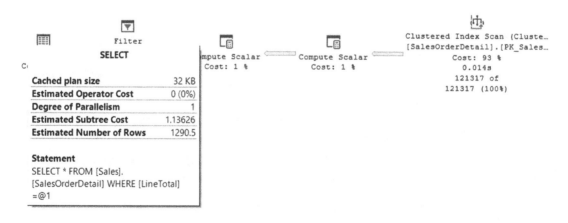

Figure 1-14. *Plan showing total cost*

Finally, keep in mind this is just a cost model; although it works perfectly fine to select a good enough execution plan, it does not mean that it is the real cost on a real execution. I have heard many people trying to compare performance efficiency of a plan with another by using these costs. This is a big mistake. As I said before, there are multiple tools to look into the real performance information of a query.

An interesting anecdote regarding the history of cost estimation in SQL Server has to do with the original meaning of the cost value. Originally, the number meant the number of seconds the query would take to execute on a particular hardware configuration. So, a cost of 1.25 would mean the query would take 1.25 seconds to execute. Obviously, the execution time would depend on the hardware, so these costs were measured at Microsoft at what was called Nick's computer, an employee working on the query processing team. This happened in the SQL Server 7 days, when the current query optimizer was written. Currently, the values should not be associated with seconds or any other measure and are just called cost units.

Statistics

We could not end a section about how the query optimizer works without at least an introduction to query optimization statistics. The SQL Server query optimizer is a cost-based optimizer. This means that the quality of the plans it produces is directly related to its cost estimations. In the same way, the estimated cost of a plan is based on a cost model defined per specific operator as well as their cardinality estimation. Cardinality estimation basically means the estimated number of rows returned by a given query.

So how does the optimizer know the number of rows returned by a query or, more specifically, by any operator in a query? This seems like technically impossible as the job of the query optimizer is just to generate an execution plan, and it never does even access the data at all.

To get an estimation about the data, SQL Server uses query optimization statistics. Statistics are, simply put, information about the data or data distribution. A cardinality estimate is the number of rows estimated to be returned by a query or a specific query operator such as a filter or a join. On the other way, selectivity can be described as a fraction of rows in a set that satisfy a specific predicate. As such, selectivity is always a value between 0 and 1, inclusive. A highly selective predicate would return a small number of rows.

Next, I will show you a very basic example of how statistics work. Let us suppose we want to optimize this query:

```
SELECT * FROM Sales.SalesOrderDetail
WHERE ProductID = 898
```

In this case, request an estimated execution plan instead of an actual execution plan. Instead of "Include Actual Execution Plan," select "Display Estimated Execution Plan" or use Ctrl-L. Our plan is shown in Figure 1-15.

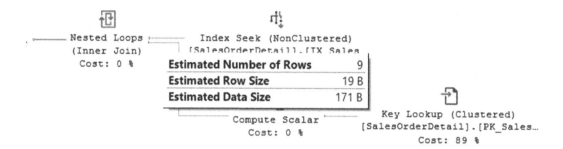

Figure 1-15. *Plan showing estimated number of rows*

Note   You can also see the estimated number of rows in the final execution plan, along with the actual number of rows.

So how does the optimizer know there are nine estimated rows before actually running the query? To answer this, we would have to look at the histogram of the statistics object. In order to do this, you can either use DBCC SHOW_STATISTICS for any version of SQL Server or the newer sys.dm_db_stats_histogram DMF for SQL Server 2016 Service Pack 1 CU2 or later. DBCC SHOW_STATISTICS can be used to display the entire statistics object, which includes a header, the density information, and the histogram. sys.dm_db_stats_histogram can be used to display the histogram of the statistics object only, and it is the same as running DBCC SHOW_STATISTICS WITH HISTOGRAM. The following statement will request the required statistics object:

```
DBCC SHOW_STATISTICS('Sales.SalesOrderDetail',
IX_SalesOrderDetail_ProductID)
```

You can get the histogram using the following statement:

```
SELECT * FROM sys.dm_db_stats_histogram (OBJECT_ID(
'Sales.SalesOrderDetail'), 3)
```

In the last example, you need the stats_id, in this case 3, which you can get from the sys.stats DMV as in the following example:

```
SELECT * FROM sys.stats
WHERE object_id = OBJECT_ID('Sales.SalesOrderDetail')
```

Although sys.stats has the benefit that it can be used programmatically to find the stats_id, for a single request, you would have to run it manually. For example, in my system, I can see that the statistic IX_SalesOrderDetail_ProductID has stats_id value of 3.

Another method used to show details about the statistics object can be using the sys.dm_db_stats_properties DMF as shown next (although the same information is available using DBCC SHOW_STATISTICS):

```
SELECT * FROM sys.dm_db_stats_properties (OBJECT_ID(
'Sales.SalesOrderDetail'), 3)
```

A small section of the histogram is next:

range_high_key	range_rows	equal_rows	distinct_range_rows	average_range_rows
889	80	161	2	40
892	116	169	2	58
894	140	145	1	140
898	227	9	3	75.66666
900	117	110	1	117
904	34	253	2	17

In this part of the histogram, only 6 steps are shown out of 200 in my test system. We can see there is a range_high_key value of 898 (where 898 was used in our search predicate), and the equal_rows value is 9, which is where the query optimizer is getting the value from. In the cases where there is no match for range_high_key, for example, 897, the average_range_rows value will be used instead, in this case 75.66666, as you can see in Figure 1-16.

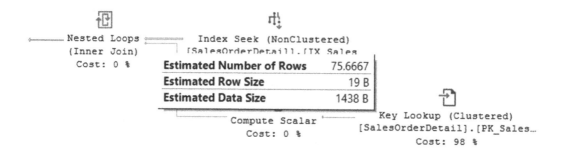

Figure 1-16. *Estimated number of rows using average_range_rows*

Plan Caching

Once an execution plan is generated by the SQL Server query optimizer, it can be stored in memory to be reused as many times as needed if the same query is executed again. Since query optimization is a very expensive operation in terms of time and system resources, reusing a query plan as much as possible can greatly enhance the performance of your databases. Plans are stored in a part of the memory called the plan cache (which was previously known as the procedure cache), and they are only removed in a few cases such as when there is SQL Server memory pressure, when some configuration changes are performed either at the instance or database level, or when certain statements (like DBCC FREEPROCACHE) are executed. The plan cache is part of the memory you allocate to SQL Server along with the buffer pool, which is used to store database pages.

I mentioned earlier that when a query or batch is sent to SQL Server for execution, it is first sent to the query optimizer so a query plan can be generated. Actually, before deciding if an optimization is needed, SQL Server first checks the plan cache to see if an execution plan already exists for the submitted query or batch. If it does, the entire optimization process could be skipped.

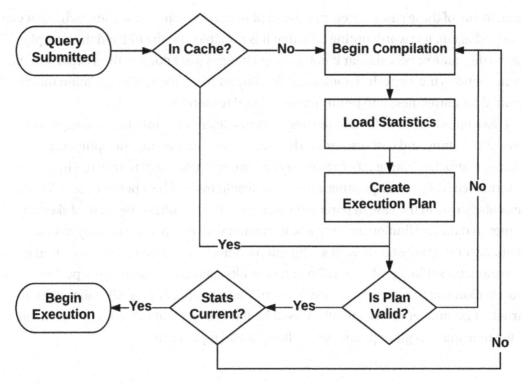

Figure 1-17. *SQL Server compilation and recompilation process*

In order to use an existing execution plan, some validations are still needed. The SQL Server compilation and recompilation process is shown in Figure 1-17, where you can notice that even after a plan for a batch is found in the plan cache, it is still validated for correctness-related reasons. This means that a plan that was used even a moment ago may no longer be valid after some database changes, for example, a change on a column or an index. Obviously, if the plan is no longer valid, a new one has to be generated by the query optimizer, and a recompilation will occur.

After a plan has been found valid for correctness-related reasons, it is next validated for optimality or performance-related reasons. A typical case in this validation is the presence of new or outdated statistics. Once again, if a plan fails this validation, the batch will be sent for optimization, and a new plan will be generated. In addition, if statistics are out of date, they will need to be automatically updated first if default SQL Server settings are used. If automatic update of statistics is disabled, which is rarely recommended, then this update will be skipped. If asynchronous update of statistics is configured, the query optimizer will use existing statistics that would be updated asynchronously later and most likely available for the next optimization that may require them. In any of these cases, a new generated plan may be kept in the plan cache so it can be reused again. It is worth noting here that it is possible that the old and the new plan may be the same or very similar if not enough changes were done in the system and the optimizer takes the same decisions as earlier. But then again this is a validation that is required for correctness and performance-related reasons.

I have emphasized so far that reusing a plan is desired in order to avoid expensive optimization time and cost resources. However, even after passing the optimality validation indicated earlier, there may be cases when reusing a plan may not help performance wise, and requesting a new plan would instead be a better choice. This is particularly true in the case of parameter-sensitive queries where, because of skewed or uneven data distribution, reusing a plan created with one parameter may not be adequate for the same query with a different parameter. This is sometimes referred to as the parameter sniffing problem, although, in reality, parameter sniffing is a performance optimization that the query optimizer uses to generate a plan especially tailored for the particular parameter values initially passed in. It is the fact that this does not work fine all the time that has given parameter sniffing its bad reputation.

Query Execution

As mentioned in the previous section, the query optimizer assembles a plan choosing from a collection of operations available on the execution engine, and the resulting plan is used by the query processor to retrieve the desired data from the database. In this section, I will describe the most common query operators, also called iterators, and the most common operations that you will see in execution plans.

Operators

Each node in an execution plan is an operator that, in order to perform its job, implements at least the following three methods:

Open(): Causes an operator to initialize itself and set up any required data structures

GetRow(): Requests a row from the operator

Close(): Performs some cleanup operations and shuts itself down

The execution of a query plan consists in calling Open() on the operator at the root of the tree, then calling GetRow() repeatedly until it returns false, and finally calling Close(). The operator at the root of the tree will in turn call the same methods on each of its child operators, and these will do the same on their child operators, and so on. For example, an operator can request rows from their child operators by calling their GetRow() method. This also means that the execution of a plan starts from left to right, if we are looking at a graphical execution plan in SQL Server Management Studio.

Since the GetRow() method produces just one row at a time, the actual number of rows displayed in the query plan is usually the number of times the method was called on a specific operator, plus an additional call to GetRow() to indicate the end of the result set. At the leaf of the execution plan trees, there are usually data access operators that actually retrieve data from the storage engine accessing structures like tables, indexes, or heaps. Although the execution of a plan starts from left to right, data flows from right to left. As the rows flow from right to left, additional operations are performed on them including aggregations, sorting, filtering, joins, and so on.

It is worth noting that processing one row at a time is the traditional query processing method used by SQL Server and that a new approach introduced with columnstore indexes can process a batch of rows at a time. Columnstore indexes were introduced with SQL Server 2012 and will be covered in detail in Chapter 7.

Note   Live Query Statistics, a query troubleshooting feature introduced with SQL Server 2016, can be used to view a live query plan while the query is still in execution, allowing you to see query plan information in real time without the need to wait for the query to complete. Since the data required for this feature is also available in the SQL Server 2014 database engine, it can also work in that version if you are using SQL Server 2016 Management Studio. Live Query Statistics is covered in Chapter 6.

A specific operation does not have to read all the rows as this is decided by the calling operator. A typical example is the top operator when called, for example, with a table scan. The table scan operator does not really need to scan the entire table if, for example, the top operator stops calling GetRow() after getting 20 rows, returning false without calling the child operator anymore. By looking at the plan, you might think that the entire table was scanned, but you can verify the number of pages read by using

STATISTICS IO or using the new `ActualRowsRead` attribute, which is available since SQL Server 2012 Service Pack 3, SQL Server 2014 Service Pack 2, or SQL Server 2016. You can see this behavior by running the following query:

```
SELECT TOP(20) *
FROM Sales.SalesOrderDetail
```

Although all iterators require some small fixed amount of memory to perform its operations (store state, perform calculations, etc.), some operators require additional memory and are called memory-consuming operators. On these operators, which include sort, hash join, and hash aggregation, the amount of memory required is generally proportional to the number of estimated rows to be processed. More details on memory required by operators will be discussed later in this chapter. The query processor implements a large number of operators that you can find at `https://msdn.microsoft.com/en-us/library/ms191158`. The following section includes an overview of the most used query operations.

Data Access Operators

SQL Server has several operators to directly access the database storage that can be summarized as scans and seeks, as shown in Table 1-3, and used on structures like heaps, clustered indexes, and nonclustered indexes. A scan reads an entire table or index, while a seek efficiently retrieves rows by navigating an index. As you can see in the table, all the listed structures support scan operations, but only the clustered and nonclustered indexes support seek operations. Although this means that you cannot directly do a seek on a heap structure, you could indirectly do it by having a nonclustered index on it.

Table 1-3. *Data Access Operators*

Structure	Scan	Seek
Heap	Table scan	
Clustered index	Clustered index scan	Clustered index seek
Nonclustered index	Index scan	Index seek

An additional operation that is not listed in Table 1-3, as it is not an operation per se, is a bookmark lookup. There might be cases when SQL Server needs to use a nonclustered index to quickly find a row in a table, but the index alone does not cover all the columns required by the query. In this case, the query processor would use a bookmark lookup, which in reality is a nonclustered index seek plus a clustered index seek (or a nonclustered index seek plus a RID lookup in the case of a heap). Graphical plans will show key lookup or RID lookup operators although text and XML plans would show the operations I have just described with a lookup keyword with the seek operation on the base table.

Newer versions of SQL Server include additional features that use structures like memory-optimized tables or columnstore indexes that have their own data access operations, which also include scan and seeks. Memory-optimized tables and columnstore indexes will be covered in Chapter 7.

Aggregations

An aggregation is an operation where the values of multiple rows are grouped together to form a single value of more significant meaning or measurement. The result of an aggregation can be a single value, such as the average salary in a company, or it can be a per-group value, such as the average salary by department. The query processor has two operators to implement aggregations, stream aggregate and hash aggregate, which can be used to solve queries with aggregation functions such as AVG or SUM or the GROUP BY or DISTINCT clauses.

Stream aggregate is used in queries with an aggregation function (like AVG or SUM) and no GROUP BY clause, and they always return a single value. Stream aggregate can also be used with GROUP BY queries with larger data sets when the data provided is already sorted by the GROUP BY clause predicate, for example, by using an index. A hash aggregate could be used for larger tables where data is not sorted, there is no need to sort it, and only a few groups are estimated. Finally, a query using the DISTINCT keyword can be implemented by a stream aggregate, a hash aggregate, or a distinct sort operator. The main difference with the distinct sort operator is that it both removes duplicates and sorts its input if no index is available. A query using the DISTINCT keyword can be rewritten as using the GROUP BY clause, and they will generate the same plan.

We have seen so far that there might be operators that require the data to be already ordered. This is the case for the stream aggregate and also the case for the merge join, which we will see next. The query optimizer may employ an existing index, or it may explicitly introduce a sort operator to provide sorted data. In some other cases, data will be sorted by using hash algorithms, which is the case of the hash aggregation shown in this section, and the hash join, covered next. Both sorting and hashing are stop-and-go or blocking operations as they cannot produce any rows until they have consumed all their input (or at least the build input in the case of the hash join). As shown in the "Memory Grants" section later, incorrect estimation of the required memory can lead to performance problems.

Joins

A join is an operation that combines records from two tables based on some common information that usually is one or more columns defined as a join predicate. Since a join processes only two tables at a time, a query requesting data from n tables must be executed as a sequence of n – 1 joins. SQL Server uses three physical join operators to implement logical joins: nested loops join, merge join, and hash join. The best join algorithm depends on the specific scenario, and, as such, no algorithm is better than the others. Let's quickly review how these three algorithms work and what their cost is.

Nested Loops Join

In the nested loops join algorithm, the operator for the outer input (shown at the top on a graphical plan) will be executed only once, while the operator for the inner input will be executed once for every row that qualifies for the join predicate. The cost of this algorithm is the size of the outer input multiplied by the size of the inner input. A nested loops join is more appropriate when the outer input of the join is small and the inner input has an index on the join key. The nested loops join can be especially effective when the inner input is potentially large, there is a supporting index, and only a few rows qualify for the join predicate, which also means only a few rows in the outer input will be searched.

Merge Join

A merge join requires an equality operator on the join predicate and its inputs sorted on this predicate. In this join algorithm, both inputs are executed only once, so its cost is the sum of reading both inputs. The query processor is not likely to choose a merge join if the inputs are not already sorted, although there may be cases, depending on the estimated cost, when it may decide to sort one or even both inputs. The merge join algorithm works by simultaneously reading and comparing a row from each input, returning the matching rows until one or both of the tables are completed.

Hash Join

Similar to the merge join, a hash join requires a join predicate with an equality operator, and both inputs are executed only once. However, unlike the merge join, it does not require its inputs to be sorted. A hash join works by creating a hash table in memory, called the build input. The second table, called the probe input, will be read and compared to the hash table, returning the rows that match. A performance problem that may occur with hash joins is a bad estimation of the memory required for the hash table, in which case there might not be enough memory allocated and may require SQL Server to use a workfile in `tempdb`. The query optimizer is likely to choose a hash join for large inputs. As with merge joins, the cost of a hash join is the sum of reading both inputs.

Parallelism

Parallelism is a mechanism used by SQL Server to execute parts of a query on multiple different processors simultaneously and then combine the output at the end to get the correct result. In order for the query processor to consider parallel plans, a SQL Server instance must have access to at least two processors or cores, or a hyperthreaded configuration, and both the affinity mask and the max degree of parallelism configuration options must allow the use of at least two processors.

The max degree of parallelism advanced configuration option can be used to limit the number of processors that can be used in parallel plans. A default value of 0 allows all available processors to be used in parallelism. On the other side, the affinity mask configuration option indicates which processors are eligible to run SQL Server threads. The default value of 0 means that all the processors can be used. SQL Server will only consider parallel plans for queries whose serial plans estimated cost exceeds the configured cost threshold for parallelism, whose default value is 5. This basically means that if you have the proper hardware, a SQL Server default configuration value would allow parallelism with no additional changes.

Parallelism in SQL Server is implemented by the parallelism operator, also known as the exchange operator, which implements the Distribute Streams, Gather Streams, and Repartition Streams logical operations.

Parallelism in SQL Server works by splitting a task among two or more instances of the same operator, each instance running in its own scheduler. For example, if a query is required to count the number of records on a small table, a single stream aggregate operator may be just enough to perform the task. But if the query is requested to count the number of records in a very large table, SQL Server may use two or more stream aggregate operators, which will run in parallel, and each will be assigned to count the number of records of a part of the table. Each stream aggregate operator will perform part of the work and would run in a different scheduler.

Updates

Update operations in SQL Server also need to be optimized so they can be executed as quickly as possible and are sometimes more complicated than SELECT queries as they not only need to find the data to update but may also need to update existing indexes, execute triggers, and reinforce existing referential integrity or check constraints.

Update operations are performed in two steps, which can be summarized as a read section followed by the requested update section. The first step determines which records will be updated and the details of the changes to apply and will read the data to be updated just like any other SELECT statement. For INSERT statements, this includes the values to be inserted, and for DELETE statements, the keys of the records to be deleted, which could be the clustering keys for clustered indexes or the RIDs for heaps. For UPDATE statements, a combination of both the keys of the records to be updated and the values to be updated is needed. In the second step, the update operations are performed, including updating indexes, validating constraints, and executing triggers, if required. The update operation will fail and roll back if it violates any constraint.

Memory Grants

Although every query submitted to SQL Server requires some memory, sorting and hashing operations require significant larger amounts of memory, which, in some cases, can contribute to performance problems. Different from the buffer cache, which keeps data pages in memory, a memory grant is a part of the server memory used to store temporary row data while a query is performing sorting and hashing operations, and it is only required for the duration of the query. This memory is required to store the rows to be sorted or to build the hash tables used by hash join and hash aggregate operators.

In rare cases, a memory grant may also be required for parallel query plans with multiple range scans.

The memory required by a query is estimated by the query optimizer when the execution plan is assembled, and it is based on the estimated number of rows and the row size in addition to the kind of operation required, such as a sort, a hash join, or a hash aggregate. Although this process usually works fine, in some cases, some performance problem may occur:

   a.   A system running multiple queries requiring sorting or hashing operations may not have enough memory available, requiring one or more queries to wait.

   b.   A plan underestimating the required memory could lead to additional data processing or to the query operator to use disk (spilling).

In the first case, SQL Server estimated the minimum memory needed to run the query, called required memory, but since there is not enough memory in the system, the query will have to wait until this memory is available. You can get information about the queries that have acquired a memory grant or that still require a memory grant to execute by looking at the sys.dm_exec_query_memory_grants DMV. For example, the following code will show queries waiting for a memory grant:

```
SELECT * FROM sys.dm_exec_query_memory_grants WHERE grant_time IS NULL
```

In the second case, usually due to bad cardinality estimations, the query optimizer may have underestimated the amount of memory required for the query and the sort operations, or the build inputs of the hash operations do not fit into the available memory. You can use the sort_warning, hash_warning, and exchange_spill extended events (or the Sort Warning, Hash Warning, and Exchange Spill trace event classes) to monitor the cases where these performance problems may be happening in your database.

The resource semaphore process is responsible for reserving and allocating memory to incoming queries. When enough memory is available in the system, the resource semaphore will grant the requested memory to queries in a first-in, first-out (FIFO) basis so they can start execution. If not enough memory is available, the resource semaphore will place the current query in a waiting queue. As memory becomes available, the resource semaphore will wake up queries in the waiting queue and will grant the requested memory so they can start executing. Additional information about the resource semaphore can be shown using the sys.dm_exec_query_resource_ semaphores, which, in addition to the regular resource semaphore described here, describes a small-query resource semaphore. The small-query resource semaphore takes care of queries that requested memory grant less than 5 MB and query cost less than three cost units. The small-query resource semaphore helps improve response time for small queries that are expected to execute very fast.

Memory-related waits can be detected with the RESOURCE_SEMAPHORE wait type, which indicates that a query memory request cannot be granted immediately because of other concurrent queries. Monitor this wait to detect excessive number of concurrent queries or excessive memory request amount. You can use the following query to see such information:

```
SELECT * FROM sys.dm_os_wait_stats
WHERE wait_type = 'RESOURCE_SEMAPHORE'
```

Note   Related wait type RESOURCE_SEMAPHORE_QUERY_COMPILE indicates excessive concurrent query compiles. RESOURCE_SEMAPHORE_MUTEX shows waits for a thread reservation when running a query, but it also occurs when synchronizing query compile and memory grant requests. More details on waits will be covered in Chapter 5.

Finally, the memory grant feedback, a feature introduced with SQL Server 2017, was designed to help with these situations by recalculating the memory required by a query and updating it in the cached query plan. The memory grant feedback comes in two flavors, batch mode and row mode, and it is covered in more detail in Chapter 10.

Locks and Latches

Latches are short-term lightweight synchronization primitives used to protect memory structures for concurrent access. They must be acquired before data can be read from or written to a page in the buffer pool depending on the access mode preventing other threads from looking at incorrect data. Latches are SQL Server internal control mechanisms and are only held for the duration of the physical operation on the memory structure. Performance problems relating to latch contention may happen when multiple threads try to acquire incompatible latches on the same memory structure.

Latches can be categorized into two main groups: page latch waits, which are reported with the PAGELATCH and PAGEIOLATCH prefixes on the sys.dm_os_wait_stats DMV, and nonpage latch waits, which use the LATCH and TRAN_MARKLATCH prefixes on the same DMV. Let's review them:

a. PAGELATCH_: They are called buffer latches as they are used for pages in the buffer pool. Pages are the fundamental unit of data storage in SQL Server, and their size is 8 KB. Pages include data and index pages for user objects along with pages that manage allocations such as the IAM (Index Allocation Map), PFS (Page Free Space), GAM (Shared Global Allocation Map), and SGAM (Shared Global Allocation Map) pages.

b. PAGEIOLATCH: Similar to the previous type of latch, they are also latches for pages, but these are used in the case where a page is not yet loaded in the buffer pool and needs to be accessed from disk. They are often referred to as I/O latches.

c. LATCH_ and TRAN_MARKLATCH: These are used for internal memory structures other than buffer pool pages and so are simply known as nonbuffer latches.

Every latch wait on the sys.dm_os_wait_stats also includes a mode, identified by two characters after the latch prefix such as SH (shared latch), EX (exclusive latch), UP (update latch), KP (keep latch), DT (destroy latch), or NL (null latch), this last one undocumented and no longer used. Since there are currently six modes running, the following will return 24 rows:

```
SELECT * FROM sys.dm_os_wait_stats
WHERE wait_type LIKE '%LATCH_%'
```

The sys.dm_os_latch_stats DMV can be used to return information about all latch waits in the system and is organized by classes. All the buffer latch waits are included in the BUFFER latch_ class, and all remaining classes are nonbuffer latches. Since latch contention in allocation pages is a common problem on the tempdb database, this topic will be explained in more detail in Chapter 4, which covers tempdb troubleshooting and configuration.

Locking, on the other hand, is a mechanism used by SQL Server to synchronize access to the same data by multiple users at the same time. There are several ways to get information about the current locking activity in SQL Server such as using the `sys.dm_tran_locks` DMV. The main difference between locks and latches is that latches are used to guarantee consistency of memory structures and that they are held for the duration of the physical operation on this memory structure. Locks are used to guarantee the consistency of a transaction and are controlled by the developer, for example, by the use of transaction isolation levels.

Note   SQL Server also uses similar structures called superlatches (sometimes called sublatches) to provide increased performance in highly concurrent workloads. SQL Server will dynamically promote a latch into a superlatch or demote it as needed.

Waits and contention on locks and latches are inevitable as part of the normal operation on a busy SQL Server instance. The challenge is to identify when these waits are excessive and may create a performance problem. Waits for any SQL Server resource are always recorded and available as inside the SQL Server code it is required to indicate what resource the code is waiting for. Waits for locks and latches are covered in great detail in Chapter 5.

Summary

This chapter covered how the SQL Server database engine works and explained everything happening in the system from the moment a connection is made to a database until a query is executed and the results are returned to the client. TDS was introduced as an application-level protocol that facilitates the interaction between clients and SQL Server. We also saw how operating system services are general-purpose services and many times inappropriate for database engine needs as they do not scale well.

We covered how the query processor works and how the query optimizer assembles an efficient execution plan using the operations provided by the database engine. With a large number of operators available in SQL Server, we covered the most used operations as well, including operators for data access, aggregations, joins, updates, and parallelism. Memory grants and locks and latches were discussed as well as many performance problems that require a basic understanding of how they work.

This introductory chapter didn't include newer database engine structures such as columnstore indexes or memory-optimized tables, which are totally new technologies and require an entire chapter. Chapter 7 is dedicated to those in-memory technologies.

CHAPTER 2

SQL Server on Linux

I started my IT career working with Unix systems and databases. That includes databases and applications on platforms like System V Release 4, IBM AIX, HP-UX, Sun Solaris, and of course Linux. Back in 1991, I was using Unix on minicomputers, and I was always wondering how I could run Unix on less expensive hardware, such as a PC, so I could better test and learn how it works. Then I discovered Linux while reading a personal computing magazine article.

I was fortunate to be among the very early Linux users when I downloaded it from the Internet and saved the images into four or five floppy disks. I know not so many people were using Linux back then because not many people even heard about it. In fact, I never knew about anyone else using or even knowing Linux existed back then. Not so many people even had access to the Internet in those days. The Internet was mostly available in only a few universities.

Although I started working with SQL Server 6.5 in the second part of the 1990s, I was also working with other database technologies in both Windows and Unix. A few years later, when I decided to specialize in and focus exclusively on SQL Server, I thought I would never work with a Unix system ever again. But that was about to change years later, by 2016.

Microsoft Announcements

It was a huge surprise for all of us in the technology world when at the Data Driven event in New York, in March 2016, Microsoft's Scott Guthrie, Executive Vice President, Cloud and Enterprise Group, announced that SQL Server would be available for the Linux platform. You can still read about the announcement here: `https://blogs.microsoft.com/blog/2016/03/07/announcing-sql-server-on-linux/`. Before that day, we would only hear occasional announcements that SQL Server will be ported to Linux, just to notice that was posted on an April 1st or April fools' day. But this time, it was no joke.

67

B. Nevarez, *High Performance SQL Server*, https://doi.org/10.1007/978-1-4842-6491-1_2

The first bits of the product, which consisted of the first public preview or CTP (Community Technology Preview) of what later would become SQL Server 2017, were released later that year in November at the Microsoft Connect() event in the same city.

Note   I was so excited about the possibilities of running SQL Server on Linux that I wrote an entire book about SQL Server on Linux myself. If you are interested in more details, you can read *SQL Server on Linux* published by McGraw-Hill.

Microsoft also released SQL Server 2016 Service Pack 1 at the same event and announced that, starting with this version, for the first time in the history of SQL Server, all the application and programmability features would be available on all the editions of the product. Features such as In-Memory OLTP, columnstore indexes, database snapshots, compression, partitioning, Always Encrypted, row-level security, dynamic data masking, and change data capture, among others, would be available on all the editions of SQL Server, from the free Express edition to Standard and Enterprise. This obviously also impacted SQL Server on Linux as it was planned to be part of the SQL Server 2017 release.

Having all the application and programmability features available on all the editions of the product would make applications more portable and could be developed and deployed on any edition and now on multiple platforms or at least Windows, Linux, and Docker. Also, as of March of 2016, the SQL Server Developer edition, starting with SQL Server 2014, was also made available for free.

After several impacting announcements on those two events, it seems like we still were not ready for yet another big surprise. Just two days after the mentioned first CTP of what later would be the first version of SQL Server for Linux was released, several sources, starting with *The Register*, indicated that the product was not a port, as almost everybody expected, but instead was using a virtualization technology based on a research project called Drawbridge. You can still read such an article, "Microsoft Linux? Microsoft running its Windows' SQL Server software on Linux," at `www.theregister.com/2016/11/18/microsoft_running_windows_apps_on_linux`.

Even when Microsoft never explicitly said it was a port, which means compiling the SQL Server code and running it as a native Linux application, it was the most logical assumption. It was strange hearing that the opposite was true for the first time from some other sources outside Microsoft. The SQL Server team went public with the architecture only a month later, mostly with the article "SQL Server on Linux: How? Introduction" which is still a good read which you can find at `https://cloudblogs.microsoft.com/sqlserver/2016/12/16/sql-server-on-linux-how-introduction/`.

Although it took less than three years to ship the final bits of the software, work still spanned two versions of the product. While work on Linux started back in late 2014 and early 2015, SQL Server 2016 was released in May of 2016. SQL Server 2017, the first release to run on Linux, would not be released until October of 2017.

Currently, only the latest two versions of SQL Server, 2017 and 2019, can run on Linux. They can run on Red Hat Enterprise Linux, SUSE Linux Enterprise Server, and Ubuntu. These versions of SQL Server can also run on Docker, which itself runs on Linux, Windows, and Mac OS platforms.

Note   Installing SQL Server on Linux or running SQL Server on Docker is outside the scope of this book. For details about how to perform this, see the installation section at `https://docs.microsoft.com/en-us/sql/linux/sql-server-linux-overview?view=sql-server-ver15`.

I will use the remainder of this chapter to explain the architecture behind SQL Server on Linux. A bit of history to bring perspective may be needed as well.

A Bit of History

Although SQL Server has been a Windows-only software product for more than two decades, not so many people know that it started in the Unix world. SQL Server was originally a Sybase product which ran in several Unix platforms and was originally called DataServer. Back in the day, in order to run software on multiple platforms, the code had to be ported and compiled for every operating system. So SQL Server started as a multiplatform technology. Windows did not even exist on those early days (or at least the server software, originally called Windows NT). Sometime later, Sybase partnered with Microsoft to take SQL Server first to OS/2 and later to Windows.

Microsoft and Sybase even had a short partnership with Ashton-Tate, and the result of this partnership released Ashton-Tate/Microsoft SQL Server 1.0 for OS/2 in May 1989. After the agreement with Ashton-Tate ended, the name of the product was changed to just Microsoft SQL Server, and its first version, 1.1, was released in the summer of 1990.

A few years later, Microsoft released a new server-based operating system, Windows NT. Its first version, Windows NT 3.1, was released in July 1993 (there was no version 1 or 2). The kernel of Windows NT was originally intended to be used on OS/2. Windows NT was written in C, C++, and assembly language. Very soon Microsoft decided to port SQL Server from OS/2 to Windows NT.

SQL Server 4.2 for OS/2 was ported to Windows NT resulting in SQL Server 4.21 and was released in 1993. In April 1994, Microsoft and Sybase announced the end of their development agreement, and each decided to develop its own SQL Server or database products. SQL Server 4.2B was the last version of the product for OS/2.

Back in those early days of SQL Server, both as a Sybase product and a Microsoft product, there was always the dilemma and decision to make about making a product portable and able to run on more than one platform or making a product designed, written, and optimized for a single operating system. This was one of the decisions Microsoft took while leaving the OS/2 platform and keeping SQL Server a Windows-only software. This same concern would return when Microsoft tried to port SQL Server to Linux. The goals of portability sometimes conflict with the goals of performance. In other words, a software project would either need a major reengineering for every supported platform or it could take a lowest common denominator approach and not fully use the features of every platform.

Note: You can learn more about the history of SQL Server by reading Chapter 1 of *Inside Microsoft SQL Server 2000* by Kalen Delaney which you can also find online at `www.sqlserverinternals.com/s/History-of-SQL-Server.pdf`.

SQLOS

As mentioned in Chapter 1, SQLOS was built for the SQL Server 2005 release. Back then, SQL Server was a Windows-only application, so SQLOS was never intended to provide platform independence or portability. It was not created to help porting the database engine to other operating systems. There was no need for a PAL.

As also indicated earlier, SQLOS main purpose was to exploit the new available hardware capabilities such as hardware with very large amounts of memory, non-uniform memory access (NUMA) systems, symmetric multithreading (SMT) and multi-CPU configuration with multiple cores per socket systems, and support for hot memory and CPU add-ons and removals. These and other new hardware and hardware trends would benefit database engines. SQLOS became the SQL Server application layer responsible for managing all operating system resources such as memory and buffer management, nonpreemptive scheduling, I/O functions, exception handling, resource governance, deadlock detection, and extended events.

As indicated, operating system services are general-purpose services and sometimes inadequate for database engine needs. Those general-purpose services may not scale well while used by a database engine. Those services could be rewritten and optimized and tailored for the specific needs of a database engine.

However, even when SQLOS was never intended to provide platform independence, unbeknownst to the SQL Server team, SQLOS would take a very important role years later when it was decided to take the database engine to Linux.

Note   For more details about SQLOS, read the paper "A new platform layer in SQL Server 2005 to exploit new hardware capabilities and their trends" by Slava Oks at `https://docs.microsoft.com/en-us/archive/blogs/slavao/platform-layer-for-sql-server`.

Project Helsinki

The SQL Server team had considered porting SQL Server to Linux a few times before. Hal Berenson, who retired from Microsoft as a distinguished engineer and general manager, describes the experience in its 2011 post "Porting Microsoft SQL Server to Linux" which you can find at `https://hal2020.com/2011/07/27/porting-microsoft-sql-server-to-linux`. The article is still a very interesting read. Rohan Kumar, general manager of Microsoft's Database Systems group, also mentioned a couple of attempts to release a Linux version of SQL Server on this interview back in 2017, which you can read here: `https://techcrunch.com/2017/07/17/how-microsoft-brought-sql-server-to-linux/`.

The project to take SQL Server to Linux was revisited again at the end of 2015 giving rise to Project Helsinki, named after the birthplace of Linus Torvalds, the creator and, historically, the principal developer of the Linux kernel. The Helsinki team was led by Slava Oks, Partner Group Engineering Manager, SQL Server; Tobias Ternstrom, Principal Program Manager, SQL Server; and Scott Konersmann, Partner Engineering Manager, SQL Server. Slava was also part of the team that built SQLOS which, as mentioned, was implemented in the SQL Server 2005 release.

It was worth noting that the project ran under strict NDA (nondisclosure agreement), and reportedly there were no leaks. Not even people with current SQL Server NDA, for example, the Microsoft MVP community, were aware of the project.

The Helsinki team envisioned to have a product on Linux to be the same as the Windows release in terms of quality, functionality, performance, application compatibility, scalability, and security. In addition, the product would require a continued fast pace of innovation in the code base in order to make sure that fixes and new features would appear simultaneously both in the Windows and Linux platforms.

Porting to Linux, also usually described as the purist approach, was usually the first approach considered. But according to the Microsoft team, doing a port would be a huge project and would face the following challenges:

With more than 40 million lines of C++ code and close to 30 years of development behind it, porting the code to compile Linux would take years to complete.

During the porting project, the live code will still be changing as new features, updates, and fixes are performed all the time. Catching up with the current code base would be another huge challenge by itself.

After decades of development in a single platform, Windows, there were a large number of operating system dependencies across the code base. Those dependencies were the biggest challenge to do a code port to Linux. The SQL Server team found dependencies in the following libraries:

   a)   Windows kernel library (ntdll.dll)

   b)   Win32 library (e.g., user32.dll)

   c)   Windows application libraries (e.g., MSXML, SQLCLR, COM components and libraries used by the SQL Server Agent and MS DTC or Microsoft Distributed Transaction Coordinator)

Among these, the Windows application libraries were the most complex dependencies. Rewriting all these libraries alone could not be completed in a reasonable time. Very soon it was clear that doing a direct port would not be acceptable. At least, Microsoft had been considering the port path before, but such project was never approved. So, the Helsinki team started looking for an alternative solution to porting.

SQLOS was not able to provide all the abstraction required. For example, there were still many Windows calls performed outside SQLOS. In addition, several components such as XML and the SQL Server Agent were external to SQL Server and not using SQLOS at all. So a consideration was to, instead of rewriting these libraries, focus on growing SQLOS into a proper abstraction layer. That is, all calls to Windows APIs would be routed through SQLOS which will interact with the underlying operating system. Because of this, a new approach was needed and a virtualization solution called Drawbridge was considered.

Drawbridge

Drawbridge was a Microsoft Research project intended as a new form of virtualization for application sandboxing based on a library OS version of Windows. Although virtualization has been extremely popular for many years now, a problem with virtualization was that it requires an entire operating system instance and a lot of services to run, making it very heavy. Research has been conducted to build a lighter version of these virtual machines with only the required resources.

Drawbridge's main purpose was to drastically reduce the virtualization resource overhead when hosting multiple virtual machines in the same hardware, in some way, something similar to what Docker would achieve sometime later. According to Microsoft, Drawbridge provided valuable insights into container technology. Docker was released as open source in March 2013, while the Drawbridge project had been completed two years earlier.

The original purpose of the Drawbridge project was to host small applications in Azure. In order to achieve that, Drawbridge took the Windows kernel to run it in user mode in a process to create a high-density container that could run Windows applications. In other words, Drawbridge was actually taking the entire Windows operating system in user mode. Later, the team started testing running Drawbridge in other operating systems. This allowed them to use this technology as a container to run Windows applications on a different platform. Linux was one of those operating systems tested.

Drawbridge contained two main components, a process called picoprocess and a library OS, sometimes called LibOS, as shown in Figure 2-1. The library OS was a Windows user mode library, which will allow Drawbridge to run Windows programs on a specified host. Such library implemented a large subset of the Win32 and Windows NT calls, as also shown in Figure 2-1.

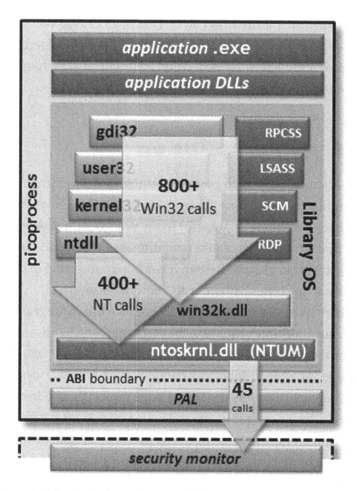

Figure 2-1. *Drawbridge Windows library OS*

The library OS implemented more than 1500 Windows calls, and since it also implemented part of the Win32 and Windows NT layers, the SQL Server team was able to host MSXML, SQLCLR, and other APIs required by other SQL Server components. By using the library OS, the team would not have to rewrite whole features like MSXML or SQLCLR. The picoprocess component was not needed for the SQL Server on the Linux project.

Note: You can find more information about the Drawbridge project on the Microsoft Research page at `www.microsoft.com/en-us/research/project/drawbridge/` and "Rethinking the Library OS from the Top Down" at `www.microsoft.com/en-us/research/publication/rethinking-the-library-os-from-the-top-down/`.

Figure 2-2. *First SQL Server boot on Linux*

Andrew Baumann, who worked on the original Drawbridge project, had already made a port of Drawbridge and had a prototype of Drawbridge running on Linux. Thanks to this prototype, the team had SQL Server booting and working on Linux in less than a month, at the end of February 2015. Figure 2-2 is a picture of the screen of this first boot, as later posted by Slava in a blog titled "SQL Server on Linux, aka project Helsinki: Story behind the idea," which you can still find at `https://docs.microsoft.com/en-us/archive/blogs/slavao/sql-server-on-linux-aka-project-helsinki-story-behind-the-idea`.

It is obvious to note that making SQL Server run on Linux was not only just a matter of running SQL Server on Drawbridge and fixing a few bugs. A Platform Abstraction Layer (PAL) was still needed to abstract the calls and libraries from the underlying operating system. Although SQLOS was not able to provide all the abstraction required, using it for the project was still a huge benefit. But using Drawbridge LibOS along with pieces of SQLOS provided the required solution. By combining these technologies, SQLPAL was born.

SQLPAL

Growing SQLOS into a SQLPAL by marrying it with Drawbridge LibOS was the perfect solution. In addition to SQLOS and Drawbridge LibOS, a new layer was required to help SQLPAL to interact with the operating system. This layer, which was called host extension, was added at the bottom of SQLOS to map calls from inside SQLPAL into operating system calls. SQLPAL would allow to bypass the Windows libraries and get the same functionality calling directly into the SQLPAL.

Even at this point in the project, as you can see from Figure 2-3, there was some duplication of services between the choices provided by SQLOS, the Drawbridge library OS, and host extension. Some unneeded or duplicated features would have to be removed. Merging duplicated features would require changes as well.

Technologies	SOS	Library OS	Host Extension
Object Management	✓	✓	✓
Memory Management	✓	✓	✓
Threading/Scheduling	✓	✓	✓
Synchronization	✓	✓	✓
I/O (Disk, Network)	✓	✓	✓

Figure 2-3. *Helsinki project functionality overlap*

The SQL Server team decided to keep the SQLOS core as the main component, sometimes called SOSv2, and use some parts of both the Drawbridge library OS and the Linux host extension. The resulting SQL Server on Linux system architecture is depicted in Figure 2-4. All SQL Server code, including SQLPAL, is compiled for Windows. The host extension is a native Linux application, compiled for Linux.

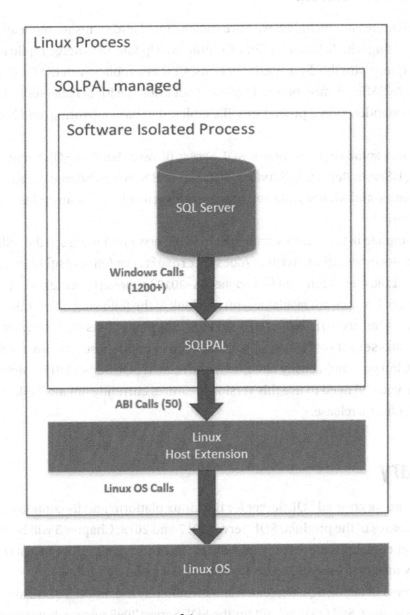

Figure 2-4. SQL Server on Linux architecture

Different than SQL Server on the Windows platform, a single Linux process hosts both the SQL Server database engine and SQL Server Agent. Also, only a single SQL Server instance can be run per server, called a default instance; named instances are not supported yet.

Finally, it is worth mentioning that SQL Server on Linux includes almost all the features of SQL Server for Windows, including both SQL Server 2017 and SQL Server 2019.

Among the features not included, we have transactional and snapshot replication (available starting with SQL Server 2017 Cumulative Update 18), merge replication, distributed query with third-party connections, CLR assemblies with the EXTERNAL_ ACCESS or UNSAFE permission set, Polybase (not available for SQL Server 2017), Stretch DB, system extended stored procedures, file tables, database mirroring, and buffer pool extension.

In addition, some services such as SQL Server Browser Service, SQL Server Analysis Services, SQL Server Reporting Services, SQL Server R Services, StreamInsight, Data Quality Services, and Master Data Services are not yet available for any release of SQL Server on Linux.

For a complete list of features available on SQL Server on Linux, see the following entry on the documentation: `https://docs.microsoft.com/en-us/sql/linux/ sql-server-linux-editions-and-components-2019?view=sql-server-ver15`. For a complete list of features not available, you can look at the following link: `https://docs. microsoft.com/en-us/sql/linux/sql-server-linux-editions-and-components- 2019?view=sql-server-ver15#Unsupported`. Keep in mind these links are for SQL Server 2019, but you could easily navigate to the related SQL Server 2017 articles as well, in case you still need to use this version. Features currently not available may be included in a future release.

Summary

In this chapter, we covered SQL Server for the Linux platform and its content applies to the latest releases of the product, SQL Server 2017 and 2019. Chapter 3 will be the only other chapter covering features only relevant to the Linux version. The rest of the book would apply mostly to every SQL Server supported version.

The success of taking SQL Server to Linux would rely mostly on SQLOS and the Drawbridge project. SQLOS was built for the SQL Server 2005 release, but it was never intended to provide platform independence or portability. Although SQLOS was not able to provide all the abstraction required, it helped make taking SQL Server to Linux much easier. Implementing the Drawbridge library OS along with pieces of SQLOS provided the required solution. By combining these technologies, SQLPAL was born.

SQL Server was finally made available for Red Hat Enterprise Linux, SUSE Linux Enterprise Server, Ubuntu, and Docker.

PART II

Design and Configuration

CHAPTER 3

SQL Server Configuration

Properly configuring SQL Server is of paramount importance for the performance of your databases and applications. Even when the product has been updated throughout the years to ensure it has the best possible configuration by default, there are still multiple cases, especially for high performance workloads, in which additional configurations and optimizations may be required.

So, how is SQL Server configured? There are several levels and methods of configuring SQL Server. For example, there are some configuration options at the instance, the database, or even at the table or object level. The traditional and most common method to perform instance-level configuration is using the `sp_configure` stored procedure, which shows at least 70 instance-level configuration options, also visible on the `sys.configurations` catalog view. There are some operating system configuration options that directly or indirectly impact SQL Server as well. Trace flags are also used to configure some items in SQL Server, and they may work at the instance, database, or other levels. A trace flag is a method to change a specific behavior in SQL Server and, by definition, was never meant to be a permanent configuration choice.

You may be asking, if these choices are best practices, recommendations, or guidelines, why do we have to enable them on any new instance all the time and why they are not enabled by default by SQL Server. The reality is some configuration options were originally designed to be enabled by default (like the auto-create and auto-update statistics options), while others over time became best practices and eventually default options in SQL Server. Some other configuration recommendations will depend on a specific workload and therefore are not enabled by default on every installation.

As usual, when the defaults are changed in a new version of a product, SQL Server provides methods to change this default back to the original behavior to minimize performance problems in case of regressions or some other dependencies your application may have had on a previous behavior.

© Benjamin Nevarez 2021
B. Nevarez, *High Performance SQL Server*, https://doi.org/10.1007/978-1-4842-6491-1_3

The configuration choices discussed in this chapter are not intended to be comprehensive, but rather I have chosen the ones primarily impacting performance, mostly at the instance level, with some focus on what is new in both SQL Server 2017 and SQL Server 2019. Some configuration choices for better administration, manageability, or recoverability may be included as well. After many possible choices, the good news is that usually the default configuration values are a good choice for most SQL Server instances or at least a good starting point.

Interestingly enough, the behavior that originally started as trace flags 2371, 1117, and 1118 is now enabled by default, starting with SQL Server 2016. Let's start the chapter discussing all those changes. Chapter 4 will cover trace flags 1117 and 1118 in greater detail.

Statistics Update

By default, SQL Server automatically creates and updates query optimization statistics. You can change this database level default, but doing so is almost never recommended as it would require the developer or administrator to manually create and update all the required statistics. Although disabling the creation of statistics is possible, it does not make much sense as the query optimizer can efficiently create the required statistics for you. Some other statistics will be created automatically when you create indexes for the columns involved in the index key. Some statistics, however, like multicolumn statistics are not created automatically and would need to be created manually (some tools like the Database Engine Tuning Advisor could help on this, though).

Updating statistics is a little bit different. SQL Server can automatically update statistics when a specific threshold is reached. Although there are two thresholds or algorithms used to accomplish this (which I'll cover in more detail in a moment), a common problem is the size of the sample used to update the statistics object. High performance databases require a more proactive approach to updating statistics instead of letting SQL Server hit any of these two thresholds with a very small sample.

The main problem I see with automatic statistics update is the traditional 20% fixed threshold of changes required to trigger the update operation, which for large tables would require a very significant amount of changes. The second algorithm mentioned, usually enabled by using trace flag 2371, improves a bit on the threshold required to automatically update statistics, but the size of sample issue remains. The statistics update is triggered during the query optimization process when you run a query but before it is executed. Since it is technically part of the execution process, only a very small sample is used. This small sample may not always be enough but at least makes sense as you may not want to use a larger sample in the middle of a query execution as it may dominate the execution time.

The previous process can be efficient for many workloads, but for more performance-demanding applications, a more proactive approach is required. This proactive approach usually means having a scheduled maintenance job to update statistics on a regular basis. This method fixes both problems mentioned earlier—not having to wait for a specific large threshold to hit and providing a better sample size, if not using the entire table (which is called a fullscan).

Note   Keep in mind that having a maintenance job does not imply that you need a maintenance window with no activity at all as this and other maintenance jobs could run along with user transactions. However, a period with low activity is obviously strongly recommended.

In my opinion, the new algorithm is not enough either, but it is certainly better than no automatic update of statistics. The benefit of the new algorithm is obvious with large tables, but a small sample used in such large tables may still be inadequate. This is the reason I recommend to proactively update statistics in the first place, but leave the automatic update enabled, just in case, as a second choice.

Although there are free tools and scripts available to update statistics, even within SQL Server, creating an efficient script to perform this update is not as easy as it sounds, especially for large databases. Your script will have to deal with some or all of the following questions: Which tables, indexes, or statistics should be updated? What percentage of the table should be used as sample size? Do I need to do a fullscan? How often do I need to update statistics? Does updating statistics impact my database performance activity? Do I need a maintenance window? Does updating statistics frequently impact my plan cache? The answer to most of these questions will depend on the particular implementation as there are so many varying factors.

First, we have to define a point at which to update statistics. For example, it is very easy to decide when to rebuild indexes as we can make such decision based on the index fragmentation level. Such information is easily available through the sys.dm_db_index_physical_stats DMV, whose documentation can be found at `https://msdn.microsoft.com/en-us/library/ms188917.aspx`. The DMV documentation even provides a fragmentation threshold and a script to get started. But doing something similar for statistics is a little bit more complicated.

Traditionally, database administrators relied on updating statistics based on the last updated date for statistics (which can be seen, e.g., using the `DBCC SHOW_STATISTICS` statement or the `STATS_DATE` function) or older columns like `rowmodctr` available on the `sys.sysindexes` compatibility view, both of which have some drawbacks. If a table hasn't changed much in a specific period of time, those statistics may still be useful. In addition, the `rowmodctr` column does not consider changes for the leading statistics column as the following solution does. Introduced with SQL Server 2012 Service Pack 1 and SQL Server 2008 R2 Service Pack 2, you can use a new DMF, `sys.dm_db_stats_properties`, to return information about a specific statistics object. One of the columns, `modification_counter`, returns the number of changes for the leading statistics column, since the last time the statistics on the object were last updated so this value can be used to decide when to update them. The point at which to update will depend on your data and could be difficult to estimate, but at least you have better choices than before.

Along with jobs for statistics maintenance, usually there also should be jobs to rebuild or reorganize indexes, which makes the choice to update statistics a bit more complicated. Rebuilding an index will update statistics with the equivalent of a table fullscan. Reorganizing an index does not touch or update statistics at all. We usually only want to rebuild indexes depending on their fragmentation level, so statistics will be updated only for those indexes. We may not want the statistics job to update those statistics again. Traditionally, this has been left to your scripts with the difficult decision about which statistics object to update and sometimes end up updating the same object twice. As mentioned, currently, this problem can be fixed or minimized by using the `sys.dm_db_stats_properties` DMF.

Finally, there is currently no documented method of knowing if statistics are being used by the query optimizer. Let us suppose an ad hoc query was executed only once, which created statistics on some columns. Assuming those statistics are never used again by a query, maintenance jobs will continue to update those statistics objects potentially as long as the columns exist.

Note: If you need a SQL Server maintenance solution, I strongly recommend using Ola Hallengren's scripts for backups, integrity checks, and index and statistics maintenance. This maintenance solution is free and can be downloaded from `https://ola.hallengren.com/`.

Standard Automatic Statistics Update

Automatically updating statistics has been available since SQL Server 7, when the query processor was rearchitected and the statistics feature was introduced. Since then, the algorithm to automatically update statistics has not changed much; for tables with more than 500 rows, the automatic update will hit when the column modification counters (colmodctrs) or changes on the statistics leading column hit 20% of changes plus 500.

Keep in mind that SQL Server 7 and SQL Server 2000 relied instead on the rowmodctrs or row-level modification counters to get the same behavior. Obviously, using rowmodctrs was not optimal as it was not based on the statistics leading column. For example, suppose there was a statistics object on column c1, 25% of changes on column c2, but no changes on c1. This will still trigger a statistics update on column c1 which was not needed at all.

A few more details about the algorithm to automatically update statistics, especially as it relates to tables with 500 rows or smaller, temporary tables, and filtered statistics, can be found at the white paper listed at the end of this section.

Trace Flag 2371

Trace flag 2371 was introduced with SQL Server 2008 R2 as a way to change and lower the threshold in which statistics are automatically updated, and, as any other trace flag, it had to be manually enabled. The new algorithm will use whatever number of changes is smaller between the new formula, defined as SQRT(1000 * number of rows), and the old one using 20% of the size of the table. If you do the math using both formulas, you can see that the threshold changes with tables of 25,000 rows in which both cases return the same value, 5000 changes. For example, with the default algorithm requiring 20% of changes, if a large table has a billion rows, it would require 200 million rows to trigger the update. Trace flag 2371 would require a smaller threshold, in this case SQRT(1000 * 1000000000) or 1 million.

Starting with SQL Server 2016, the behavior of trace flag 2371 is enabled by default when you use the compatibility levels 130, 140, and 150, which basically includes the latest three versions of the product.

Finally, as covering statistics in full detail is outside the scope of this book, I would recommend the Microsoft white paper "Statistics Used by the Query Optimizer in Microsoft SQL Server 2008," which you can still find at `https://msdn.microsoft.com/en-us/library/dd535534(SQL.100).aspx`. Although written for SQL Server 2008, its contents are still relevant for all the supported versions of the product.

tempdb Configuration

The `tempdb` database has multiple configuration options that may greatly impact the performance of your SQL Server instance. In addition, there are several changes introduced with SQL Server 2016 that you need to be aware of. Those include the ability to automatically create multiple data files during setup based on the number of available processors on the system, or the new default `tempdb` configuration, which integrates the behavior of trace flags 1117 and 1118. These and other changes are covered in Chapter 4, which is dedicated to tempdb.

Query Optimizer Hotfix Servicing Model

Starting with SQL Server 2000 Service Pack 3, query optimizer hotfixes were provided disabled by default and required different trace flags to enable them (e.g., using some of the trace flags with values between 4101 and 4135). The reason for requiring to explicitly enable them was to have execution plan stability and avoid plan regressions. Although the purpose of those updates was to fix some other problems, since they also included query optimizer improvements, regressions were still possible. For later versions (starting with SQL Server 2005 Service Pack 3 Cumulative Update 6, SQL Server 2008 Service Pack 1 Cumulative Update 7, and SQL Server 2008 R2 RTM), Microsoft decided to combine most of the query optimizer upgrades into a single trace flag, 4199. There were still a few particular cases that required their own trace flag, but the majority was using 4199. The plan was to put together under the same trace flag all those updates that could be enabled by default in a future release. That future release was SQL Server 2016.

Starting with SQL Server 2016, while using the latest compatibility level, all the query optimizer–related hotfixes, which in previous versions required trace flag 4199, will now be automatically enabled. Should you encounter a plan regression or any other problem, you just need to go back to a previous compatibility level to disable those query optimizer updates, assuming trace flag 4199 is disabled.

Trace flag 4199 will now be used to enable new query optimizer hotfixes, released after the SQL Server RTM version. Finally, if you use a previous compatibility level and disable trace flag 4199, you are disabling query optimizer hotfixes released both before and after the SQL Server RTM.

Table 3-1 shows a summary of all possible scenarios mentioned when using the compatibility level and trace flag 4199 as defined in the SQL Server documentation.

Table 3-1. *Trace Flag 4199 Servicing Model for SQL Server*

SQL Server Version	Database Compatibility Level	TF 4199	QO Changes from All Previous Database Compatibility Levels	QO Changes Post-RTM
SQL Server 2016	100 to 120	Off	Disabled	Disabled
		On	Enabled	Enabled
	130 (Default)	Off	Enabled	Disabled
		On	Enabled	Enabled
SQL Server 2017	100 to 120	Off	Disabled	Disabled
		On	Enabled	Enabled
	130	Off	Enabled	Disabled
		On	Enabled	Enabled
	140 (Default)	Off	Enabled	Disabled
		On	Enabled	Enabled
SQL Server 2019	100 to 120	Off	Disabled	Disabled
		On	Enabled	Enabled
	130 to 140	Off	Enabled	Disabled
		On	Enabled	Enabled
	150 (Default)	Off	Enabled	Disabled
		On	Enabled	Enabled

As you may guess, the service model described in Table 3-1 will be applied to future versions of the product where, for example, a newer compatibility level could be used to enable the query optimizer hotfixes before that version and the previous compatibility level to disable them in case of a performance regression (again, assuming trace flag 4199 is disabled). For more details, see "SQL Server Query Optimizer Hotfix Trace Flag 4199 Servicing Model" at `https://support.microsoft.com/en-us/kb/974006`.

In addition, also new with SQL Server 2016, you can enable query optimizer hotfixes at the database level, regardless of their compatibility level, by using the `QUERY_OPTIMIZER_HOTFIXES` option of the new `ALTER DATABASE SCOPED CONFIGURATION` syntax. You can use this syntax as in the following statement:

```
ALTER DATABASE SCOPED CONFIGURATION SET QUERY_OPTIMIZER_HOTFIXES = ON
```

For more details about the new `ALTER DATABASE SCOPED CONFIGURATION` statement, see `https://msdn.microsoft.com/en-us/library/mt629158.aspx`.

Finally, enabling query optimizer hotfixes is also possible at the query level using either the trace flag 4199 along with the `QUERYTRACEON` hint or the USE HINT 'ENABLE_QUERY_OPTIMIZER_HOTFIXES' query hint. For example, the following two queries are equivalent:

```
SELECT * FROM Sales.SalesOrderDetail
ORDER BY OrderQty
OPTION (QUERYTRACEON 4199)

SELECT * FROM Sales.SalesOrderDetail
ORDER BY OrderQty
OPTION (USE HINT('ENABLE_QUERY_OPTIMIZER_HOTFIXES'))
```

Note   Although it is common to find a large variety of trace flags used with the QUERYTRACEON hint online, only a few are documented and supported by Microsoft. You can see such a list at `https://support.microsoft.com/en-us/kb/2801413`. Many of my own posts and articles include such undocumented trace flags, and, as usual, I always clarify that they are undocumented, not supported, and not intended to be used in a production environment.

---

max degree of parallelism

This configuration setting has been a topic of debate, especially in the last few years when having a large number of processors started to become common in new hardware.

Basically, the "max degree of parallelism" configuration option defines the degree of parallelism that the query processor can use for a single query, or said in a different way, the number of logical processors that a query can use at execution time. When using the default value, which is 0, SQL Server can decide at runtime the number of logical processors it can use to execute a parallel plan, up to a maximum of 64. Keep in mind that this does not mean that every parallel query would use the maximum of processors available all the time. For example, if your system has 64 logical processors and you are using the default configuration, it is still very possible that a query can use only eight processors and run with eight threads. Again, this is a decision the query processor makes at execution time.

Microsoft came up with the recommendation of using a maximum of eight, as documented at https://support.microsoft.com/en-us/kb/2806535. Basically, this best practice asks to have the "max degree of parallelism" configuration option the same as the number of logical processors in the system, up to a maximum of eight. And since it is getting very common to have eight processors or more, eight might be a common configuration these days. And once again, changing this setting to eight does not mean that every parallel query will use eight threads.

However, keep in mind that the recommendation by Microsoft is just that, a recommendation or a guideline. The document itself specifies that the guideline is applicable for typical SQL Server activity and that, depending on your workload or application patterns, some other values for this setting may be considered and thoroughly tested as well. For example, assuming your system has 16 logical processors and a workload with a small number of queries running at the same time, a max degree of parallelism value of 16 can be considered. On the other hand, for a workload with a large number of queries in the same system, a value of four could also be the best choice.

First of all, the hardware running SQL Server must be capable of running parallel queries, which, based on current trends, includes almost every server today, even with most configurations in virtual machines for a production instance. Second, the affinity mask configuration option (which has now been deprecated) or the ALTER SERVER CONFIGURATION SET PROCESS AFFINITY statement must allow the use of multiple processors, which they both do by default. Finally, the query processor must decide if using parallelism can in fact improve the performance of a query.

There is also a list of features that do not support parallelism in the first place, even if your query is expensive enough to warrant it. Among those features, we have scalar-valued user-defined functions; miscellaneous built-in functions such as

ERROR_NUMBER(), OBJECT_ID(), and @@TRANCOUNT; CLR user-defined functions with data access; dynamic cursors; TOP clause; sequence functions; multistatement table-valued user-defined functions; and global scalar aggregates. An execution plan can also tell you why parallelism was not used by looking at the NonParallelPlanReason attribute.

Also, parallelism is only considered for expensive queries, which again are defined by another configuration setting—the "cost threshold for parallelism," whose default value is five and which, again, some database administrators may consider increasing as well. This threshold means that parallelism would only be considered by the query processor if an initially created serial plan has the cost of five or more cost units, so it does not mean that a parallel plan is always selected. For example, it is totally possible that the query processor initially estimates a cost of 5.5 for a serial plan, decides to inspect a parallel choice, and, after finding a parallel plan of 6.3, decides to stick with the serial choice as the lowest cost choice is selected. But for more expensive queries, most likely a parallel plan would be produced. When a parallel plan is selected for execution, the plan itself does not define the degree of parallelism; this will be defined at runtime by the query processor. It is totally possible for the same plan to change the degree of parallelism from one execution to the next one.

In addition, even if you decide to set a specific value for the max degree of parallelism configuration option, it is not a hard limit. Any user can run a query with the MAXDOP query hint asking or recommending the query processor to use more processors to run a parallel query. The only way to specify a hard limit on the degree of parallelism is using the Resource Governor, a feature introduced with SQL Server 2008.

Another common misunderstanding of parallelism, as explained in Chapter 5, is when people see a large number of CXPACKET waits, in which case they assume parallelism is the problem and decide to change this configuration or some other setting to minimize or eliminate parallelism. As explained, most of the time, parallelism itself is not the problem, and probably we are all aware of cases of people setting the configuration value to one to eliminate parallelism, which obviously is totally wrong. There might be some extreme cases when you want to set the value to one and totally disable parallelism from the instance, but there must be a very good researched reason. There are also some applications, like Microsoft SharePoint, which explicitly require setting the max degree of parallelism setting to one.

Finally, introduced with SQL Server 2016, you can also use the MAXDOP set option of the new ALTER DATABASE SCOPED CONFIGURATION statement covered earlier to override the max degree of parallelism configured at the server level for the specified database.

Next, I will show you an example of how the max degree of parallelism works. In my test environment with a SQL Server default configuration and eight logical processors, the following query creates a parallel plan of cost 4.33126. This information is shown in the execution plan in Figure 3-1.

```
SELECT * FROM Sales.SalesOrderDetail
ORDER BY OrderQty
```

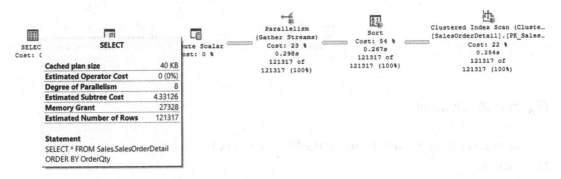

Figure 3-1. Parallel plan

In this plan, two operations are executed in parallel, the sort operation and the clustered index scan. Notice that parallelism works at the operator level, so not all the operators in a parallel plan are required to run in parallel. The actual execution plan even tells me how many rows each thread processed for this particular execution for both operations, as shown next from an XML plan fragment:

```
<RunTimeInformation>
        <RunTimeCountersPerThread Thread="8" ActualRows="12549" ... />
        <RunTimeCountersPerThread Thread="7" ActualRows="17828" ... />
        <RunTimeCountersPerThread Thread="6" ActualRows="12369" ... />
        <RunTimeCountersPerThread Thread="5" ActualRows="12432" ... />
        <RunTimeCountersPerThread Thread="4" ActualRows="18531" ... />
        <RunTimeCountersPerThread Thread="3" ActualRows="11934" ... />
        <RunTimeCountersPerThread Thread="2" ActualRows="18202" ... />
        <RunTimeCountersPerThread Thread="1" ActualRows="17472" ... />
        <RunTimeCountersPerThread Thread="0" ActualRows="0" ... />
</RunTimeInformation>
```

Assuming you want to change the max degree of parallelism setting to one:

```
sp_configure 'max degree of parallelism', 1
RECONFIGURE
```

Running again the previous SELECT statement would obviously create the serial plan shown in Figure 3-2.

Figure 3-2. *Serial plan*

But you could override it by using the MAXDOP query hint as shown next, using MAXDOP 8:

```
SELECT * FROM Sales.SalesOrderDetail
ORDER BY OrderQty
OPTION (MAXDOP 8)
```

The previous query again creates a parallel plan using eight threads. You can try a few other values for MAXDOP and observe its behavior. Finally, do not forget to change the max degree of parallelism setting back to the default:

```
sp_configure 'max degree of parallelism', 0
RECONFIGURE
```

cost threshold for parallelism

As introduced in the previous section, the cost threshold for parallelism configuration setting, whose default value is five, defines the cost at which the query processor starts considering parallel plans during the query optimization process. Whether to use this default or a higher value and which value to use is becoming a new topic of debate. The main problem with some of the recommendations online is that there is no definitive research or performance data—let alone a recommendation from Microsoft—about increasing this value and which value to use for a specific workload.

Although the default five could be a good choice for many workloads, you may also consider increasing this value for some specific scenarios. Which value to use would depend on your workload and should be thoroughly tested. For example, if you decide to change this configuration value from 5 to 25, this roughly means that all your plans whose original serial cost was estimated between 5 and 25 will no longer be considered to be parallelized and continue as serial plans. You have the choice to either research such queries to see if the new serial choice does not impact the execution performance, especially if those are critical queries or are executed frequently, or you could also just test your workload as a whole.

Keep in mind that the default value is not a bad choice either. After all, parallelism improves query performance, and, when a parallel plan is selected, the query processor compared the serial plan against the parallel alternative and selected the best choice. Assuming the cost estimation is adequate, it will perform better. Also, as explained in Chapter 5, seeing a large number of CXPACKET waits alone does not mean that you need to change this or the max degree of parallelism configuration settings.

Finally, a reminder that this configuration setting works in conjunction with the max degree of parallelism setting, meaning that if a parallel query plan was selected for execution, its degree of parallelism will be defined just before execution influenced by this last configuration setting.

Instant File Initialization

Instant file initialization is a feature that can dramatically improve the performance of creation and restore of databases or operations such as adding, restoring, or expanding data files. It can be enabled by granting the "Perform Volume Maintenance Task" privilege to the SQL Server database engine service account. Unfortunately, their performance benefits apply only to data files and not to transaction log files.

When SQL Server requests file space to Windows, by default, the file has to be first initialized by filling it with zeros. This operation can be time-consuming, especially for large file sizes or large growth operations. When using instant file initialization, however, SQL Server can skip zeroing the files, making the operation almost instantaneous. The only downside to using this feature is that files will not be zero initialized, and information previously available in those files may be visible using some advanced techniques. In addition, as indicated, this performance improvement cannot be used with transaction log files, so they still have to be zero initialized. This is one reason why it is a good idea to presize your transaction log files so that (depending upon transactional demand) growths are unlikely and can be avoided.

To enable instant file initialization, you need to grant the "Perform Volume Maintenance Task" privilege to the SQL Server database engine service account by using the Local Security Policy application (`secpol.msc`) as documented in `https://msdn.microsoft.com/en-us/library/ms175935(v=sql.130).aspx`. Starting with SQL Server 2016, you can also grant this privilege at the setup level during the SQL Server installation process by checking the box "Grant Perform Volume Maintenance Task privilege to SQL Server Database Engine Service," as shown in Figure 3-3.

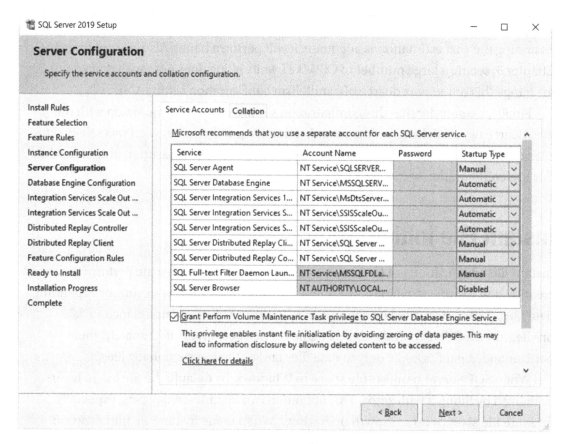

Figure 3-3. *"Perform Volume Maintenance Task" privilege during setup*

The setup screen also shows the security warning I mentioned earlier, which reads, "This privilege enables instant file initialization by avoiding zeroing of data pages. This may lead to information disclosure as it could allow deleted content to be accessed by an unauthorized principal." Granting the "Perform Volume Maintenance Task" privilege can also be specified for a command-line installation using the /SQLSVCINSTANTFILEINIT parameter.

Cardinality Estimator

Another important choice impacting the performance of your application while using any of the latest releases of SQL Server is the choice of a cardinality estimator. SQL Server introduced the original cardinality estimator when the query processor was rearchitected back in SQL Server 7. More recently, starting with SQL Server 2014, a new cardinality estimator was introduced to overcome some of the limitations of the original. Beginning with that version, you have to choose one or the other, and most of the time the choice will depend on the database compatibility level.

But what is a cardinality estimator? A cardinality estimator is a component of the query optimizer used during optimization to estimate the number of rows every operation in a query would return. This information is essential to help the query optimizer estimate the cost of each operation and, by doing that, make the best decision about the physical operations to use to assemble an execution plan.

The new cardinality estimator includes a variety of changes compared to the original, which are documented on the Microsoft white paper "Optimizing Your Query Plans with the SQL Server 2014 Cardinality Estimator," located at https://msdn.microsoft.com/en-us/library/dn673537.aspx. The new cardinality estimator includes some additional updates for the latest releases as well.

You may be asking, if the new cardinality estimator fixes limitations of the old one, why there is still the choice of using the old cardinality estimator. The answer is plan performance regressions. Due to the complexity of the query optimization process, even in cases when a problem is fixed, a regression can create a performance problem on a query that had an acceptable execution time before. This is sometimes called "two or more wrongs make a right" when, for example, two bad estimations, one overestimating and the second underestimating, cancel each other out, giving a good estimation as a result. After only one of the estimations is fixed, it is possible to now get a bad estimation, and the query optimizer may end up selecting a bad performing execution plan.

The new cardinality estimator can be enabled using the latest database compatibility level of the version of SQL Server being used. For example, it is 120 for SQL Server 2014, 130 for SQL Server 2016, 140 for SQL Server 2017, and 150 for the latest version. The compatibility level can also be explicitly changed using the following statement:

```
ALTER DATABASE AdventureWorks SET COMPATIBILITY_LEVEL = 150
```

Any older database compatibility levels would use the old cardinality estimator. The oldest compatibility level in the current release is SQL Server 2008 (100).

There are a couple more choices to define the cardinality estimator to use during query optimization. If you need to use the old cardinality estimator but need to retain the new database compatibility levels, you can use the LEGACY_CARDINALITY_ESTIMATION option of the new ALTER DATABASE SCOPED CONFIGURATION:

```
ALTER DATABASE SCOPED CONFIGURATION
SET LEGACY_CARDINALITY_ESTIMATION = ON
```

An alternate choice to enable the old cardinality estimator is to use trace flag 9481, which can be defined at the server level or at the query level if using the QUERYTRACEON query hint as shown next:

```
SELECT * FROM Person.Address WHERE City = 'Burbank' AND PostalCode = '91502'
OPTION (QUERYTRACEON 9481)
```

optimize for ad hoc workloads

Query optimization is an expensive operation, so SQL Server tries to keep the created execution plans in an area of the memory called the plan cache (or procedure cache in some older versions of SQL Server). This saves optimization time and resources in case the same query needs to be executed again. However, a well-known problem with workloads with a large number of ad hoc queries is that execution plans may be kept in the plan cache, never be reused again, therefore wasting this plan cache memory.

A plan always has to be generated for a query to be executed, but when you use the "optimize for ad hoc workloads" configuration option, SQL Server will not keep the execution plan the first time it is compiled and executed. Instead, it will keep a small plan stub that will use only a small fraction of the memory required for the entire plan. If the same query is executed a second time, the database engine will know by looking at the plan stub that this is a second execution and will perform a new optimization, but this time will keep the resulting plan in cache. In other words, the plan stub is replaced by this new query plan which can be used for subsequent executions.

Although you could enable this configuration option on almost any SQL Server instance, this choice is mostly recommended for instances with ad hoc workloads. A small drawback for some other workloads is that every valid and reused query will have to be optimized a second time for the plan to be kept in cache.

SQL Server Enterprise Edition

If you are looking for the best possible performance for your database and application, you need to use the Enterprise edition of SQL Server. The document "Editions and supported features of SQL Server 2019 (15.x)" at `https://docs.microsoft.com/en-us/sql/sql-server/editions-and-components-of-sql-server-version-15` compares scalability limits and features supported by the various editions of SQL Server 2019. You can access the same documents for SQL Server 2017 and other older versions from those pages as well.

SQL Server Enterprise edition supports all the memory and processors supported by the operating system. In the case of Windows Server 2016 Standard or Datacenter edition, it means up to 24 TB of memory and 512 cores could be available for SQL Server. For Windows Server 2019 Standard or Datacenter edition, it goes up to 24 TB of memory and an unlimited number of cores. SQL Server Standard edition, on the other hand, will be limited to the lesser of 4 sockets or 24 cores and 128 GB of memory.

As mentioned in Chapter 2, starting with SQL Server 2016 Service Pack 1, several features which used to be Enterprise-only are now available on all the editions of the product. Such features include In-Memory OLTP, columnstore indexes, database snapshots, compression, partitioning, Always Encrypted, row-level security, dynamic data masking, and change data capture, among others.

As you can see in the previous document, there are still plenty of features that are only available on SQL Server Enterprise edition. Just to list the most important ones, especially from the performance point of view, we have

- Resource Governor
- Online nonclustered columnstore index rebuild
- In-memory optimized tempdb metadata
- Partitioned table parallelism

- NUMA aware and large page memory and buffer array allocation

- Read-ahead

- Advanced scanning

- Automatic tuning

- Batch mode for rowstore

- Row mode memory grant feedback

- Batch mode adaptive joins

- Batch mode memory grant feedback

- Distributed partitioned views

- Parallel index operations

- Automatic use of indexed views by the query optimizer

- Parallel consistent check

- Star join query optimizations

- Global batch aggregation

- Always On availability groups (see the following note)

- Online index create and rebuild

- Resumable online index rebuilds

- Fast recovery

Note   SQL Server Standard edition provides Basic Always On availability groups which support a failover environment for a single database and a single replica. Basic availability groups are intended to replace the deprecated database mirroring feature and provide a similar level of feature support.

Memory Configuration

SQL Server can automatically and dynamically manage memory without any change to the default memory configuration. This can work perfectly fine most of the time when SQL Server is installed as a single instance on a dedicated server. In this case, you could leave the default settings of max server memory and min server memory, as no other application or server component is competing for the server memory. SQL Server is designed to dynamically allocate memory only when needed and, in order to avoid the operating system to page memory to disk, release it if not much is available. If you are targeting for a high performance SQL Server installation, it is strictly recommended to have a server dedicated just for your production SQL Server instance, as other applications or components on the same server may compete for memory and other server resources.

However, in some cases, you may want to tune the memory configuration for some specific cases—for example, if you want to restrict the memory available to SQL Server or if you are seeing memory problems. Configuring memory using these settings is essential if you are using more than one instance of SQL Server, but, then again, multiple instances are not recommended for a high performance production installation. In order to estimate the max server memory, you should consider how much memory is needed by the operating system and other required server components, if any. As documented on `https://msdn.microsoft.com/en-us/library/ms178067.aspx`, max server memory accounts for the following:

   a. Buffer pool memory

   b. All caches

   c. Memory grants

   d. Compile memory

   e. Lock manager memory

   f. CLR memory

It also accounts for basically any memory clerk defined on `sys.dm_os_memory_clerks`. Memory not controlled by the max server memory configuration setting includes the following:

   a. Memory heaps

   b. Linked server providers other than SQL Server

   c. Thread stacks

   d. Non-SQL Server DLLs

Max server memory is the high-water mark, and, except as indicated next, SQL Server cannot use more memory than the specified value on this configuration setting. Starting with the 2012 release, SQL Server might allocate more memory than the configured value for max server memory when there is insufficient contiguous free memory because of memory fragmentation. SQL Server can perform overcommitment instead of rejecting the memory request and, by doing that, briefly exceeding the configured max server memory setting.

When configuring min server memory, SQL Server does not immediately allocate all the minimum memory. As before, it will only allocate more memory when its workload requires it. But once the min server memory is reached, memory is never released under that point.

For example, to configure the max memory to 492 GB, you could run the following statements:

```
sp_configure 'max server memory', 503808
GO
RECONFIGURE
```

To get back to its default, run the following:

```
sp_configure 'max server memory', 2147483647
GO
RECONFIGURE
```

You can use the sys.dm_os_sys_info and sys.dm_os_process_memory DMV to get general information about the memory in the system. Some other memory configuration choices are 32-bit related, but this architecture is currently disappearing. In fact, SQL Server 2016 was the first database engine release to be no longer available for the 32-bit architecture. Another SQL Server architecture, Itanium, was also deprecated with SQL Server 2008 R2 and Windows Server 2008 R2 a few years ago.

Lock Pages in Memory

Lock Pages in Memory is a Windows policy that prevents the operating system from paging data in physical memory to disk, which is usually an expensive operation. Although this configuration option may be less relevant than earlier versions, it is still available in all the latest versions of SQL Server. While trace flag 845 was required in the

Standard edition of SQL Server 2012 and other older versions, it is not needed for later versions of the product. Trace flag 845 was never required for the Enterprise edition of SQL Server.

To enable Lock Pages in Memory, you need to enable the policy with the same name for the service account used by the SQL Server database engine using the Windows group policy tool (gpedit.msc). For details on how to perform this, see https://msdn. microsoft.com/en-us/library/ms190730.aspx.

backup compression default

The backup compression default is another interesting option that can be helpful to compress your database backups, and it is disabled by default. Although compressing SQL Server backups may have some overhead for processor usage, it will minimize I/O, increasing the backup speed in addition to saving disk space. Optionally, you can set compression at the backup level using the COMPRESSION set option of the DATABASE BACKUP statement, but it is recommended to have it as a server default.

Backup compression was introduced with SQL Server 2008, and it is currently only available on the Enterprise and Standard editions.

query governor cost limit

The "query governor cost limit" configuration option allows you to define the cost limit of a query executed in your SQL Server instance, where cost limit refers to the estimated cost of the execution plan. You can also get the same behavior on a per-connection basis using the SET QUERY_GOVERNOR_COST_LIMIT statement.

For example, briefly change the query governor cost limit to 20 by running the following statements:

```
sp_configure 'query governor cost limit', 20
RECONFIGURE
```

Trying to run an expensive query like the following will result in the error message "The query has been canceled because the estimated cost of this query (%d) exceeds the configured threshold of %d":

```
SELECT * FROM Sales.SalesOrderDetail s1 CROSS JOIN Sales.SalesOrderDetail s2
```

Don't forget to set back the configuration to its default value:

```
sp_configure 'query governor cost limit', 0
RECONFIGURE
```

blocked process threshold

The blocked process threshold is a useful configuration option that you can use to specify a threshold in which a blocked process alert should be generated. The threshold is specified in seconds, and the default for this configuration option is 0, which means that no alert is generated. After this configuration setting has been configured, an alert still has to be explicitly defined for some action to be taken. Run the following statement to change the blocked process threshold to five seconds:

```
sp_configure 'blocked process threshold (s)', 5
RECONFIGURE
```

One of the choices available to create an alert is to use the blocked_process_report extended event and create a session as shown:

```
CREATE EVENT SESSION blocked_process_test ON SERVER
ADD EVENT sqlserver.blocked_process_report
GO
ALTER EVENT SESSION blocked_process_test ON SERVER
STATE = START
```

After the session has been created and started, it will start capturing events every time a process has been blocked for five seconds.

Don't forget to set the configuration value back to its default after you finish your testing.

```
sp_configure 'blocked process threshold (s)', 0
RECONFIGURE
GO
ALTER EVENT SESSION blocked_process_test ON SERVER
STATE = STOP
GO
DROP EVENT SESSION blocked_process_test ON SERVER
```

Advanced Trace Flags

In an article published a few years ago called "Tuning Options for SQL Server When Running in High-Performance Workloads," Microsoft documented an interesting list of trace flags that can be useful to improve the performance of SQL Server when running in high performance workloads. You can find the article at `https://support.microsoft.com/en-us/kb/920093`, and, in this section, I'll provide a summary of the listed trace flags.

First of all, these are advanced trace flags that may have secondary effects, so they are only recommended after all the traditional tuning choices have been exhausted. In addition, since some of these recommendations may be a bit extreme, the article warns about evaluating the effects of your workload on a test system before a production implementation. The listed trace flags are as follows:

   a. Using trace flag 652 to disable page prefetching scans, that is, read-ahead reads. If you know that your workload can benefit from disabling read-ahead reads, this could be a choice that you may want to consider.

   b. Using trace flag 8744 to disable prefetching for ranges, used by the nested loops join operator.

   c. Using trace flag 661 to disable the ghost record removal process. Enabling this trace flag improves performance as deleted records don't have to be removed, but it obviously has an impact on disk usage and the performance of scan operations.

   d. Using trace flag 834 to enable Windows large page allocations for the memory that is allocated for the buffer pool. This trace flag requires the Lock Pages in Memory privilege assigned to the SQL Server database engine service account, as covered earlier. Currently, columnstore indexes are not supported if you are using this trace flag so keep this in mind. Columnstore indexes are covered in Chapter 7.

   e. Using trace flag 836 to enable the max server memory option for the buffer pool. This trace flag applies only to 32-bit versions of SQL Server, but I really hope you are not using that architecture anymore.

f. Using trace flag 2301 to enable advanced decision support optimizations. Trace flag 2301 is also covered in more detail in the article "Query Processor Modeling Extensions in SQL Server 2005 SP1" at `https://blogs.msdn.microsoft.com/ianjo/2006/04/24/query-processor-modelling-extensions-in-sql-server-2005-sp1/`.

g. Using trace flag 8020 to disable working set monitoring.

h. Using several trace flags to disable various ring buffers, including 8011 to disable the resource monitor ring buffer, 8012 to disable the ring buffer for schedulers, 8018 to disable the exception ring buffer, and 8019 to disable the stack collection for the exception ring buffer. Disabling these ring buffers improves the performance of SQL Server, but ironically they also provide diagnostic information that can help you to troubleshoot problems. I would not recommend disabling these ring buffers, but again this is something you can consider and hopefully only on a short-term basis.

Configuring SQL Server on Linux

As mentioned earlier, the latest two versions of SQL Server, 2017 and 2019, can run on both Windows and Linux operating systems. In addition, they can run on Docker which itself can run on Windows, Linux, and Mac OS. All the configurations mentioned so far in this chapter can also be applied to a Linux system. The rest of this chapter, however, will focus on configurations that only apply to Linux implementations. These configurations fall mostly in two categories: configuration using the mssql-conf utility and operating system configurations.

Although you can use the setup option of the mssql-conf utility to install and configure SQL Server, this section assumes you have SQL Server and the command-line tools already installed. For details on how to install this, you can refer to the SQL Server documentation or my book *SQL Server on Linux* published by McGraw-Hill. Just for completeness, this is what you most likely would run to install and initially configure SQL Server:

```
sudo /opt/mssql/bin/mssql-conf setup
usermod: no changes
Choose an edition of SQL Server:
  1) Evaluation (free, no production use rights, 180-day limit)
  2) Developer (free, no production use rights)
  3) Express (free)
  4) Web (PAID)
  5) Standard (PAID)
  6) Enterprise (PAID) - CPU Core utilization restricted to 20 physical/40
     hyperthreaded
  7) Enterprise Core (PAID) - CPU Core utilization up to Operating System
     Maximum
  8) I bought a license through a retail sales channel and have a product
     key to enter.

Details about editions can be found at
https://go.microsoft.com/fwlink/?LinkId=2109348&clcid=0x409

Use of PAID editions of this software requires separate licensing through a
Microsoft Volume Licensing program.
By choosing a PAID edition, you are verifying that you have the appropriate
number of licenses in place to install and run this software.

Enter your edition(1-8): 2
The license terms for this product can be found in
/usr/share/doc/mssql-server or downloaded from:
https://go.microsoft.com/fwlink/?LinkId=2104294&clcid=0x409

The privacy statement can be viewed at:
https://go.microsoft.com/fwlink/?LinkId=853010&clcid=0x409

Enter the SQL Server system administrator password:
Confirm the SQL Server system administrator password:
Configuring SQL Server...

ForceFlush is enabled for this instance.
ForceFlush feature is enabled for log durability.
Setup has completed successfully. SQL Server is now starting.
```

Although you can configure multiple settings in several ways, for example, running SQL Server Management Studio on Windows while opening a session to your SQL Server instance running on Linux, in other cases, using the mssql-conf tool is the only way to perform those changes. Configuring a global trace flag or a TCP/IP port is a good example of requiring the mssql-conf tool, but in the Windows world, we would use SQL Server Configuration Manager. As mentioned earlier in Chapter 2, SQL Server Configuration Manager is not available on Linux.

To see the available mssql-conf choices, run the utility without arguments:

```
# /opt/mssql/bin/mssql-conf
usage: mssql-conf [-h] [-n]  ...

positional arguments:

    setup               Initialize and setup Microsoft SQL Server
    set                 Set the value of a setting
    unset               Unset the value of a setting
    list                List the supported settings
    get                 Gets the value of all settings in a section or of an
                        individual setting
    traceflag           Enable/disable one or more traceflags
    set-sa-password     Set the system administrator (SA) password
    set-collation       Set the collation of system databases
    validate            Validate the configuration file
    set-edition         Set the edition of the SQL Server instance
    validate-ad-config
                        Validate configuration for Active Directory
                        Authentication
    setup-ad-keytab     Create a keytab for SQL Server to use to
                        authenticate AD
                        users

optional arguments:
  -h, --help            show this help message and exit
  -n, --noprompt        Does not prompt the user and uses environment
                        variables
                        or defaults.
```

It may not be immediately clear from that output but you can use the mssql-conf in two different ways. The first is using one of the listed arguments, such as traceflag or set-sa-password, which enables or disables one or more trace flags or sets the system administrator password, respectively. The second is using the set or unset arguments to set or unset the value of a specific setting. For example, a popular setting could be memory.memorylimitmb, which can be used to set the SQL Server memory limit. You can see the list of all the available settings by using the following command:

```
/opt/mssql/bin/mssql-conf list
```

SQL Server 2019 currently returns 60 entries, and I will mention the most useful ones in a moment. But first let me show you how to use mssql-conf to configure all three mentioned examples. To enable a trace flag at the instance level, for example, 3226, you could run this:

```
# /opt/mssql/bin/mssql-conf traceflag 3226 on
SQL Server needs to be restarted in order to apply this setting. Please run
'systemctl restart mssql-server.service'.
```

Run 'systemctl restart mssql-server.service' as recommended. In the same way, the following command will disable the trace flag from the system:

```
# /opt/mssql/bin/mssql-conf traceflag 3226 off
```

To set the system administrator password, use set-sa-password as in the following example:

```
/opt/mssql/bin/mssql-conf set-sa-password
Enter the SQL Server system administrator password:
Confirm the SQL Server system administrator password:
Configuring SQL Server...

ForceFlush is enabled for this instance.
ForceFlush feature is enabled for log durability.
The system administrator password has been changed.
Please run 'sudo systemctl start mssql-server' to start SQL Server.
```

Next is an example using the set argument with a specific setting, in this case memory.memorylimitmb:

```
/opt/mssql/bin/mssql-conf set memory.memorylimitmb 503808
SQL Server needs to be restarted in order to apply this setting. Please run
'systemctl restart mssql-server.service'.
```

This would set the SQL Server limit memory to 503,808 MB or 492 GB. As mentioned, memory.memorylimitmb is one of the 60 possible settings in SQL Server 2019. Next are some of the most useful settings:

coredump.captureminiandfull	Choose to capture both mini and full core dumps
coredump.coredumptype	Choose the type of dump memory file to collect
filelocation.defaultdatadir	Change the default data directory location
filelocation.defaultdumpdir	Change the default dump directory location
filelocation.defaultlogdir	Change the default log directory location
filelocation.masterdatafile	Change the default master database data file directory location
filelocation.masterlogfile	Change the default master database log file directory location
filelocation.masterdatafile	Change the name of the master database data file
filelocation.masterlogfile	Change the name of the master database log file
filelocation.errorlogfile	Change the default error log file directory location
filelocation.defaultbackupdir	Change the default backup directory location
hadr.hadrenabled	Enable availability groups for high availability and disaster recovery
language.lcid	Set the locale identifier for SQL Server to use
memory.memorylimitmb	Set the SQL Server memory limit
network.rpcport	Configure rpcport for Microsoft Distributed Transaction Coordinator (MSDTC)
network.tcpport	Change SQL Server TCP port for incoming connections
sqlagent.enabled	Enable SQL Server Agent

(continued)

sqlagent.databasemailprofile	Set the default database mail profile
sqlagent.errorlogfile	Configure SQL Server Agent log file path
sqlagent.errorlogginglevel	Configure SQL Server Agent logging level
telemetry.customerfeedback	Configure customer feedback
telemetry.userrequestedlocalauditdirectory	Set a directory to add local audit files

A final practical example would be to enable the SQL Server Agent, which uses the sqlagent.enabled from the previous list:

```
# /opt/mssql/bin/mssql-conf set sqlagent.enabled true
SQL Server needs to be restarted in order to apply this setting. Please run
'systemctl restart mssql-server.service'.
```

Finally, you can see the configured changes by looking at the contents of the /var/opt/mssql/mssql.conf file as shown next:

```
# more /var/opt/mssql/mssql.conf
[sqlagent]
enabled = true

[EULA]
accepteula = Y

[memory]
memorylimitmb = 503808

[traceflag]
traceflag0 = 3226
```

Using Environment Variables

You can also configure a SQL Server instance in Linux using environment variables, although this will only assist with the initial installation using the mssql-conf setup command on the Linux host or as a new SQL Server container in Docker. To configure SQL Server after setup for either of these scenarios, just use the mssql-conf utility as explained earlier.

These are the variables supported as of SQL Server 2019 (all except the last four are available for SQL Server 2017):

ACCEPT_EULA	Sets a value to confirm your acceptance of the End-User Licensing Agreement
MSSQL_SA_PASSWORD	Configures the sa user password
MSSQL_PID	Sets the SQL Server edition or product key
MSSQL_LCID	Sets the language ID to use for SQL Server
MSSQL_COLLATION	Sets the default collation for SQL Server
MSSQL_MEMORY_LIMIT_MB	Sets the maximum amount of memory, in MB, that SQL Server can use. By default, it is 80% of the total physical memory
MSSQL_TCP_PORT	Configure the TCP port that SQL Server listens on. The default port is 1433
MSSQL_IP_ADDRESS	Sets the IP address
MSSQL_BACKUP_DIR	Sets the default backup directory location
MSSQL_DATA_DIR	Changes the directory where the new SQL Server database data files are created
MSSQL_LOG_DIR	Changes the directory where the new SQL Server database log files are created
MSSQL_DUMP_DIR	Changes the directory where SQL Server will save the memory dumps and other troubleshooting files by default
MSSQL_ENABLE_HADR	Enables availability groups
MSSQL_AGENT_ENABLED	Enables SQL Server Agent
MSSQL_MASTER_DATA_FILE	Sets the location of the master database data file
MSSQL_MASTER_LOG_FILE	Sets the location of the master database log file
MSSQL_ERROR_LOG_FILE	Sets the location of the error log files

For example, you can use environmental variables in the following way to install SQL Server Developer edition, specifying a password for sa and accepting the SQL Server End-User Licensing Agreement:

```
sudo ACCEPT_EULA='Y' MSSQL_PID='Developer' MSSQL_SA_PASSWORD='Pa$$w0rd' /
opt/mssql/bin/mssql-conf setup
```

Performance Best Practices

Similar to the Windows world, you usually do not have to worry about performing a large number of operating system configurations in Linux in order to run and optimize SQL Server for performance. Obviously, selecting the right hardware or, in a virtualized platform, the right configurations for a virtual machine is still essential. Properly configuring storage, as covered in Chapter 11, is extremely important as well.

However, there are a few configuration guidelines for SQL Server on Linux that you could take advantage from, which I will cover next. Some SQL Server administrators, new to the Linux world, may be intimidated by performing these configuration changes on their own, so it may be recommended that they work closely with their system administrators. Sometimes, the same is true even for Windows systems where we usually have to work very closely with both the system and the storage administrators to take advantage of the available hardware, operating system, and storage.

I will use this last section of the chapter to describe some of those configuration guidelines, starting with memory configuration.

Memory and the Out-of-Memory Killer

By default, SQL Server uses only up to 80% of the available physical memory in Linux, so you may want to use mssql-conf and the memory.memorylimitmb setting to configure it to a higher value. This setting configures the memory limit, and its value must be specified in MB. An example using the memory.memorylimitmb setting was provided in the previous section where we set the memory limit to 492 GB.

However, a system with improper configured memory can also create problems. You will need to make sure you are leaving enough memory for the operating system and possibly any other processes running in the same system. Since many applications allocate their required memory up front and usually do not utilize all this memory, the

Linux kernel was designed with the ability to overcommit memory to make memory usage more efficient. And what is worst, a system running low in memory may lead the kernel to start killing processes in order to free up memory and stay operational. Since SQL Server is most likely the process using most of the memory, it would also be likely the process killed.

If you suspect the SQL Server was killed for this reason, you should inspect the contents of the /var/log/messages file and look for a message indicating that the sqlservr process was actually killed because the system was running out of memory. If you find this evidence, the best way to avoid this problem is to properly configure the required memory for SQL Server, leaving enough memory for Linux and any other processes running in the same system.

Kernel Settings

For those of us who have worked with other databases in the Unix world (e.g., Oracle), the need to configure kernel settings will not be surprising. In this section, I will discuss CPU and disk kernel settings Microsoft recommends for a Linux environment. You may also want to look at the documentation on your Linux distribution on how to perform these configurations. In this section, I will cover the basics for Red Hat Enterprise Linux.

In Red Hat Enterprise Linux, you can also use performance tuning profiles. Linux provides predefined tuning profiles, and we can also create our own, as we will do next. In order to do this, we will use the tuned-adm tool.

To get started, we can use tuned-adm to get a list of the available tuning profiles in the system:

```
# tuned-adm list
Available profiles:
- accelerator-performance    - Throughput performance based tuning with
                               disabled higher latency STOP states
- balanced                   - General non-specialized tuned profile
- desktop                    - Optimize for the desktop use-case
- hpc-compute                - Optimize for HPC compute workloads
- intel-sst                  - Configure for Intel Speed Select Base
                               Frequency
- latency-performance        - Optimize for deterministic performance at
                               the cost of increased power consumption
```

```
- network-latency            - Optimize for deterministic performance at
                               the cost of increased power consumption,
                               focused on low latency network performance
- network-throughput         - Optimize for streaming network throughput,
                               generally only necessary on older CPUs or
                               40G+ networks
- powersave                  - Optimize for low power consumption
- throughput-performance     - Broadly applicable tuning that provides
                               excellent performance across a variety of
                               common server workloads
- virtual-guest              - Optimize for running inside a virtual guest
- virtual-host               - Optimize for running KVM guests
Current active profile: virtual-guest
```

The following command shows what the active tuning profile is (which was also shown in the previous example):

```
# tuned-adm active
Current active profile: virtual-guest
```

Originally, when SQL Server for Linux was just released with the 2017 version, Microsoft recommended using the throughput-performance profile. If you still need this profile, you can enable it using the next command:

```
# tuned-adm profile   throughput-performance
```

However, starting with Red Hat Enterprise Linux 8.0, an mssql profile was codeveloped with Red Hat to offer the best performance-related tuning for SQL Server implementations. By the way, you can verify your Red Hat Enterprise Linux system version by running cat /etc/os-release. For example, I get the following partial output:

```
# cat /etc/os-release
NAME="Red Hat Enterprise Linux"
VERSION="8.2 (Ootpa)"
ID="rhel"
ID_LIKE="fedora"
VERSION_ID="8.2"
PLATFORM_ID="platform:el8"
PRETTY_NAME="Red Hat Enterprise Linux 8.2 (Ootpa)"
```

This is the profile proposed by Microsoft and Red Hat, which, as you may see, includes the mentioned system-defined throughput-performance profile. The include parameter in a profile definition file allows you to base your own tuned profiles on existing profiles.

```
#
# A tuned configuration for SQL Server on Linux
#

[main]
summary=Optimize for Microsoft SQL Server
include=throughput-performance

[cpu]
force_latency=5

[sysctl]
vm.swappiness = 1
vm.dirty_background_ratio = 3
vm.dirty_ratio = 80
vm.dirty_expire_centisecs = 500
vm.dirty_writeback_centisecs = 100
vm.transparent_hugepages=always
vm.max_map_count=1600000
net.core.rmem_default = 262144
net.core.rmem_max = 4194304
net.core.wmem_default = 262144
net.core.wmem_max = 1048576
kernel.numa_balancing=0
kernel.sched_latency_ns = 60000000
kernel.sched_migration_cost_ns = 500000
kernel.sched_min_granularity_ns = 15000000
kernel.sched_wakeup_granularity_ns = 2000000
```

In order to implement the proposed profile, follow the following steps.

Create the mssql directory as shown next:

```
# mkdir /usr/lib/tuned/mssql
```

Save the profile definition shown earlier with a file named tuned.conf under /usr/lib/tuned/mssql.

Update the permissions accordingly, in this case, so that anyone could execute the tuned.conf file:

```
chmod +x /usr/lib/tuned/mssql/tuned.conf
```

At this moment, you could verify that the profile is available. Run the following command, only partial output shown:

```
# tuned-adm list
Available profiles:
- mssql                        - Optimize for Microsoft SQL Server
```

You can then enable the profile running:

```
# tuned-adm profile mssql
```

Finally, validate that it is enabled:

```
# tuned-adm active
Current active profile: mssql
```

Tables 3-2 and 3-3 show the Microsoft recommended CPU and disk settings. You may notice that some of those values were included in the previous custom mssql tuning profile. Let us discuss more about those settings and values next.

Table 3-2. Recommended CPU-Related Kernel Settings

Setting	Value	Details
CPU frequency governor	performance	See the **cpupower** command in your distribution's documentation
ENERGY_PERF_BIAS	performance	See the **x86_energy_perf_policy** command in your distribution's documentation
min_perf_pct	100	See your documentation on intel p-state
C-States	C1 only	See your Linux or system documentation on how to ensure C-States is set to C1 only

Table 3-3. *Recommended Disk-Related Kernel Settings*

Setting	Value	Details
disk readahead	4096	See the blockdev command
sysctl settings	kernel.sched_min_granularity_ns = 10000000	See the sysctl command
	kernel.sched_wakeup_granularity_ns = 15000000	
	vm.dirty_ratio = 40	
	vm.dirty_background_ratio = 10	
	vm.swappiness = 10	

Table 3-3 shows the sysctl command, which is used to configure kernel parameters at runtime. Although the settings listed in the table were already configured and enabled at the mssql profile created earlier in this section, I will show you how this command works. You can use the sysctl command to see a current kernel value as in the following example:

```
# sysctl kernel.sched_min_granularity_ns
kernel.sched_min_granularity_ns = 15000000
```

This returns the value we just set on the profile; you may see a default value too. If you wanted to set a new value, you could use

```
# sysctl -w kernel.sched_min_granularity_ns=10000000
kernel.sched_min_granularity_ns = 10000000
```

You can display all the kernel settings currently configured in the system by using the --all option:

```
# sysctl --allsysctl
```

My current installation returned 942 values.

As also indicated in Table 3-3, you can use the blockdev command to set the disk readahead property. Let us start with a report of all the devices in the system:

```
# blockdev --report
RO    RA   SSZ   BSZ   StartSec          Size   Device
rw  8192   512  4096          0   21474836480   /dev/sdb
rw  8192   512  4096       2048   21472739328   /dev/sdb1
rw  8192   512  4096          0   68719476736   /dev/sda
```

We can now use the --getra and --setra options to read and set the readahead values, respectively:

```
# blockdev --getra /dev/sda
8192
# blockdev --setra 4096 /dev/sda
# blockdev --report
```

Running the report again will show 4096, as recommended in Table 3-3.

The profile created earlier also disables auto numa balancing on a multinode NUMA system. Disabling this performance configuration is required as this property is enabled by default.

```
# sysctl kernel.numa_balancing
kernel.numa_balancing = 1
# sysctl -w kernel.numa_balancing=0
```

Finally, another property set in the tuning profile was vm.max_map_count. Its default value, 65536, may not be high enough for a SQL Server instance. It is recommended to change this value to 256K or 262,144 as shown next:

```
# sysctl vm.max_map_count
vm.max_map_count = 65536
# sysctl -w vm.max_map_count=262144
vm.max_map_count = 262144
```

Additional Configurations

Three important additional configurations to consider in regard to a Linux system running SQL Server are transparent huge pages, swap files, and the last accessed date and time file property.

Notice that the vm.transparent_hugepages value was set to "always" on our tuned profile. Transparent huge pages are an abstraction layer which uses large-sized pages of memory such as 2 MB and 1 GB which are recommended for applications using large amounts of memory like SQL Server. However, in case of high memory paging activity in SQL Server deployments, you may want to use the value "madvise." In this scenario, transparent huge pages are disabled system-wide but are still available to applications that make a madvise call to allocate memory in the madvise region. The following is one way to accomplish this, where the value in brackets shows the active value:

```
more /sys/kernel/mm/transparent_hugepage/enabled
[always] madvise never
# echo madvise > /sys/kernel/mm/transparent_hugepage/enabled
# more /sys/kernel/mm/transparent_hugepage/enabled
always [madvise] never
```

You can also modify our tuning profile, replacing always with madvise, and make the mssql profile active again by running the following commands:

```
# tuned-adm off
# tuned-adm profile mssql
```

Same as in the Windows platform, properly configuring a swap file on Linux is important for the performance of SQL Server. A swap file can be used when the available physical memory is full and inactive pages are moved to the swap space. For details on how to implement and maintain a swap file, please refer to your Linux distribution documentation.

Linux writes a date and time timestamp every time it performs a read operation in a file. This means it technically generates write activity every time a file is accessed. Although this attribute can be required for some applications, it is not required and it is very expensive for a database system like SQL Server.

It is recommended to disable this behavior on the file systems used by SQL Server. In order to perform that, you would have to add the noatime attribute to the associated mount options on such file systems.

Check your operating system documentation for comprehensive instructions to perform this operation. One method is to edit the /etc/fstab file as shown next. The following commands show part of the /etc/fstab file:

```
more /etc/fstab
/dev/mapper/rootvg-usrlv /usr          xfs     defaults                 0 0
```

Edit the file to add noatime on the options column:

```
more /etc/fstab
/dev/mapper/rootvg-usrlv /usr          xfs     defaults,noatime         0 0
```

Use the mount command to reload the file system information:

```
# mount -o remount /
```

Summary

This chapter covered SQL Server configuration settings that can help in the performance of your databases and applications. We also discussed how some configuration choices are set to the best possible values or a good starting point by default. However, as workloads vary from one installation to another, some additional configurations may be required, especially for high performance installations.

We also saw how some behaviors that were originally implemented as a trace flag, probably as a temporary solution to fix a particular problem, eventually made it to the database engine as a configuration default. This was the case of trace flags 2371, 1117, and 1118, whose behavior is now enabled by default starting with SQL Server 2016. We covered trace flag 2371 in this chapter, and although we also briefly covered trace flags 1117 and 1118, they are covered in greater detail in Chapter 4.

Some configurations for performance should be considered if you use other SQL Server features such as Always On availability groups, compression, or encryption, just to name a few. Some other features, like in-memory technologies, are extremely critical for performance and will be covered in more detail in Chapter 7.

Finally, we covered configuring SQL Server on Linux. This included ways to configure SQL Server settings, for example, by using the mssql-conf tool, and to configure Linux settings to improve the performance of SQL Server.

CHAPTER 4

tempdb Troubleshooting and Configuration

`tempdb` is a system database used for holding temporary objects that can be user or system created. Unlike other databases, `tempdb` is recreated every time SQL Server starts. The various uses of `tempdb` can be generally categorized into three groups: user, internal, and version store objects.

a. **User objects**: Used for objects created directly by users like global and local temporary tables, table variables, or temporary stored procedures.

b. **Internal objects**: Used for internal objects including worktables to store temporary data for sorting, spools, and cursor and service broker information and workfiles for hash join and hash aggregate operations. Users cannot directly create these internal objects.

c. **Version store objects**: Used for row versioning for snapshot isolation levels, online index operations, AFTER triggers, and MARS (multiple active result sets).

The performance problems discussed in this chapter mostly impact the first two areas, user and internal objects. One of these performance problems—one I learned the hard way the day we went live with a new application in my earlier years working as a database administrator—is `tempdb` contention. The creation of a large number of user objects in a short period of time can contribute to latch contention of allocation pages, also called DML (Data Modification Language) contention. Contention of system catalogs, also called DDL (Data Definition Language) contention, although not common, is also possible in some heavy use scenarios.

121

© Benjamin Nevarez 2021
B. Nevarez, *High Performance SQL Server*, https://doi.org/10.1007/978-1-4842-6491-1_4

Regarding internal objects, some query processor operations, such as storing intermediate runs for sorts or hash tables for hash joins and hash aggregates, may create performance problems when using `tempdb` as these operations were originally designed to work on server memory instead of disk. In this last case, `tempdb` is not the problem per se, but rather the fact that these operations need to use `tempdb`, which is obviously slower than memory access.

SQL Server 2019 introduces probably the biggest tempdb performance improvement in the history of the product. Starting with this version, it is possible to configure tempdb to use memory-optimized metadata, an In-Memory OLTP–based feature. By enabling this configuration, tempdb metadata can now be moved into latch-free nondurable memory-optimized tables eliminating metadata contention entirely.

Since memory-optimized tempdb metadata is an optional configuration in SQL Server 2019 and DML contention is still a performance concern on all the versions of the product, I will still start this chapter covering the problem in greater detail. Memory-optimized tempdb metadata is covered later in this chapter.

DML Contention

As mentioned earlier, one of the two biggest performance problems that `tempdb` faces is latch contention in allocation pages, which is also called DML contention as it is mostly due to `INSERT`, `UPDATE`, and `DELETE` operations on temporary tables. To analyze the problem and talk about workarounds and possible solutions, let's start with an introduction to allocation pages. Latches were introduced in Chapter 1. As shown in Figure 4-1, every database data file starts with a file header page, followed by the PFS, GAM, SGAM, BCM, and DCM pages.

Every Database File

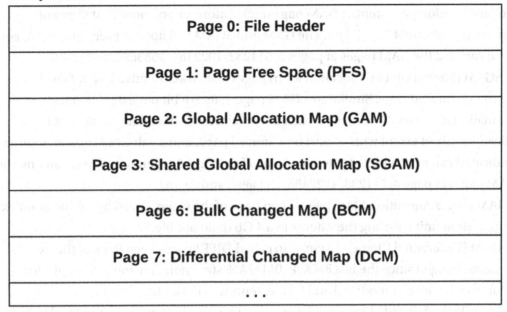

Figure 4-1. *Data file pages*

The PFS (Page Free Space) page records the allocation status of each page in a database file and is the first page on a database after the file header page. Each byte in the PFS page records information about one specific page, which means the PFS page can cover only a limited number of pages, in this case, 8088. In a large enough database, a new PFS page will be available every 8088 pages in a data file, roughly every 64 MB, so you can find PFS pages at pages 1, 8088, 16176, 24264, and so on. Bits 0–2 of each byte in the PFS page indicate if the page is empty or the percentage full if it is not, while bits 3–7 keep other page information not related to our topic.

GAM and SGAM are related to extents, so let me start by explaining pages and extents. As covered in Chapter 1, a page is the fundamental unit of data storage in SQL Server, and its size is 8 KB. An extent is eight pages and its size is therefore 64 KB. SQL Server traditionally uses two kinds of extents, mixed and dedicated extents. Mixed extents are used for small objects that can, at least initially, fit in one page. By using a mixed extent, they can allocate up to eight distinct objects. On the other hand, a dedicated extent, also called uniform extent, is used for larger objects in which all eight pages are used by the same object.

GAM (Global Allocation Map) pages keep track of allocated extents using only one bit of information per extent. A GAM page tracks information about 64,000 extents, which covers almost 4 GB of data. The GAM and SGAM will appear every 511,232 pages, so you can find the GAM pages at pages 3, 511232, 1022464, 1533696, and so on.

SGAM (Shared Global Allocation Map) pages keep track of mixed extents with at least one unused page. Similar to a GAM page, it uses a bit per extent and has information about 64,000 extents, which covers almost 4 GB of data. A value of 1 indicates a mixed extent with at least one unused page, and a value of 0 indicates either a dedicated extent or a mixed extent without a free page. As mentioned, you can find the SGAM pages at page 4, 511233, 1022465, 1533697, and so on.

IAM (Index Allocation Map) pages keep track of the extents used by a table or index per allocation unit covering the extents in a 4 GB database file.

DCM (Differential Changed Map, also called DIFF) pages keep track of the extents that have changed since the last BACKUP DATABASE statement, having a value of 1 for extents that have been modified and 0 for extents that have not.

BCM (Bulk Changed Map) pages keep track of extents that have been modified by bulk-logged operations since the last BACKUP LOG statement, having a value of 1 for extents that have been modified and 0 for extents that have not. It is also called ML, or Minimally Logged.

You can verify if a page is a PFS, GAM, or SGAM page by using the undocumented statement DBCC PAGE, which has the following syntax:

```
DBCC PAGE ( {'dbname' | dbid}, filenum, pagenum [, printopt={0|1|2|3} ])
```

Note   Although DBCC PAGE is an undocumented and unsupported statement and should be used at your own risk, it is relatively safe and used extensively by the SQL Server community.

The page type will be displayed as m_type on the page header. Although there are many page types, some of the interesting values for the purpose of this chapter include the following:

1: Data page

2: Index page

8: GAM page

9: SGAM page

10: IAM page

11: PFS page

15: File header page

16: DCM map page

17: BCM map page

As an example, run

```
DBCC TRACEON(3604)
DBCC PAGE('tempdb', 1, 1, 0)
```

where the first three parameters are the database name, file ID, and page number, respectively. The last choice, printopt 0, requests to just print the page header information of the page we want to inspect. DBCC TRACEON(3604) is required to send the output of the statement to SQL Server Management Studio, which you can see using the Messages tab. Part of the output is shown next, where m_type 11 shows it is a PFS page, in this case the first PFS page in the file:

```
m_pageId = (1:1)                      m_headerVersion = 1
m_type = 11
m_typeFlagBits = 0x1                  m_level = 0
m_flagBits = 0x0
m_objId (AllocUnitId.idObj) = 99  m_indexId (AllocUnitId.idInd) = 0
Metadata:
AllocUnitId = 6488064
Metadata: PartitionId = 0             Metadata: IndexId = 0
Metadata: ObjectId = 99
```

Using the values 2, 3, 6, and 7 for pagenum will return the GAM, SGAM, DCM, and BCM pages, respectively. You can play with the other values mentioned such as 8088, 16176, 24264, and so on, for additional PFS pages, assuming the file is large enough.

New with SQL Server 2019, the sys.dm_db_page_info DMF is finally a documented and supported way to get information about a page in a database. Although DBCC PAGE has more functionality, the sys.dm_db_page_info DMF still can be extremely helpful in many cases. DBCC PAGE will still be needed for cases when the entire contents of the page are needed.

The parameters for sys.dm_db_page_info are very similar to those required by DBCC PAGE. You would need to provide the database id, file id, page id, and a mode, which determines the level of detail of the returned information. The values for mode could be LIMITED and DEFAULT. For example, our last DBCC PAGE statement could be run in the following way:

```
SELECT * FROM sys.dm_db_page_info(2, 1, 1, 'DETAILED')
```

For more details about SQL Server pages and extents, see "Pages and Extents Architecture" at `https://technet.microsoft.com/en-us/library/cc280360(v=sql.105).aspx`. For more details about `DBCC PAGE`, see `https://blogs.msdn.microsoft.com/sqlserverstorageengine/2006/06/10/how-to-use-dbcc-page/`.

Describing tempdb Latch Contention

Every time a new object has to be created in tempdb, which is usually a temporary table, and at least one row is inserted, two new pages must be allocated from a mixed extent and assigned to the new object. One is an IAM page and the second one is a data page. During this process, SQL Server also has to access and update the very first PFS page and the very first SGAM page in the data file.

As discussed in Chapter 1, only one thread can change an allocation page at a time, by requesting a latch on it. When there is high activity and a large number of temporary tables being created and dropped in tempdb, contention on the PFS and SGAM pages is possible. Remember that this is not an I/O problem as allocation pages are in this case already in memory. Obviously, this contention impacts the performance of the processes creating those tables since they may have to wait and SQL Server may appear unresponsive for short periods of time. Keep in mind that although user databases also use allocation pages, they are not likely to have a latch contention problem since not as many objects are created at the same time as in tempdb.

Back in the SQL Server 2000 days, when temporary tables were deleted, these pages would need to be deallocated, requiring a new latch on the PFS page and potentially another latch on the SGAM page. An optimization introduced with SQL Server 2005, temporary table caching, improved this mechanism by caching one IAM page and one data page when the temporary table is deleted, which could be reused if the same temporary table or table variable had to be created again, avoiding access to the allocation bitmap pages. However, this caching mechanism has some limitations, and latch contention is not completely avoided on systems with heavy tempdb use.

The easiest way to check if you have a latch contention problem on `tempdb` allocation pages is to look for `PAGELATCH_XX` waits on the database activity. Please note that they are not the same as `PAGEIOLATCH_XX` waits. Run the following code:

```
SELECT * from sys.dm_os_waiting_tasks
WHERE wait_type LIKE 'PAGE%LATCH%'
AND resource_description LIKE '2:%'
```

Optionally, you could also try the following:

```
SELECT * FROM sys.dm_exec_requests
WHERE wait_type LIKE 'PAGE%LATCH%'
AND wait_resource LIKE '2:%'
```

or

```
SELECT * FROM sysprocesses
WHERE lastwaittype LIKE 'PAGE%LATCH%'
AND waitresource LIKE '2:%'
```

Note   Traditionally, sysprocesses has been widely used to get these latch waits, and it is very likely you will still see it in old code examples and other sources. Since this was a SQL Server 2000 system table and only included in newer versions as a view for backward compatibility, it should not be used in new code anymore.

The `resource_description` column in `sys.dm_os_waiting_tasks` has a large number of formats depending on the resource that is being consumed. In the case of latch contention, the format we are interested in is `<db-id>:<file-id>:<page-in-file>`, which represents the database ID (which is always 2 for tempdb), file ID, and page in file, respectively. If you see `resource_description` as 2:1:1 and 2:1:3, you know immediately that they are the PFS and SGAM pages, respectively. The `wait_type` would usually be `PAGELATCH_UP` although `PAGELATCH_EX` can also appear, and the file ID most likely would be 1. File IDs greater than 1 are not common as creating additional files is a workaround to this issue as shown in the next section.

Fixing tempdb Latch Contention

In my opinion, there is no perfect solution to the latch contention problem as the database engine should be able to escalate and work fine as the number of operations increase. An obvious solution may be to minimize the number of temporary tables created in tempdb at the same time, but this may not be easy to implement as it would require code and application changes. Keep in mind that internal objects, like the ones created by sort and hash operations, are not created explicitly by users and do not require the allocation methods discussed in this section. These internal objects are, however, a performance problem for other reasons that we will discuss later.

The workaround to these problems has historically been one or a combination of some of the following choices, prior to SQL Server 2016:

1. Using multiple data files

2. Enabling trace flag 1118

3. Enabling trace flag 1117

Let's cover these in the following sections.

Using Multiple Data Files

One possible solution to the latch contention problem is to use multiple data files for tempdb. By using multiple files, allocation bitmaps will be spread onto these files, minimizing contention as SQL Server will balance incoming requests across them. Using multiple files can help with both PFS and SGAM pages, and using trace flag 1118, as shown next, can greatly minimize the use of SGAM pages as well.

One question that has been debated for years is what the optimal number of files for tempdb should be. The fact that applications could use tempdb in different ways and have different workloads has proved difficult to recommend a specific number for every scenario. Fortunately, there is a good recommendation that can work on most use cases and consists of creating one data file per logical processor available to the SQL Server instance, up to a maximum of eight files. As shown later, starting with SQL Server 2016, this recommendation is now a default configuration option for tempdb when you install the software. As mentioned in Chapter 1, SQL Server creates a scheduler per logical processor available to SQL Server, so the number of logical processors is also the maximum number of concurrent threads. Having multiple files means multiple PFS and

SGAM pages, which means more allocations can happen at a time, reducing contention as threads are not waiting for one set of allocation pages. But this is a general guideline, and there might be cases where a high `tempdb` usage may still show contention. In these cases, it is recommended to create additional data files in multiples of four, up to the number of logical processors available in the system.

As explained in the next section, data files on `tempdb` should be created with the same size and have the same autogrowth setting.

Trace Flags 1117 and 1118

Since SQL Server uses SGAM pages to look for mixed extents with at least one unused page, a possible workaround to SGAM contention could be to avoid mixed extents altogether and, instead, exclusively use uniform extents. Trace flag 1118 has been available since SQL Server 2000 to do just this. By disabling most of the single-page allocations and, instead, using dedicated extents, you reduce the contention on SGAM pages. A downside with using trace flag 1118 is that every object will use a dedicated extent, which requires eight pages. If the object is small enough to fit in only one page, this is effectively wasting space. That is, if the object only requires 8 KB of space, it will have to use 64 KB, thus wasting 56 KB of storage. The other downside is that this configuration takes effect at the instance level, impacting user databases as well. SGAM pages will still be used, as IAM pages will still need to be single-page allocations from mixed extents, but SGAM contention will most likely be eliminated or greatly minimized.

Trace flag 1117 is related to how SQL Server increases the size of database files when enabling even growth of all files in a filegroup. This discussion requires an introduction to three important points:

    a.   Do not rely on autogrowth.

    b.   Configure database instant file initialization.

    c.   Create data files of equal size.

Do not rely on the default autogrowth configuration, but leave it enabled with a proper file growth configuration, so it can be used as a last resort choice. A production environment most likely will have a dedicated drive for `tempdb`, if not a dedicated drive for data files and another for the transaction log file. If you are in this situation, simply allocate all the space possible to the `tempdb` files. This will help to avoid growing the database files during production operations, causing unnecessary overhead. At the same time, it will minimize fragmentation.

Configure database instant file initialization, which is covered in detail in Chapter 3 and briefly described in the next section.

Create data files of equal size. A mechanism called the proportional fill algorithm used by SQL Server considers the current size of the database files, at least at the filegroup level. This algorithm determines the order files are utilized and written to. It attempts to spread the allocations across the pages in a round-robin fashion. There is an unfortunate behavior when files are not the same size. Instead of spreading GAM allocations evenly between all the data files on a database, it would favor the largest file instead. Because of this, it is critical to have all the data files the same size.

Trace flag 1117 helps you to avoid this problem by growing all the `tempdb` files together at the same time by the configured increment. However, as in the case of trace flag 1118, trace flag 1117 applies to the entire SQL Server instance, working at the filegroup level on user databases. You may need to review this setting if it might be a problem for filegroups on your user databases.

As we will see in the next section, the behavior of trace flags 1117 and 1118 can now be configured at the database level.

SQL Server 2016 Enhancements

SQL Server 2016 introduced several important enhancements for tempdb, so let us discuss them in this section. As mentioned in the introduction to this chapter, some of the previous `tempdb` recommendations are now either configured or enabled by default in SQL Server 2016. Let's start with the SQL Server setup process.

One of the screens during the SQL Server installation, shown in the previous chapter in Figure 3-3, now gives you the choice to grant the "Perform Volume Maintenance Task" privilege to the SQL Server database engine service account, automatically enabling instant file initialization. In previous versions of SQL Server, this was a choice that you would have to configure separately from the SQL Server setup or configuration process.

By default, when a database is created or restored (or when a file is added, expanded, or restored), files are first initialized by filling them with zeros. In some cases, depending on the file size, this may be time-consuming. By enabling instant file initialization, SQL Server skips zeroing the files, making the process almost instantaneous. The only downside of skipping this process, as warned on the mentioned setup screen in Figure 3-3, is that avoiding zeroing data pages "may lead to information disclosure as it could allow deleted content to be accessed by an unauthorized principal." Please refer to Chapter 3 for more details about the instant file initialization feature.

Later in the setup process, SQL Server allows you to configure tempdb. Different from previous versions of SQL Server, the installation process now recommends the number of data files to be the same as the logical processors available in the system, up to a maximum of eight. This will be the default configuration if you take no action, as shown in Figure 4-2.

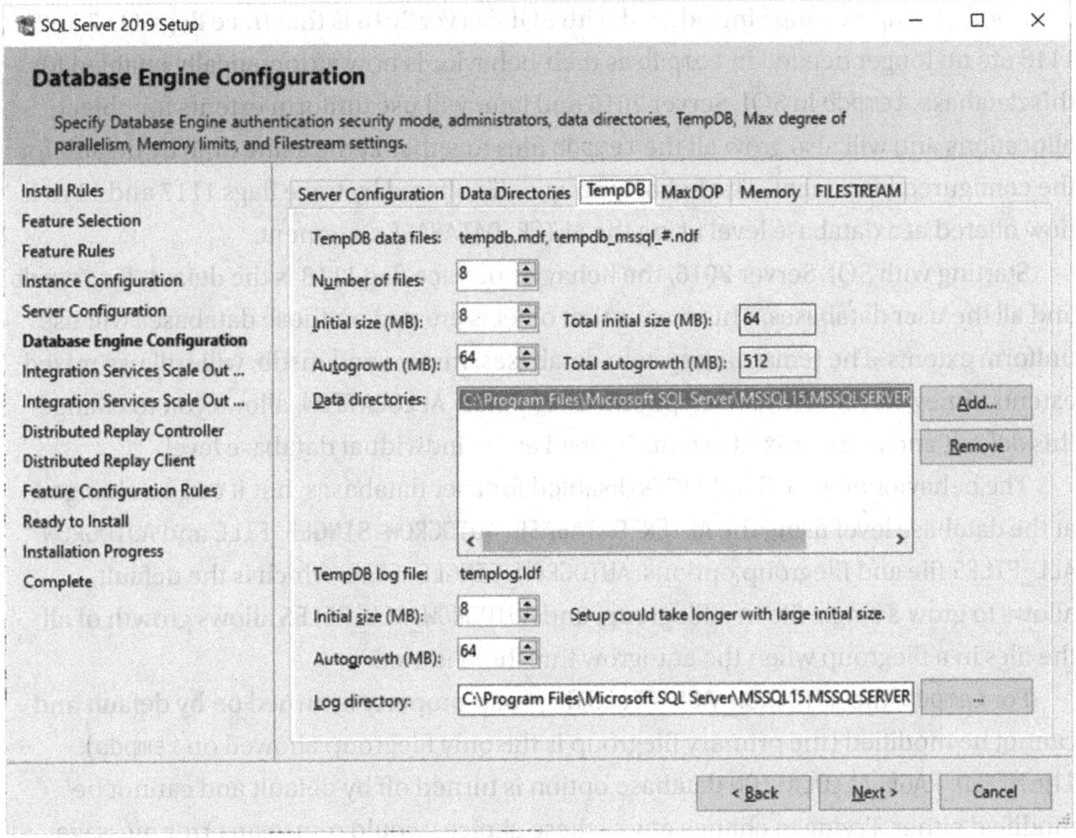

Figure 4-2. Tempdb configuration during setup

Note As suggested in Figure 4-2, please also be sure you properly configure the initial data file and autogrowth sizes according to your application workload and requirements.

This default number of data files will also be automatically configured if you perform a command-line installation, and, optionally, you have the choice to specify a different value by using the /SQLTEMPDBFILECOUNT installation parameter. For more details about this and other tempdb-related setup parameters, see "Install SQL Server from the Command Prompt" at https://docs.microsoft.com/en-us/sql/database-engine/install-windows/install-sql-server-from-the-command-prompt.

At the time of writing, creating a Microsoft Azure SQL Server 2019 image still provisions a single data file for a multiprocessor virtual machine. As a result, you may still need to manually configure the number of files accordingly.

Another major change introduced with SQL Server 2016 is that trace flags 1117 and 1118 are no longer needed in tempdb as their behavior is now automatically enabled for this database. tempdb in SQL Server 2016 and later will use uniform extents for object allocations and will also grow all the tempdb files together at the same time by default for the configured increment. The behavior originally offered by trace flags 1117 and 1118 is now offered at a database level using the ALTER DATABASE statement.

Starting with SQL Server 2016, the behavior of trace flag 1118 is the default for tempdb and all the user databases. This means that objects created on those databases will use uniform extents. The remaining system databases, master and msdb, will still use mixed extents. A new ALTER DATABASE option, MIXED_PAGE_ALLOCATION, allows you to change this default and to use mixed extents instead at the individual database level.

The behavior of trace flag 1117 is disabled for user databases, but it can be changed at the database level using the ALTER DATABASE AUTOGROW_SINGLE_FILE and AUTOGROW_ALL_FILES file and filegroup options. AUTOGROW_SINGLE_FILE, which is the default, allows to grow a single file in a filegroup, and AUTOGROW_ALL_FILES allows growth of all the files in a filegroup when the autogrow threshold is met.

For tempdb, the AUTOGROW_ALL_FILES filegroup property is turned on by default and cannot be modified (the primary filegroup is the only filegroup allowed on tempdb). The MIXED_PAGE_ALLOCATION database option is turned off by default and cannot be modified either. Trying to change any of these choices would return an error message indicating that the option cannot be set in the tempdb database. This means that tempdb is configured exactly as best practices would advise through trace flags prior to SQL Server 2016.

Finally, keep in mind that even with these configurations and defaults available starting with SQL Server 2016, contention may still be possible on systems with heavy tempdb use, so the additional information provided in this chapter may still be useful to help with those problems.

What Is New in SQL Server 2019

SQL Server 2017 was mostly a vehicle to ship the Linux release, and so there was not much in significant enhancements for tempdb. Probably the only improvement was that the setup process now allows specifying an initial tempdb file size of up to 256 GB per file, but that is pretty much it. Actually, it is ironic that one of the improvements of SQL Server 2016, which is the ability to create multiple data files during the installation, did not even make it into the Linux release in 2017.

Starting with SQL Server 2019, you can now also create multiple data files during a new SQL Server on Linux installation, same as with a SQL Server on Windows installation.

A second improvement for the latest version is an improvement on PFS updates. For this release, PFS pages, which were described earlier in this chapter, can now be updated using a shared latch instead of an exclusive latch, greatly helping alleviate page latch contention on PFS pages. This behavior is enabled by default on all the instance databases obviously including tempdb.

But without a doubt, the most important tempdb enhancement of the SQL Server 2019 release is memory-optimized tempdb metadata. I cover this feature in the next section.

Memory-Optimized tempdb Metadata

As mentioned at the beginning of this chapter, SQL Server 2019 introduces probably the biggest tempdb performance improvement in the history of the product, finally providing relief to a problem that has been impacting SQL Server for many years. Starting with this version, you can now configure tempdb to use memory-optimized metadata, a feature based on the In-Memory OLTP technology. By enabling this tempdb configuration, tempdb metadata can now be moved into latch-free nondurable memory-optimized tables and by doing that technically eliminating metadata contention.

To enable memory-optimized tempdb metadata, you can use the following statement:

```
ALTER SERVER CONFIGURATION SET MEMORY_OPTIMIZED TEMPDB_METADATA = ON
```

You can verify the feature is enabled at any time by running the following code:

```
SELECT SERVERPROPERTY('IsTempdbMetadataMemoryOptimized')
```

Enabling the feature will require to restart the SQL Server service. The same is true if you decide to disable the feature later for any reason.

This feature still has a few limitations, but it is still a huge improvement, and we hope those limitations could be eliminated in the coming cumulative updates or newer versions of the product. The current limitations of the feature are

a) As we will cover in Chapter 7, a current limitation of In-Memory OLTP is that a single transaction may not access memory-optimized tables in more than one database. The same is true for tempdb, and so this means that you cannot access system views in tempdb in the same transaction where you access a memory-optimized table in a user database.

b) Columnstore indexes cannot be created on temporary tables while memory-optimized tempdb metadata is enabled.

c) Using the COLUMNSTORE or COLUMNSTORE_ARCHIVE parameter of the sp_estimate_data_compression_savings is not supported.

d) As mentioned, enabling or disabling the feature will require a SQL Server service restart.

As you can see, the first limitation in this list is, in fact, an In-Memory OLTP limitation, and since it impacts mostly catalog or system views, perhaps it is not very restricting for your applications. Finally, if you need to disable this feature, you could run the following statement, which requires a SQL Server service restart:

```
ALTER SERVER CONFIGURATION SET MEMORY_OPTIMIZED TEMPDB_METADATA = OFF
```

Let us run a complete example. The following code creates a temporary table and inserts a single row on it. We will create an expensive workload by running this code thousands of times simultaneously. An easy way to accomplish this is to use the ostress utility. Save the following code into a file with a name like tempdbtest.sql:

```
CREATE TABLE #tempdbtest (id int, name char(7000))
INSERT INTO #tempdbtest VALUES (1, 'tempdb test')
```

Note   You can download the ostress utility as part of the RML Utilities for SQL Server at `www.microsoft.com/en-us/download/details.aspx?id=4511`.

Prepare your system to run the following:

```
ostress -n5000 -itempdbtest.sql
```

Basically, this runs the code we save in the file tempdbtest.sql using 5000 connections simultaneously. You may need to provide a file path too.

We are going to monitor waits in two different ways, using Performance Monitor (perfmon) and querying the sys.dm_os_waiting_tasks DMV. Be ready to run the following query while the load is running. We know you can miss some waits while running the query interactively, so we want to complement it with the Performance Monitor data. sys.dm_os_waiting_tasks and PAGE_LATCH waits were covered earlier in the chapter. Additional ways to collect wait information are covered in the next chapter.

```
SELECT * FROM sys.dm_os_waiting_tasks
WHERE wait_type LIKE 'PAGE%LATCH%'
AND resource_description LIKE '2:%'
```

Open Performance Monitor and add the following counters:

> Object: SQLServer:Wait Statistics
>
> Counter: Page latch waits
>
> Instance: All
>
> Average wait time (ms)
>
> Cumulative wait time (ms) per second
>
> Waits in progress
>
> Waits started per second

Run the first load using ostress. You may be able to see Performance Monitor data similar to what I show in Figure 4-3.

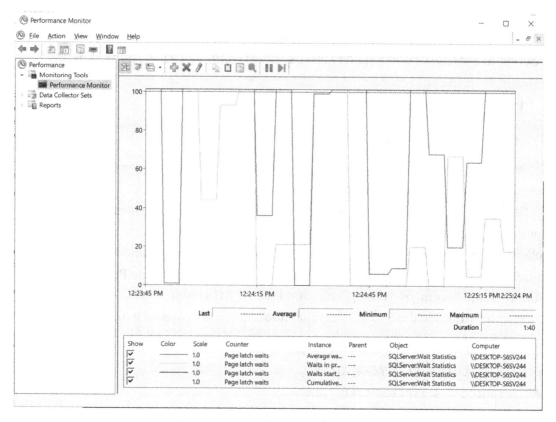

Figure 4-3. *Performance Monitor showing PAGE_LATCH waits*

You can also interactively run the sys.dm_os_waiting_tasks DMV query. We are just interested in getting a small sample, so there is no need to run multiple times. This is an example of what I get on my system:

waiting_task_address	session_id exec_context_id wait_duration_ms wait_type
0x00000187F8053848	115 0 217 PAGELATCH_EX
0x00000187E55BB848	59 0 235 PAGELATCH_EX
0x00000187E55BB088	108 0 235 PAGELATCH_EX
0x00000187F8053C28	123 0 210 PAGELATCH_EX

As you can see, there are plenty of PAGELATCH_EX waits in the system. Numbers are not important for this exercise. Now execute the following to enable memory-optimized tempdb metadata. Restart the SQL Server service.

```
ALTER SERVER CONFIGURATION SET MEMORY_OPTIMIZED TEMPDB_METADATA = ON
```

After SQL Server is back online, run the ostress load again. Look at the Performance Monitor data and run the waits query again. Both will show no PAGELATCH_EX waits at all. The Performance Monitor screen is shown in Figure 4-4 which shows no waits at all (you have got to believe I was really running the load).

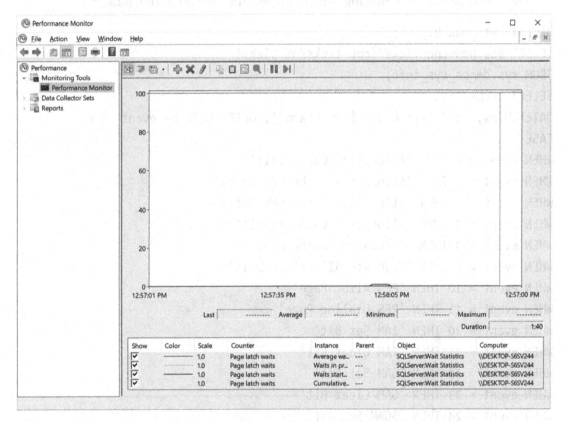

Figure 4-4. *Performance Monitor without page latch waits*

To end the exercise, you can disable the memory-optimized tempdb metadata feature, if you wish, as shown earlier. I will cover waits in more detail in the following chapter.

tempdb Events

You can analyze allocation and deallocation information in the tempdb database by inspecting the allocation ring buffer, which can be enabled using undocumented trace flag 1106. But be aware that enabling it would definitely impact the performance of your system, so don't use it on a production or busy system. Here is an example of how it works. Start by enabling trace flag 1106.

```
DBCC TRACEON (1106, -1)
```

Then you can use the following code to inspect the allocation ring buffer:

```
DECLARE @ts_now bigint;
SELECT @ts_now=cpu_ticks/(cpu_ticks/ms_ticks)
FROM sys.dm_os_sys_info;
SELECT record_id,
DATEADD(ms, -1 * (@ts_now - [timestamp]), GETDATE()) as event_time,
CASE
WHEN event = 0 THEN 'Allocation Cache Init'
WHEN event = 1 THEN 'Allocation Cache Add Entry'
WHEN event = 2 THEN 'Allocation Cache RMV Entry'
WHEN event = 3 THEN 'Allocation Cache Reinit'
WHEN event = 4 THEN 'Allocation Cache Free'
WHEN event = 5 THEN 'Truncate Allocation Unit'
WHEN event = 10 THEN 'PFS Alloc Page'
WHEN event = 11 THEN 'PFS Dealloc Page'
WHEN event = 20 THEN 'IAM Set Bit'
WHEN event = 21 THEN 'IAM Clear Bit'
WHEN event = 22 THEN 'GAM Set Bit'
WHEN event = 23 THEN 'GAM Clear Bit'
WHEN event = 24 THEN 'SGAM Set Bit'
WHEN event = 25 THEN 'SGAM Clear Bit'
WHEN event = 26 THEN 'SGAM Set Bit NX'
WHEN event = 27 THEN 'SGAM Clear Bit NX'
WHEN event = 28 THEN 'GAM Zap Extent'
WHEN event = 40 THEN 'Format IAM Page'
WHEN event = 41 THEN 'Format Page'
```

```
WHEN event = 42 THEN 'Reassign IAM Page'
WHEN event = 50 THEN 'Worktable Cache Add IAM'
WHEN event = 51 THEN 'Worktable Cache Add Page'
WHEN event = 52 THEN 'Worktable Cache RMV IAM'
WHEN event = 53 THEN 'Worktable Cache RMV Page'
WHEN event = 61 THEN 'IAM Cache Destroy'
WHEN event = 62 THEN 'IAM Cache Add Page'
WHEN event = 63 THEN 'IAM Cache Refresh Requested'
ELSE 'Unknown Event'
END as event_name,
session_id as s_id,
page_id,
allocation_unit_id as au_id
FROM
(
SELECT
xml_record.value('(./Record/@id)[1]', 'int') AS record_id,
xml_record.value('(./Record/SpaceMgr/Event)[1]', 'int') AS event,
xml_record.value('(./Record/SpaceMgr/SpId)[1]', 'int') AS session_id,
xml_record.value('(./Record/SpaceMgr/PageId)[1]', 'varchar(100)') AS
page_id,
xml_record.value('(./Record/SpaceMgr/AuId)[1]', 'varchar(100)') AS
allocation_unit_id,
timestamp
FROM
(
SELECT timestamp, convert(xml, record) as xml_record
FROM sys.dm_os_ring_buffers
WHERE ring_buffer_type = N'RING_BUFFER_SPACEMGR_TRACE'
) AS the_record
) AS ring_buffer_record
-- WHERE session_id = 52
ORDER BY record_id
```

To test it, try creating a temporary table, for example, using the following code. You can try running each line at a time and run the previous code to inspect the allocation ring buffers and see which events are created on each statement. You can uncomment the `session_id` part and specify a session ID value in case you need to filter out for a specific session if you are getting too many events from other sessions:

```
CREATE TABLE #temp (c1 int, c2 varchar(20), c3 datetime)
INSERT INTO #temp VALUES (1, 'test', GETDATE())
DROP TABLE #temp
```

You could see some output like the following:

record_id	event_name	s_id	page_id	au_id
0	PFS Alloc Page	52	1:321	34:1
1	Format Page	52	1:321	34:1
2	GAM Clear Bit	52	1:336	34:4
3	PFS Alloc Page	52	1:336	34:4
4	IAM Set Bit	52	1:336	34:4
5	Allocation Cache Add Entry	52	1:336	34:4
6	Format Page	52	1:336	34:4

Don't forget to disable trace flag 1106 before continuing:

```
DBCC TRACEOFF (1106, -1)
```

Note   Going into detail for each of the events is outside the scope of the book, but you could use it as a troubleshooting and learning tool.

The previous code works with SQL Server 2012 and later versions. You could use the following code for versions older than SQL Server 2012 as the name of the ring buffer was named `RING_BUFFER_ALLOC_TRACE` back then, and the script requires some other small changes as well:

```
DECLARE @ts_now bigint;
SELECT @ts_now=cpu_ticks/(cpu_ticks/ms_ticks)
FROM sys.dm_os_sys_info;
```

```
SELECT record_id,
DATEADD(ms, -1 * (@ts_now - [timestamp]), GETDATE()) as event_time,
CASE
WHEN event = 0 THEN 'Allocation Cache Init'
WHEN event = 1 THEN 'Allocation Cache Add Entry'
WHEN event = 2 THEN 'Allocation Cache RMV Entry'
WHEN event = 3 THEN 'Allocation Cache Reinit'
WHEN event = 4 THEN 'Allocation Cache Free'
WHEN event = 5 THEN 'Truncate Allocation Unit'
WHEN event = 10 THEN 'PFS Alloc Page'
WHEN event = 11 THEN 'PFS Dealloc Page'
WHEN event = 20 THEN 'IAM Set Bit'
WHEN event = 21 THEN 'IAM Clear Bit'
WHEN event = 22 THEN 'GAM Set Bit'
WHEN event = 23 THEN 'GAM Clear Bit'
WHEN event = 24 THEN 'SGAM Set Bit'
WHEN event = 25 THEN 'SGAM Clear Bit'
WHEN event = 26 THEN 'SGAM Set Bit NX'
WHEN event = 27 THEN 'SGAM Clear Bit NX'
WHEN event = 28 THEN 'GAM Zap Extent'
WHEN event = 40 THEN 'Format IAM Page'
WHEN event = 41 THEN 'Format Page'
WHEN event = 42 THEN 'Reassign IAM Page'
WHEN event = 50 THEN 'Worktable Cache Add IAM'
WHEN event = 51 THEN 'Worktable Cache Add Page'
WHEN event = 52 THEN 'Worktable Cache RMV IAM'
WHEN event = 53 THEN 'Worktable Cache RMV Page'
WHEN event = 61 THEN 'IAM Cache Destroy'
WHEN event = 62 THEN 'IAM Cache Add Page'
WHEN event = 63 THEN 'IAM Cache Refresh Requested'
ELSE 'Unknown Event'
END as event_name,
session_id as s_id,
page_id,
allocation_unit_id as au_id
```

```
FROM
(
SELECT
xml:record.value('(./Record/@id)[1]', 'int') AS record_id,
xml:record.value('(./Record/ALLOC/Event)[1]', 'int') AS event,
xml:record.value('(./Record/ALLOC/SpId)[1]', 'int') AS session_id,
xml:record.value('(./Record/ALLOC/PageId)[1]', 'varchar(100)') AS page_id,
xml:record.value('(./Record/ALLOC/AuId)[1]', 'varchar(100)') AS
allocation_unit_id,
timestamp
FROM
(
SELECT timestamp, convert(xml, record) as xml:record
FROM sys.dm_os_ring_buffers
WHERE ring_buffer_type = N'RING_BUFFER_ALLOC_TRACE'
) AS the_record
) AS ring_buffer_record
-- WHERE session_id = 52
ORDER BY record_id
```

In addition to the DMVs and views covered earlier, you could use also extended events to capture and monitor events related to contention on latches on allocation pages. An obvious benefit of tracing events is that you don't have to be looking at the moment the problem is happening as the information can be collected for you to review later. The following events are available:

> latch_suspend_begin: Occurs when an executing task must suspend while waiting for a latch to become available in the requested mode

> latch_suspend_end: Occurs when the executing task is resumed after waiting for a latch

> latch_suspend_warning: Occurs when there is a timeout waiting for a latch possibly causing performance problems

Some of the interesting fields you can see by capturing these events are the following:

address: The memory address where the latch resides

database_id: The database ID of the page the latch protects

duration: The amount of time in microseconds that the requestor waited for the latch (not available on latch_suspend_begin)

file_id: The file ID of the page the latch protects

is_superlatch: Indicates if the latch is a super latch

mode: The mode of the latch request

page_id: The page ID of the page the latch protects

For example, the following code creates a session for the extended events related to latches. Notice we are filtering for database_id 2 and page_id 1 and 3.

```
CREATE EVENT SESSION [test] ON SERVER
ADD EVENT sqlserver.latch_suspend_begin (
    WHERE (database_id = 2 AND (page_id = 1 OR page_id =3))
),
ADD EVENT sqlserver.latch_suspend_end (
    WHERE (database_id = 2 AND (page_id = 1 OR page_id =3))
),
ADD EVENT sqlserver.latch_suspend_warning (
    WHERE (database_id = 2 AND (page_id = 1 OR page_id =3))
)
GO
```

Once the session has been created, you can start it by running the following code:

```
ALTER EVENT SESSION [test] ON SERVER
STATE = START
GO
```

The following is a sample of one captured data event for latch_suspend_end, showing contention. You can easily see the events using the Watch Live Data feature (which you can find on SQL Server Management Studio, looking at the Management folder ➤ Extended Events ➤ Sessions, right-clicking your active session, and selecting Watch Live Data).

address	513679079488
database_id	2
duration	42990
file_id	1
is_superlatch	False
mode	UP
page_id	1

Finally, don't forget to close and drop the session to finish this exercise:

```
ALTER EVENT SESSION [test] ON SERVER
STATE = STOP
GO
DROP EVENT SESSION [test] ON SERVER
GO
```

DDL Contention

It is worth clarifying that the contention of allocating pages discussed in this section is sometimes referred to as DML contention, as it is mostly due to INSERT, UPDATE, and DELETE operations on temporary tables. This would be different, for example, from DDL contention, which can also happen in tempdb but is certainly less common than DML contention, and relates to the contention on the system catalogs needed to record information about the user-created objects. To see if you have DDL contention in tempdb, you can use the same methods described earlier for DML contention, but, instead of looking at contention of the allocation pages, you may see contention on pages belonging to the system catalog tables. Unfortunately, fixing DDL contention would require minimizing the number of user objects created and dropped in tempdb.

tempdb Spill Warnings

Although every query in SQL Server requires some memory to perform its work, some query operations, like hash, sort, and exchange, may require significantly larger amounts of memory, depending on the amount of data they need to process. This memory is required to store the rows to be sorted or to build the hash tables used by hash join and hash aggregate operators. In some cases, a memory grant may also be required for parallel query plans with multiple range scans. The query optimizer usually does a good job estimating how much memory will be required, and if the memory is available, it will be provided to the operator at execution time.

However, as mentioned in Chapter 1, hash, sort, and parallelism or exchange operators can create performance problems in the cases when not enough memory is allocated and they are instead forced to do additional data processing or to use the tempdb database (spilling to disk). These problems are usually due to bad cardinality estimations where the query optimizer may underestimate the amount of memory required for the query. Since the query may be granted less memory than needed, the sort operations or the build input of the hash operations may not fit into this available memory. Once the query is executing, it has to continue despite not having enough memory to run.

You can use the sort_warning, hash_warning, and exchange_spill extended events (or the Sort Warning, Hash Warning, and Exchange Spill trace event classes) to monitor the cases where these performance problems may be happening in your system. Starting with SQL Server 2016, you can also use the Live Query Statistics feature, explained in Chapter 6, which may help to take a look at these performance problems in real time too, as these operations can take a huge part of the query execution.

In addition to the performance problems, as accessing disk is several times slower than memory, there might be disk space problems as these operations may use a large amount of space to create internal objects on tempdb. I've seen problem queries writing dozens or hundreds of GBs of data to tempdb on this scenario. We will discuss more on how to monitor how much disk space is used in tempdb in the next section.

Since the main reason for this problem is that the query optimizer underestimates the required memory, the best plan of action to fix it is to make sure statistics do exist and are up to date. Additional recommendations will be given depending on the problem, as shown in the next three sections.

Sort Warning

Sort warnings are created by queries requiring sorts, for example, when using the ORDER BY clause. The sort_warning extended event provides additional data to troubleshoot this problem, which includes the actual number of sorted rows, granted memory, used memory, and the number of pages read from and written to the worktable. You should pay special attention to the sort_warning_type column, which shows whether a single additional pass or multiple passes were required to obtain the sorted output. This warning type information is also available on the Sort Warning trace event using the EventSubClass column. The event also includes the column query_operation_node_id, which you can use to identify which operator is causing the tempdb spill, or you can also look at an execution plan to look for a warning on a sort operator or a SpillToTempDb property. A typical solution to avoid sort warnings is to add a proper index to the query. More details about indexes will be covered in Chapter 9.

Hash Warning

Hash warnings are created when hash joins do not have enough memory to create their hash table. A hash join works by creating a hash table in memory called the build input. The second input of the join, called the probe input, will be read and compared to the hash table, returning the rows that match. The query optimizer will select the smaller of both join tables as the build input and will usually correctly estimate how much memory is required for its hash table. The query processor can even reverse those roles at execution time if the estimation was incorrect, choosing the new smaller input as the build input.

But there might still be performance problems when there is a bad estimation of the memory required for this hash table. Since the query might not have enough memory allocated, it may require SQL Server to use a workfile in tempdb.

When the build input does not fit into the available memory, SQL Server first has to split its rows into several partitions, which are processed separately. If any of those partitions still do not fit into the available memory, they are split into subpartitions, which are again processed separately. This splitting process will continue until each partition fits into the available memory or until the maximum recursion level is reached. The maximum recursion level is shown on the recursion_level column of the event (or the IntegerData column on SQL trace) and corresponds to the number of times the build input was subpartitioned. This entire process is called hash recursion.

When hash recursion has reached the maximum recursion level, the query processor will try instead a different process called hash bailout to process the remaining data. SQL Server will show if hash recursion or hash bailout was used during execution on the hash_warning_type event column (or the EventSubClass column in a Hash Warning trace event).

Similar to the sort warning discussed earlier, the hash_warning extended event provides additional troubleshooting data like including the actual number of uniquely hashed rows, granted memory, used memory, and the number of pages read from and written to the worktable.

To avoid hash warning problems, in addition to the general recommendation about statistics mentioned earlier, you can try using a different join type. Or, if you have limited memory on the server, increase the memory available. Using a different join type may require using a query hint and should be carefully tested to verify that, in fact, it improves the performance of a query.

Exchange Warning

Finally, the exchange warning, which is less common than the other two, occurs when the communication buffers in a parallel plan have been temporarily written to the tempdb database. As discussed in Chapter 1, the exchange operator is responsible for implementing parallelism in SQL Server by using multiple processors simultaneously to execute a query. The exchange warning problem only occurs in cases when you have multiple ordered range scans. In this case, you may try to avoid using the ORDER BY clause, try to avoid the multiple range scans, try to use an index hint to access the tables in a different way, or even go to the extreme of avoiding parallel plans, for example, by using the MAXDOP query hint.

Monitoring Disk Space

Although monitoring disk space on tempdb does not directly fall into the performance area per se, seeing unexpected large amounts of disk space used can sometimes be an indication of performance issues or other problems. Most of the disk space–related issues in tempdb are created by versioning, when any of the two flavors of snapshot isolation is used, or by internal objects created by sorts or hash joins, as covered in the previous section.

You can use the sys.dm_db_file_space_usage DMV to return space usage information for each file in a database. In fact, in older versions of SQL Server, this DMV was only applicable to tempdb but was later extended to include information for every database, although the internal objects and version store–related columns still apply only to tempdb. The following query is commonly used to report the space used by the different objects:

```
USE tempdb
GO
SELECT
SUM (user_object_reserved_page_count) * 1.0 / 128 as user_object_mb,
SUM (internal_object_reserved_page_count) * 1.0 / 128 as internal_objects_mb,
SUM (version_store_reserved_page_count) * 1.0 / 128  as version_store_mb,
SUM (unallocated_extent_page_count) * 1.0 / 128 as free_space_mb,
SUM (mixed_extent_page_count) * 1.0 / 128 as mixed_extents_mb
FROM sys.dm_db_file_space_usage
```

Sometimes, you may need to look for a specific process which can be causing the disk space problem. In this case, you could use sys.dm_db_task_space_use DMV, which returns page allocation and deallocation activity by task and is applicable only to the tempdb database. An example is the following query, borrowed from the tempdb white paper mentioned in the summary of this chapter:

```
SELECT t1.session_id, t1.request_id, t1.task_alloc,
  t1.task_dealloc, t2.sql_handle, t2.statement_start_offset,
  t2.statement_end_offset, t2.plan_handle
FROM (SELECT session_id, request_id,
    SUM(internal_objects_alloc_page_count) AS task_alloc,
    SUM (internal_objects_dealloc_page_count) AS task_dealloc
  FROM sys.dm_db_task_space_usage
  GROUP BY session_id, request_id) AS t1,
  sys.dm_exec_requests AS t2
WHERE t1.session_id = t2.session_id
  AND (t1.request_id = t2.request_id)
ORDER BY t1.task_alloc DESC
```

Summary

tempdb is a special system database that is shared with all the databases and activities on the SQL Server instance, and it is used for holding temporary objects or intermediate result sets. In this chapter, we covered tempdb from a SQL Server performance point of view. An additional recommendation for the reader is the Microsoft white paper "Working with tempdb in SQL Server 2005," which, although covering an older version of SQL Server, still contains a lot of relevant and useful information. You can find this white paper at https://technet.microsoft.com/en-us/library/cc966545.aspx.

Two of the most common performance problems related to tempdb are latch contention of allocation pages and tempdb spills when not enough memory is available for some query processor operations like sorts, hash joins, or exchange using range scans. New defaults introduced with SQL Server 2016 help to avoid or minimize the tempdb contention problem by automatically configuring multiple data files during installation and including the behavior that previous versions require to explicitly configure trace flags 1117 and 1118.

In addition, memory-optimized tempdb metadata, introduced with SQL Server 2019, is the most promising tempdb new feature in years. This feature was designed to remove metadata contention by moving tempdb system tables into latch-free nondurable memory-optimized tables.

PART III

Monitoring

CHAPTER 5

Analyzing Wait Statistics

One of my main recommendations for troubleshooting a performance problem when a particular issue is lacking information is to run a SQL trace or extended event session to find out the most expensive queries. This method will usually show us the most expensive queries based on one or more metrics including duration, CPU usage, logical and physical reads, writes, rows, and so on. Many times the metric of choice is duration, or how long the query took to execute. We usually assume this entire duration is usable work, which of course can be optimized. In a lot of cases, this method can find the troubled queries, and tuning them solves the performance problem.

However, something that is hidden or not obvious in this duration metric is how much time the query spent performing usable work and how much time it spent doing nothing, basically waiting for something else to happen. It is important to know both values as both can be either optimized or addressed. For example, a query may show a duration of 30 seconds—20 seconds spent doing work, like scanning a table, and the remaining 10 seconds spent waiting for system resources or being blocked. Query tuners will usually miss the waiting part, and they can optimize the work part as most tools only show that information. For example, they can easily find table scans in an execution plan where an index seek is more appropriate.

It is also true that sometimes optimizing the work part may also indirectly optimize the wait part, but not every time. Blocking may still be happening, so we may have just fixed half the problem. In some other cases, waiting may dominate the duration, so optimizing other areas will only give a modest performance improvement. These cases show why wait analysis is an important part of performance troubleshooting. In summary, performance problems happen because SQL Server is either doing excessive work or maybe doing nothing but waiting too long for resources to be available. Although a query spending a long time waiting does not really use resources, it will appear slow to the final user.

153

© Benjamin Nevarez 2021
B. Nevarez, *High Performance SQL Server*, https://doi.org/10.1007/978-1-4842-6491-1_5

Fortunately, SQL Server tracks every wait happening in the database engine, and this information is available in multiple ways. While this information is available in all the versions of the product, the DMVs and techniques shown in this chapter were introduced in SQL Server 2005 and later versions.

The waits performance tuning methodology, also called troubleshooting waits and queues, is a widely used tuning methodology originally introduced with the Microsoft white paper "SQL Server 2005 Waits and Queues" by Tom Davidson, which you can still find at https://technet.microsoft.com/en-us/library/cc966413.aspx.

Once we know what SQL Server is waiting for, we should have all the information we need to fix the problem, right? Unfortunately, it is not that simple. The waits and queues performance methodology usually requires some experience and additional analysis from other sources, including looking at system-wide performance data. Waits happen all the time in SQL Server. In fact, often even large numbers of waits does not mean there is a problem. In many cases, it is perfectly normal for SQL Server to wait for something. Some specific waits, usually called benign waits, can be ignored at all times so it is also important to filter them out of our analysis.

When we get wait information, we usually just get a number so the challenge is knowing when the waits are abnormal or excessive. In most cases, you will have to correlate the wait information with some other information that you can obtain in SQL Server from diverse sources, including DMVs, performance counters, SQL trace, extended events, and so forth, and then interpret and correlate the resulting data.

Introduction

Chapter 1 introduced SQLOS and explained that SQL Server uses a nonpreemptive scheduler, in which a task voluntarily releases control periodically and will run as long as its quantum allows it or until it gets suspended on a synchronization object. We also learned that, in a few cases, a task can run in preemptive mode when the task is running code outside the SQL Server domain. Both cases are represented in Figure 5-1, which shows the task execution process that was explained in Chapter 1. In this chapter, we expand on this topic and explain how this task execution process fits into the waits and queues performance methodology.

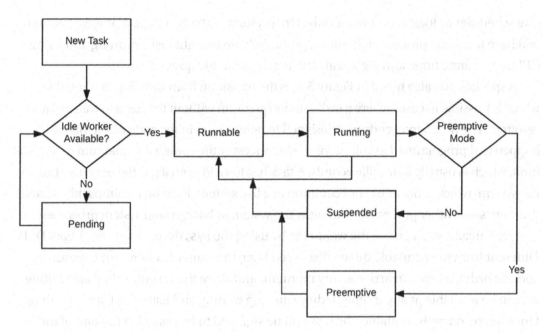

Figure 5-1. *Task execution process*

From the point of view of the user, a request is always running. After all, when we run a query, it appears to be executing all the time. But, as we can see in Figure 5-1, a request sometimes is running and sometimes is waiting. When it is running, it is using processor time to perform useful work. When it is suspended, it is waiting for something—maybe a resource, maybe a synchronization object—or maybe it is waiting for work to be assigned. The task is said to be in a waiter list. When it is runnable, the task is ready to execute, but it first has to wait for its processor slice, and it is said to be in the runnable queue. The time spent on the runnable queue, waiting for processor time, is called signal wait time. When any of these parts take too long, either running or waiting, it is very important to understand why, as there might be a possibility of improvement in any case. SQL Server tracks all the information about why a request is waiting, how long it is waiting, and what it is waiting for.

As covered in Chapter 1, SQL Server has a scheduler per logical processor, and, in addition, there are some hidden schedulers used for internal tasks and one more used for the DAC (Dedicated Administrator Connection). You can identify them by looking at the status column of the sys.dm_os_schedulers DMV. An interesting column on this DMV, quantum_length_us, shows the quantum used by the scheduler, which is usually 4 milliseconds (or 4000 microseconds). In addition, keep in mind that Figure 5-1 shows one scheduler or logical processor only. On a system with eight logical processors, you will have the same process eight times, potentially up to eight tasks running and using CPU at the same time, and eight waiter lists and runnable queues.

A special case, also noted in Figure 5-1, is the transition from Running to Runnable, which is possible in cases where a task uses its quantum without the need to wait for any resource. The SQL Server code was designed to detect areas in the code when this can happen and programmed to voluntarily yield processor time when the quantum reaches its limit, which is usually four milliseconds. A task has to yield even if it is the only user task in the system, which is obviously not common in a live system. Even on an almost idle system, there are some other processes running in the system as background system processes.

Technically, you can see the waiter list by using the `sys.dm_os_waiting_tasks` DMV. Different from the runnable queue discussed later, the waiter list does not have any specific order, a task can arrive at any moment, and since the resource they are waiting on can be available at any moment, they can stop waiting and leave the list at any time. Once the resource is available, the task will be signaled to be placed at the end of the runnable queue. The `resource_description` column of the `sys.dm_os_waiting_tasks` DMV shows the resource the task is waiting for, which can have a large number of possible values but which are nicely documented at `https://msdn.microsoft.com/en-us/library/ms188743.aspx`.

The runnable queue usually works as a FIFO list, meaning that tasks are placed in this queue and serviced in the order they arrive, the only exception being when Resource Governor is configured to change this priority, but that is a special configuration and is not common. `runnable_tasks_count` on the `sys.dm_os_schedulers` DMV shows the number of workers on the runnable queue for a specific scheduler.

The task execution process shown in Figure 5-1 will continue until the query execution is complete, except for a few cases when a query is canceled, timed out, or not able to complete for some other reason. The new Query Store feature, covered in the next chapter, allows you to track these queries in cases where you want to troubleshoot them as well.

The task execution status, Running, Runnable, or Suspended, can be shown using the status column on `sys.dm_exec_requests`, which, as covered in Chapter 1, returns information about each request that is executing within SQL Server. There are two additional task execution statuses in SQL Server, Background and Sleeping. Background is used for background system processes. Sleeping can be used for any connection, whether a user or system process, that had done work and was now connected but not actively working or waiting to do work. As indicated earlier, the wait information is available in several DMVs and other sources and will be covered in detail in the next section.

As mentioned, waits happen in SQL Server all the time, and you can see this information in several ways including running the sys.dm_exec_requests DMV. Let us build a simple example to show you how to get this information. Open a SQL Server Management Studio session and run the following statements:

```
BEGIN TRANSACTION
UPDATE Sales.SalesOrderDetail
SET OrderQty = 5
WHERE SalesOrderDetailID = 121317
```

Notice that a transaction is started but not yet committed or rolled back. Open another session and run this:

```
SELECT * FROM Sales.SalesOrderDetail
WHERE SalesOrderDetailID = 121317
```

Then open a third session and run this:

```
SELECT * FROM Sales.SalesOrderDetail
ORDER BY OrderQty
```

Since the first session has locks in an open transaction on the Sales. SalesOrderDetail table, the other two sessions will be blocked. Run this on a new session:

```
SELECT * FROM sys.dm_exec_requests r JOIN sys.dm_exec_sessions s
ON r.session_id = s.session_id
WHERE s.is_user_process = 1
```

Note   The only reason we join with sys.dm_exec_sessions is to use the is_user_ process column, which indicates if the session is a system or user process. We can no longer just rely on the session_id value as was done in previous versions of SQL Server.

You should see something like this, summarized to fit the page:

session_id	status	Command	blocking_ session_id	wait_type	last_wait_type	wait_resource
59	suspended	SELECT	55	LCK_M_S	LCK_M_S	KEY: 5:720575 94057588736 (722affd45fb5)
64	running	SELECT	0	NULL	MEMORY_ ALLOCATION_EXT	
65	suspended	SELECT	0	CXPACKET	CXPACKET	

Session 55 is blocking session 59. (It is also blocking 65, but not shown here, more on that later.) Session 59 is the first SELECT and it is waiting on a KEY resource. Session 65 is the second SELECT and is waiting on CXPACKET waits. Session 55 is the open transaction, and it is not even shown on sys.dm_exec_requests as it is currently technically not executing anything. The UPDATE statement has been completed, but the transaction is still open. Sessions 59 and 65 are suspended and on the waiter list. Even in this system with four processors, only one task is running, 64, which is the session running the DMV.

Run the following statement on the first session:

```
ROLLBACK TRANSACTION
```

Note   A major limitation when looking at waits using the sys.dm_exec_ requests DMVs is when analyzing parallel queries. This DMV only displays an entry per session, so it only displays information about the parent task and not about the child tasks. An alternate solution to troubleshoot these parallel queries will be provided later in the chapter.

Multiple scenarios can happen after the transaction is rolled back; I will describe the scenario I captured shortly. Now, in reality, this is a very simplified example. Many more waits are happening during the execution of these tasks, and, as shown in the next section, SQL Server provides methods to capture those waits if we need that detail of wait information.

After the transaction was rolled back, the KEY resource required by session 59 became available, so session 59 was signaled and placed in the runnable queue. Eventually, session 59 got access to processor time and was able to finish their work. There is the possibility that session 59 could have waited again for something else, but it would have been difficult to capture those waits by manually running this DMV. It can be captured by other methods, however, as mentioned earlier.

Session 65 was also able to continue. Once the resource it was waiting for was available, it was placed on the runnable queue and eventually got processor time and continued running. Since this is a more expensive query, it is very likely it got some more waits and placed on the waiter list and runnable queue probably multiple times. The one I captured is where session 65 is on the waiter list on ASYNC_NETWORK_IO. The sort requested by this query may run fast enough so you may not even see it or you may see some other wait. Runnable status may be so brief that you cannot capture it unless you look at a busier system.

session_id	status	command	blocking_session_id	wait_type	last_wait_type	wait_resource
64	running	SELECT	0	NULL	MEMORY_ALLOCATION_EXT	
65	suspended	SELECT	0	ASYNC_NETWORK_IO	ASYNC_NETWORK_IO	

Finally, if you run the DMV again, both SELECT statements will be completed so you no longer see any output from the DMV, except session 64 for the DMV execution.

This simplified scenario is summarized in Figure 5-2, which includes two additional sessions, 52 and 53, not captured on the DMVs but shown for completeness, as runnable tasks are hard to capture in an example with just a few transactions.

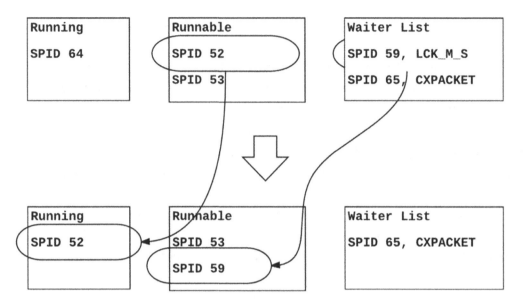

Figure 5-2. *Task execution process example*

In Figure 5-2, spid 64 is originally executing, and spid 52 is at the top of the runnable queue. After spid 64 completes (or leaves the running state for any of the reasons mentioned earlier), spid 52 moves from runnable to running, and spid 53 is now at the top of the runnable queue. Since the lock that spid 59 was waiting on is now available, it is signaled to move to the end of the runnable queue. For a brief time, spid 65 remains on the waiter list, as shown in Figure 5-2, but since it is indirectly waiting for the same resource as 59, it will be eventually moved to the runnable queue as well.

You may have noticed that we filtered out the system processes. SQL Server also has some dedicated threads, and we usually should not worry about their waits. For example, run the following query a few times while examining the wait type and wait time:

```
SELECT * FROM sys.dm_exec_requests
WHERE wait_type = 'REQUEST_FOR_DEADLOCK_SEARCH'
```

The lock or deadlock monitor is usually waiting on a REQUEST_FOR_DEADLOCK_SEARCH wait type up to five seconds between deadlock detection events. wait_time will never be more than five seconds (measured in milliseconds). The command column shows the type of task the internal system process performs, in this case LOCK MONITOR. There are several other system processes with similar waits as shown later in the "Timer Wait Types" section.

Although the wait time is reset as shown on `sys.dm_exec_requests`, it is in fact accumulated and available on `sys.dm_os_wait_stats`. For example, the following query

```
SELECT * FROM sys.dm_os_wait_stats
WHERE wait_type = 'REQUEST_FOR_DEADLOCK_SEARCH'
```

can show the next output.

wait_type	waiting_tasks_count	wait_time_ms	max_wait_time_ms	signal_wait_time_ms
REQUEST_FOR_DEADLOCK_SEARCH	20	100118	5014	100118

This information shows that the time was reset 20 times; in other words, there have been 20 separate waits, and the maximum wait time was 5014 milliseconds. Since the process is not waiting for a resource per se, the signal wait time is the same as the wait time.

Wait Information

Although we can see wait-related information on `sys.dm_exec_requests` and `sys.dm_os_waiting_tasks`, these DMVs are most focused on real-time information or useful when we need data about a particular process that is currently executing. Many times we would want to accumulate the statistical wait information or collect it for later analysis. There are three main ways to achieve this, using the `sys.dm_os_waits` DMV, SQL Server Extended Events, and, introduced with SQL Server 2016, the `sys.dm_exec_session_wait_stats` DMV. Let us review each one and see in which scenarios each one could be the best choice.

sys.dm_os_wait_stats

The `sys.dm_os_wait_stats` DMV has been the traditional way to get wait information on a SQL Server instance, and even when the DMV was introduced in SQL Server 2005, the same information was available in earlier versions using the DBCC `SQLPERF('waitstats')` statement, which still works on the current version, although it is no longer documented and was deprecated a long time ago. You could just get the wait information running the following statement, but usually we would want to do additional filtering and data aggregation, as shown later:

```
SELECT * FROM sys.dm_os_wait_stats
```

You may also query the following catalog to list the available wait types:

```
SELECT * FROM sys.dm_xe_map_values WHERE name = 'wait_types'
```

The `sys.dm_os_wait_stats` DMV shows all the waits that have occurred since the last time the SQL Server instance started or the wait statistics were last cleared and lists all the wait types available, even the ones for which waits haven't occurred yet, in which case wait time and count values will be 0. The DMV shows 1080 waits for SQL Server 2019, and a large number of them are undocumented. Since this DMV returns a numeric value, you will have to use it with some other information, compare it to a baseline, compare it with another snapshot taken at a different time, and probably do additional analysis to get value from it. For example, is a value of 10808265 for `wait_time_ms` good or bad?

Another difference with `sys.dm_exec_requests` and `sys.dm_os_waiting_tasks` is that these DMVs show wait information for waits that are still in progress, while `sys.dm_os_wait_stats` only accumulates the information once the wait is completed. For example, if you refresh multiple times the query using `sys.dm_exec_requests` shown earlier, you would notice that the wait time for the CXPACKET and LCK_M_S wait increases for as long as the processes continue to be blocked by another session. Once the wait is completed, the wait statistics will be registered on `sys.dm_os_wait_stats`.

The SQL Server documentation traditionally categorizes waits into three categories:

    a.   Resource: The task is waiting on a resource that is either not available or that is being used by some other task such as I/O, locks, or latches.

    b.   Queue: The task is waiting for work to be assigned. It is usually used by system background tasks.

    c.   External: The task is waiting for an external process such as a linked server query or an extended procedure to complete.

Some other sources add some other categories like I/O, which in our case would be part of the Resource category, or separate locks and latches into its own synchronization category.

The `sys.dm_os_wait_stats` DMV has the following columns:

> `wait_type`: Wait type, most of them documented at `https://msdn.microsoft.com/en-us/library/ms179984.aspx`. I'll cover the most important ones later in this chapter.

> `waiting_tasks_count`: Number of waits for the specified wait type.

> `wait_time_ms`: Total wait time in milliseconds. This time includes signal wait time as described next.

> `max_wait_time_ms`: Maximum wait time in milliseconds for the specified wait type.

> `signal_wait_time_ms`: Signal wait time in milliseconds. As described earlier, this is the time the task waits in the runnable queue, waiting for processor time.

There are multiple wait types that should not be a concern, and it is typical to filter them out when collecting or aggregating wait information. Here is an example of what such a query would look like:

```
SELECT
    wait_type,
    wait_time_ms,
    wait_time_ms * 100.0 / SUM(wait_time_ms) OVER() AS percentage,
    signal_wait_time_ms * 100.0 / wait_time_ms as signal_pct
FROM sys.dm_os_wait_stats
WHERE wait_time_ms > 0
AND wait_type NOT IN (
        'BROKER_DISPATCHER', 'BROKER_EVENTHANDLER',
        'BROKER_RECEIVE_WAITFOR', 'BROKER_TASK_STOP',
        'BROKER_TO_FLUSH', 'BROKER_TRANSMITTER',
        'CHECKPOINT_QUEUE', 'CHKPT',
        'CLR_AUTO_EVENT', 'CLR_MANUAL_EVENT',
        'CLR_SEMAPHORE', 'DBMIRROR_DBM_EVENT',
        'DBMIRROR_DBM_MUTEX', 'DBMIRROR_EVENTS_QUEUE',
```

```
            'DBMIRROR_WORKER_QUEUE', 'DBMIRRORING_CMD',
                'DIRTY_PAGE_POLL', 'DISPATCHER_QUEUE_SEMAPHORE',
            'EXECSYNC', 'FSAGENT',
            'FT_IFTS_SCHEDULER_IDLE_WAIT', 'FT_IFTSHC_MUTEX',
            'HADR_CLUSAPI_CALL', 'HADR_FILESTREAM_IOMGR_IOCOMPLETION',
            'HADR_LOGCAPTURE_WAIT', 'HADR_NOTIFICATION_DEQUEUE',
                'HADR_TIMER_TASK', 'HADR_WORK_QUEUE',
                'KSOURCE_WAKEUP', 'LAZYWRITER_SLEEP',
                'LOGMGR_QUEUE', 'ONDEMAND_TASK_QUEUE',
                'PWAIT_ALL_COMPONENTS_INITIALIZED', 'QDS_ASYNC_QUEUE',
                'QDS_PERSIST_TASK_MAIN_LOOP_SLEEP', 'QDS_SHUTDOWN_QUEUE',
                'QDS_CLEANUP_STALE_QUERIES_TASK_MAIN_LOOP_SLEEP',
                'REQUEST_FOR_DEADLOCK_SEARCH',
                'RESOURCE_QUEUE', 'SERVER_IDLE_CHECK',
                'SLEEP_BPOOL_FLUSH', 'SLEEP_BUFFERPOOL_HELPLW',
                'SLEEP_DBSTARTUP', 'SLEEP_DCOMSTARTUP',
                'SLEEP_MASTERDBREADY', 'SLEEP_MASTERMDREADY',
                'SLEEP_MASTERUPGRADED', 'SLEEP_MSDBSTARTUP',
                'SLEEP_SYSTEMTASK', 'SLEEP_TASK',
                'SLEEP_TEMPDBSTARTUP', 'SLEEP_WORKSPACE_ALLOCATEPAGE',
                'SNI_HTTP_ACCEPT', 'SP_SERVER_DIAGNOSTICS_SLEEP',
                'SQLTRACE_BUFFER_FLUSH', 'SQLTRACE_INCREMENTAL_FLUSH_SLEEP',
                'SQLTRACE_WAIT_ENTRIES', 'WAIT_FOR_RESULTS',
                'WAITFOR', 'WAITFOR_TASKSHUTDOWN',
                'WAIT_XTP_HOST_WAIT', 'WAIT_XTP_OFFLINE_CKPT_NEW_LOG',
                'WAIT_XTP_CKPT_CLOSE', 'XE_DISPATCHER_JOIN',
                'XE_DISPATCHER_WAIT', 'XE_TIMER_EVENT')
ORDER BY percentage DESC
```

A great choice for collecting wait information is to enable the SQL Server Data Collection feature, which was introduced with SQL Server 2008. This feature will allow you to collect not only waits but a great variety of performance information and persist it in a database. It also includes a number of graphs and reports to present the collected data. Figure 5-3 shows an example of a partial Data Collection report with wait statistics, aggregated by multiple categories. For more details about enabling and using the Data Collection feature, please refer to the SQL Server documentation.

Wait Category	Completed Waits	Wait Time (ms/sec)	% of Total Wait Time
⊞ Other	13	5.560	67.13%
⊟ Logging	480	1.864	22.51%
WRITELOG	480	1.864	22.51%
⊟ Buffer I/O	73	0.554	6.69%
PAGEIOLATCH_EX	50	0.451	5.45%
PAGEIOLATCH_SH	16	0.101	1.22%
PAGEIOLATCH_UP	7	0.002	0.02%
ASYNC_IO_COMPLETION	0	0.000	0.00%
IO_COMPLETION	0	0.000	0.00%
⊞ Lock	10	0.141	1.70%
⊞ Network I/O	437	0.093	1.13%
⊞ CPU	973	0.047	0.56%
⊞ Buffer Latch	227	0.024	0.29%
⊞ Latch	27	0.000	0.00%
⊞ Memory	0	0.000	0.00%

Figure 5-3. *Data Collection SQL Server waits report*

Finally, it is possible to clear wait statistics using the following statement although it may not always be desirable as this historical information may be used by other tools:

```
DBCC SQLPERF('sys.dm_os_wait_stats', CLEAR)
```

Waits are obviously also cleared when SQL Server is restarted. Additional information about waits can be obtained using the Wait Statistics SQL Server object on the sys.dm_os_performance_counters DMV, for example:

```
SELECT * FROM sys.dm_os_performance_counters
WHERE object_name = 'SQLServer:Wait Statistics'
```

The previous query works against a SQL Server default instance. If you have a named instance, you would need to replace the instance name accordingly, so that the SQLServer prefix of object_name would become MSSQL$<instance>. You may try the following if not sure how to specify the instance name:

```
SELECT * FROM sys.dm_os_performance_counters
WHERE object_name like '%Wait Statistics%'
```

Information available on the sys.dm_os_performance_counters DMV requires additional processing to be properly interpreted, as covered in Chapter 8.

sys.dm_exec_session_wait_stats

The sys.dm_exec_session_wait_stats, which was introduced with SQL Server 2016, is finally a long-requested method to find the waits per session, which previously required to run a potentially expensive SQL Server Extended Event session. The columns in this DMV are exactly the same as sys.dm_os_wait_stats. In the same way as sys.dm_os_wait_stats, but different from sys.dm_exec_requests and sys.dm_os_waiting_tasks, this DMV only reports waits that have been completed. For example, if a task waited 3000 milliseconds for a resource, the last two DMVs can report the progress, like 1500 or 2500, but sys.dm_exec_session_wait_stats will only report 0 if the task is still waiting or 3000 when the wait is completed. The next example will examine the waits completed for session 52.

```
SELECT * FROM sys.dm_exec_session_wait_stats
WHERE session_id = 52
```

Extended Events

There are three extended events related to waits in SQL Server: wait_completed, wait_info, and wait_info_external. wait_completed and wait_info are very similar and share most of their fields. They both capture waits happening in the system, but wait_info captures both when the wait begins and when the wait ends, as defined in the field opcode, which has the values "Begin" and "End." wait_completed only captures completed waits. The other common fields are duration and signal_duration, which are the duration and signal duration in milliseconds, and wait_resource and wait_type, which are the resource on which the wait is waiting and the wait type, respectively. wait_info is also produced both when there is a scheduler yield operation and when the thread gets processor time again. wait_info_external is when SQL Server runs an external task running in preemptive mode.

As mentioned, waits happen in SQL Server all the time, even on an idle system that is not executing any user queries. You should be extremely careful while capturing these events as it may generate a lot of data. You should only troubleshoot for short periods of time or filter out waits as much as possible.

Let's run the following exercise to see some of those waits. First, create a new extended event session for the wait_info event. (Make sure you use the correct drive and folder according to your test environment.) You may want to collect the waits for the entire instance or specify filters to limit the number of events. In this case, you want to see the waits for a specific query, so a good filter could be your session ID. Find the spid in your session and replace it accordingly in the following statement, which creates an extended event session called waits:

```
CREATE EVENT SESSION waits ON SERVER
ADD EVENT sqlos.wait_info (
        WHERE (sqlserver.session_id = 58))
ADD TARGET package0.event_file
   (SET FILENAME = 'C:\data\waits.xel')
```

Then start the session and run the query you want to analyze—in this case, a sort statement—and close the session.

```
ALTER EVENT SESSION waits ON SERVER STATE = START
GO
USE AdventureWorks2017
GO
SELECT * FROM Sales.SalesOrderDetail
ORDER BY OrderQty
GO
ALTER EVENT SESSION waits ON SERVER STATE = STOP
```

The following statement will display the captured data. For example, my test system shows just a few thousand events.

```
SELECT *, CAST(event_data AS XML) AS 'event_data'
FROM sys.fn_xe_file_target_read_file('C:\data\waits*.xel', NULL, NULL, NULL)
```

Just for reference, the event_data column for one of the events in my captured data looks like this:

```
<event name="wait_info" package="sqlos" timestamp="2016-05-
10T06:12:27.996Z">
  <data name="wait_type">
    <value>191</value>
    <text>CXPACKET</text>
  </data>
```

```xml
<data name="opcode">
  <value>1</value>
  <text>End</text>
</data>
<data name="duration">
  <value>8</value>
</data>
<data name="signal_duration">
  <value>0</value>
</data>
<data name="wait_resource">
  <value>0x0000007128e19ec0</value>
</data>
</event>
```

You can see the fields mentioned earlier for the wait_info event. In this case, the wait type is CXPACKET, opcode End, and some captured values for duration, signal_duration, and wait_resource.

Let's save the data in a temporary table to make it easier to do some additional processing:

```sql
CREATE TABLE #waits (
    event_data XML)
GO
INSERT INTO #waits (event_data)
SELECT CAST (event_data AS XML) AS event_data
FROM sys.fn_xe_file_target_read_file (
    'C:\data\waits*.xel', NULL, NULL, NULL)
```

Finally, run the following query to perform some aggregations:

```sql
SELECT
    waits.wait_type,
    COUNT (*) AS wait_count,
    SUM (waits.duration) AS total_wait_time_ms,
    SUM (waits.duration) - SUM (waits.signal_duration) AS total_resource_
    wait_time_ms,
    SUM (waits.signal_duration) AS total_signal_wait_time_ms
```

```
FROM
    (SELECT
        event_data.value ('(/event/@timestamp)[1]', 'DATETIME') AS
        datetime,
        event_data.value ('(/event/data[@name=''wait_type'']/text)[1]',
        'VARCHAR(100)') AS wait_type,
        event_data.value ('(/event/data[@name=''opcode'']/text)[1]',
        'VARCHAR(100)') AS opcode,
        event_data.value ('(/event/data[@name=''duration'']/value)[1]',
        'BIGINT') AS duration,
        event_data.value ('(/event/data[@name=''signal_duration'']/value)
        [1]', 'BIGINT') AS signal_duration
    FROM #waits
    ) AS waits
WHERE waits.opcode = 'End'
GROUP BY waits.wait_type
ORDER BY total_wait_time_ms DESC
```

A summary output for my test including just the top events is shown next.

wait_type	wait_count	total_wait_time_ms	total_resource_wait_ time_ms	total_signal_ wait_time_ms
CXPACKET	5301	11662	11649	13
NETWORK_IO	7057	482	478	4
LATCH_EX	23	19	9	10
LATCH_SH	4	14	0	14

Finally, close and drop the extended event session and delete the temp table.

```
DROP EVENT SESSION waits ON SERVER
```

```
DROP TABLE #waits
```

In this exercise, we filtered on session ID, but you can filter on some other fields as well. An example is shown in the next section, which discusses the system_health session and which default code filters out by wait type and duration.

system_health Extended Event Session

The system_health session is an extended event session that automatically collects system data that can be used to troubleshoot performance problems. It is configured by default on every SQL Server installation, and it starts when the instance starts, running all the time. Although the system_health session can be closed and deleted, it is not recommended to do so as its execution does not have any noticeable performance impact.

The system_health session collects information about multiple areas (for details, see https://msdn.microsoft.com/en-us/library/ff877955.aspx), and it also captures a number of waits. The following code is a partial definition of the SQL Server system_ health describing the wait types captured and filtering out based on the wait duration:

```
ADD EVENT sqlos.wait_info(
    ACTION(package0.callstack,sqlserver.session_id,sqlserver.sql_text)
    WHERE ([duration]>(15000) AND ([wait_type]>=N'LATCH_NL' AND ([wait_
type]>=N'PAGELATCH_NL'
AND [wait_type]<=N'PAGELATCH_DT' OR [wait_type]<=N'LATCH_DT' OR [wait_
type]>=N'PAGEIOLATCH_NL'
AND [wait_type]<=N'PAGEIOLATCH_DT' OR [wait_type]>=N'IO_COMPLETION' AND
[wait_type]<=N'NETWORK_IO' OR [wait_type]=N'RESOURCE_SEMAPHORE' OR [wait_
type]=N'SOS_WORKER' OR
[wait_type]>=N'FCB_REPLICA_WRITE' AND [wait_type]<=N'WRITELOG' OR [wait_
type]=N'CMEMTHREAD' OR [wait_type]=N'TRACEWRITE' OR [wait_type]=N'RESOURCE_
SEMAPHORE_MUTEX') OR [duration]>(30000)
AND [wait_type]<=N'LCK_M_RX_X'))),
ADD EVENT sqlos.wait_info_external(
    ACTION(package0.callstack,sqlserver.session_id,sqlserver.sql_text)
    WHERE ([duration]>(5000) AND ([wait_type]>=N'PREEMPTIVE_OS_GENERICOPS'
AND
[wait_type]<=N'PREEMPTIVE_OS_ENCRYPTMESSAGE' OR
[wait_type]>=N'PREEMPTIVE_OS_INITIALIZESECURITYCONTEXT' AND
[wait_type]<=N'PREEMPTIVE_OS_QUERYSECURITYCONTEXTTOKEN' OR
[wait_type]>=N'PREEMPTIVE_OS_AUTHZGETINFORMATIONFROMCONTEXT' AND
[wait_type]<=N'PREEMPTIVE_OS_REVERTTOSELF' OR
[wait_type]>=N'PREEMPTIVE_OS_CRYPTACQUIRECONTEXT' AND
```

```
[wait_type]<=N'PREEMPTIVE_OS_DEVICEOPS' OR
[wait_type]>=N'PREEMPTIVE_OS_NETGROUPGETUSERS' AND
[wait_type]<=N'PREEMPTIVE_OS_NETUSERMODALSGET' OR
[wait_type]>=N'PREEMPTIVE_OS_NETVALIDATEPASSWORDPOLICYFREE' AND
[wait_type]<=N'PREEMPTIVE_OS_DOMAINSERVICESOPS' OR
[wait_type]=N'PREEMPTIVE_OS_VERIFYSIGNATURE' OR [duration]>(45000) AND
([wait_type]>=N'PREEMPTIVE_OS_SETNAMEDSECURITYINFO' AND
[wait_type]<=N'PREEMPTIVE_CLUSAPI_CLUSTERRESOURCECONTROL' OR
[wait_type]>=N'PREEMPTIVE_OS_RSFXDEVICEOPS' AND
[wait_type]<=N'PREEMPTIVE_OS_DSGETDCNAME' OR
[wait_type]>=N'PREEMPTIVE_OS_DTCOPS' AND
[wait_type]<=N'PREEMPTIVE_DTC_ABORT' OR
[wait_type]>=N'PREEMPTIVE_OS_CLOSEHANDLE' AND
[wait_type]<=N'PREEMPTIVE_OS_FINDFILE' OR
[wait_type]>=N'PREEMPTIVE_OS_GETCOMPRESSEDFILESIZE' AND
[wait_type]<=N'PREEMPTIVE_ODBCOPS' OR
[wait_type]>=N'PREEMPTIVE_OS_DISCONNECTNAMEDPIPE'AND
[wait_type]<=N'PREEMPTIVE_CLOSEBACKUPMEDIA' OR
[wait_type]=N'PREEMPTIVE_OS_AUTHENTICATIONOPS' OR
[wait_type]=N'PREEMPTIVE_OS_FREECREDENTIALSHANDLE' OR
[wait_type]=N'PREEMPTIVE_OS_AUTHORIZATIONOPS' OR
[wait_type]=N'PREEMPTIVE_COM_COCREATEINSTANCE' OR
[wait_type]=N'PREEMPTIVE_OS_NETVALIDATEPASSWORDPOLICY' OR
[wait_type]=N'PREEMPTIVE_VSS_CREATESNAPSHOT'))))
```

In addition, the system_health event session uses sp_server_diagnostics_ component_result, which by itself collects a variety of diagnostic data and health information including some waits. For more information about sp_server_ diagnostics_component_result, see https://msdn.microsoft.com/en-us/library/ ff878233.aspx. The sp_server_diagnostics_component_result is defined as follows:

```
ADD EVENT sqlserver.sp_server_diagnostics_component_result(SET collect_
data=(1)
    WHERE ([sqlserver].[is_system]=(1) AND [component]<>(4)))
```

Finally, keep in mind that although the system_health session collected information is captured to both the file and ring buffer targets, it may only hold recent events, and it is not persisted but recycled as shown next. You may need to perform some additional steps to persist this information to disk.

```
ADD TARGET package0.event_file(SET filename=N'system_health.xel',max_file_
size=(5), max_rollover_files=(4)),
ADD TARGET package0.ring_buffer(SET max_events_limit=(5000),
max_memory=(4096))
```

The definition shows that the file target has a max_file_size, which is the maximum file size in megabytes, of 5 MB and max_rollover_files or maximum number of files to retain in the file system of four, making a maximum of 20 MB of information. The file target can be read using the following query:

```
SELECT *, CAST(event_data AS XML)
FROM sys.fn_xe_file_target_read_file('system_health*.xel', NULL, NULL, NULL)
```

In the same way, the system_health session uses the ring buffer target with a max_events_limit of 5000, meaning that it will keep to a maximum of 5000 events in the ring buffer, and older events will be dropped as this limit is reached. It also defines a maximum amount of memory of 4096 kilobytes. By default, the oldest events are dropped when these limits are reached, but another configuration option, occurrence_number, allows you to configure the number of events kept before being discarded depending on the event type.

You can use the following query as a starting point to start inspecting the system_health session captured information, especially the ring buffer target:

```
SELECT CAST(t.target_data AS xml)
FROM sys.dm_xe_session_targets t
JOIN sys.dm_xe_sessions s
ON s.address = t.event_session_address
WHERE s.name = 'system_health'
```

> **Note**   You may need to increase the number of characters retrieved from the server for XML data in your SQL Server Management Studio session if you find an unexpected end of file parsing error while trying to open the XML column. To do that, use the Tools menu and select Options ➤ Query Results ➤ SQL Server ➤ Results to Grid ➤ Maximum Characters Retrieved, and change XML data to Unlimited (the default value is 2 MB).

Similar to the `system_health` session, SQL Server has provided a default trace for many versions of the product. Although it does not capture any wait information, the default trace persists some activity and changes primarily related to SQL Server configuration options. Along with SQL trace, the default trace has been deprecated.

Example: Analyzing CXPACKET Waits

Since there are many wait types, more than a thousand as of SQL Server 2019, analyzing even the most common ones would require an entire book. Later in the chapter, I'll describe the most common waits. In this section, I'll show you how to troubleshoot one of the most common ones: the CXPACKET waits. Let's create a problem that can demonstrate this kind of wait.

If you run the following query, most likely it will run for a few seconds without a problem using a sort operator and a parallel plan:

```
SELECT * FROM Sales.SalesOrderDetail
ORDER BY OrderQty
```

In my test system with four logical processors, I am able to see a parallel plan with four threads for both a clustered index scan and a sort operation. However, let's assume we have a performance problem and we see CXPACKET waits. Let's simulate waits by blocking one row. Run this on another session:

```
BEGIN TRANSACTION
UPDATE Sales.SalesOrderDetail
SET OrderQty = 5
WHERE SalesOrderDetailID = 121317
```

Notice that the UPDATE statement completes but the transaction remains open. (No COMMIT or ROLLBACK TRANSACTION statement has been issued just yet.)

Run the previous SELECT statement again on a different Management Studio session. If you use the new Live Query Statistics feature, you can see that it is using a parallel plan and the process blocks on the sort operator, as shown in Figure 5-4. Even when the clustered index scan operator has processed 121,199 rows, no rows will ever be processed by the sort operator until the blocking ends. The new Live Query Statistics feature is covered in more detail in the next chapter.

Figure 5-4. *Live Query Statistics on a blocked query*

Run the following statement using the session ID number of the query running the SELECT ORDER BY statement, which in my case is 52:

SELECT * FROM sys.dm_exec_requests WHERE session_id = 52

This is what I get on my test system:

session_id	request_id	Status	command	blocking_session_id	wait_type	wait_time	last_wait_type	wait_resource
52	0	suspended	SELECT	0	CXPACKET	219773	CXPACKET	

It is common that once people troubleshooting waits see the CXPACKET wait type, they tend to assume it is a parallelism problem and perform some incorrect configuration or query changes focused on disabling parallelism. (By the way, not shown in the previous output and introduced in SQL Server 2016, you can also see the DOP or degree of parallelism and parallel_worker_count columns, which in my case both show four.)

Another issue is that sys.dm_exec_requests does not show what the problem is, and some other tools are required. The sys.dm_os_waiting_tasks DMV can be more effective on this. Run the following query remembering to update the session_id to your executing query:

```
SELECT * FROM sys.dm_os_waiting_tasks WHERE session_id = 52
```

Now we get this data:

session_id	exec_context_id	wait_duration_ms	wait_type	blocking_session_id	blocking_exec_context_id	resource_description
52	3	1256486	LCK_M_S	55	NULL	pagelock fileid=1 pageid=28576 dbid=5 subresource=FULL id=lockdbc49b0380 mode=IX associated ObjectId=72057594057588736
52	4	1256486	CXPACKET	52	NULL	exchangeEvent id=Portdbf1ce8300 WaitType=e_waitPortOpen nodeId=2
52	0	1256605	CXPACKET	52	1	exchangeEvent id=Portdbf1ce8300 WaitType=e_waitPortOpen nodeId=2
52	2	1255426	CXPACKET	52	4	exchangeEvent id=Portdbf1ce8300 WaitType=e_waitPortOpen nodeId=2
52	1	1256486	CXPACKET	52	3	exchangeEvent id=Portdbf1ce8300 WaitType=e_waitPortOpen nodeId=2

We can see that the main process, execution context 0, is being blocked by the same process context id 1, and context id 1 is being blocked by context id 3. All of them show CXPACKET waits. However, context id 3 is being blocked by a different session with a LCK_M_S wait, which is the session running the UPDATE statement. This is a good example to show that something that seems to be one wait type problem in reality is related to a different wait type. In other words, something that looks like a parallelism problem in reality is not. Not shown on the output, you could see the same information and come to the same conclusion by looking at the waiting_task_address, which shows the address of the waiting task, and blocking_task_address, which is the task that is currently holding the resource the task is waiting on. Listed also is resource_description, which is also very helpful to understand the resource being consumed.

Run the following statement on the session running the UPDATE:

```
ROLLBACK TRANSACTION
```

The blocking will end and the sort will be able to finish as well.

Finally, how do we find the statement that is blocking? After all, the statement has already been executed, and it won't appear on some of the typical DMVs. Even the old sysprocesses compatibility catalog view will only show "AWAITING COMMAND" if you query it to see what the specific session ID is doing now. A couple of easy solutions are to use the old DBCC INPUTBUFFER statement and the new sys.dm_exec_input_buffer DMF.

DBCC INPUTBUFFER displays the last statement executed by SQL Server for the specified session ID. An example on how to use it follows:

```
DBCC INPUTBUFFER(55)
```

The new sys.dm_exec_input_buffer DMF (dynamic management function) introduced in SQL Server 2014 Service Pack 2 can take the same parameters as DBCC INPUTBUFFER, as shown next:

```
SELECT * FROM sys.dm_exec_input_buffer(55, NULL)
```

Both will return, with some minor output differences, the executed statement BEGIN TRANSACTION UPDATE Sales.SalesOrderDetail SET OrderQty = 5 WHERE SalesOrderDetailID = 121317.

This example shows how troubleshooting CXPACKET waits may show problems with other kinds of waits, in this case, LCK_M_S or blocking, which happen to be the root cause of the problem. Also, remember that, in general, troubleshooting waits would also require additional information from some other sources. In some cases, parallelism could, in fact, be the problem. Most of them can usually be fixed by updating related table statistics, creating appropriate indexes, or using other traditional query-tuning and optimization techniques.

Latches and Spinlocks

Latches and spinlocks are two synchronization mechanisms considered an important part of a waits performance methodology. As covered in Chapter 1, latches are short-term lightweight synchronization primitives used to protect memory structures for concurrent access and multiple wait types, using the PAGELATCH, PAGEIOLATCH, LATCH, and TRAN_MARKLATCH prefixes, available on the previously mentioned DMVs to track them. Since probably the most common latch problem is related to contention on allocation pages in tempdb, I cover them in more detail in Chapter 4. You can get additional information about latch contention by reading the Microsoft white paper "Diagnosing and Resolving Latch Contention on SQL Server," which you can find at Diagnose and resolve latch contention on SQL Server.

As also introduced in Chapter 1, spinlocks are lightweight synchronization primitives used by the SQL Server engine to protect access to some internal data structures, but they go to a deeper level than a latch. Structures protected by spinlocks are usually held only for an extremely short time, which makes them a better choice compared to latches. Using a latch will require the task to yield its processor time if the resource is not available, which is a very expensive operation. Different from latches, though, spinlocks will run in a loop for a period of time periodically checking for the availability of a resource.

Although it is very unlikely that you will have to troubleshoot problems with spinlocks, spinlock contention could happen on some systems that have both high concurrency and a high number of processors. At the same time that new versions of SQL Server continue to improve scalability, the new hardware has more and more processors that compete for resources and, in some cases, create concurrency problems, which usually result in a high CPU usage. But as suggested, just because you see high concurrency and high CPU usage, you should not immediately assume it is spinlock contention and try some other more common troubleshooting techniques first.

The starting point to troubleshoot spinlock contention is through the sys.dm_os_spinlock_stats DMV, which until recently did not even appear in the documentation and currently is just barely documented. When almost all of the 396 spinlock type descriptions just show as "Internal use only," it sure still remains as a very obscure topic.

So currently, the main source for information to troubleshoot spinlock contention still is the Microsoft white paper "Diagnosing and Resolving Spinlock Contention on SQL Server," which you can find at Diagnose and resolve spinlock contention on SQL Server. As a matter of fact, troubleshooting spinlock contention could be a very advanced topic that may require deep knowledge of the SQL Server engine. For example, the case mentioned in the white paper required involvement of the SQL Server customer support team and finally led to the discovery of a bug, which has been since corrected.

Let's run the DMV:

```
SELECT * FROM sys.dm_os_spinlock_stats
ORDER BY spins DESC
```

You could also visualize the different spinlock types querying the following catalog (although it no longer works for SQL Server 2019):

```
SELECT map_value, map_key, name FROM sys.dm_xe_map_values
WHERE name = 'spinlock_types'
```

I get 396 rows querying sys.dm_os_spinlock_stats in SQL Server 2019, a sample of which is next. Again, similar to other waits, large numbers alone do not mean a problem with spinlock contention.

name	collisions	spins	spins_per_collision	sleep_time	backoffs
LOCK_HASH	107232	31777250	296.3411	15	7623
RESQUEUE	72620	21237701	292.4497	29	3134
SOS_SCHEDULER	16726	14204588	849.252	2	1154
BLOCKER_ENUM	18572	5098250	274.5127	0	267
SECURITY_CACHE	12965	4939500	380.9873	0	2643
SOS_SUSPEND_QUEUE	5648	1975750	349.8141	14	157

Let's briefly discuss the meaning of the columns. A collision happens when a task tries to access a resource that is not available and the DMV keeps the number of collisions for each specific spinlock type. In the same way, if the resource is not available, a task executes a loop waiting for the resource, and every loop is counted as spin.

A spin uses CPU, which is why spinlock contention symptom shows as high CPU usage. A thread does not attempt to access the resource on each spin, as you can see by looking at the spins_per_collision column. Instead, a task will perform multiple spins before attempting to access a resource again. As you guessed, spins_per_collision is just collision divided by spins. A thread will not continue to spin indefinitely, so after a certain number of spins, it may determine to avoid using excessive CPU and yield. This operation is called a backoff. After a backoff operation, the thread will go to sleep.

Similar to wait statistics, latches and spinlock statistics can also be cleared using the DBCC SQLPERF statement. The following will clear latches statistics:

```
DBCC SQLPERF('sys.dm_os_latch_stats', CLEAR)
```

The following statement will clear spinlock statistics. But, once again, clearing spinlock statistics is undocumented, and it is only available since SQL Server 2012.

```
DBCC SQLPERF('sys.dm_os_spinlock_stats', CLEAR)
```

Common Waits

Finally, since there are a large number of wait types and it would be impossible to describe them all, a chapter about waits wouldn't be complete without describing at least the most common ones, along with recommendations on how to fix or minimize them. In fact, with so many waits available, there is currently no single document to describe them all. The original white paper described earlier, "SQL Server 2005 Waits and Queues," used to be the official wait list, but it has not been updated since 2006. The sys.dm_os_wait_stats SQL Server documentation at https://msdn.microsoft.com/en-us/library/ms179984.aspx documents a large number of waits, but there are still dozens or hundreds with little or no documentation. At the time of this writing, Paul Randal, formerly a Program Manager with the SQL Server Storage Engine team, has published a wait types and latch classes library, but it is also a work in progress. You can find these two sources at www.sqlskills.com/help/waits/ and www.sqlskills.com/help/latches. In this section, I'll cover some of the most common wait types you will see in your production environments.

CXPACKET

This is the parallel processing wait. Having these waits in your system does not necessarily mean that there is a problem, or a problem with parallelism. Unfortunately, some wrong advice online shows otherwise, which has given parallelism a bad reputation. As a consequence, a bad reaction to this wait by many people is to sometimes disable parallelism. The reality is we may need to do additional research to see if, in fact, parallelism is the problem. As covered in the example earlier in this chapter, to troubleshoot CXPACKET wait, we should start by looking at the waits on the additional child parallel threads.

In addition, starting with SQL Server 2016 Service Pack 2 and SQL Server 2017 CU3, CXPACKET waits are separated into CXPACKET and CXCONSUMER waits, mostly separating the waits for the producer and consumer threads, respectively. So CXPACKET now only applies to waits related to the synchronization of the query processor exchange operator and producing rows for consumer threads. Consumer thread waits are now tracked separately using the CXCONSUMER wait type.

CXCONSUMER

As mentioned earlier, starting with SQL Server 2016 Service Pack 2 and SQL Server 2017 CU3, CXPACKET waits are now separated into CXPACKET and CXCONSUMER waits. CXCONSUMER are consumer threads waiting for a producer thread to send rows and can usually be safely ignored.

PAGELATCH_* and PAGEIOLATCH_*

Latches and latch-related waits were introduced in Chapter 1 and also covered earlier in this chapter. In addition, latch waits related to contention on allocation pages on tempdb are covered in great detail in Chapter 4.

ASYNC_NETWORK_IO

Although the name of this wait type may suggest a network problem, a most common scenario is a client processing data problem. Usually, the recommendation is to make sure the client is processing the data fast enough or to validate that the client itself does not have a performance problem. Network connectivity problem is less common but also a recommended check.

SOS_SCHEDULER_YIELD

As covered in Chapter 1 and at the beginning of this chapter, SQL Server uses a nonpreemptive scheduler so when a task uses its quantum, it is programmed to yield CPU voluntarily. The task is never suspended and instead goes directly from running to runnable as there is no need to wait for a resource or anything else. This wait on the runnable queue is reflected as a SOS_SCHEDULER_YIELD wait and usually does not mean there is a problem. Since wait_time includes signal_wait_time on the previously discussed DMVs, for a task waiting on SOS_SCHEDULER_YIELD, both values will be the same or very close.

This wait type can also mean spinlock contention, but as explained earlier it is not common.

THREADPOOL

As explained in Chapter 1, workers in SQL Server are created in an on-demand fashion until the "max worker threads" configured value is reached, and if there are not enough workers for query execution, tasks may have to wait, and you will see this wait type. This does not mean that the value of "max worker threads" has to be increased as using the default value of 0 is usually the recommended choice. Some other waits or performance issues should be investigated as well. Queries showing these waits most likely should be optimized, especially if they have parallel plans using a large number of threads.

The "max worker threads" configured value does not take into account the workers required for the background system process, and its default value allows SQL Server to automatically configure the number of maximum worker threads. For more details, see the following Books Online entry: https://msdn.microsoft.com/en-us/library/ms190219.aspx.

PREEMPTIVE_*

The PREEMPTIVE_ prefix includes a large number of waits (225 in SQL Server 2019), all of which occur when the SQLOS scheduler switches to preemptive mode to perform a specific external operation. In preemptive mode, you will see the task status as Running as in reality its execution is outside the control of the SQLOS.

OLEDB

You will see OLEDB waits when a task is waiting for data from a SQL Server Native Client OLE DB provider. You should look at these sources, which in many cases are linked servers or SSIS packages, for the possibility of optimizations. Executing DMVs or DBCC CHECK commands will also show OLEDB waits as internally they are implemented as special OLEDB calls.

IO_COMPLETION

This wait type occurs for a large variety of I/O waits related to reads and writes other than database pages. Some examples of these I/O operations include reading and writing sort or hash workfiles on tempdb, reading and writing records or any other information from the transaction log (other than WRITELOG explained next), or reading and writing eager spools to tempdb. As mentioned previously, I/O waits on data pages appear as PAGEIOLATCH_ waits.

WRITELOG

WRITELOG occurs when a thread is waiting for SQL Server to write a log block to the transaction log, mostly as a result of a transaction commit or a checkpoint operation. Keep in mind that every update operation requires a transaction, even if one has not been explicitly created, for example, using the BEGIN/COMMIT TRANSACTION statements. Although some recommendations online ask for reducing the amount of changes to the database, assuming that has been optimized, the remaining thing to do is to use a faster I/O subsystem, at least for the transaction log file. In addition, you could also consider implementing delayed durability, a feature introduced with SQL Server 2014.

Timer Wait Types

There are several wait types that are usually used by background system processes on which large waiting times do not necessarily mean there is a problem. One example of these waits was covered earlier when I showed the REQUEST_FOR_DEADLOCK_SEARCH wait. Let's update the previous query to include some of these wait types so we can also take a look at which tasks use them:

```
SELECT session_id, command, wait_type, wait_time FROM sys.dm_exec_requests
WHERE wait_type IN ('BAD_PAGE_PROCESS',
'BROKER_EVENTHANDLER',
'BROKER_TRANSMITTER',
'CHECKPOINT_QUEUE',
'DBMIRROR_EVENTS_QUEUE',
'DBMIRRORING_CMD',
'KSOURCE_WAKEUP',
'LAZYWRITER_SLEEP',
'LOGMGR_QUEUE',
'ONDEMAND_TASK_QUEUE',
'REQUEST_FOR_DEADLOCK_SEARCH',
'SQLTRACE_BUFFER_FLUSH',
'WAITFOR')
```

I get the following output on my test system:

session_id	Command	wait_type	wait_time
1	LAZY WRITER	LAZYWRITER_SLEEP	938
3	LOG WRITER	LOGMGR_QUEUE	79
4	SIGNAL HANDLER	KSOURCE_WAKEUP	445305651
5	LOCK MONITOR	REQUEST_FOR_DEADLOCK_SEARCH	4736
6	BRKR TASK	BROKER_TRANSMITTER	445366653
12	RESOURCE MONITOR	ONDEMAND_TASK_QUEUE	42312
14	CHECKPOINT	CHECKPOINT_QUEUE	9784594
25	BRKR EVENT HNDLR	BROKER_EVENTHANDLER	445322210
29	BRKR TASK	BROKER_TRANSMITTER	445366652
55	WAITFOR	WAITFOR	100651

As you can see, especially if you run the query a few times monitoring its output, some of the wait times are extremely large, while the times for other waits seem to reset periodically.

The wait time for some of these wait types will be reset to 0 after a specific number of seconds. For example, the lazy writer will be reset after 1 second and the resource monitor task after 60 seconds. Some of these background tasks have a dedicated worker thread, so instead of creating a new task every time they need to do some work, they are just suspended between work intervals. In the sample output, WAITFOR was explicitly executed by a user query running the WAITFOR statement, so session ID 55 was not a background process.

Some of these interesting background processes are as follows:

- a. Lazy writer

- b. Log writer

- c. Signal handler

- d. Lock monitor

- e. Resource monitor

- f. Checkpoint

You can use the status column of the sys.dm_exec_requests to list all the sessions running as background tasks as in the following query:

```
SELECT session_id, command, wait_type, wait_time, status FROM sys.dm_exec_
requests
WHERE status = 'background'
```

What Is New on SQL Server 2019

SQL Server 2019 introduces two changes related to wait statistics. The first one is a new wait type, WAIT_ON_SYNC_STATISTICS_REFRESH, which shows accumulated waits spent on synchronous statistics refresh operations. In addition, the command column of the sys.dm_exec_request DMV will now show SELECT (STATMAN) if a SELECT statement is waiting for such a synchronous statistics.

Keep in mind that a synchronous statistics refresh operation is a regular update of optimization statistics performed in the middle of a query optimization process and is obviously not the same as an asynchronous statistics refresh operation that you configure manually by using the AUTO_UPDATE_STATISTICS_ASYNC option of the ALTER DATABASE statement. More details about statistics and statistics maintenance are provided in Chapters 1 and 3.

Blocking

Blocking itself is a large topic that would require a chapter of its own, if not an entire book. Since covering blocking in depth is outside the scope of this book, I will use this section to cover the basics and will refer to additional information at the end. Blocking is related to lock waits, and some of the best ways to troubleshoot them is to use the sys. dm_tran_locks or sys.dm_os_waiting_tasks DMVs where they will show as LCK_ wait types. Locks can be acquired to the RID, key, page, extent, table, metadata, database, and other levels. There are also several resource lock modes including Shared (S), Update (U), Exclusive (X), Intent, Schema, Bulk Update (BU), and Key-range.

Such a variety of choices creates a large number of locks and lock wait types, 63 on all the currently supported versions of SQL Server, identified by the LCK prefix such as LCK_M_S shown in earlier examples, LCK_M_U, LCK_M_X, and so on, and many different resource formats depending on the resource, all documented at sys.dm_os_waiting_ tasks (https://msdn.microsoft.com/en-us/library/ms188743.aspx) on the lock resource owner section. For example, the page resource format is

```
pagelock fileid=<file-id> pageid=<page-id> dbid=<db-id>
subresource=<pagelock-subresource>
```

As usual, do not automatically assume that locks alone are the root cause of a performance problem as minimizing the size of the transaction and other optimizations could be possible to avoid or minimize such waits. A bad piece of advice that I see a lot of times is to just use the NOLOCK hint to avoid locks. That does not mean that the NOLOCK hint should never be used. The hint exists for a reason, but I see it abused everywhere. Developers should understand how NOLOCK really works and if it makes sense for the business transaction they are using it for. Alternate solutions like implementing snapshot isolation should be considered as well.

The blocked process threshold configuration option uses the deadlock monitor background thread shown earlier and can be configured using `sp_configure`. The default configuration is 0, meaning that no blocked process reports are generated. An example configuring the blocked process threshold to five seconds is next.

```
sp_configure 'blocked process threshold', 5
RECONFIGURE
```

Note   You can use "blocked process threshold" or "blocked process threshold(s)" or technically any other unique string that is part of the configuration name. This is also true for any other configuration option.

Deadlocks occur when two or more processes permanently block each other. However, you usually won't have time to react to those waits. The SQL Server engine will detect them within five seconds and kill one of the processes involved. Although automatically taken care of by the database engine, they are still a problem, and SQL Server offers several tools to troubleshoot them. There are also several recommendations published in the documentation about how to deal with them including keeping transactions shorter and accessing the objects in the same order. Deadlocks are detected by the deadlock monitor background thread.

For more additional information about locking, see "Locking in the Database Engine" at `https://technet.microsoft.com/en-us/library/ms190615(v=sql.105).aspx`.

In-Memory OLTP

Although In-Memory OLTP, sometimes known by its original project name Hekaton, is covered in detail in Chapter 7, in this section I will introduce its performance benefits especially as it relates to waits by locks and latches. In-Memory OLTP includes several performance benefits based on new hardware trends such as the following:

a.   Tables and indexes are optimized for memory-only use.

b.   New natively compiled stored procedures are compiled to native code.

c.   No locks and latches are needed.

Based on new optimistic concurrency methods that rely on versioning, this new technology does not use locks and latches, and blocking is eliminated. However, transaction conflicts still have to be taken care of, and, in some cases, transactions may have to be resubmitted. It is worth noting that this new versioning process is entirely memory based and is not the same as the tempdb versioning technology introduced with SQL Server 2005 and used by features like snapshot isolation, MARS, or triggers.

Summary

This chapter introduced the waits performance methodology, which can be used to fix performance problems especially when other traditional methods are not able to pinpoint the performance issue. An advanced methodology will usually require looking at and correlating with other performance information on the SQL Server instance or even with clients or other data sources interacting with SQL Server. In addition, since waits happen in a SQL Server instance all the time, additional knowledge and baselining is required to understand when waits are, in fact, a problem.

## CHAPTER 6

The Query Store

Have you ever had a performance problem due to the fact that a query unexpectedly got a different execution plan? Have you ever found a plan regression after a SQL Server upgrade and wanted to know what the previous execution plan for a query was? The Query Store, a feature introduced with SQL Server 2016, can help you to troubleshoot and solve these and other performance problems related to changes in execution plans.

The Query Store automatically captures the history of queries, execution plans, and runtime statistics, and it allows you to find regressions in query plans, identify expensive queries, and even force the query processor to use a previously captured execution plan. Currently available in all the editions of SQL Server, this feature was originally released as a cloud-first feature on Azure SQL Database.

This chapter covers the Query Store as a collection and troubleshooting tool and shows how you can use it to quickly fix a performance problem by forcing an existing execution plan. However, as with the use of query hints, forcing a plan is not considered a long-term solution, and traditional query-tuning techniques may still be required to fix a query performance problem. This chapter also covers Live Query Statistics, another query performance–related feature introduced with SQL Server 2016.

Why Is a Query Slow?

To understand the benefits of the Query Store, let me start talking about the query troubleshooting process. You can use the Query Store, or some other tools, to find out if the reason we have a performance problem is because one or more queries are slow, and then identify what those queries are. Once you have detected that a performance problem is due to a slow query, the next step is to find out why. Obviously, not every query performance problem is related to plan changes. There could be multiple reasons why a query that has been performing well is suddenly slow. Sometimes this could be related to blocking or waiting for some other system resources, which I covered in Chapter 5. In many cases, the reason is that something may have changed, but the

189

© Benjamin Nevarez 2021
B. Nevarez, *High Performance SQL Server*, https://doi.org/10.1007/978-1-4842-6491-1_6

challenge may be to find out what it is. Usually, we don't have a baseline about system resource usage, query execution statistics, or performance history. In fact, often we have no idea what the old plan was. It may be the case that a change, for example, in data, schema, or query parameters, made the query processor produce a new plan. It may also be the extreme case that after getting more data, an increasing workload, or some other changes, the new plan, although taking longer to execute than before, may be the new "good plan" for the new database state.

Plan Changes

The Picasso Database Query Optimizer Visualizer tool, developed by the Indian Institute of Science, can be used to show why the plans in a query change and how many different plans could be selected for the same query based on the selectivity of their predicates. An example diagram of the Picasso Database Query Optimizer Visualizer tool is shown in Figure 6-1.

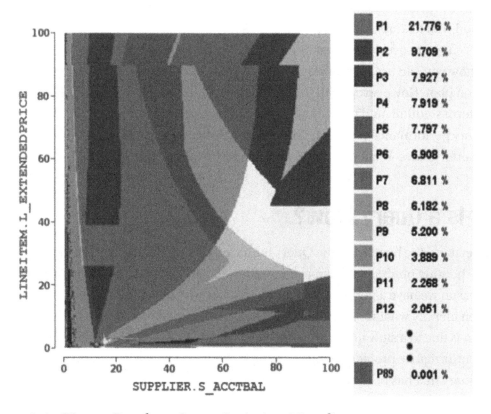

Figure 6-1. *Picasso Database Query Optimizer Visualizer*

Each color in the diagram is a different plan for the same query, and each plan is selected based on the selectivity of the predicates. It is interesting to note that when a boundary in the graph is crossed and a different plan is selected, most of the time the cost and performance of both plans should be similar, as the selectivity or estimated number of rows only changed slightly. This could happen, for example, when a new row is added to a table that qualifies for the used predicate. However, in some cases, mostly due to limitations in the query optimizer cost model in which it is unable to model something correctly, the new plan can have a large performance difference compared to the previous one, creating a problem for your application and its users. It is worth clarifying that the plans shown in the diagram are the final plans selected by the query optimizer for the same query depending on the selectivity of the parameters used. They are not some of the many alternatives the optimizer has to consider selecting only one. You can find more information about the Picasso Database Query Optimizer Visualizer tool at http://dsl.cds.iisc.ac.in/projects/PICASSO.

Another well-known problem with plans is performance issues due to regressions after changes on SQL Server cumulative updates (CUs), service packs, or version upgrades. A major concern that comes to mind with changes inside the query optimizer is plan regressions, which have been considered a big obstacle to query optimizer improvements. Regressions are problems introduced after a fix has been applied to the query optimizer, and it is sometimes referred to as the classic "two or more wrongs make a right." For example, this can happen when two bad estimations, one overestimating a value and the second one underestimating it, cancel each other out, luckily giving a good estimate and therefore producing a good execution plan overall. Correcting only one of these values after a query optimizer improvement may now lead to a bad estimation that may negatively impact the choice of plan selection, causing a regression in performance.

How the Query Store Can Help

By collecting query and plan information, gathering runtime statistics, and allowing you to force an existing query plan, the Query Store can be useful in the following scenarios:

   a) Plan regressions

   b) SQL Server upgrades

   c) Application/hardware changes

d)   Identify expensive queries

e)   Identify ad hoc workloads

Plan Regressions

In previous versions of SQL Server, there was no easy way to know if a plan regression had occurred as you could only see the current version of a specific plan. By storing the history of query plans in the system and capturing the performance of each one over time, the Query Store allows you to identify queries that have got slower over time. The "Regressed Queries" report can be used to identify queries for execution metrics that have recently regressed and may be creating performance problems in your database.

SQL Server Upgrades

You can use the Query Store and the database compatibility level or COMPATIBILITY_LEVEL setting to minimize the risk of SQL Server upgrades. The compatibility level sets certain database behaviors to be compatible with a specified version of SQL Server. For example, you can upgrade to SQL Server 2019 and still keep the COMPATIBILITY_LEVEL setting to 140 (SQL Server 2017), which allows you to use the previous version of the query processor. By enabling the Query Store, you can collect query and performance data to create a baseline and later change the COMPATIBILITY_LEVEL setting to 150 (SQL Server 2019) to use the latest version of the query processor. If a plan regression is found, you will be able to use the Query Store to mitigate the problem at different levels, which could include forcing a specific execution plan, tuning a query, or changing back to the original COMPATIBILITY_LEVEL setting. This scenario can also be used with SQL Server cumulative updates (CUs) or service packs, although in this case the database compatibility level remains the same.

Note   As covered in Chapter 3, trace flag 4199 can also be used to control whether query optimizer fixes are enabled after you upgrade to SQL Server 2019 and use the database COMPATIBILITY_LEVEL 150. Also, as mentioned in Chapter 1, starting with SQL Server 2017, service packs are no longer used, and the new servicing model is based on cumulative updates.

Application/Hardware Changes

Similar to the concept of SQL Server upgrades mentioned before, you could use the Query Store to test major changes in your system including database, application, or hardware changes. Again, you can collect query and plan data to create a baseline, implement the required changes, and use the Query Store to analyze the workload and identify any performance regression.

Identify Expensive Queries

Although you can identify expensive queries in previous versions of SQL Server using DMVs or some other statements or available performance data, these methods usually have several limitations. Some other techniques used in the past would require capturing an expensive trace and performing some complicated analysis to get similar information. As I will explain later, the Query Store removes some of these limitations and allows you to quickly identify the most expensive queries in your database based on a specific execution metric. To access this information, use the "Top Resource Consuming Queries" report in the Query Store folder in SQL Server Management Studio. Choose an execution metric of interest to identify the queries that have the biggest impact to database resource consumption for a provided time interval.

Note   Keep in mind that even after you find the expensive queries in your system, you still may need to apply standard query-tuning techniques to improve their performance. Query tuning is beyond the scope of this book. A good reference for this topic is the author's previous book *Microsoft SQL Server 2014 Query Tuning & Optimization*.

Identify Ad Hoc Workloads

You can use the Query Store to identify ad hoc workloads, which are typically characterized with a relatively large number of different queries executed very rarely and usually only once. Ad hoc workloads spend a significant portion of system resources in query optimization and use a large amount of memory in the plan cache. Identifying ad hoc workloads is covered later in this chapter.

Architecture

The Query Store directly interacts with the query processor. As shown in Figure 6-2, every time SQL Server compiles or executes a query, a message is sent to the Query Store.

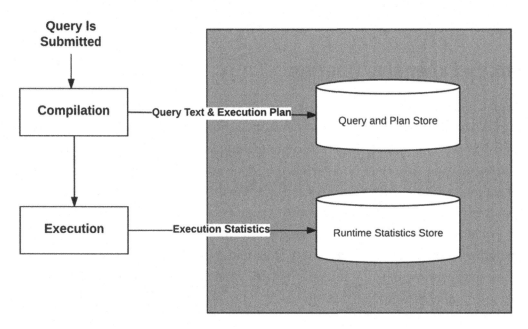

Figure 6-2. *Query Store workflow overview*

A more detailed query compilation and execution flow is also shown in Figure 6-3.

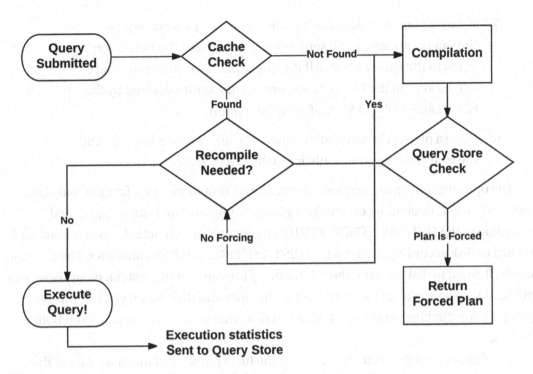

Figure 6-3. *Query compilation and execution*

The query compilation and execution flow is as follows:

1. When a query is submitted to SQL Server for execution, SQL Server will try to find an existing execution plan in the plan cache.

2. If no plan is found, it will proceed to run the query compilation and optimization process. After an execution plan is generated, it will send the query text and query plan to the Query Store.

3. If the query is configured to use an existing plan in the Query Store, the query processor will try to create a plan using the information provided in the forced plan.

4. After any of the three previously listed scenarios—plan found in cache, new optimization, or plan forced—the query processor will check if a recompile is needed.

5. If a new plan is created during the recompile process, again, the query processor will send the query text and the new query plans to the Query Store. All the query plans for the same query will be kept in the Query Store, up to a maximum defined by the MAX_PLANS_PER_QUERY configuration option.

6. Once a plan is chosen and executed, the query processor will send the runtime execution statistics to the Query Store.

The optimization and execution information is kept in memory first and only later persisted to disk, depending on the Query Store configuration. Data is aggregated according to the INTERVAL_LENGTH_MINUTES parameter, which defaults to one hour, and flushed to disk according to the DATA_FLUSH_INTERVAL_SECONDS parameter. The data can also be flushed to disk earlier if there is memory pressure on the system. In any case, you will be able to access all of the data, both in memory and disk, when you run the sys. query_store_runtime_stats catalog, as it is designed to retrieve the data from both sources.

The definition of the query text starts at the first character of the first token of the statement and ends at the last character of the last token. Space and comments inside do count, but if they are before or after, they are not considered part of the query text. A query also has to be on the same object to be considered the same query. If the same query is used in two different stored procedures, it would be considered a different query, and the object_id of the object is kept in the Query Store catalogs. It is recommended that you use ALTER instead of DROP and CREATE statements when maintaining objects to keep the same object_id value (in addition to other benefits like keeping permissions and so forth).

Note   If you still need to use the DROP and CREATE statements, SQL Server 2016 also introduces the new DROP IF EXISTS syntax, which allows you to conditionally drop an object only if it already exists. For an example with stored procedures, see the SQL Server documentation at https://msdn.microsoft. com/en-us/library/ms174969.aspx.

Enabling, Purging, and Disabling the Query Store

The Query Store is disabled by default. To enable it on the current database, you can use the ALTER DATABASE CURRENT SET QUERY_STORE = ON statement. Once the Query Store is enabled, it will start collecting the plans and query performance data, and you can analyze that data by looking at the Query Store catalog views. The information is available immediately after compilation and execution.

You can analyze the information collected either proactively to understand the query performance changes in your application or retroactively in case you have a performance problem. Once you look at the different metrics stored, which are very similar to what is stored, for example, in the sys.dm_exec_query_stats DMV, you can make the decision to optimize for a specific metric like query duration, CPU time, logical IO reads, logical IO writes, physical reads, and so on. Once you identify the problem, you can use traditional query-tuning techniques to try to fix the problem, or you can use the Query Store to force a previous plan. The plan has to be captured in the Query Store to be forced, which obviously means it is a valid plan (or at least it was at the moment when it was collected—more on that later) and it was previously generated by the query optimizer. To force a plan, you need both the plan_id and query_id, which can be found in the sys.query_store_plan catalog view. Technically, you could also force a plan using a plan guide without the Query Store, but it would be more complicated and you would still have to manually collect and find the required plan in the first place.

You can query the Query Store current configuration values, even if it is disabled, by running the following statement:

```
SELECT * FROM sys.database_query_store_options
```

This will return the following data:

desired_state	0
desired_state_desc	OFF
actual_state	0
actual_state_desc	OFF
readonly_reason	0
current_storage_size_mb	0

(continued)

flush_interval_seconds	900
interval_length_minutes	60
max_storage_size_mb	100
stale_query_threshold_days	30
max_plans_per_query	200
query_capture_mode	1
query_capture_mode_desc	ALL
size_based_cleanup_mode	1
size_based_cleanup_mode_desc	AUTO

To enable the Query Store on the AdventureWorks2017 database, use the following statement:

```
ALTER DATABASE AdventureWorks2017 SET QUERY_STORE = ON
```

Note   The AdventureWorks2017 database may already have the Query Store enabled when you initially restore it.

After enabling the Query Store, only the state will be changed. All the other default values will remain the same. You could also change one or more configuration values when you enable the Query Store, as shown later. If you display the sys.database_query_store_options catalog view again, you can see that both the desired_state and actual_state columns have now the value 2 and that the desired_state_desc and actual_state_desc switched to READ_WRITE. These two states are used to differentiate the desired operation mode explicitly set by the user and the actual or real state. The most common case when these values may be different is when the READ_WRITE mode is requested but the Query Store has to automatically switch to READ_ONLY due to lack of disk space.

Alternatively, you can use SQL Server Management Studio to perform the same operations. Right-click your database and select Properties. Then select the Query Store page. On General, Operation Mode (Requested), select Read Write. Keep in mind that when using SQL Server Management Studio, several values are populated by default, but you can change any of these values and click OK when done. The Query Store page is shown in Figure 6-4.

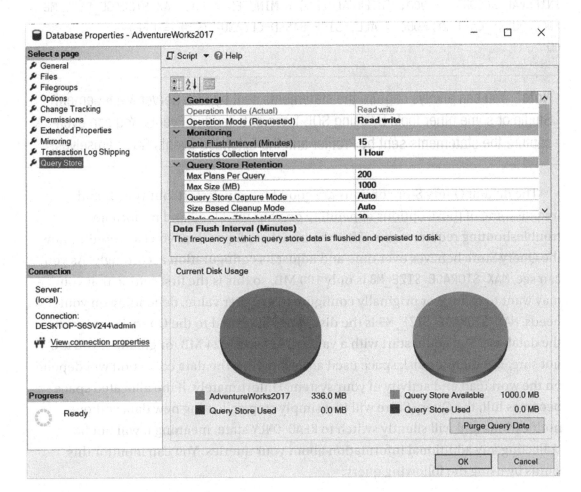

Figure 6-4. *Query Store configuration*

By default, the following statements and values will be sent to SQL Server:

```
ALTER DATABASE AdventureWorks2017 SET QUERY_STORE = ON
GO
ALTER DATABASE AdventureWorks2017 SET QUERY_STORE (OPERATION_MODE = READ_
WRITE, CLEANUP_POLICY = (STALE_QUERY_THRESHOLD_DAYS = 367), DATA_FLUSH_
INTERVAL_SECONDS = 900, INTERVAL_LENGTH_MINUTES = 60, MAX_STORAGE_SIZE_MB =
100, QUERY_CAPTURE_MODE = ALL, SIZE_BASED_CLEANUP_MODE = OFF)
GO
```

Note   You can always capture the statements sent by SQL Server Management Studio or some other tools by using SQL Trace or Extended Events. You can even capture the statements sent by Profiler and the Extended Events GUI themselves!

The default Query Store options are good for a quick start, but you should update some of those options depending on your workload and performance troubleshooting requirements. After the initial configuration, you can monitor how the Query Store behaves over time and adjust its configuration accordingly. As you can see, MAX_STORAGE_SIZE_MB is only 100 MB, so this is the first setting that you may want to change or originally configure to a higher value, depending on your needs. MAX_STORAGE_SIZE_MB is the disk space allocated to the Query Store inside the database. You could start with a value of at least 1024 MB, or greater if you are not sure, but monitor disk space used accordingly as the data collection will depend on the workload and activity of your system. Unfortunately, if the allocated space becomes full, the Query Store will just simply stop collecting new data without notifications and will silently switch to READ_ONLY state, meaning it will not be collecting any additional information about your queries. You can monitor this status by using the following query:

```
SELECT actual_state_desc, desired_state_desc, current_storage_size_mb,
    max_storage_size_mb, readonly_reason
FROM sys.database_query_store_options
```

In my testing, I was able to go over the configured size allocated for a brief time without a problem as it looks like the space used is not validated in real time. It only went to READ_ONLY state some time later, as shown in the following configuration values:

actual_state_desc	READ_ONLY
desired_state_desc	READ_WRITE
current_storage_size_mb	4
max_storage_size_mb	1
readonly_reason	65536

Currently, the catalog view does not show a description for readonly_reason, but the documentation shows that 65536 means the Query Store has reached the size limit set by the MAX_STORAGE_SIZE_MB option. The documentation incorrectly says that you need to change the status back to READ_WRITE after expanding the MAX_STORAGE_SIZE_MB value, but my testing shows that it is not needed. Expanding MAX_STORAGE_SIZE_MB will automatically return the Query Store to the READ_WRITE state:

```
ALTER DATABASE AdventureWorks2017 SET QUERY_STORE (MAX_STORAGE_SIZE_MB = 2048)
```

Keep in mind that although you can change the size of the Query Store, its internal tables are always stored in the database primary filegroup, and this currently cannot be changed. Alternatively, you can activate query capture and cleanup policies to control the disk space used, as explained later.

As the SQL Server Management Studio generated code showed earlier, you can change more than one attribute at a time, separating them with commas, using the following syntax:

```
ALTER DATABASE database_name SET QUERY_STORE (<query_store_option> [,... n])
```

If you need to purge the Query Store data, you can select the "Purge Query Data" button on the Query Store page, as shown earlier in Figure 6-4. This will send the following statement, which you could have also typed directly to get the same results:

```
ALTER DATABASE AdventureWorks2017 SET QUERY_STORE CLEAR ALL
```

To disable the Query Store once again, you can use SQL Server Management Studio and select Off on Operation Mode (Requested), or you can use the following statement:

```
ALTER DATABASE AdventureWorks2017 SET QUERY_STORE = OFF
```

In addition to `MAX_STORAGE_SIZE_MB`, the following options can be configured in the Query Store:

a. `OPERATION_MODE`: Updates the operation mode of the Query Store and can be `OFF`, `READ_ONLY`, and `READ_WRITE`. As mentioned earlier, the state of the Query Store can be seen using `desired_state_desc` and `actual_state_desc` from the `sys.database_query_store_options` catalog view. It can be `OFF` when the Query Store is disabled and `READ_ONLY` and `READ_WRITE` when it is enabled. When the Query Store is enabled, it will usually be in the `READ_WRITE` state. The Query Store can automatically go to the `READ_ONLY` state if there is a disk space problem, as explained earlier, or if you manually change the operation mode.

b. `MAX_PLANS_PER_QUERY`: Indicates the maximum number of plans maintained for each query, and its default value is 200. The Query Store gives you the possibility to explore how many different plans could be created for a specific query in a production workload, something that was not possible before, unless you use a third-party tool like the Picasso Database Query Optimizer Visualizer.

c. `INTERVAL_LENGTH_MINUTES`: Defines the time interval at which runtime execution statistics data is aggregated into the Query Store and the default value is 60 minutes. It would not be feasible to store each and every query execution as some of them could be executed thousands or millions of times in a short period of time. The Query Store will store one row per query with aggregated runtime statistics for the specified interval.

For example, if a query is executed 2000 times in one hour, the interval in the `sys.query_store_runtime_stats` catalog view will show 2000 `count_executions`, but the performance data will be aggregated for all those executions. Using a lower value can be useful in cases where you want finer granularity, but it will also use more disk space.

d. CLEANUP_POLICY: Defines the data retention policy of the Query Store. At the moment, the only possible value is STALE_QUERY_THRESHOLD_DAYS, which specifies the number of days for which the information for a query is retained in the Query Store. Its default value, as shown in an ALTER DATABASE statement at the beginning of this section, is 367 days. This configuration value will also impact the required disk space for the Query Store, and 367 days may be too high for some workloads so you may need to configure it to a lower value.

e. DATA_FLUSH_INTERVAL_SECONDS: Defines the frequency at which data written to the Query Store is persisted to disk. Its default value is 900 seconds or 15 minutes. As shown in the architecture section, data collected by the Query Store is immediately available, but for performance reasons it is only written to disk asynchronously.

Finally, the Query Store also has configuration options to define query capture and cleanup policies. Defining the query capture policy can be done with the QUERY_CAPTURE_MODE, which has the values ALL, AUTO, and NONE, which are described as

a. ALL: Defines that all the queries are captured. It is the default value.

b. AUTO: Indicates to only capture relevant queries based on execution count and resource consumption. When this option is used, queries with low compile and execution times and executed infrequently are not collected. Thresholds for frequency, compile, and execution times are internally determined and cannot be manually configured.

c. NONE: Requests the Query Store to stop capturing new queries. When this configuration choice is used, the Query Store will collect compile and runtime statistics only for queries that were captured already. This configuration should be used with caution since important information for new queries will be missed.

The cleanup policy is defined using the SIZE_BASED_CLEANUP_MODE configuration option and has the values OFF (the default) and AUTO. OFF means that the policy is disabled and no data is automatically deleted. If the AUTO value is defined, the policy will be automatically activated when size on disk reaches 90% of the value defined in MAX_ STORAGE_SIZE. The cleanup policy removes the least expensive and oldest queries first and stops at approximately 80% of the disk space defined at MAX_STORAGE_SIZE.

Using the Query Store

In the previous section, we saw how to enable and configure the Query Store. Let's now see it in action running some queries. In our examples, we can examine the data immediately as soon it is collected. In a production environment, however, you may want to wait some time until a representative workload is collected, which would depend on your application and could be, for example, an entire day or a week. Let's test it with one of my favorite queries on the AdventureWorks2017 database, which has the advantage that it is extremely simple and, in this case, can show parameter-sensitive problems. Create the following stored procedure:

```
CREATE PROCEDURE test (@pid int)
AS
SELECT * FROM Sales.SalesOrderDetail
WHERE ProductID = @pid
```

Note   Keep in mind that this is a simplified exercise to show how the Query Store works. You could certainly solve problems with parameter-sensitive queries using some other techniques, but it would take a lot more effort to simulate a plan regression in a small database like AdventureWorks2017. And, yes, the Query Store could also be used to find parameter-sensitive queries (or more commonly known as queries with parameter sniffing–related problems).

Depending on the values provided to the procedure, two possible execution plans could be created. This is equivalent to the Picasso diagram in Figure 6-1, showing only two colors. Executing the stored procedure with ProductID 898 will create a plan with index seek and key lookup operators, and using a value of 870 will instead select a table scan. In both cases, the created plan will be adequate for the provided parameters. Trying any other possible value will still create any of these two plans, assuming a new optimization is required and performed. But as a parameter-sensitive query or procedure, performance problems may occur when reusing an existing plan that may not be adequate for the provided parameter.

For example, running the procedure for ProductID 898 with a plan that uses a table scan may cause a bit of a performance problem as the entire table has to be scanned to return only nine rows. But the highest performance problem will happen when the ProductID 870 is used with the index seek/key lookup plan as it performs 14,000 logical reads for a table that can be scanned with only 1200 reads. The reason for the performance problem is that the index seek/key lookup combination is very expensive and is only a good solution when a small number of rows are returned. Let's create that scenario and see if the Query Store can detect that performance problem. First, run SET STATISTICS IO ON to enable SQL Server to display information regarding the amount of disk activity generated by our queries, and ALTER DATABASE SET QUERY_STORE CLEAR ALL to clear any information currently stored by the Query Store. Run the following statements:

```
SET STATISTICS IO ON
GO
ALTER DATABASE AdventureWorks2017 SET QUERY_STORE CLEAR ALL
```

Run the first query to create a table scan plan. You can optionally visualize the plan in SQL Server Management Studio by selecting Include Actual Execution Plan.

```
EXEC test @pid = 870
```

Running the previous statement will show 1248 logical reads, which you can see on the Messages tab (you may have small variations on this value depending on a few factors). If you later try the following query, it will reuse the table scan plan, so it will have the same number of logical reads (assuming the plan has not been removed from the plan cache):

```
EXEC test @pid = 898
```

In fact, any parameter used will use the same plan and the performance will be the same. At least in this case, the performance is stable and consistent, although probably not a perfect solution for the latest case, which has to scan the entire table to return only nine rows.

But a higher performance variation will occur with the plan using the index seek and key lookup operators. Let's suppose that the current plan is evicted from the plan cache and that the next execution uses the ProductID 898, creating a new optimization and a new plan. To simulate that, we will use the DBCC FREEPROCCACHE statement, which, although not the best method to accomplish this, is a simple way to do it so we can focus on our main point. Run the following query:

```
DBCC FREEPROCCACHE
GO
EXEC test @pid = 898
GO
EXEC test @pid = 870
```

Note   DBCC FREEPROCCACHE will remove all the plans from the entire plan cache, so be careful not to run such a statement on a production environment.

Logical reads for these executions were 29 (to obtain nine rows) and 14,077 (to obtain 4688 rows), respectively. 14,077 is a huge number for a table in which a table scan operation only takes 1266 logical reads as shown earlier. This time, the execution time is not stable, and it will depend on the parameter supplied and, more exactly, on the number of index seeks/key lookups required. In other words, a plan using a table scan will always have the same performance, depending on the number of pages in the table. But the plan with index seeks/key lookups will depend on the number of rows read, so it can range from very cheap to very expensive.

Making sure you executed the previous queries, we can now run this query to display some of the information collected by the Query Store:

```
SELECT rs.avg_logical_io_reads, qt.query_sql_text,
    q.query_id, qt.query_text_id, p.plan_id, rs.runtime_stats_id,
    rsi.start_time, rsi.end_time, rs.avg_rowcount, rs.count_executions
FROM sys.query_store_query_text AS qt
JOIN sys.query_store_query AS q
    ON qt.query_text_id = q.query_text_id
JOIN sys.query_store_plan AS p
    ON q.query_id = p.query_id
```

```
JOIN sys.query_store_runtime_stats AS rs
    ON p.plan_id = rs.plan_id
JOIN sys.query_store_runtime_stats_interval AS rsi
    ON rsi.runtime_stats_interval_id = rs.runtime_stats_interval_id
```

We get the following output; only the required rows are displayed:

avg_logical_io_reads	1249	7054
query_sql_text	(@pid int)SELECT * FROM	(@pid int)SELECT * FROM
query_id	1	1
query_text_id	1	1
plan_id	1	2
runtime_stats_id	1	2
avg_rowcount	2348.5	2348.5
count_executions	2	2

This shows that for plan_id 1, the one with the table scan, the average logical IO reads was 1249 as the entire table has 1249 pages. For plan_id 2, the plan with the index seek and key lookup operators, the average was 7054, which is roughly 29 plus 14,077 divided by 2, as there were two executions.

SQL Server Management Studio can also show you this and other Query Store information. Right-click Regressed Queries on the Query Store folder under the database and select View Regressed Queries. The report will give you the choice to select CPU Time (us), Duration (us), Logical Reads, Logical Writes, Memory Consumption (KB), and Physical Reads. Click "View regressed queries in a grid format with additional details." Figure 6-5 shows the report with logical reads.

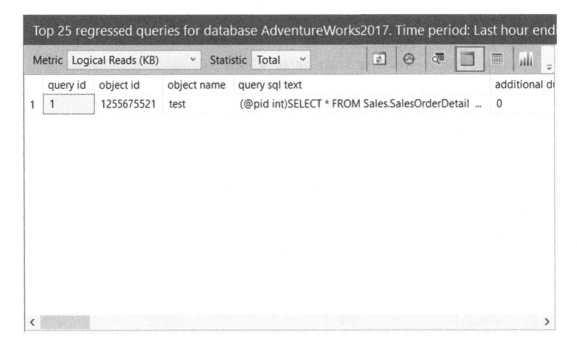

Figure 6-5. *Top 25 regressed queries sorted by logical reads*

Click the query we are interested in. (You may have different query_id even if you have followed the same steps here.) You would see a screen similar to Figure 6-6 on the top-right pane that shows both plans, represented by two small circles. Clicking a circle will show runtime information for each plan, and the graphical plan will be displayed at the bottom pane (not shown in Figure 6-6).

Note   Older versions of the Query Store will show logical reads in pages. The latest version shows the same information on KBs. For example, you may see 7054 for Avg Logical Reads or 56,432 for Avg Logical Reads (KB). As we learned in Chapter 1, a data page is 8 KB.

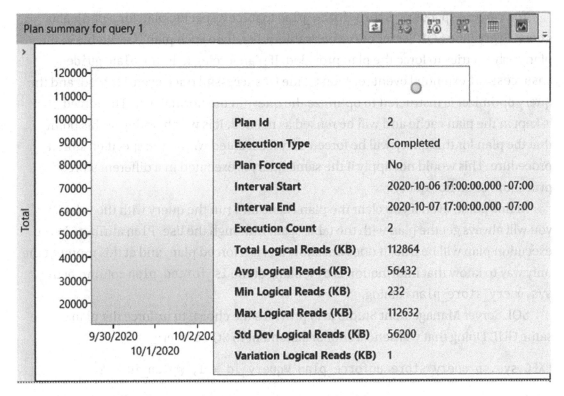

Plan summary for query 1

Plan Id	2
Execution Type	Completed
Plan Forced	No
Interval Start	2020-10-06 17:00:00.000 -07:00
Interval End	2020-10-07 17:00:00.000 -07:00
Execution Count	2
Total Logical Reads (KB)	112864
Avg Logical Reads (KB)	56432
Min Logical Reads (KB)	232
Max Logical Reads (KB)	112632
Std Dev Logical Reads (KB)	56200
Variation Logical Reads (KB)	1

Figure 6-6. *Plan summary for query pane*

At this point, you could research why there is such a big difference in the performance for both plans and try to apply any of the traditional query-tuning techniques. A solution that the Query Store provides and one that is immediately available without needing any query-tuning effort is to force any of the available execution plans, assuming you want to use that plan for every execution of that particular query.

So, what to do next? Although not a perfect solution for this example (this is why parameter-sensitive queries are difficult to fix and usually require some other methods), suppose that we want consistent performance and decided to use the plan with the table scan. Let's force that plan by selecting the plan on the "Plan summary for query" pane and clicking "Force Plan" when the plan is displayed on the bottom pane. Plan summary also gives you the choice to force a plan. You can only force a plan when it is saved in the Query Store. Answer "Yes" when asked for confirmation. If you capture the query in a trace, you would see a similar statement being sent:

```
EXEC sys.sp_query_store_force_plan @query_id = 1, @plan_id = 1
```

You can use `sp_query_store_force_plan` to force a specific plan for a particular query. Every time SQL Server encounters this query, if no such plan is available in the plan cache, it tries to force the plan provided. If plan forcing fails, the `plan_guide_unsuccessful` extended event (or Plan Guide Unsuccessful trace event) is fired, and the query optimizer is instructed to optimize the query in the normal way. The forced plan is kept in the plan cache and will be reused as needed. It is worth noting at this point that the plan for this query will be forced only if executed within the specified stored procedure. This would not apply if the same query is executed in a different stored procedure or ad hoc query.

At this point, even if you clear the plan cache and run the query with the value 898, you will always get the plan with the table scan. Although the `Use  Plan` attribute in the execution plan will be true, it does not show this is a forced plan, and at this moment the only way to know that information is by looking at the `is_forced_plan` column of the `sys.query_store_plan` catalog.

SQL Server Management Studio also provides the choice to unforce the plan on the same GUI. Doing that will send a similar statement to SQL Server:

```
EXEC sys.sp_query_store_unforce_plan @query_id = 1, @plan_id = 1
```

Forcing a plan uses plan guides in the background. When a plan is forced, SQL Server implicitly adds a `USE  PLAN` hint with the fragment of the XML plan associated with that statement, so you no longer need to use a plan guide anymore. Also, keep in mind when using a plan guide alone, the query optimizer is not guaranteed to produce the exact requested forced plan, but at least something similar to it. In addition, you should be aware that there may be some cases where forcing a plan does not work, a typical example being when the schema has changed. So, if a stored plan uses an index but the index no longer exists, it would be impossible to reuse and force such plan. In this case, SQL Server will perform a normal optimization, and it will record the fact that the forcing plan operation failed in the `sys.query_store_plan` catalog. Plan forcing failure is explained later in this chapter. For more details about the elements of a query plan that can be forced with the Query Store and `USE  PLAN`, see `https://technet.microsoft.com/en-us/library/ms186954(v=sql.105).aspx`.

Purging or disabling the Query Store will also disable any forced query plans. Once you purge a plan, there is no way to force it back as the plan has been permanently removed from the Query Store database. However, if you disable the Query Store while a plan was configured as forced, it will be forced back once the Query Store is enabled again, assuming the plan was not deleted by some other means. Unforcing the previous plan in our example and running the procedure with the ProductID 898 again will perform a normal query optimization, creating the original plan with the index seek/key lookup combination, and the Use Plan attribute will not appear in the execution plan anymore.

Finally, forcing a plan should not be considered a long-term solution as, similar to using query hints, the database data and schema can change, and the forced plan can no longer be optimal. Again, using traditional query-tuning techniques should be required to fix the problematic query.

Performance Troubleshooting

As mentioned in the previous section, you can analyze the information collected by the Query Store, either proactively to understand the query performance changes in your application or reactively in case you have a performance problem. The Query Store can be used to find out the expensive queries pretty much in the same way we used to do it with the sys.dm_exec_query_stats DMV. The Query Store provides some additional benefits to using this DMV including the following:

a. Using the sys.dm_exec_query_stats DMV provides a view of only the plans currently in the plan cache. Only the current version of a plan exists, and even this version can be removed from the plan cache at any time. The Query Store persists all the history of plans for every query.

b. Not every plan gets cached and therefore exposed by the sys. dm_exec_query_stats DMV. All the plans are stored by the Query Store, even incomplete queries, as explained later.

To display the most expensive queries in a database, you can use the "Top Resource Consuming Queries" report in SQL Server Management Studio, which allows you to select different metrics including CPU time, duration, execution count, logical reads, logical writes, memory consumption, and physical reads. An example for CPU time is shown in Figure 6-7.

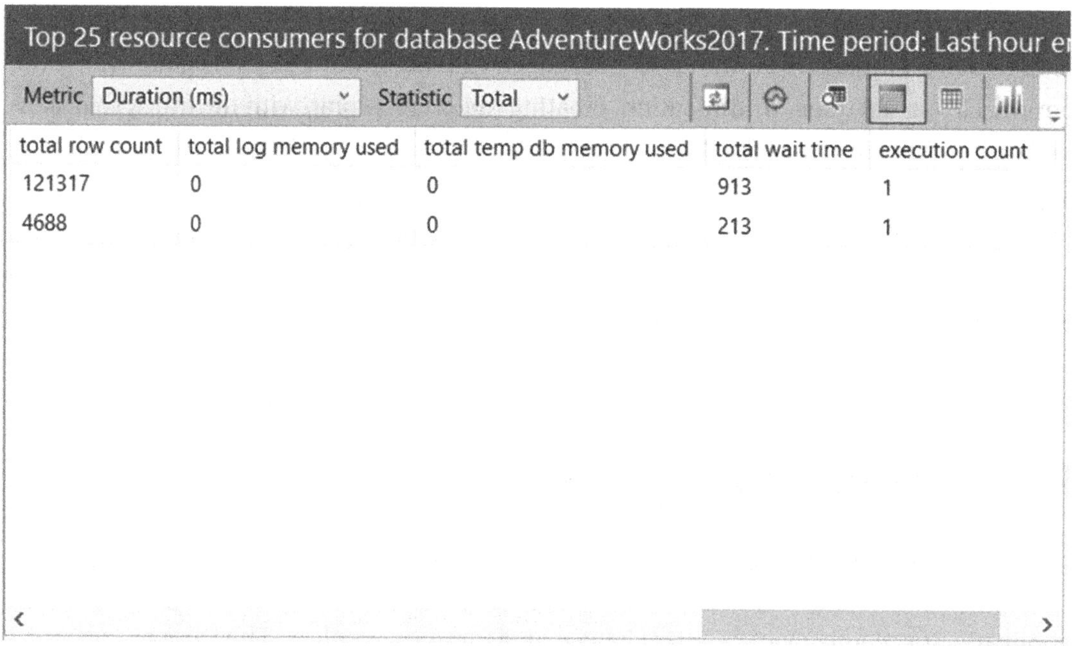

Figure 6-7. *Top 25 resource consumers report*

For additional flexibility, you can write your own queries using the runtime statistics collected on `sys.query_store_runtime_stats` along with the other Query Store catalog views.

As one of my favorite techniques, I can run a trace or extended event session against SQL Server Management Studio, run the Top Resource Consuming Queries report selecting the metric I need, and see which query is being submitted to the engine. For example, when running the report for CPU time shown in Figure 6-7, I saw the following query being submitted, copied here with some minor edits, including removing a filter selecting specific intervals to get most expensive queries during the last hour:

```
SELECT TOP 25
    p.query_id query_id,
    qt.query_sql_text query_text,
    CONVERT(float, SUM(rs.avg_cpu_time * rs.count_executions)) total_cpu_time,
    SUM(rs.count_executions) count_executions,
    COUNT(DISTINCT p.plan_id) num_plans
```

```
FROM sys.query_store_runtime_stats rs
    JOIN sys.query_store_plan p ON p.plan_id = rs.plan_id
    JOIN sys.query_store_query q ON q.query_id = p.query_id
    JOIN sys.query_store_query_text qt ON q.query_text_id = qt.query_text_id
GROUP BY p.query_id, qt.query_sql_text
ORDER BY total_cpu_time DESC
```

As covered earlier, you can use the Query Store to identify ad hoc workloads in your database. Since ad hoc workloads can consist of a large number of different queries, they usually spend a significant portion of system resources in query optimization and use a large amount of memory in the plan cache. To identify an ad hoc workload, you can use "Top Resource Consuming Queries," as explained earlier, and select Execution Count as the metric for the report. A large number of queries on the graph or report showing an execution count of 1 may reveal an ad hoc workload. You may also need to visualize more than the default of 25 queries and include a larger value. In order to do that, select Configure (look for it at the top-right region of the screen), then Return, and specify a new value on the Top section. Once the report is displayed, you can also click the exec count column to start with the queries with an execution count value of 1, as shown earlier in Figure 6-7.

If you have a large number of ad hoc queries, you may want to enable the "optimize for ad hoc workloads" configuration option, which SQL Server can use to improve the efficiency of the plan cache. When this configuration is enabled, SQL Server minimizes the memory used by the plan cache by storing only a small compiled plan stub in the plan cache instead of the full compiled execution plan for queries that are executed only once. For more details about the "optimize for ad hoc workloads" configuration option, see Chapter 3.

An alternate solution to reusing plans, although more drastic, is to force parameterization at the database level. This configuration can be useful in cases where multiple similar ad hoc queries can benefit from using the same execution plan. Forcing the same plan may not always be a good solution, so this is a choice that requires careful and thorough testing. Forcing parameterization at the database level can be implemented by using the ALTER DATABASE SET PARAMETERIZATION FORCED statement.

Incomplete Queries

A very interesting feature that you can use with the Query Store is to see the final status of a query, which is especially helpful to find information about queries that didn't complete successfully. This is something that was very difficult to accomplish using other current methods in SQL Server. You can find this information by looking at the execution_type and execution_type_desc columns of the sys.query_store_runtime_stats catalog view. The possible values for the column execution_type as documented are as follows:

> 0: Regular execution (successfully finished)
>
> 3: Client-initiated aborted execution
>
> 4: Exception-aborted execution

Most of your queries will return the value 0, meaning they were successfully executed, so let's run an example to see how it works when queries are not executed successfully. Clear the Query Store so it is easier to manage the available results in our queries:

```
ALTER DATABASE AdventureWorks2017 SET QUERY_STORE CLEAR ALL
```

Run the following query (be careful, the query would run for a long time if left executing):

```
SELECT * FROM Sales.SalesOrderDetail s1 CROSS JOIN Sales.SalesOrderDetail s2
```

Let the query run for five seconds or so and cancel it. Now run the following query:

```
SELECT COUNT(*) FROM Sales.SalesOrderDetail s1 CROSS JOIN Sales.
SalesOrderDetail s2
```

Different from the previous execution, which was canceled, this query should finish quickly with an error message complaining about an arithmetic overflow error converting expression to data type int.

Finally, run the following query, which should finish successfully in less than a second:

```
SELECT COUNT_BIG(*) FROM Sales.SalesOrderDetail s1 CROSS JOIN Sales.
SalesOrderDetail s2
```

Let's inspect the execution type value by running the following query:

```
SELECT rs.avg_logical_io_reads, qt.query_sql_text,
    q.query_id, execution_type_desc, qt.query_text_id, p.plan_id,
    rs.runtime_stats_id,
    rsi.start_time, rsi.end_time, rs.avg_rowcount, rs.count_executions
FROM sys.query_store_query_text AS qt
JOIN sys.query_store_query AS q
    ON qt.query_text_id = q.query_text_id
JOIN sys.query_store_plan AS p
    ON q.query_id = p.query_id
JOIN sys.query_store_runtime_stats AS rs
    ON p.plan_id = rs.plan_id
JOIN sys.query_store_runtime_stats_interval AS rsi
    ON rsi.runtime_stats_interval_id = rs.runtime_stats_interval_id
```

The output should contain the following data:

avg_logical_io_reads	query_sql_text	execution_type_desc
942	select count(*) from sales.SalesOrderDetail s1 cross join sales.SalesOrderDetail s2	Exception
343572	select * from sales.SalesOrderDetail s1 cross join sales.SalesOrderDetail s2	Aborted
942	select count_big(*) from sales. SalesOrderDetail s1 cross join sales. SalesOrderDetail s2	Regular

As you can see, the Query Store was able to track all the previous queries and provide us with the status of the query or type of query execution, along with the runtime and performance information. This could be very helpful in scenarios when a query fails and you need to see additional information like resources used, duration, and so on. Keep in mind that a query must be valid, and a plan should be generated and should start executing for it to be tracked after a failure or cancelation. If a query fails to compile, there is nothing to be tracked. For example, if a query tries to use a table that does not exist, no plan will be generated, and there will be no query execution. For example, if you run

```
SELECT * FROM authors
```

you will receive an "Invalid object name" error, and there will be no optimization or execution at all and, therefore, no information captured by the Query Store.

A common problem with tracking queries that didn't complete successfully is related to the default query timeout setting for .NET applications, which is 30 seconds. You can test a .NET application default timeout using the following code. Since the default .NET timeout is not changed and the query executed in the code will definitely run for more than 30 seconds, you will get the Exception type of query execution as mentioned before:

```
using System;
using System.Data.SqlClient;

public class Test {

    public static void Main() {
        string connectionString = "Data Source=(local);Initial
        Catalog=AdventureWorks2017;Integrated Security=SSPI";
        string queryString = "SELECT * FROM Sales.SalesOrderDetail s1
        CROSS JOIN Sales.SalesOrderDetail s2";
        using (SqlConnection connection = new SqlConnection
        (connectionString)) {
            connection.Open();
            SqlCommand command = new SqlCommand(queryString, connection);

            try {
                command.ExecuteNonQuery();
            }
            catch (SqlException e) {
                Console.WriteLine("Got expected SqlException due to command
                timeout ");
                Console.WriteLine(e);
            }
        }
    }
}
```

Note   You don't need Visual Studio installed to test this example, just the Microsoft .NET framework, which should be already installed if you also have SQL Server. A typical installation would have one or more versions of the Microsoft .NET framework at the `C:\Windows\Microsoft.NET` folder, where you can find the Microsoft Visual C# Compiler or `csc.exe`. The provided code may need to be updated if you are not using a default SQL Server instance or if you are not using Windows authentication.

A simple way to compile the code could be running the following, assuming the code is saved in a file named test.cs:

```
"C:\Windows\Microsoft.NET\Framework64\v4.0.30319\csc.exe" test.cs
Microsoft (R) Visual C# Compiler version 4.8.3752.0
for C# 5
Copyright (C) Microsoft Corporation. All rights reserved.
```

Running the created executable test.exe would produce the following expected error:

```
Got expected SqlException due to command timeout
System.Data.SqlClient.SqlException (0x80131904): Execution Timeout
Expired.  The timeout period elapsed prior to completion of the operation
or the server is not responding. ---> System.ComponentModel.Win32Exception
(0x80004005): The wait operation timed out
```

Since I've mentioned that the Query Store tracks all the queries executed in the configured database, you may be asking if it captures queries using the `RECOMPILE` hint, maintenance statements, or cross-database queries. Let me answer with the following examples. Create a small table on a test database to prepare for running a cross-database query:

```
USE Test
CREATE TABLE Orders (SalesOrderID int)
INSERT INTO Orders VALUES (43659)
```

Go back to AdventureWorks2017. Again, clear the Query Store so it is easy to look at the query stored in the catalog views:

```
USE AdventureWorks2017
GO
ALTER DATABASE AdventureWorks2017 SET QUERY_STORE CLEAR ALL
```

Run the following statements making sure to update the backup destination to a valid path:

```
ALTER INDEX IX_SalesOrderDetail_ProductID ON Sales.SalesOrderDetail REBUILD
GO
DBCC CHECKDB
GO
SELECT * FROM Sales.SalesOrderDetail
WHERE ProductID = 898
OPTION (RECOMPILE)
GO
BACKUP DATABASE AdventureWorks2017 TO  DISK = 'c:\data\delete_me.bak'
GO
SELECT * FROM Sales.SalesOrderDetail a JOIN Test.dbo.Orders b
ON a.SalesOrderID = b.SalesOrderID
```

Inspect which queries were captured by the Query Store using the previous query. All of them except the DBCC CHECKDB and BACKUP DATABASE statements were captured.

Force Failure

As mentioned earlier, plan forcing should be a temporary solution while a long-term solution is researched and implemented. Similar to the case of using query hints, forced plans should be monitored, as performance may degrade after changes in your database. There is also the possibility that SQL Server may fail to force a specified plan. The Query Store provides information regarding force plan failure using the columns last_force_failure_reason and last_force_failure_reason_desc of the sys.query_store_plan catalog view. The documented values for these columns are as follows:

> 8637: ONLINE_INDEX_BUILD: Query tries to modify data while target table has an index that is being built online.

8683: `INVALID_STARJOIN`: Plan contains invalid StarJoin specification.

8684: `TIME_OUT`: Optimizer exceeded number of allowed operations while searching for plan specified by forced plan.

8689: `NO_DB`: A database specified in the plan does not exist.

8690: `HINT_CONFLICT`: Query cannot be compiled because plan conflicts with a query hint.

8694: `DQ_NO_FORCING_SUPPORTED`: Cannot execute query because plan conflicts with use of distributed query or full-text operations.

8698: `NO_PLAN`: Query processor could not produce query plan because forced plan could not be verified to be legal for query.

8712: `NO_INDEX`: Index specified in plan no longer exists.

8713: `VIEW_COMPILE_FAILED`: Could not force query plan because of a problem in an indexed view referenced in the plan.

<other value>: `GENERAL_FAILURE`: General forcing error (not covered with preceding reasons).

A trivial example to show this feature would be to disable an existing index that is used in a forced plan. Clean the Query Store and plan cache:

```
ALTER DATABASE AdventureWorks2017 SET QUERY_STORE CLEAR ALL
GO
DBCC FREEPROCCACHE
```

Create the indexed plan by running the following code (it assumes the procedure was created as shown earlier):

```
EXEC test @pid = 898
```

Just for the purpose of this exercise, it is assumed that you may have at least another plan, and you want to force the one with the seek index operator. Run the following query to obtain its `plan_id`:

```
SELECT plan_id, q.query_id, query_sql_text FROM sys.query_store_plan p
JOIN sys.query_store_query AS q
        ON p.query_id = q.query_id
```

```
JOIN sys.query_store_query_text qt
      ON q.query_text_id = qt.query_text_id
WHERE query_sql_text LIKE '%SELECT * FROM Sales.SalesOrderDetail%'
```

Inspect the results to find the query text "(@pid int)SELECT * FROM Sales. SalesOrderDetail WHERE ProductID = @pid". Get the query_id and plan_id values. In my case, query_id is 1 and plan_id is 1. Run the following to force the required plan:

```
EXEC sys.sp_query_store_force_plan @query_id = 1, @plan_id = 1
```

You can optionally perform this process in SQL Server Management Studio as explained earlier. Verify that the query runs, that the plan using an index seek is used, and that the Use Plan attribute in the execution plan is set to true. Finally, disable the index:

```
ALTER INDEX IX_SalesOrderDetail_ProductID ON Sales.SalesOrderDetail DISABLE
```

If you run the query again, forcing the plan will fail as the index used by the plan is no longer available. You will instead get a normal query optimization and a plan using a table scan. The following query, first updating the plan_id to the one you used earlier

```
SELECT * FROM sys.query_store_plan
WHERE plan_id = 1
```

will return force_failure_count 1, which is the number of times that forcing this plan has failed. Remember that this value shows optimization attempts and not query executions. The results also show that the last_force_failure_reason is 8712 and last_force_failure_reason_desc NO_INDEX, which were expected as documented at the beginning of this section. But if you enable or rebuild the index, the plan will continue to be forced. Run the following statement:

```
ALTER INDEX IX_SalesOrderDetail_ProductID ON Sales.SalesOrderDetail REBUILD
```

The forced plan will be used again by the query processor, and the values for force_ failure_count, last_force_failure_reason, and last_force_failure_reason_desc on the sys.query_store_plan catalog will be reset to 0, 0, and NONE, respectively.

Wait Statistics

As mentioned in the previous chapter, starting with SQL Server 2016, it is now possible to track wait statistics at the session or query level, by using the sys.dm_exec_session_wait_stats DMV. Obviously, I am talking at the database engine level. Even when the Query Store was released during the same version, collecting wait information on the Query Store was not implemented until SQL Server 2017. This feature was without a doubt the most important improvement to the Query Store since the original release.

Wait statistics are enabled by default in the Query Store. For example, you can create a new database and, without enabling the Query Store, take a look at the sys.database_query_store_options to verify that wait_stats_capture_on is enabled. So if you enable the Query Store, the wait statistics feature will be automatically enabled along with it.

You can also explicitly enable wait statistics by running the following statement:

```
ALTER DATABASE AdventureWorks2017 SET QUERY_STORE
(WAIT_STATS_CAPTURE_MODE = ON)
```

In a similar way, you can disable the feature using the same statement with WAIT_STATS_CAPTURE_MODE = OFF.

Wait types in the Query Store are grouped into wait categories, in a similar way as the data collection feature, as shown in Figure 5-3 in Chapter 5. Let us try a quick exercise to see how the feature works. After making sure the wait statistics feature is enabled, try running some expensive queries. A simple example could be running the following SELECT statements ten times each:

```
SELECT * FROM Person.Person
GO 10
SELECT * FROM Sales.SalesOrderDetail
GO 10
```

You can immediately access the wait information after the queries are completed. In order to do that, you can use SQL Server Management Studio and run the Query Wait Statistics report from the Query Store folder. You may see a report similar to what I show in Figure 6-8. The graph is based on the "wait category" metric, but you can change it to other choices such as avg wait time, min wait time, max wait time, std dev wait time, total wait time, or execution count. My example shows our two queries, called Query ID 1 and 2, including their wait information.

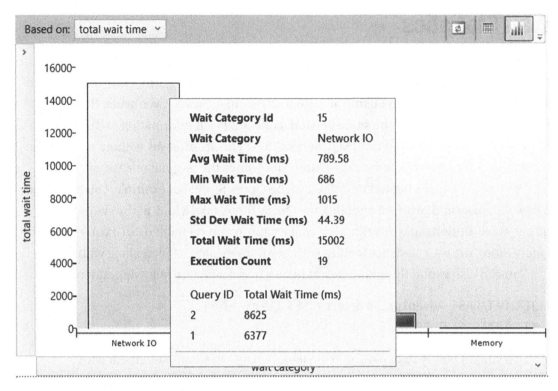

Figure 6-8. *Query Store wait statistics*

Clicking any wait category will take us to a second screen where we can see the wait information per query, including any available execution plans, as you can see in Figure 6-9.

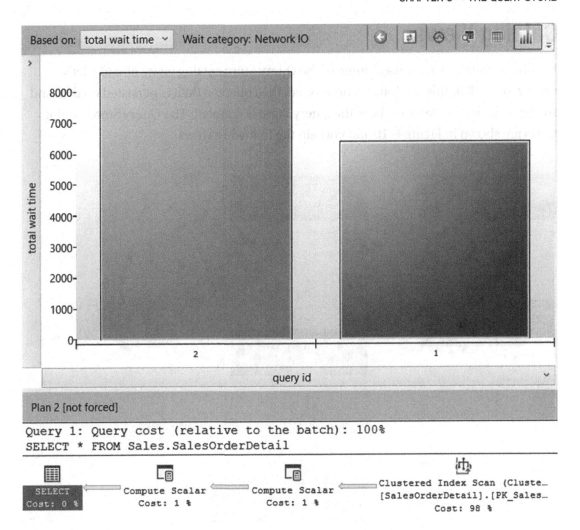

Figure 6-9. *Query wait statistics*

Finally, as mentioned earlier, waits are grouped in categories, instead of listing
a particular wait such as CXPACKET or ASYNC_NETWORK_IO. For example, all the
LCK_M_% waits are grouped in the Lock category, all LATCH_% into the Latch category,
PAGELATCH_% into Buffer Latch, PAGEIOLATCH_% into Buffer IO, CXPACKET and
others into Parallelism, ASYNC_NETWORK_IO and others into Network IO, and
SOS_SCHEDULER_YIELD alone is listed as CPU, just to list the most common ones we
usually see. You can see the entire list by looking at sys.query_store_wait_stats in the
documentation. You can also see more details about waits in Chapter 5.

Catalog Views

Finally, although we have used some of the Query Store catalog views already, let's review them all in this section. As mentioned, the collected data is persisted on disk and stored in the user database where the Query Store is enabled. The Query Store catalog views are shown in Figure 6-10 and contain the following views.

Figure 6-10. *Query Store catalog views*

sys.query_store_query_text	Query text information
sys.query_store_query	Query information, including query hash, parameterization, compilation, and optimization information
sys.query_store_plan	Execution plans, including history

(*continued*)

`sys.query_store_runtime_stats`	Query runtime statistics. The Query Store stores aggregate statistics on an interval for every executed plan. The interval is defined by the configuration option `INTERVAL_LENGTH_MINUTES`
`sys.query_store_runtime_stats_ interval`	Start and end time for intervals
`sys.query_context_settings`	Query context settings information

The collected data is only captured when the query execution ends (including when a query is canceled or interrupted as shown earlier). The `query_hash` column of the `sys.query_store_query` catalog view is the MD5 hash of the individual query, based on the logical query tree, and it also includes optimizer hints. Also, as indicated earlier, an identical query will be considered distinct if used in an ad hoc query or in a stored procedure or in a different stored procedure.

Queries with different context settings, that is, using different plan-affecting SET options, are considered distinct. Plan-affecting SET options can impact the choice of an execution plan, as they affect things like the results of evaluating constant expressions during the optimization process. The plan-affecting SET options are the following:

ANSI_NULL_DFLT_OFF

ANSI_NULL_DFLT_ON

ANSI_NULLS

ANSI_PADDING

ANSI_WARNINGS

ARITHABORT

CONCAT_NULL_YIELDS_NULL

DATEFIRST

DATEFORMAT

FORCEPLAN

LANGUAGE

NO_BROWSETABLE

NUMERIC_ROUNDABORT

QUOTED_IDENTIFIER

You can find more information about the plan-affecting SET options by reading the Microsoft white paper "Plan Caching in SQL Server 2008" at https://msdn.microsoft.com/en-us/library/ee343986(v=sql.100).aspx.

Finally, in addition to sp_query_store_force_plan and sp_query_store_unforce_plan, covered earlier, the Query Store provides the following stored procedures:

sp_query_store_remove_query: Removes a query, as well as all its associated plans and runtime statistics from the Query Store

sp_query_store_remove_plan: Removes a specific plan from the Query Store

sp_query_store_reset_exec_stats: Clears the runtime statistics for a specific query plan from the Query Store

sp_query_store_flush_db: Flushes the in-memory portion of the Query Store data to disk

Live Query Statistics

Live Query Statistics is another query troubleshooting feature introduced with SQL Server 2016 that you can use to view a live query plan while the query is still in execution. Using this feature, which can also be used with SQL Server 2014 as explained later, you can see query plan information in real time without the need to wait for the query to complete. Live Query Statistics can be useful to determine which part of a query could be running slow and to troubleshoot queries which either never finish, fail after many hours, or just take many hours to complete. Usually, a challenge with queries taking a long time to execute is the lack of runtime execution statistics (like the information provided by the sys.dm_exec_query_stats DMV or the SET STATISTICS IO and SET STATISTICS TIME statements) or an actual execution plan. Often using an estimated execution plan is not enough for troubleshooting a query problem. For example, since it only provides estimated information, it cannot be used to detect cardinality estimation problems.

Live Query Statistics uses information that is available through the sys.dm_exec_query_profiles DMV. Since this DMV was introduced with SQL Server 2014, Live Query Statistics could also be used against this version of SQL Server provided that you use

SQL Server 2016 Management Studio or later, as Live Query Statistics is implemented in this tool. Keep in mind that this feature uses a significant number of system resources so it should only be used in troubleshooting scenarios. There are several ways to enable this feature in SQL Server Management Studio, including selecting Include Live Query Statistics on the SQL Editor toolbar or using similar choices on the Tools menu or Activity Monitor. To test how Live Query Statistics works, enable the feature using any of the three previous methods, and run the following query against the AdventureWorks2017 database.

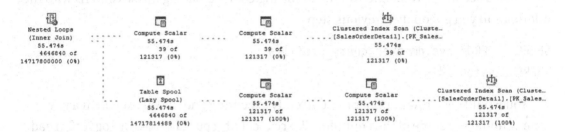

Figure 6-11. *Live Query Statistics execution*

```
SELECT * FROM Sales.SalesOrderDetail s1 CROSS JOIN Sales.SalesOrderDetail s2
```

This should show a plan similar to the one in Figure 6-11 in which Live Query Statistics shows both the overall query progress and the progress and elapsed time for the query plan operators, and the information is being updated as the query is being executed. At the time of writing, Hekaton natively compiled stored procedures are not supported by the Live Query Statistics feature.

Currently, Live Query Statistics does not reveal as much information as the DMV so you may also want to query it as well. To better understand the information available through Live Query Statistics, we could examine the data provided by the DMV. The DMV returns a rich list of performance information including row count, rewinds, rebinds, elapsed time, CPU time, number of table or index scans, logical reads, physical reads, read-aheads, LOB logical reads, LOB physical reads, and LOB read-aheads, among others. (Please refer to the documentation for the entire list.) The counters are per operator per thread.

In order to use the sys.dm_exec_query_profiles DMV, you will first need to enable the runtime execution plan statistics collection, using either the SET STATISTICS PROFILE ON or SET STATISTICS XML ON statements, on the same session where you would be running the query that will be the focus of the live statistics. For an example, follow the following exercise. Open a session where you plan to run the query to get information from and obtain its session ID. (You can look at the SQL Server Management Studio editor or run a statement like SELECT @@SPID.) Run the following statement:

```
SET STATISTICS PROFILE ON
```

Now run

```
SELECT * FROM Sales.SalesOrderDetail s1 CROSS JOIN Sales.SalesOrderDetail s2
```

Open a second session and run the following code, replacing the session ID with the information you got on the previous step:

```
SELECT * FROM sys.dm_exec_query_profiles
WHERE session_id = 55
```

You would get a row per operator currently executing and, if you execute it a few times, should see some of the counters, like row_count, cpu_time_ms, or logical_read_count, updating its information as the query is being executed. To end the exercise, don't forget to cancel the first query as it would take a long time to run and use a lot of resources.

Finally, SQL Server Management Studio also includes a plan comparison tool that you can use to compare execution plans for troubleshooting purposes. This tool can be useful in query-tuning scenarios like testing changes in queries or changes in objects used by the queries like indexes. For more information about this tool, see http://blogs.msdn.com/b/sql_server_team/archive/2015/10/12/comparison-tool-released-with-latest-ssms.aspx.

Summary

The Query Store and Live Query Statistics are two of the most important database engine features introduced with SQL Server 2016 designed to help you in query performance troubleshooting. The Query Store allows you to troubleshoot query performance by collecting optimization and execution runtime statistics, helping you to pinpoint queries that may have regressed. Its data can also be used to find expensive queries that can be candidates for additional query tuning. Finally, the Query Store can be used to force a specific plan for a query, which can be useful if plan regression has been found.

While the Query Store works with data of queries already completed, the Live Query Statistics can be used to troubleshoot queries while they are still running, something that can be useful for queries that either never finish, fail after many hours, or take many hours to complete.

PART IV

Performance Tuning and Troubleshooting

CHAPTER 7

SQL Server In-Memory Technologies

This chapter covers in-memory databases along with some other new technologies and paradigms that radically depart from the traditional disk-based rowstore architecture and query processing algorithms that most relational databases have been using for a few decades now. Current relational databases were architected back in the late 1970s, when hardware was totally different from what it is today, and databases were too large to fit in memory and assumed to be kept on disk. In addition to faster processors and declining memory cost, memory capacity in current hardware has increased in a way that most transactional databases could now fit entirely into it.

Microsoft first introduced in-memory database technologies in the analytical and data warehouse arena. This technology, a column-based storage engine, was first available as part of the PowerPivot add-in for Excel and later included in the Analysis Services product. It eventually made it into the SQL Server relational engine in the form of columnstore indexes when it was introduced in SQL Server 2012 and has now had very important enhancements throughout several releases. Although this technology is a column-based storage, it is worth noting that it is also a memory-optimized technology, and, in fact, it is sometimes called In-Memory Columnstore. With columnstore indexes, SQL Server introduced yet another new paradigm, batch execution mode, a query processing improvement when compared against the traditional row-based execution that SQL Server had been using in all its releases.

© Benjamin Nevarez 2021
B. Nevarez, *High Performance SQL Server*, https://doi.org/10.1007/978-1-4842-6491-1_7

In-memory technologies debuted into the transactional arena when In-Memory OLTP (Online Transaction Processing), widely known as Hekaton because of the name of its project announced in late 2012, was introduced with SQL Server 2014. In-Memory OLTP also introduced a new kind of stored procedure, called natively compiled, which is compiled to machine native code and loaded as in-process DLL (dynamic-link library) into memory. Similar to the beginning of columnstore indexes, Hekaton suffered considerable limitations on its initial release. Fortunately, it has greatly improved with the recent versions of the product, allowing more applications to be migrated to it.

While SQL Server 2012 introduced columnstore indexes for analytical and data warehouse workloads and SQL Server 2014 In-Memory OLTP for transactional databases, the SQL Server 2016 release combined both technologies to provide real-time analytics by allowing you to create a columnstore index on operational tables. These columnstore indexes are now updatable and can be created, as mentioned, on operational tables, which can be either a regular disk-based or a memory-optimized Hekaton table.

Although this chapter may contain more code than the remaining chapters of the book, the main focus is to show the new in-memory features, their characteristics, and performance benefits. It is not meant to be a programming guide, so implementing a feature may require a look at the SQL Server documentation.

Since this chapter covers new technologies and paradigms, it also uses different terminology from the rest of the book. It uses the term "disk-based table" to refer to traditional tables in order to differentiate them from the new memory-optimized tables. Natively compiled stored procedures are also contrasted with the traditional stored procedures. In addition, it uses the term "rowstore" to refer to the traditional row storage as compared to the new column-based technologies (or columnstore).

In-Memory OLTP

In the paper "OLTP Through the Looking Glass, and What We Found There," Michael Stonebraker et. al researched with an open source database to show where query execution time is spent in modern database systems. Their results showed that for this particular database system, the query execution time is dominated by components such as the buffer manager, latching, locking, and logging, comprising 34.6%, 14.2%, 16.3%, and 11.9% of the execution time, respectively. These four areas make about 77% of the execution time.

Note   The "OLTP Through the Looking Glass, and What We Found Their" paper is a recommended reading. You can find it online at `http://nms.csail.mit.edu/~stavros/pubs/OLTP_sigmod08.pdf`.

The SQL Server performance engineering team performed a similar analysis that showed where time is spent in a SQL Server OLTP system as a percentage of the total query execution. The results of their analysis were similarly interesting, indicating that the communication stack used 10% of the total query execution time. I/O and thread management accounted for another 10%, while the storage engine including access methods, transaction, lock, and log managers used 45%. Finally, the query processor accounted for 35% of the total time used in execution. Understanding where time is spent in an OLTP system was a critical part of their research, which allowed them to focus on the components of a database system that has more opportunity for additional optimizations.

Hekaton is a memory-optimized engine for OLTP workloads that benefits from current hardware and was designed to minimize the query execution time spent on some of the previously listed components. In-Memory OLTP achieves better performance with the following features:

- Memory-optimized engine: Data is always in memory, and the Hekaton engine data structures and algorithms are optimized for memory access. New structures include memory-optimized nonclustered indexes and hash indexes.

- Multiversion concurrency control and optimistic concurrency: Locks and latches are eliminated so we no longer have contention for latches and spinlocks, user waits for locks, or blocking. Similar to the snapshot isolation level introduced with SQL Server 2005, the Hekaton engine uses versioning, although its versions are stored in memory instead of the `tempdb` database.

- Native code: The query optimizer is still used to produce an execution plan, but this plan is additionally translated into C code, compiled into a DLL, and loaded in memory. Native code executes faster than traditional interpreted query plans.

Hekaton was released with SQL Server 2014, and, similar to columnstore indexes, it started with a considerable number of limitations. The main limitation was that after a table was created, it could not be changed in any way. It was not possible to add or remove columns or indexes or change any of its properties. `ALTER TABLE` can now be used with memory-optimized tables starting with SQL Server 2016 to change most of the table properties. But similar to the traditional disk-based tables, you still want to design your memory-optimized tables in the best possible way from the beginning since performing changes after production may require a maintenance window with potentially database downtime.

Memory-optimized data structures currently include tables and table variables, while natively compiled modules include stored procedures, triggers, and scalar and table-valued user-defined functions. These memory-optimized data structures are defined using the new `MEMORY_OPTIMIZED` and `NATIVE_COMPILATION` clauses. Memory-optimized data is not stored in data pages unlike traditional database engine storage structures. Rows are always in memory, and tables require at least one index. In Hekaton, tables must fit entirely in memory, and all its data is always in memory all the time. However, you do not have to move the entire database to memory, and you can select which tables of a database to be migrated. You can also choose which stored procedures to migrate to natively compiled form.

Even though both columnstore indexes and Hekaton are in-memory technologies, none of the three performance benefits of Hekaton directly apply to columnstore indexes as they are used in different workloads and have different architecture. Locks and latches are still held in columnstore indexes, and they do not implement natively compiled code. Performance benefits of columnstore indexes are more related to their column-based storage, high compression, and batch processing execution algorithms. Columnstore indexes are covered in the next section.

Note   Although both columnstore indexes and Hekaton are in-memory technologies, only the latter requires a table to entirely fit in memory. Columnstore indexes are usually used for very large tables and are not required to fit entirely in memory.

Interestingly, just a few days after SQL Server 2012 was released, Microsoft's technical fellow David Campbell hinted about a new in-memory engine for transactional workloads in his paper "The Coming In-Memory Database Tipping Point," which is a recommended reading. You can find it at `https://blogs. technet.microsoft.com/dataplatforminsider/2012/04/09/the- coming-in-memory-database-tipping-point`. Hekaton was publicly announced later that same year at a conference in Seattle.

Enhancements After the Initial Release

Starting with SQL Server 2016, In-Memory OLTP now includes the ability to change tables and native procedures by using the `ALTER TABLE` and `ALTER PROCEDURE` statements.

The original version of Hekaton also had a serious limitation regarding memory as the total in-memory size of all the tables in a database should not exceed 256 GB. With the SQL Server 2016 release, this limit was originally extended to 2 TB and was not exactly a hard limit but a supported limit. Weeks after SQL Server 2016 RTM was released, Microsoft announced it was removing such limits and supporting any amount of memory available by the operating system.

Parallelism is now possible with table scan operations. Although not a big requirement for pure OLTP workloads, it can now benefit operational analytic queries, as covered later in this chapter.

Statistics used by the query optimizer are now automatically updated, as is the case with disk-based tables. You can now also specify a sample when manually updating statistics, as `FULLSCAN` was the only choice available in SQL Server 2014. However, updated statistics do not immediately benefit natively compiled modules in the same way they do with traditional stored procedures. That is, an update of statistics, either manual or automatic, does not trigger a new optimization on natively compiled modules. You will have to manually recompile them, for example, using the `sp_ recompile` system stored procedure.

Finally, starting with SQL Server 2017, Hekaton has removed the original limitation of a maximum of eight indexes per table or table type. Although you can now define as many indexes as you like, the same recommendation for disk-based tables applies, and you should only define the indexes that are really needed.

Memory-Optimized Tables

Let's start playing with the technology. First, we need to create a database with Hekaton enabled. In order to achieve this, we need to create a filegroup with the CONTAINS MEMORY_OPTIMIZED_DATA clause, as shown in the following code. You can optionally add such a filegroup to an existing database, but only one such filegroup is allowed per database. Make sure you have the required drive and folder if you are running this in your system or change accordingly.

Create a database:

```
CREATE DATABASE Test
ON PRIMARY (NAME = Test_data,
FILENAME = 'C:\DATA\Test_data.mdf', SIZE=500MB),
FILEGROUP Test_fg CONTAINS MEMORY_OPTIMIZED_DATA
(NAME = Test_fg, FILENAME = 'C:\DATA\Test_fg')
LOG ON (NAME = Test_log, Filename='C:\DATA\Test_log.ldf', SIZE=500MB)
```

In the next example, I will try to create a table exactly as it appears in AdventureWorks as a quick exercise to understand some of the changes you need to do when migrating disk-based tables to In-Memory OLTP. In order to do this, I will use the script functionality available in SQL Server Management Studio (e.g., right-clicking the table and choosing Script Table as CREATE TO and New Query Editor Window).

Note   All the Hekaton examples in this chapter will use the Test database we have just created.

This is the minimum version that can be successfully created as a disk-based table (just removing three columns that require a user-defined data type, which is not supported in Hekaton). I am adding the WITH (MEMORY_OPTIMIZED=ON) clause so you can test on your system.

```
CREATE TABLE dbo.SalesOrderHeader(
        SalesOrderID int IDENTITY(1,1) NOT FOR REPLICATION NOT NULL,
        RevisionNumber tinyint NOT NULL,
        OrderDate datetime NOT NULL,
        DueDate datetime NOT NULL,
        ShipDate datetime NULL,
```

```
    Status tinyint NOT NULL,
    SalesOrderNumber  AS (isnull(N'SO'+CONVERT(nvarchar(23),
    SalesOrderID),N'*** ERROR ***')),
    CustomerID int NOT NULL,
    SalesPersonID int NULL,
    TerritoryID int NULL,
    BillToAddressID int NOT NULL,
    ShipToAddressID int NOT NULL,
    ShipMethodID int NOT NULL,
    CreditCardID int NULL,
    CreditCardApprovalCode varchar(15) NULL,
    CurrencyRateID int NULL,
    SubTotal money NOT NULL,
    TaxAmt money NOT NULL,
    Freight money NOT NULL,
    TotalDue  AS (isnull((SubTotal+TaxAmt)+Freight,(0))),
    Comment nvarchar(128) NULL,
    rowguid uniqueidentifier ROWGUIDCOL  NOT NULL,
    ModifiedDate datetime NOT NULL,
    CONSTRAINT PK_SalesOrderHeader_SalesOrderID PRIMARY KEY CLUSTERED (
    SalesOrderID ASC
    )
) WITH (MEMORY_OPTIMIZED = ON)
```

Trying to run the CREATE TABLE statement returns some of the following error messages or recommendations:

a. Clustered indexes, which are the default for primary keys, are not supported with memory-optimized tables. Specify a NONCLUSTERED index instead.

b. Computed columns are not supported with memory-optimized tables (computed columns are supported starting with SQL Server 2017).

c. The feature ROWGUIDCOL is not supported with memory-optimized tables.

Finally, up next is a working version, using the dbo schema:

```
CREATE TABLE dbo.SalesOrderHeader(
        SalesOrderID int PRIMARY KEY NONCLUSTERED NOT NULL,
        RevisionNumber tinyint NOT NULL,
        OrderDate datetime NOT NULL,
        DueDate datetime NOT NULL,
        ShipDate datetime NULL,
        Status tinyint NOT NULL,
        CustomerID int NOT NULL,
        SalesPersonID int NULL,
        TerritoryID int NULL,
        BillToAddressID int NOT NULL,
        ShipToAddressID int NOT NULL,
        ShipMethodID int NOT NULL,
        CreditCardID int NULL,
        CreditCardApprovalCode varchar(15) NULL,
        CurrencyRateID int NULL,
        SubTotal money NOT NULL,
        TaxAmt money NOT NULL,
        Freight money NOT NULL,
        Comment nvarchar(128) NULL,
        ModifiedDate datetime NOT NULL
) WITH (MEMORY_OPTIMIZED = ON)
```

Fortunately, SQL Server provides a better way to help you find and evaluate incompatibilities while migrating your tables to In-Memory OLTP. A tool called the Table Memory Optimization Advisor (or just Memory Optimization Advisor on recent versions) can help you to migrate your disk-based tables to memory-optimized tables. To run this tool, right-click the Sales.SalesOrderHeader table on the AdventureWorks2017 database and select Memory Optimization Advisor. Running the migration validation part will show the screen in Figure 7-1, which indicates that it cannot proceed with the migration and provides additional information and recommendations.

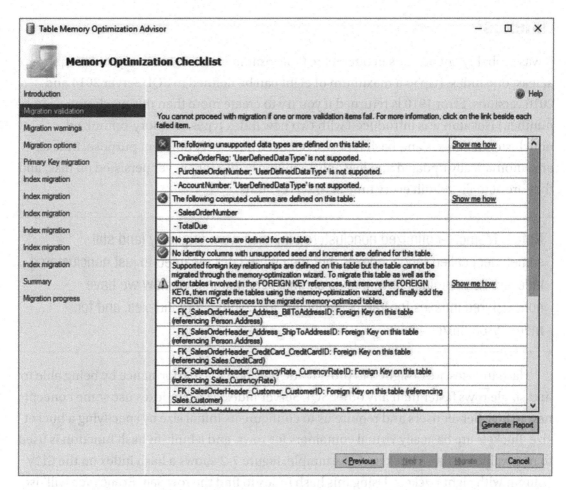

Figure 7-1. *Table Memory Optimization Advisor*

SQL Server provides a similar tool for stored procedures and other code called the Stored Procedure Native Compilation Advisor (or just Native Compilation Advisor), which you can find by right-clicking the code object you want to review. SQL Server 2016 and later also includes the Transaction Performance Analysis Overview report, which can help you to decide which tables and code to move first to Hekaton. To run this report, right-click your database and select Report and Standard Reports. SQL Server 2014 provides similar reports, but you would have to enable and configure them using the Data Collector tool.

Indexes

It was probably not obvious in our create table example earlier, but every table requires at least one index. (Up to a maximum of eight can be defined in SQL Server 2014 and 2016 versions. Error 1910 is returned if you try to create more than this maximum number.) Hekaton was introduced with two new index types, memory-optimized nonclustered indexes and hash indexes, but each has a very different purpose. Indexes are automatically updated and live only in memory; they are never persisted on disk, and they are actually rebuilt every time SQL Server starts.

Note   Memory-optimized nonclustered indexes were originally (and still sometimes) called range indexes, but they were later renamed to just nonclustered indexes. This naming convention is confusing sometimes as now we have nonclustered indexes for traditional tables, for columnstore indexes, and for memory-optimized tables.

Hash indexes are designed to provide the best possible performance by being able to find single rows faster than any other SQL Server index. Hash indexes use some concepts new to SQL Server users and require us to configure its initial size by specifying a bucket size. Buckets are basically virtual containers for rows, and a built-in hash function is used to map values to those buckets. For example, Figure 7-2 shows a hash index on the City column with eight buckets. Using this hash index to find the row San Francisco will use the hash function that will return bucket 2, and the Hekaton engine will find the row there.

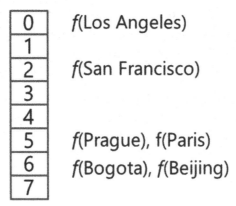

Figure 7-2. Hash indexes showing hash collisions

However, collisions may also occur while using the hash index. If you try to find the row Prague, the hash function will correctly return bucket 5. However, since there is more than one row, the engine will have to search a linked list to find the requested row. Although having a small number of rows is not an issue, a performance problem may appear when there is a large number of rows on each bucket. The hash function will always efficiently find the correct bucket, but traversing a long list may be a performance concern. We can monitor such information by looking at the avg_chain_length column of the sys.dm_db_xtp_hash_index_stats DMV, which records the average number of rows of all the hash buckets in the index.

Unfortunately, the bucket count cannot be changed dynamically, and, in SQL Server 2014, it would require the creation of a new table with the new BUCKET_COUNT configuration. SQL Server 2016 and later now allows using the ALTER TABLE statement to change the bucket size, but it is still a major change to the table structure, and it is a blocking operation that you may want to perform only during a maintenance window as most likely it will require an application outage. Because of this limitation, it is extremely important to estimate and plan what the best value for the number of buckets to use is. Since the best performance is achieved when a small number of rows is available per bucket, the main recommendation is to configure the BUCKET_COUNT value to be the same or twice the number of unique rows in the index.

Let me show you some examples with a smaller version of SalesOrderHeader. Creating a hash index requires the NONCLUSTERED HASH keyword along with a BUCKET_COUNT definition:

```
CREATE TABLE dbo.SalesOrderHeader(
        SalesOrderID int PRIMARY KEY NONCLUSTERED HASH WITH
                (BUCKET_COUNT = 10000),
        OrderDate datetime NOT NULL,
        ShipDate datetime NULL,
        Status tinyint NOT NULL,
        CustomerID int NOT NULL,
) WITH (MEMORY_OPTIMIZED = ON)
```

After the table is being populated, you can do an analysis of the bucket usage by using the sys.dm_db_xtp_hash_index_stats:

```
SELECT OBJECT_NAME(object_id), * FROM sys.dm_db_xtp_hash_index_stats
```

The column `total_bucket_count` will show the total number of hash buckets in the index, which is rounded to the next power of 2. For the example shown where 10,000 buckets are requested, the index will be created with 16,384.

Nonclustered indexes are memory-optimized b-tree indexes and more similar to the nonclustered indexes we are used to on disk tables. They just require the `NONCLUSTERED` keyword.

```
CREATE TABLE dbo.SalesOrderHeader(
      SalesOrderID int PRIMARY KEY NONCLUSTERED,
      OrderDate datetime NOT NULL,
      ShipDate datetime NULL,
      Status tinyint NOT NULL,
      CustomerID int NOT NULL,
) WITH (MEMORY_OPTIMIZED = ON)
```

Note   Although a heavy computer science level paper, you can learn more about the new range indexes on the paper "The Bw-Tree: A B-Tree for New Hardware Platforms" by Justin Levandoski et. al, which you can find online at `www.microsoft.com/en-us/research/publication/the-bw-tree-a-b-tree-for-new-hardware`.

As a summary, hash indexes provide the best performance to search rows with equality predicates (once again, assuming `BUCKET_COUNT` has been correctly configured and maintained). Hash indexes cannot be used to find rows using nonequality predicates or even using the order of the hash index. If no better index is found, the previous operations would require a hash index scan. Memory-optimized nonclustered indexes behave pretty much like a disk-based nonclustered index. You can perform all the typical operations including searching rows with equality and nonequality predicates and using the order of the index, range predicates, although, as mentioned, hash indexes are superior on equality searches.

Natively Compiled Modules

As mentioned earlier, there are three types of natively compiled modules in SQL Server 2016 and later, including stored procedures, scalar and table-valued user-defined functions, and triggers. Only stored procedures were available when Hekaton was originally introduced in SQL Server 2014. Let's review all of them here. The following code is a basic definition of a natively compiled stored procedure:

```
CREATE PROCEDURE test
WITH NATIVE_COMPILATION, SCHEMABINDING,
EXECUTE AS OWNER
AS
BEGIN ATOMIC WITH (
TRANSACTION ISOLATION LEVEL = SNAPSHOT,
LANGUAGE = 'us_english')
SELECT SalesOrderID, OrderDate, CustomerID
FROM dbo.SalesOrderHeader
END
```

An example of its execution follows:

```
EXEC test
```

User-defined functions are sometimes mentioned as concern for performance problems. Natively compiled user-defined functions perform better but still should only be used when appropriate. Next is the most basic scalar user-defined function to show the required syntax:

```
CREATE FUNCTION test_function()
RETURNS int
WITH NATIVE_COMPILATION, SCHEMABINDING
AS BEGIN ATOMIC WITH (TRANSACTION ISOLATION LEVEL = SNAPSHOT, LANGUAGE =
'English')
        RETURN 1
END
```

You would call it using the following:

```
SELECT dbo.test_function()
```

This is an example of a table-valued user-defined function:

```
CREATE FUNCTION dbo.test_tvf()
RETURNS TABLE
WITH NATIVE_COMPILATION, SCHEMABINDING
AS
        RETURN SELECT SalesOrderID, OrderDate, Status FROM dbo.
SalesOrderHeader
```

You would call it using the following:

```
SELECT * FROM dbo.test_tvf()
```

Similarly, this is the code you would use for a trigger. Natively compiled triggers are only available on memory-optimized tables, and these are the only kind of triggers allowed on these tables.

```
CREATE TRIGGER Insert_SalesOrderHeader
ON dbo.SalesOrderHeader
WITH NATIVE_COMPILATION, SCHEMABINDING
FOR INSERT, UPDATE, DELETE
AS BEGIN ATOMIC WITH (TRANSACTION ISOLATION LEVEL = SNAPSHOT, LANGUAGE =
'us_english')
        -- trigger code
END
```

In order to avoid unnecessary runtime checks for natively compiled modules, which have to be performed at execution time, some choices must be defined at compile time. The required options for any natively compiled module are as follows:

> SCHEMABINDING: Binds the natively compiled module to the schema of the underlying table or tables.

> EXECUTE AS: Specifies the security context under which to execute the natively compiled module.

> ATOMIC: Indicates that the entire block is executed as an atomic block and the entire block is either committed or rolled back. Part of the ANSI SQL standard.

TRANSACTION ISOLATION LEVEL: Defines the transaction isolation level, but only the following three choices are available: SNAPSHOT, REPEATABLE READ, and SERIALIZABLE. Different from the traditional SQL Server code, there is no default transaction isolation level for natively compiled modules so this option has to be specified.

LANGUAGE: Specifies the language environment for the code.

Two other options, although not required, are DATEFIRST and DATEFORMAT, which specify the first day of the week and the date format. If not specified, they are inferred from the LANGUAGE option.

Changing Tables and Natively Compiled Modules

ALTER TABLE is now available to change most of the properties of a table including adding and removing columns, adding and removing indexes, or changing the value for BUCKET_COUNT on a hash index. CREATE INDEX and DROP INDEX are not allowed with memory-optimized tables; ALTER TABLE has to be used instead. Let's look at a few examples assuming the following initial table:

```
CREATE TABLE dbo.SalesOrderHeader(
        SalesOrderID int PRIMARY KEY NONCLUSTERED NOT NULL,
        RevisionNumber tinyint NOT NULL,
        OrderDate datetime NOT NULL,
        DueDate datetime NOT NULL,
        ShipDate datetime NULL,
        Status tinyint NOT NULL,
        CustomerID int NOT NULL,
        SalesPersonID int NULL,
        TerritoryID int NULL,
        BillToAddressID int NOT NULL,
        ShipToAddressID int NOT NULL,
        ShipMethodID int NOT NULL,
        CreditCardID int NULL,
        CreditCardApprovalCode varchar(15) NULL,
        CurrencyRateID int NULL,
```

```
    SubTotal money NOT NULL,
    TaxAmt money NOT NULL,
    Freight money NOT NULL,
    Comment nvarchar(128) NULL,
    ModifiedDate datetime NOT NULL
) WITH (MEMORY_OPTIMIZED = ON)
```

a. Add a column. The following code adds three columns (by the way, these three columns were originally removed from the disk-based table as they were based on user-defined data types):

```
ALTER TABLE dbo.SalesOrderHeader
ADD OnlineOrderFlag bit NOT NULL,
PurchaseOrderNumber nvarchar(25) NULL,
AccountNumber nvarchar(25) NULL
```

b. Add an index. The following code adds a nonclustered index and a hash index:

```
ALTER TABLE dbo.SalesOrderHeader
ADD INDEX IX_ModifiedDate (ModifiedDate),
INDEX IX_CustomerID HASH (CustomerID) WITH (BUCKET_COUNT = 10000)
```

c. Change the bucket count of an index. The following code rebuilds an index and changes the bucket count to 100,000:

```
ALTER TABLE dbo.SalesOrderHeader
ALTER INDEX IX_CustomerID
REBUILD WITH (BUCKET_COUNT = 100000)
```

d. Remove columns or indexes. The following code removes the three columns added earlier:

```
ALTER TABLE dbo.SalesOrderHeader
DROP COLUMN OnlineOrderFlag, PurchaseOrderNumber, AccountNumber
```

Making changes to a table may interfere with the SCHEMABINDING property of natively compiled modules. Assume you have the following natively compiled stored procedure, which uses several columns from SalesOrderHeader:

```
CREATE PROCEDURE dbo.test
WITH NATIVE_COMPILATION, SCHEMABINDING, EXECUTE AS owner
AS
BEGIN ATOMIC
WITH (TRANSACTION ISOLATION LEVEL = SNAPSHOT, LANGUAGE = 'us_english')
SELECT SubTotal, ModifiedDate FROM dbo.SalesOrderHeader
END
```

Trying to drop a column from the table one of the columns referenced by the procedure

```
ALTER TABLE   dbo.SalesOrderHeader
       DROP COLUMN SubTotal
```

would return the following error:

```
Msg 5074, Level 16, State 1, Line 1
The object 'test' is dependent on column 'SubTotal'.
Msg 4922, Level 16, State 9, Line 1
ALTER TABLE DROP COLUMN SubTotal failed because one or more objects access
this column.
```

However, you will be able to drop any other column not referenced by this procedure or any other schema-bound object:

```
ALTER TABLE dbo.SalesOrderHeader
       DROP COLUMN TaxAmt
```

Fortunately, using a star (*) to select all the columns in a table is not allowed in this case. Trying it would get error 1054, complaining that such a syntax is not allowed in schema-bound objects.

New with SQL Server 2016, you can also alter natively compiled stored procedures. Other natively compiled objects like triggers and scalar and table-valued user-defined functions can be altered as well. For example, the following code alters the previously created stored procedure to remove one column from the SELECT list and change the isolation level:

```
ALTER PROCEDURE dbo.test
WITH NATIVE_COMPILATION, SCHEMABINDING, EXECUTE AS owner
AS
BEGIN ATOMIC
WITH (TRANSACTION ISOLATION LEVEL = REPEATABLE READ, LANGUAGE = 'us_
english')
SELECT SubTotal FROM dbo.SalesOrderHeader
END
```

Native Compilation

Native compilation applies to the creation of both memory-optimized tables and
natively compiled modules. In both cases, C code is generated, compiled, and linked,
and finally a DLL is created and loaded into memory in-process with the SQL Server
executable for performance. You can find the list of DLLs currently loaded in the
system by looking at the sys.dm_os_loaded_modules DMV as shown next, which in my
test system lists several files pointing to the C:\Program Files\Microsoft SQL Server\
MSSQL15.MSSQLSERVER\MSSQL\DATA\xtp\ folder.

```
SELECT * FROM sys.dm_os_loaded_modules
WHERE description = 'XTP Native DLL'
```

A concern sometimes raised in the database community is about the security access
of the created files. In summary, I will tell you that you should not worry about it. When
a DLL file is created, it is automatically loaded in memory, and there is no need to back
up the created files or do any maintenance to them. Those files are not needed anymore.
Every time SQL Server starts, it creates new DLLs for memory-optimized tables. Natively
compiled modules are compiled only when they are executed the first time. Technically,
the created DLL files have the same security access as the data files. Once inside the
previously listed xtp folder, you will find additional folders named after the database ID
of the configured database, containing files with the following extensions (a set of these
files is created per memory-optimized table and natively compiled module):

.c	C language source code
.dll	Dynamic-link library file
.obj	Object file generated by C compiler
.out	Log file generated by C compiler (includes parameters used by compiler)
.pdb	Symbol file generated by C compiler
.xml	MAT (Mixed Abstract Tree) file

Note   The In-Memory OLTP feature was originally called extreme transaction processing, and the XTP acronym remains in a large number of places in SQL Server.

In my system, the C compiler and Microsoft linker are located on C:\Program Files\ Microsoft SQL Server\MSSQL15.MSSQLSERVER\MSSQL\Binn\Xtp\VC\bin as cl.exe and link.exe, respectively. A small C code fragment shown for illustration purposes is next. (Generated code is not intended for human consumption.)

```c
#include "hkenggen.h"
#include "hkrtgen.h"
#include "hkgenlib.h"

#define ENABLE_INTSAFE_SIGNED_FUNCTIONS
#include "intsafe.h"

#define HOTPATCH_BUFFER_SIZE 256

typedef struct _PATCH_BUFFER {
    unsigned short PointerIndex;
    unsigned short Fill1;
    unsigned short BufferSize;
    unsigned short Fill2;
    unsigned __int64 Buffer[(HOTPATCH_BUFFER_SIZE - 8) / sizeof(__int64)];
} PATCH_BUFFER;

PATCH_BUFFER HotPatchBuffer = {0, 0, HOTPATCH_BUFFER_SIZE, 0};
```

```
int memcmp(const void*, const void*, size_t);
void *memset(void*, int, size_t);

#pragma deprecated (memcpy)


#define offsetof(s,f)    ((size_t)&(((s*)0)->f))


struct NullBitsStruct_322100188
{
        unsigned char hkc_isnull_3:1;
};
```

> **Note**   For more details about the Hekaton compiler architecture, you can read the paper "Hekaton: SQL Server's Memory-Optimized OLTP Engine" by Cristian Diaconu et. al, which you can find online at www.microsoft.com/en-us/ research/publication/hekaton-sql-servers-memory-optimized-oltp-engine.

Memory-Optimized Table Variables

Starting with SQL Server 2016, you can now use memory-optimized table variables to replace traditional table variables or temporary tables. Memory-optimized table variables offer several times better performance than their tempdb counterparts, and among their benefits are that they are always in memory and don't use tempdb. Consequently, they don't suffer from the tempdb limitations like I/O access or contention allocation.

> **Note**   New on SQL Server 2019, you can now configure tempdb to use memory-optimized metadata, a feature based on the In-Memory OLTP technology. By enabling this tempdb configuration, tempdb metadata can now be moved into latch-free nondurable memory-optimized tables and by doing that technically eliminating metadata contention. You can find more details at Chapter 4, where we covered tempdb troubleshooting and configuration.

Let's take a look at one example. The following code creates a regular temporary table and its equivalent memory-optimized table variable. Notice that two steps are required to create a memory-optimized table variable. First, we must create a type using the MEMORY_ OPTIMIZED = ON clause, which like any other memory-optimized table requires an index. Then we must declare a memory-optimized table variable using the type.

```
CREATE TABLE #temp (
        CustomerID int,
        Name varchar(40)
)
GO
CREATE TYPE test
AS TABLE (
        CustomerID int INDEX IX_CustomerID,
        Name varchar(40)
)
WITH (MEMORY_OPTIMIZED = ON)
GO
DECLARE @mytest test

SELECT * FROM @mytest
SELECT * FROM #temp
```

You may have a similar behavior using a memory-optimized table with SCHEMA_ONLY durability, but the main difference is that the table schema remains part of the database after SQL Server is restarted or the database is brought offline by some other methods. Tables with SCHEMA_ONLY durability are also useful in some other business scenarios like session state for web applications and staging tables for ETL (Extract, Transform, and Load) purposes.

Current Limitations

Although SQL Server 2019 is the fourth release of Hekaton, there are still some limitations you need to be aware of before deciding to start working on a project using this feature. You can find such information in "Transact-SQL Constructs Not Supported by In-Memory OLTP" at https://msdn.microsoft.com/en-us/library/dn246937. aspx and "Unsupported SQL Server Features for In-Memory OLTP" at https://msdn. microsoft.com/en-us/library/dn133181.aspx.

Both documents offer links for previous SQL Server versions, but it is strongly recommended that you implement new Hekaton projects on the later version instead.

Columnstore Indexes

Although column-based storage technology research dates back to the 1970s, their first implementations on database engines appeared only in the 1990s, 20 years later. Columnstore storage provides performance benefits on data warehouse databases as usually only a small number of the columns in a fact table may be needed for star join queries. Although they are also an in-memory technology in SQL Server, different from Hekaton, columnstore indexes are usually used in very large tables and are not required to entirely fit in memory. Figure 7-3 shows a comparison between a row-based and a column-based storage, in which we see that instead of hosting all the columns in a row, database pages contain data from only one specific column.

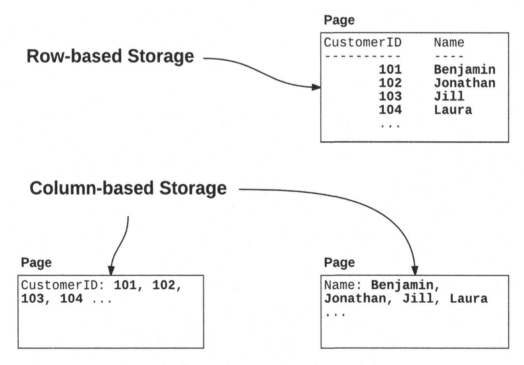

Figure 7-3. Rowstore and columnstore compared

> **Note** A seminal paper and a great reference for the topic is "C-store: A Column-oriented DBMS" by Mike Stonebraker et. al, which you can find online at `https://web.stanford.edu/class/cs245/readings/c-store.pdf`.

Columnstore index technology was first introduced in the SQL Server 2012 release, which started as a read-only nonclustered columnstore index that could be created on a heap or clustered index. Since this was a read-only structure, it would only make sense on a data warehouse, as opposed to an operational system (but as we will see soon, on recent versions of SQL Server, columnstore indexes could be created on operational system as well).

There were typically three workarounds to update read-only columnstore index data including using partitioning and partition switching, simply recreating the index, or using UNION ALL to combine data from the read-only columnstore index and a regular updatable table. These workarounds are no longer needed on subsequent versions. In the query processing side, columnstore index technology also introduced batch mode processing, a vector-based or vectorized execution method designed to improve the query performance by processing multiple rows at a time instead of using the traditional operators that process a row at a time.

The next generation of the feature included the choice to create an updatable clustered columnstore index. In this case, the columnstore index became the table or primary storage. In other words, columnstore storage can now replace the entire rowstore structure. This was introduced in SQL Server 2014, and the choice of a read-only nonclustered columnstore index was still available, if this was the only columnstore index in the table. Keep in mind that, as a nonclustered index, it would have to copy the required columns from the base table so additional storage was required. But it can also benefit from high compression ratios, making this additional required storage only 10% on average. No additional indexes were supported on the clustered columnstore index, not even rowstores, and there was no columnstore index support for memory-optimized tables.

Starting with SQL Server 2016, it is now possible to create an updatable nonclustered columnstore index, which could be created on either a heap or a clustered index (previously only a read-only version was possible). This updatable nonclustered columnstore index can be created on OLTP tables, which can help with real-time analytical queries, as covered later in this chapter, and can support a filtered condition as well. An updatable columnstore index can be created on OLTP memory-optimized tables as well although all the columns have to be included and no filtered condition is allowed. Compression delay is available to help on some performance scenarios.

It is worth mentioning that having a read-only nonclustered columnstore index, the default behavior in SQL Server 2014, is no longer possible in later versions of the product, although you can simulate their behavior, if needed, using a read-only filegroup. Finally, rowstore-based nonclustered indexes can now be created on a clustered columnstore index.

In summary, columnstore indexes started with some limitations, making SQL Server 2016 the third release improving on the features of this technology. If, for any reason, you are still under a previous version, you could use the following document to determine which features are available for the specific release: `https://msdn.microsoft.com/en-us/library/dn934994.aspx`.

Columnstore indexes include several performance benefits such as the following:

- Columnar storage: Since data warehouse star join queries usually select only a few columns of a fact table, reading only the pages for the required columns has huge I/O savings. Pages hosting columns not required for a query do not have to be read at all.

- Compression: Since data from the same column is stored in the same pages, similar data are kept contiguously, which means a high compression ratio, again saving I/O resources.

- Batch mode processing: Columnstore index technology uses a vector-based or vectorized execution model by which their engine processes multiple rows at the same time (typically up to 900). This processing is done at the query operation level, and more operations are included on each release. This contrasts the traditional query execution model, which processes just one row at a time, and it is used in all the versions of SQL Server. For a list of operations supporting batch mode processing for each SQL Server release, see `https://msdn.microsoft.com/en-us/library/dn935005.aspx`.

- Segment elimination: As mentioned earlier, data for the same column is stored in the same page, and multiple pages are grouped into a segment. Similar to the concept of partition elimination, segments can be eliminated depending on the values used as filters in a query.

- Aggregate pushdown: Starting with SQL Server 2016, aggregates are pushed down and precalculated at the storage engine. Aggregations can be pushed down to the scan operation, improving query performance by orders of magnitude.

Examples

The first example shows how to create a nonclustered columnstore index and works on every version of the product since SQL Server 2012. As a nonclustered index, it assumes a table already exists so I will start by creating one in AdventureWorksDW2017.

Note As indicated in Chapter 1, you can download the AdventureWorksDW2017 from https://docs.microsoft.com/en-us/sql/samples/ adventureworks-install-configure.

```
USE AdventureWorksDW2017
GO

CREATE TABLE dbo.FactResellerSalesNew(
        ProductKey int NOT NULL,
        OrderDateKey int NOT NULL,
        DueDateKey int NOT NULL,
        ShipDateKey int NOT NULL,
        ResellerKey int NOT NULL,
        EmployeeKey int NOT NULL,
        PromotionKey int NOT NULL,
        CurrencyKey int NOT NULL,
        SalesTerritoryKey int NOT NULL,
        SalesOrderNumber nvarchar(20) NOT NULL,
        SalesOrderLineNumber tinyint NOT NULL,
        RevisionNumber tinyint NULL,
        OrderQuantity smallint NULL,
        UnitPrice money NULL,
        ExtendedAmount money NULL,
        UnitPriceDiscountPct float NULL,
        DiscountAmount float NULL,
        ProductStandardCost money NULL,
        TotalProductCost money NULL,
        SalesAmount money NULL,
        TaxAmt money NULL,
```

```
        Freight money NULL,
        CarrierTrackingNumber nvarchar(25) NULL,
        CustomerPONumber nvarchar(25) NULL,
        OrderDate datetime NULL,
        DueDate datetime NULL,
        ShipDate datetime NULL,
        CONSTRAINT PK_SalesOrderNumber_SalesOrderLineNumber PRIMARY KEY
        CLUSTERED (
        SalesOrderNumber ASC,
        SalesOrderLineNumber ASC)
)
```

We can now create the nonclustered columnstore index by selecting a subset of the table columns:

```
CREATE NONCLUSTERED COLUMNSTORE INDEX ncsi_FactResellerSalesNew ON dbo.
FactResellerSalesNew (
        SalesOrderNumber, SalesOrderLineNumber, ProductKey, OrderDateKey,
DueDateKey, ShipDateKey,
        ResellerKey, EmployeeKey, PromotionKey, CurrencyKey,
SalesTerritoryKey, RevisionNumber,
        OrderQuantity, UnitPrice, ExtendedAmount, UnitPriceDiscountPct,
DiscountAmount, ProductStandardCost,
        TotalProductCost, SalesAmount, TaxAmt, Freight,
CarrierTrackingNumber, CustomerPONumber,
        OrderDate, DueDate, ShipDate)
```

As indicated earlier, starting with SQL Server 2016, the nonclustered columnstore index is now updatable, so we can load the data after the index is created. (If you are testing this code in an earlier version of SQL Server, where a columnstore index may be read-only, you may want to load the data first.)

```
INSERT INTO dbo.FactResellerSalesNew SELECT * FROM dbo.FactResellerSales
```

Next is an example of a star join query taking benefit of the index and running in batch execution mode as shown in the plan in Figure 7-4.

```
SELECT ProductKey, SUM(SalesAmount) FROM dbo.FactResellerSalesNew
GROUP BY ProductKey
```

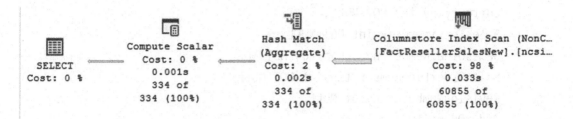

Figure 7-4.   *Columnstore index on a fact table*

Next, try to create a clustered columnstore index:

```
CREATE CLUSTERED COLUMNSTORE INDEX csi_FactResellerSalesNew ON dbo.
FactResellerSalesNew
```

There are two main reasons this would not work. The immediate one is that our table already has a clustered index, and obviously only one is allowed per table. Even if you remove the clustered index, or use `CREATE CLUSTERED COLUMNSTORE INDEX WITH (DROP_EXISTING = ON)`, the next limitation is that only one columnstore index is allowed per table, and SQL Server will complain showing error 35339.

Next, clean up by dropping the index:

```
DROP INDEX dbo.FactResellerSalesNew.ncsi_FactResellerSalesNew
```

Obviously, dropping the index is not required if you are also dropping the table, as shown:

```
DROP TABLE FactResellerSalesNew
```

For the next exercise, create a version of the table without a clustered index:

```
USE AdventureWorksDW2017
GO

CREATE TABLE dbo.FactResellerSalesNew(
        ProductKey int NOT NULL,
        OrderDateKey int NOT NULL,
        DueDateKey int NOT NULL,
        ShipDateKey int NOT NULL,
        ResellerKey int NOT NULL,
        EmployeeKey int NOT NULL,
        PromotionKey int NOT NULL,
```

```
    CurrencyKey int NOT NULL,
    SalesTerritoryKey int NOT NULL,
    SalesOrderNumber nvarchar(20) NOT NULL,
    SalesOrderLineNumber tinyint NOT NULL,
    RevisionNumber tinyint NULL,
    OrderQuantity smallint NULL,
    UnitPrice money NULL,
    ExtendedAmount money NULL,
    UnitPriceDiscountPct float NULL,
    DiscountAmount float NULL,
    ProductStandardCost money NULL,
    TotalProductCost money NULL,
    SalesAmount money NULL,
    TaxAmt money NULL,
    Freight money NULL,
    CarrierTrackingNumber nvarchar(25) NULL,
    CustomerPONumber nvarchar(25) NULL,
    OrderDate datetime NULL,
    DueDate datetime NULL,
    ShipDate datetime NULL)
```

Now you can create a clustered columnstore index, which will basically convert the entire table storage from a rowstore into a columnstore. This could happen from either a heap like in this example or from a row-based clustered index, as shown later.

```
CREATE CLUSTERED COLUMNSTORE INDEX csi_FactResellerSalesNew ON dbo.
FactResellerSalesNew
```

You can load data as shown previously as clustered columnstore indexes have always been updatable since they were introduced with SQL Server 2014. Similarly, trying to create a nonclustered columnstore index at this point would return error 35339.

You could also create the table directly as a clustered columnstore. This is an example using only a few columns of the previous table:

```
DROP TABLE dbo.FactResellerSalesNew
GO
CREATE TABLE dbo.FactResellerSalesNew (
```

```
ProductKey int NOT NULL,
OrderDateKey int NOT NULL,
DueDateKey int NOT NULL,
ShipDateKey int NOT NULL,
ResellerKey int NOT NULL,
EmployeeKey int NOT NULL,
PromotionKey int NOT NULL,
CurrencyKey int NOT NULL,
SalesTerritoryKey int NOT NULL,
INDEX csi_FactResellerSalesNew CLUSTERED COLUMNSTORE)
```

We saw earlier that we cannot create a nonclustered columnstore on a clustered columnstore (or more than one clustered index of any kind as a matter of fact), but we can create a rowstore nonclustered index. An example is shown next:

```
CREATE INDEX IX_ProductKey ON dbo.FactResellerSalesNew(ProductKey)
```

Assuming a table is a rowstore clustered index, you can convert it to a columnstore clustered index using the DROP_EXISTING clause. Run the following statement to create a rowstore:

```
DROP TABLE dbo.FactResellerSalesNew
GO
CREATE TABLE dbo.FactResellerSalesNew (
        ProductKey int NOT NULL,
        OrderDateKey int NOT NULL,
        DueDateKey int NOT NULL,
        ShipDateKey int NOT NULL,
        ResellerKey int NOT NULL,
        EmployeeKey int NOT NULL,
        PromotionKey int NOT NULL,
        CurrencyKey int NOT NULL,
        SalesTerritoryKey int NOT NULL)
```

If you run the following query, the type_desc column will return HEAP as the description of index type:

```
SELECT * FROM sys.indexes
```

```
WHERE object_id = OBJECT_ID('dbo.FactResellerSalesNew')
```

Run the following code to create a row-based clustered index:

```
CREATE CLUSTERED INDEX IX_ProductKey ON dbo.FactResellerSalesNew
(ProductKey)
```

This time, `type_desc` will be `CLUSTERED` but still rowstore based. By running the following statement, the storage will be changed from clustered rowstore to clustered columnstore. `type_desc` on sys.indexes will return `CLUSTERED COLUMNSTORE`.

```
CREATE CLUSTERED COLUMNSTORE INDEX IX_ProductKey ON dbo.
FactResellerSalesNew
WITH (DROP_EXISTING = ON)
```

You can also convert a columnstore to a rowstore, either to a heap or a clustered index. Dropping the columnstore will create a heap like in the following example. Following the previous example, dropping the index will return `type_desc` to `HEAP`:

```
DROP INDEX dbo.FactResellerSalesNew.IX_ProductKey
```

Alternatively, instead of dropping the index, you run the next code; `type_desc` will go back to a row-based clustered index:

```
CREATE CLUSTERED INDEX IX_ProductKey ON
dbo.FactResellerSalesNew(ProductKey)
WITH (DROP_EXISTING = ON)
```

Finally, columnstore indexes can also get fragmented just like regular b-tree indexes. You can use the `dm_db_column_store_row_group_physical_stats` DMV to find out the fragmentation level:

```
SELECT OBJECT_NAME(object_id),
        100 * (ISNULL(deleted_rows,0)) / total_rows AS fragmentation, *
FROM sys.dm_db_column_store_row_group_physical_stats
```

You can look into removing fragmentation when its level reaches 20% or more, and, similar to disk-based indexes, you can use the `ALTER INDEX REORGANIZE` and `ALTER INDEX REBUILD` statements. A basic example for ALTER INDEX REORGANIZE is next:

```
ALTER INDEX csi_FactResellerSalesNew ON dbo.FactResellerSalesNew REORGANIZE
```

Similarly, the basic syntax for `ALTER INDEX REBUILD` is shown next:

```
ALTER INDEX csi_FactResellerSalesNew ON dbo.FactResellerSalesNew REBUILD
```

Fragmentation in columnstore indexes works differently than with rowstores, and the technical details are outside the scope of this book. For a way to get started, look at Columnstore Indexes Defragmentation at `https://msdn.microsoft.com/en-us/library/dn935013.aspx`.

Operational Analytics

As covered earlier, starting with SQL Server 2016, you now have the capability of running real-time analytical queries directly on OLTP systems by implementing updatable columnstore indexes on OLTP tables. Nonclustered columnstore indexes are not new, but they were read-only structures on previous versions of SQL Server and now can be implemented on OLTP disk-based tables. A clustered columnstore index can be created on memory-optimized tables to provide operational analytics as well.

To better understand the benefit of real-time analytical queries on a transactional system, let's quickly review the traditional data warehouse or analytics architecture, which is pictured in Figure 7-5. In this architecture, we usually have OLTP and data warehouse/analytics workloads separated in two different servers and data being moved from one or more locations into the data warehouse using ETL jobs.

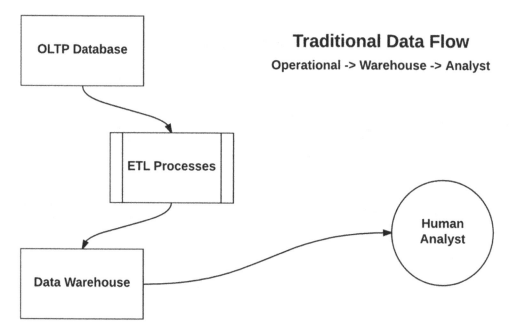

Figure 7-5. *Traditional data warehouse/analytics architecture*

SQL Server operational analytics can be used in scenarios where real-time data is required by running queries directly in an OLTP environment. The simplified architecture is shown in Figure 7-6.

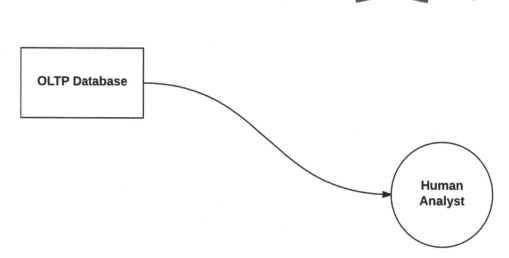

Figure 7-6. *SQL Server operational analytics*

This architecture has the following advantages:

- No data latency: Operational analytics are real time. As soon as a transaction is committed, its data can be picked up by an analytical query. A typical data warehouse, however, requires ETL jobs scheduled to run periodically, for example, once a day. In this case, the data in the data warehouse could be up to one day old. Some analytical needs may require real-time or close to real-time data.

- No ETL needed: You access the transactional data directly from the OLTP database.

- Cost: No need of additional server infrastructure or software licenses. Of course, this assumes that your server performance and available resources can support both transactional and analytical workloads at the same time.

- No changes required to the OLTP application. Changes will be required to your analytical queries, of course, if they already exist.

Obviously, while having the best performance on OLTP workloads is of paramount importance, you may have concerns about performance after adding additional columnstore indexes and analytical workloads. The disadvantages of this new architecture are the following:

- No data from additional sources: Since the columnstore indexes are created on the transactional database, real-time queries target a single data source. You can access real-time data from your OLTP database and potentially data from other SQL Server databases on the same or even another instance. Typical data warehouses integrate data from multiple sources including other relational or nonrelational data sources.

- Analytical queries are faster on a star schema: Data warehouses usually implement a star schema. Data in an OLTP schema is more normalized, typically using a third normal form (3NF) to minimize duplication of data and ensure referential integrity. However, columnstore indexes provide better performance than accessing the OLTP normalized tables directly.

- Performance considerations: Although creating and maintaining an additional nonclustered index may not be a performance problem, some considerations must be taken while running new analytical queries to the same database. Your server should be able to support this new workload. Some performance recommendations are shown next.

- No cubes or other preaggregated data: More sophisticated aggregations or analytical queries may still need the traditional data warehouse approach.

As hinted, some recommendations to improve performance while running both operational and analytical workloads on the same database include the following:

- Using Always On availability groups to run queries on a secondary replica: You can offload your analytical workload to an Always On availability group secondary replica. Columnstore indexes will still have to be updated on the primary replica, but analytical queries are executed against the secondary replica, with minimal performance disruption on the primary.

- Using a columnstore filtered index: This solution can be used for the case where there is contention while both transactional and analytical workloads access the most current or "hot" data. Since every insert, delete, and update operation needs to be reflected in the columnstore index, you can consider avoiding those rows that are having frequent updates. This is accomplished by filtering out those rows from the columnstore index. Analytical queries will still have access to all the data by using both the columnstore index for most of the data and the transactional table for the most recent data. This is done transparently and it is up to the query optimizer to decide how to do this. An example on how to do this is shown later in this chapter.

- Using compression delay: In cases where it is not easy or practical to define a filtered index, an alternate choice could be to delay compression on the columnstore index. As explained earlier, rows are compressed on such indexes, but because of the same phenomenon explained with filtered indexes, sometimes "hot" data may change frequently. If rows are compressed too early, they may need to be recompressed multiple times as data is continuously being updated. The COMPRESSION_DELAY option may be used to help with this compression overhead. For more details about this choice, see https://msdn.microsoft.com/en-us/library/dn817827.aspx.

Now, let's look at examples using both disk-based and memory-optimized tables.

Using Disk-Based Tables

Since we want to run these examples on an OLTP database, we will now switch back to the AdventureWorks2017 database. Let us create a nonclustered columnstore index on the SalesOrderHeader table:

```
CREATE NONCLUSTERED COLUMNSTORE INDEX SalesOrderHeader_ncci ON Sales.
SalesOrderHeader (
        SalesOrderID, RevisionNumber, OrderDate, DueDate, ShipDate, Status,
        OnlineOrderFlag, PurchaseOrderNumber, AccountNumber, CustomerID,
        SalesPersonID,
        TerritoryID, BillToAddressID, ShipToAddressID, ShipMethodID,
        CreditCardID,
        CreditCardApprovalCode, CurrencyRateID, SubTotal, TaxAmt, Freight,
        Comment,
        ModifiedDate)
```

Creating such an index is everything we need to start running analytical queries. For example, the following query will use the nonclustered columnstore index as shown in the plan in Figure 7-7, in which scan operation is running in batch execution mode:

```
SELECT MAX(TotalDue)
FROM Sales.SalesOrderHeader
```

Figure 7-7. Nonclustered columnstore index on an OLTP table

Of course, it is up to the query optimizer to decide whether to use the columnstore index or any other data structure. If you look at the cost of the previous query, it will show 0.017469 cost units. Running the next query asking the query optimizer not to use such an index would estimate a cost of 0.569733, which obviously is more expensive. You could also test just dropping the index without the hint to get the same behavior and cost.

```
SELECT MAX(TotalDue)
FROM Sales.SalesOrderHeader
OPTION (IGNORE_NONCLUSTERED_COLUMNSTORE_INDEX)
```

Note   The IGNORE_NONCLUSTERED_COLUMNSTORE_INDEX hint asks the query optimizer to ignore any nonclustered columnstore index in a query. You could use it in cases when SQL Server, for some reason, is not giving you a good execution plan.

Now I'll show you an exercise where using a filtered nonclustered columnstore index can be useful, but we need to drop the current index first. Trying to create a second nonclustered columnstore is not supported and would get you error message 35339.

```
DROP INDEX Sales.SalesOrderHeader.SalesOrderHeader_ncci
```

Let's make the assumption that "hot" data has a status of 1. (For some reason, this is not implemented in AdventureWorks2017, and the entire table has a value of 5.) Let's update a few rows with the most recent ship date:

```
UPDATE Sales.SalesOrderHeader
SET Status = 1
WHERE ShipDate = '2014-07-07 00:00:00.000'
```

Run the following statement to create a filtered nonclustered columnstore index to contain all the rows with status 5, which is most of the rows in the table:

```
CREATE NONCLUSTERED COLUMNSTORE INDEX SalesOrderHeader_ncci ON Sales.
SalesOrderHeader (
        SalesOrderID, RevisionNumber, OrderDate, DueDate, ShipDate, Status,
        OnlineOrderFlag, PurchaseOrderNumber, AccountNumber, CustomerID,
        SalesPersonID, TerritoryID, BillToAddressID, ShipToAddressID,
```

ShipMethodID, CreditCardID, CreditCardApprovalCode, CurrencyRateID,
SubTotal, TaxAmt, Freight, Comment, CreditCardApprovalCode,
CurrencyRateID, SubTotal, TaxAmt, Freight, Comment, ModifiedDate)
WHERE Status = 5

Trying to run the previous analytical query would not yet choose the columnstore
index even when the query processor can benefit from it and access all the data where
status is 5. The reason is simple: there is no cheap way to access the few remaining rows,
where status is 1, without a table scan of the base table. So the query is doing a regular
table scan anyway. In order to help, it is recommended to have a row-based clustered or
nonclustered index in the Status column. Let's try the second choice:

```
CREATE INDEX IX_Status ON Sales.SalesOrderHeader(Status)
```

Once this rowstore index is created, running the previous analytical query will use
the nonclustered columnstore index for most of the data and the rowstore nonclustered
index for the remaining required rows, as shown in the partial execution plan in
Figure 7-8.

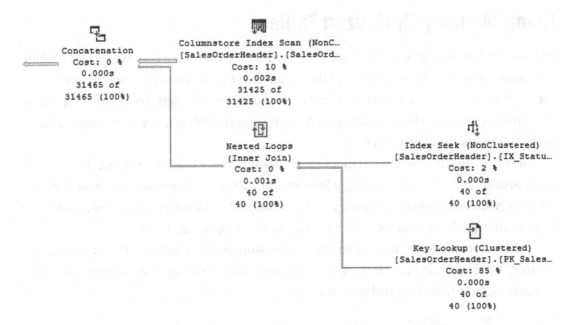

Figure 7-8. *Query using a filtered columnstore index*

A more complicated analytical query like the following will produce a plan similar to Figure 7-8, using a columnstore for most of the data plus navigating to additional rows using a rowstore index:

```
SELECT SalesPersonID, SUM(TotalDue), AVG(TotalDue)
FROM Sales.SalesOrderHeader
WHERE TerritoryID > 3
GROUP BY SalesPersonID
```

Finally, to clean up, drop both indexes created in this exercise and set the Status column to their original values:

```
DROP INDEX Sales.SalesOrderHeader.IX_Status
DROP INDEX Sales.SalesOrderHeader.SalesOrderHeader_ncci

UPDATE Sales.SalesOrderHeader
SET Status = 5
WHERE ShipDate = '2014-07-07 00:00:00.000'
```

Using Memory-Optimized Tables

We just saw how to create a nonclustered columnstore index on a disk-based OLTP table. There are some important differences if we want to perform the same operation on memory-optimized tables. First of all, we cannot use a nonclustered columnstore; only a columnstore clustered index is allowed. Also, as required by memory-optimized tables, the entire index has to fit in memory.

However, this does not mean that this will require twice the memory as the columnstore index usually has a high level of compression. Data from Microsoft shows an average of ten times compression, so the additional columnstore index would only require about 10% more of memory than the memory-optimized table.

Let's create the table. Notice that the columnstore index is defined when the table is created. The index can also be created on an existing memory-optimized table, and an example on how to do that is shown later.

```
CREATE TABLE SalesOrderHeader (
        SalesOrderID int PRIMARY KEY NONCLUSTERED NOT NULL,
        RevisionNumber tinyint NOT NULL,
        OrderDate datetime NOT NULL,
```

```
    DueDate datetime NOT NULL,
    ShipDate datetime NULL,
    Status tinyint NOT NULL,
    CustomerID int NOT NULL,
    SalesPersonID int NULL,
    TerritoryID int NULL,
    BillToAddressID int NOT NULL,
    ShipToAddressID int NOT NULL,
    ShipMethodID int NOT NULL,
    CreditCardID int NULL,
    CreditCardApprovalCode varchar(15) NULL,
    CurrencyRateID int NULL,
    SubTotal money NOT NULL,
    TaxAmt money NOT NULL,
    Freight money NOT NULL,
    Comment nvarchar(128) NULL,
    ModifiedDate datetime NOT NULL,
    INDEX SalesOrderHeader_cci CLUSTERED COLUMNSTORE)
WITH (MEMORY_OPTIMIZED = ON)
```

In order to run some basic analytical queries, we need to populate with some data. Trying to copy data directly from AdventureWorks2017 would return the following error, so let's do it in two steps, using a temporary table:

```
Msg 41317, Level 16, State 5, Line 1
A user transaction that accesses memory optimized tables or natively
compiled modules cannot access more than one user database or databases
model and msdb, and it cannot write to master.
```

Run the following statement to copy the data to a temporary table:

```
SELECT
    SalesOrderID,
    RevisionNumber,
    OrderDate,
    DueDate,
    ShipDate,
```

```
    Status,
    CustomerID,
    SalesPersonID,
    TerritoryID,
    BillToAddressID,
    ShipToAddressID,
    ShipMethodID,
    CreditCardID,
    CreditCardApprovalCode,
    CurrencyRateID,
    SubTotal,
    TaxAmt,
    Freight,
    Comment,
    ModifiedDate
INTO #temp
FROM AdventureWorks2017.Sales.SalesOrderHeader
```

And, finally, insert the data into the memory-optimized table:

```
INSERT INTO dbo.SalesOrderHeader (
    SalesOrderID,
    RevisionNumber,
    OrderDate,
    DueDate,
    ShipDate,
    Status,
    CustomerID,
    SalesPersonID,
    TerritoryID,
    BillToAddressID,
    ShipToAddressID,
    ShipMethodID,
    CreditCardID,
    CreditCardApprovalCode,
    CurrencyRateID,
```

```
    SubTotal,
    TaxAmt,
    Freight,
    Comment,
    ModifiedDate)
SELECT * FROM #temp
```

After you successfully populated the table, you can run some analytical queries similar to the ones in the previous section, which in both cases will take benefit of the columnstore indexes created previously:

```
SELECT MAX(SubTotal)
FROM dbo.SalesOrderHeader

SELECT SalesPersonID, SUM(SubTotal), AVG(SubTotal)
FROM dbo.SalesOrderHeader
WHERE TerritoryID > 3
GROUP BY SalesPersonID
```

You can also add a columnstore index to an existing memory-optimized table. As an example, follow the next code, assuming this table already exists:

```
CREATE TABLE SalesOrderHeader (
        SalesOrderID int PRIMARY KEY NONCLUSTERED NOT NULL,
        RevisionNumber tinyint NOT NULL,
        OrderDate datetime NOT NULL,
        DueDate datetime NOT NULL,
        ShipDate datetime NULL,
        Status tinyint NOT NULL,
        CustomerID int NOT NULL,
        SalesPersonID int NULL,
        TerritoryID int NULL,
        BillToAddressID int NOT NULL,
        ShipToAddressID int NOT NULL,
        ShipMethodID int NOT NULL,
        CreditCardID int NULL,
        CreditCardApprovalCode varchar(15) NULL,
        CurrencyRateID int NULL,
```

```
       SubTotal money NOT NULL,
       TaxAmt money NOT NULL,
       Freight money NOT NULL,
       Comment nvarchar(128) NULL,
       ModifiedDate datetime NOT NULL)
WITH (MEMORY_OPTIMIZED = ON)
```

You just would need to add the following statement to get the same results as before:

```
ALTER TABLE SalesOrderHeader ADD INDEX SalesOrderHeader_cci CLUSTERED
COLUMNSTORE
```

A current limitation is that you need to include all the columns of the in-memory table on the columnstore index. Nonclustered columnstore indexes are not supported with memory-optimized tables. Trying to add such an index with the ALTER TABLE ADD INDEX statement as shown previously would return the following error message:

```
Msg 10794, Level 16, State 76, Line 1
The feature 'NONCLUSTERED COLUMNSTORE' is not supported with memory
optimized tables.
```

Summary

This chapter covered SQL Server in-memory technologies, and, although the main purpose was to present databases optimized for memory, some related trends and paradigms were introduced as well including natively compiled modules, column-based databases, and batch processing. These new trends complement or compete with traditional technologies such as interpreted execution, row-based storage, and row-at-a-time query execution, respectively. Both columnstore indexes and In-Memory OLTP were originally released with serious limitations but have been improved in subsequent releases.

We covered In-Memory OLTP and columnstore indexes, two features that, although originally released with some limitations, have been improved throughout several SQL Server releases. The chapter concluded by covering operational analytics that now allow a columnstore index to be created on either disk-based or memory-optimized transactional tables to allow the execution of real-time analytical queries.

We expect the technologies and paradigms presented in this chapter to represent the future in SQL Server and relational database technologies in general.

CHAPTER 8

Performance Troubleshooting

This chapter discusses what information to look for when troubleshooting SQL Server performance problems, both examining real-time data and collecting information for later analysis. Performance information in SQL Server is exposed in several ways, and different tools are usually used to either see or collect that data. One of the new and very promising tools, the Query Store, was fully explained in Chapter 6. I am sure the Query Store will become the main tool for query performance troubleshooting for SQL Server 2016 and above. In addition to query performance, there are many performance areas that do not fall into the query troubleshooting category.

Proactively collecting information is critical for high performance systems. You cannot just rely on getting the current available information after you have been asked to look at a performance problem. The required information may already be gone by the time you connect to the SQL Server instance to research it. Collected data, however, may show directly and quickly what the problem is. In addition, you may need a baseline and probably performance trends to understand how your system works and proactively figure out when things are starting to deviate from a desirable or expected behavior, either because of an unexpected problem or an increasing workload.

This chapter covers a large variety of performance information including performance counters, information provided through objects like DMVs or DMFs (dynamic management functions) and SQL Server events, which currently cover extended events and the currently deprecated SQL Trace, better known by the client tool used to access it, SQL Profiler. This performance information is provided by SQL Server and in some other cases by Windows Server or even by other Windows applications,

B. Nevarez, *High Performance SQL Server*, https://doi.org/10.1007/978-1-4842-6491-1_8

services, or drivers. Having said that, the number of performance counters, events, or management objects is so vast, and more and more are introduced with every release or even service pack that only the most important or useful ones will be described here. Many more were used and described in other chapters of the book as well. I will also provide you links to the documentation if you need to see the entire list or more details.

Note   This chapter does not teach how to use the tools since it is assumed the reader has a basic knowledge and experience using them. The Query Store is an exception since it is a new tool, but it was covered in detail in Chapter 6.

Finally, in many of the cases, providing magic values for some performance counters or other performance information has been historically a problem and sometimes the reason for bad advice about those values comes from the Internet. There is also the case when some of those values were once good recommendations in the past, but don't make so much sense anymore. A classic example is the famous value of 300 for Page Life Expectancy (PLE), which is no longer a good recommendation, if it ever was. So the recommendation, in most cases, is not to look for a specific magic value and instead compare to a baseline.

Performance Counters

Performance counters are objects that provide information to monitor system activity. Although available from Windows, they show information not only about the operating system but also about some other Windows applications, services, and drivers. As a Windows application itself, SQL Server provides a rich number of performance counters, but it is common that, when troubleshooting SQL Server problems, performance counters from the operating system as well as some other Windows services or drivers may be required.

Similar to the information provided by waits, as covered in Chapter 5, the values provided by performance counters can sometimes be difficult to interpret and may require either experience or a baseline from the system to compare with. As indicated earlier, there are also some cases of bad advice online where values recommended may not be exactly a good choice for your system or, even if there were a valid recommendation in the past, may not be a good value anymore.

Performance counters use three basic terms: objects, counters, and instances. SQL Server performance objects have the format SQLServer:<object name> and may contain multiple counters. For example, the SQLServer:Databases object contains counters such as Data File(s) Size (KB) or Log Growths, both of which are explained later. Some objects may have multiple instances. Using the same example, for SQLServer:Databases, the instances in this case are represented by the system and user databases available on the server. You could get performance information from either one, some, or the total of all the instances combined. The SQL Server performance counter names will change slightly depending on whether you have a default or named instance. For example, SQLServer:Databases defines a counter on a default SQL Server instance, but will be called MSSQL$<instance name>:Databases on a named instance.

Note   A performance counter instance and a SQL Server instance both use the term "instance," but they are not related concepts.

There are a large number of SQL Server performance counters, most of them starting with the name SQLServer and some more starting with SQLAgent. Outside these two groups, there are several objects for SQL Server In-Memory OLTP called SQL Server <version> XTP, for example, SQL Server 2017 XTP Storage or SQL Server 2017 XTP Transactions. You can get the entire list and details of the SQL Server performance counters at https://technet.microsoft.com/en-us/library/ms190382.aspx and the SQL Server In-Memory OLTP performance counters at https://technet.microsoft.com/en-us/library/dn511015.aspx.

SQL Server also provides the sys.dm_os_performance_counters DMV, which, although can be easily queried, unfortunately only covers SQL Server counters, so you still need to look outside for the remaining Windows counters that you may need. In addition, sys.dm_os_performance_counters requires additional processing to its data, which we will discuss later.

Although collecting performance counter data does not usually impact the performance of a system, some care should be taken not to collect too many counters or to have a frequent update interval. The main tool used to display and collect performance counters is Windows Performance Monitor, although there are some other related popular tools as well, such as the PAL (Performance Analysis of Logs) tool. PAL is used to analyze performance counter data and can be found at https://pal.codeplex.com. Introduced with SQL Server 2008, there was the choice to correlate information from performance counters and SQL Trace events using Performance Monitor and Profiler. These days, with Profiler and SQL Trace deprecated, it is not clear yet if we will have a replacement tool to do the same with extended events in the future.

Finally, the Data Collector, a tool introduced with SQL Server 2008 and called the MDW (Management Data Warehouse) on some documents, can be used to collect the most important performance counters along with some other information. An immediate benefit of enabling this tool is that you don't have to decide which performance counters to collect. The Data Collector will configure the most useful according to troubleshooting scenarios from Microsoft technical support. You could, however, fine-tune this list by including additional performance counters. Removing performance counters is also possible but rarely needed.

In the following section, I'll cover some of the most useful performance counters, but as mentioned earlier, there are many more and you can refer to the previously listed documentation for the entire list or some additional details.

Comparing Batches and Transactions

Measuring batch requests per second and transactions per second is the main indicator of the throughput of your SQL Server instance. It shows how much work your instance is currently performing. Now keep in mind that with a server with a heavy workload, these counters may show the maximum capacity of the instance, but if the server is not busy enough, it just means that it is able to process all the requests being sent by the client application and more can be handled if needed. On the other hand, especially if you see a performance problem, wait analysis may show that the application is sending more requests than the SQL Server instance can handle, and the wait information may indicate what the limitations are.

For example, if a SQL Server instance shows 10,000 batch requests per second, it could mean that either it is the maximum the instance can handle or the maximum the application is submitting. It could be possible for this instance to handle 12,000 batch requests per second if it were requested.

In addition, the same value of batch requests per second may not mean exactly the same throughput between one SQL Server instance and another as their workloads could be different. For example, one instance may be running pure OLTP transactions, while another may be an OLTP system with some batch processing, and yet another a reporting or analytical system handling more expensive queries. I have yet to see a pure OLTP production system, if it really exists.

The definitions of these counters are straightforward:

SQLServer:Databases Transactions/sec: Transaction per second

SQLServer:SQL Statistics Batch Requests/sec: Number of batch requests received per second

SQLServer:Transactions: Total number of active transactions

To better visualize and compare batch requests per second and transactions per second, let's look at the following exercise. First, create a table:

```
CREATE TABLE t1 (id int IDENTITY(1,1), name varchar(20))
```

Run the following batch containing ten implicit transactions each. To have enough time to visualize the server activity, we are running the batch 10,000 times by using the GO command. Feel free to adjust for your test system if needed.

```
BEGIN
INSERT INTO t1 VALUES ('Hello')
INSERT INTO t1 VALUES ('Hello')
INSERT INTO t1 VALUES ('Hello')
INSERT INTO t1 VALUES ('Hello')
INSERT INTO t1 VALUES ('Hello')
INSERT INTO t1 VALUES ('Hello')
INSERT INTO t1 VALUES ('Hello')
INSERT INTO t1 VALUES ('Hello')
INSERT INTO t1 VALUES ('Hello')
INSERT INTO t1 VALUES ('Hello')
END
GO 10000
```

Figure 8-1 shows one snapshot I took on Performance Monitor in the middle of the execution. Notice that the number of transactions per second is roughly ten times the number of batch requests per second, as expected.

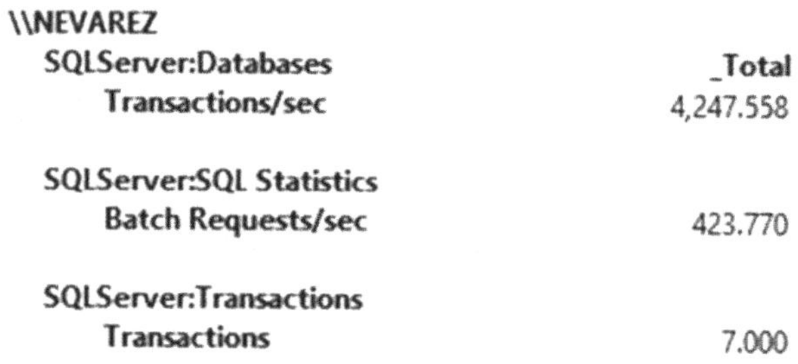

\\NEVAREZ
SQLServer:Databases
_Total
Transactions/sec
4,247.558
SQLServer:SQL Statistics
Batch Requests/sec
423.770
SQLServer:Transactions
Transactions
7.000

Figure 8-1. *Comparing batch requests/sec and transactions/sec*

You could also visualize the same information using the line graph in Performance Monitor, although these are not graphed using the same scale. (For example, the value 3,919.333 in Figure 8-2 is shown at 39.19 on the vertical axis.) You can change the vertical scale using Performance Monitor Properties, as shown in Figure 8-3.

Counter: \\NEVAREZ\SQLServer:Databases(_Total)\Transactions/sec
Value: 3,919.333
Time: 12:51:31 AM, 6/28/2016.
Show
Color
Scale
Counter
Instance
Parent
Object
Computer
0.01
Transactions/sec
_Total
SQLServer:Databases
\\NEVAREZ
1.0
Batch Requests/sec
SQLServer:SQL Statistics
\\NEVAREZ
1.0
Transactions
SQLServer:Transactions
\\NEVAREZ

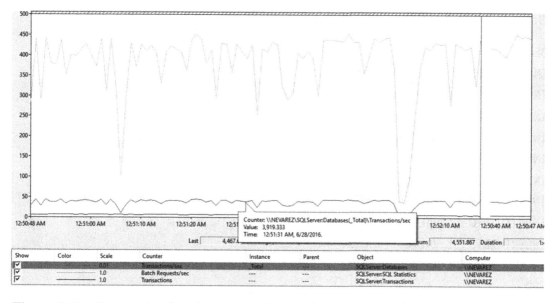

Figure 8-2. *Comparing batch requests/sec and transactions/sec graph*

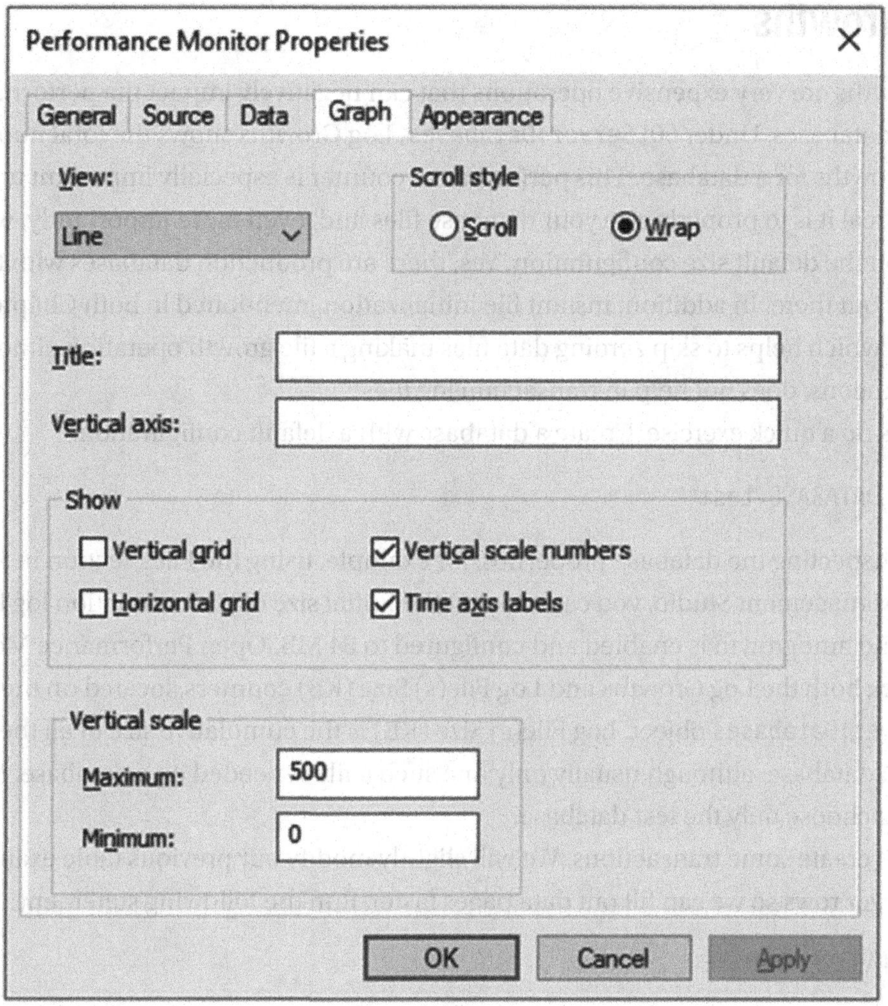

Figure 8-3. *Performance Monitor vertical scale configuration*

To clean up, drop the table:

```
DROP TABLE t1
```

Log Growths

Log growths are very expensive operations that can negatively impact the performance of your databases. Under `SQLServer:Databases`, Log Growths shows the total number of log growths for a database. This performance counter is especially important to show how critical it is to properly size your database files and, even more importantly, why not to rely on the default size configuration. Yes, there are production databases with these defaults out there. In addition, instant file initialization, mentioned in both Chapters 3 and 4, which helps to skip zeroing data files making a file growth operation almost instantaneous, does not help in transaction log files.

Let's do a quick exercise. Create a database with a default configuration:

```
CREATE DATABASE test
```

By inspecting the database properties, for example, using the Files section in SQL Server Management Studio, you can see that the initial size of the transaction log file is 8 MB, and autogrowth is enabled and configured to 64 MB. Open Performance Monitor and track both the Log Growths and Log File(s) Size (KB) counters, located on the `SQLServer:Databases` object. Log File(s) Size (KB) is the cumulative size of all the log files in a database, although usually only one such a file is needed on a database. Make sure you choose only the test database.

Let's create some transactions. We will slightly modify our previous table example to have larger rows so we can fill out data pages faster. Run the following statement:

```
USE DATABASE test
GO
CREATE TABLE t1 (id int IDENTITY(1,1), name char(8000))
```

Add data to stress the transaction log file:

```
BEGIN
INSERT INTO t1 VALUES ('Hello')
INSERT INTO t1 VALUES ('Hello')
INSERT INTO t1 VALUES ('Hello')
INSERT INTO t1 VALUES ('Hello')
INSERT INTO t1 VALUES ('Hello')
INSERT INTO t1 VALUES ('Hello')
INSERT INTO t1 VALUES ('Hello')
```

```
INSERT INTO t1 VALUES ('Hello')
INSERT INTO t1 VALUES ('Hello')
INSERT INTO t1 VALUES ('Hello')
END
GO 30000
```

Originally, Log Growths will show 0 and Log File(s) Size (KB) 8184, which corresponds to the 8 MB mentioned earlier. Review Performance Monitor carefully as you run the code. It may be easier to follow in this case if you choose to visualize the data as a report. It should not take long until Log Growths reaches 10 so you can cancel the query when it reaches such value. Ten file increments of 64 MB each plus the original 8 MB should give a size of 648 MB, which is the file size I see at the end of this exercise. In other words, Log File(s) Size (KB) will show 663,544 and Log Growths 10. Drop the database to end the exercise.

As we previously discussed, it is strongly recommended to size the transaction log file to the maximum required size to avoid log growths or, even worse, transaction failures and potential application outages, if the file becomes full without the possibility to expand. Usually, finding the optimal file size requires some testing, and, unfortunately, an unexpected activity or long transaction may still happen that requires the log to grow. However, by following the previous recommendations, you can avoid or minimize those chances.

A performance problem related to transaction log file growth operation could be very difficult to troubleshoot if you are not tracing or collecting data since, usually after the file size has increased, the performance will return to normal with no information to show what the problem was. The PREEMPTIVE_OS_WRITEFILEGATHER wait type may also show that a file is being zero-initialized, but depending on how you capture waits, you may not have additional information to point to a specific database or file. For more details about troubleshooting performance with waits, see Chapter 5.

Finally, you may be able to see those events using the SQL Server default trace and visualize its information immediately by running the Disk Usage report. To run the report, right-click the test database and select Reports ➤ Standard Reports ➤ Disk Usage. Information is shown in the Data/Log Files Autogrow/Autoshrink Events section. Keep in mind that the default trace has a limited file size and older events will be eventually deleted.

Data File(s) Size (KB)

Similar to Log File(s) Size (KB) explained in the previous section, the Data File(s) Size (KB) performance counter shows the cumulative size of all the data files in the database. Unlike transaction log files, it is very common to have multiple data files in a database.

Although there is no corresponding counter like Log Growths for data files, you can use the Data File(s) Size (KB) counter to figure out when a data file growth operation occurred. Once again, properly sizing your data files and enabling instant file initialization can help you avoid performance problems related to data file growth operations.

> **Note**   The SQL Server default trace and the Disk Usage report can be helpful to show data file autogrow events as well.

Page Reads/Sec

Under SQLServer:Buffer Manager, Page reads/sec shows the number of physical database pages read by SQL Server. Troubleshooting a problem with excessive Page reads/sec would require additional information, such as finding out which queries are performing large number of reads or analyzing the output of some DMVs like sys.db_io_virtual_file_stats or sys.dm_db_index_usage_stats. Taking a look at memory information can be helpful as well.

Troubleshooting a problem related to queries would require traditional query optimization techniques, including analyzing the query execution plan, seeing if one or more indexes are required, finding if excessive table scans or index seeks are being performed, or researching if a parameter-sensitive query is impacting I/O operations.

> **Note**   As shown later in this chapter, starting with SQL Server 2016 and SQL Server 2014 Service Pack 2, you can find operator-level performance information in an execution plan, including I/O statistics.

Page Writes/Sec

Under SQLServer:Buffer Manager, Page writes/sec shows the number of physical database page writes issued per second. Most of the recommendations mentioned on Page reads/sec may also apply here. You can also try to correlate this counter with the Log Flush counters explained later.

Page Life Expectancy

The Page Life Expectancy (PLE) performance counter, under the SQLServer:Buffer Manager object, shows the average number of seconds a data page will stay in the buffer pool. Although there is still a lot of advice online about considering a value of 300 and lower as the threshold where PLE is a problem, this is no longer a good recommendation. This recommendation was originally published by Microsoft many years ago based on the paper "The Five-Minute Rule for Trading Memory for Disc Accesses and the Five-Byte Rule for Trading Memory for CPU Time." The rule refers to the tipping point between when a page should be kept in memory and accessed from disk based on cost—both price and performance.

Note   The paper is still an interesting read, and you can find it online at www. hpl.hp.com/techreports/tandem/TR-86.1.pdf. In addition, the five-minute rule was reviewed 10 and 20 years later, and you can read about the new findings by looking at "The Five-Minute Rule Ten Years Later and Other Computer Storage Rules of Thumb" at http://research.microsoft.com/en-us/um/people/gray/5_min_rule_sigmod.pdf and "The Five-Minute Rule 20 Years Later and How Flash Memory Changes the Rules" at http://cacm.acm.org/magazines/2009/7/32091-the-five-minute-rule-20-years-later.

Based on most current hardware trends, you will be better by having a baseline and considering an issue only if the PLE drops for an extended period of time. PLE dropping for a short time may not be a problem, as some expensive queries and jobs may cause it, but it should be able to recover soon.

A second item to consider regarding PLE is if you are using a non-uniform memory access (NUMA) architecture, something that is very common these days. If you are using NUMA, you should use PLE from the SQLServer:Buffer Node object, as SQLServer:Buffer Manager will show a general value for all the NUMA nodes. In this scenario, there could be a case where the PLE for a NUMA node has a problem and may need your attention, but if you focus on the general PLE, such a problem may not be apparent. In a similar way, a major change in one node—for example, a maintenance job dropping the PLE in a large way—may also impact the general value, making the problem look like a system-wide problem.

Buffer Cache Hit Ratio

This performance counter, also from SQLServer:Buffer Manager, shows the percentage of pages that were returned from the buffer pool without having to resort to disk. This ratio is calculated considering only the last few thousand page accesses, and a 100% or close to 100% ratio is desirable.

% Processor Time

An essential performance counter to monitor and straightforward to understand, % Processor Time, under the Processor object, measures the average percentage of time the processor spends executing non-idle threads, and it is the primary indicator of processor activity.

Obviously, the first thing to validate after high processor usage is if it is SQL Server related, which, in a dedicated server, is most likely going to be the case. Having said that, a high performance installation requires to run SQL Server not only on its own server but also as the only SQL Server instance. But even in such configurations, it is good to discard the cases when some other Windows service or application may be the problem. I've seen such cases in production too.

To analyze the percentage of time the processor spends executing a specific process, you can use the % Processor Time, this time under the Process object. While looking at this counter in Performance Monitor, you may want to select the SQL Server process or a few other processes you suspect are consuming processor time. Your server may list a large number of instances (in this case, processes). The database engine service is called sqlservr (corresponding to the executable file C:\Program Files\Microsoft SQL Server\MSSQL15.MSSQLSERVER\MSSQL\Binn\sqlservr.exe. Some other SQL Server services may be running as well, for example, the SQL Server Agent (named SQLAGENT. EXE), the SQL Server Browser (sqlbrowser.exe), and a few others, depending on your installation choices.

Once you verify it is, in fact, SQL Server using the majority of the processor time, the next thing to do is to find what internal processes inside SQL Server may be utilizing such resources, for example, by looking at the most expensive queries. You could use the Query Store or data collected by the Data Collector feature or some other tool. If you are not collecting any performance data, you can just simply look at the current data from the sys.dm_exec_query_stats DMV, assuming the problem query is still in the plan cache. An example of such query follows, which will list the 20 most expensive queries by CPU usage:

```
SELECT TOP 20 qstats.query_hash,
        SUM(qstats.total_worker_time) / SUM(qstats.execution_count) AS
        avg_total_worker_time,
        MIN(qstats.statement_text) AS statement_text
FROM (SELECT qs.*, SUBSTRING(st.text, (qs.statement_start_offset/2) + 1,
        ((CASE statement_end_offset
        WHEN -1 THEN DATALENGTH(ST.text)
        ELSE qs.statement_end_offset END
        - qs.statement_start_offset)/2) + 1) AS statement_text
FROM sys.dm_exec_query_stats qs
CROSS APPLY sys.dm_exec_sql_text(qs.sql_handle) AS st) AS qstats
GROUP BY qstats.query_hash
ORDER BY avg_total_worker_time DESC
```

Additionally, you can also look at the currently executing queries using the sys.dm_exec_requests DMV, as in the following query:

```
SELECT TOP 20 SUBSTRING(t.text, (r.statement_start_offset/2) + 1,
        ((CASE statement_end_offset
        WHEN -1 THEN DATALENGTH(t.text)
        ELSE r.statement_end_offset END
        - r.statement_start_offset)/2) + 1) AS statement_text, *
FROM sys.dm_exec_requests r
CROSS APPLY sys.dm_exec_sql_text(r.sql_handle) t
ORDER BY cpu_time DESC
```

Notice that in both queries the data is sorted by processor time, using the `total_worker_time` column in the first case and `cpu_time` in the second one. As mentioned in Chapter 6, both `sys.dm_exec_query_stats` and `sys.dm_exec_requests` also include other columns that you could use to easily update any of the previous queries to sort on a different performance metric, such as logical or physical reads. Finally, once you find out which queries are consuming your processor resources, you can focus on their tuning and optimization.

Processor Queue Length

This counter, listed under the `System` object, indicates the number of threads in the processor queue for all the processors. A large number in the Processor Queue Length counter usually means that there are more threads than the current processors can service in an efficient way. Similar to the % Processor Time counter, finding and optimizing expensive queries could be a good way to improve the performance of your system.

Latches

The `SQLServer:Latches` object contains several counters that can help you to monitor the number of latch requests that had to wait and their average latch wait time in milliseconds. Latches are short-term, lightweight synchronization primitives used to protect memory structures for concurrent access and are covered in more detail in Chapters 1 and 5. The performance counters also provide information about the number of latches that are currently SuperLatches, the number of latches that have been promoted to SuperLatches, and the number of SuperLatches that have been demoted to regular latches.

Locks

Similar to latches, the `SQLServer:Locks` object includes a variety of counters providing information such as lock requests per second, lock waits per second, lock timeouts per second, and the number of deadlocks per second, along with information such as the average amount of wait time in milliseconds for each lock request that resulted in a wait. Locking and blocking were also introduced in Chapter 5.

LogicalDisk and PhysicalDisk

The LogicalDisk and PhysicalDisk objects provide a large variety of counters that can help you to monitor I/O operations in your system. LogicalDisk and PhysicalDisk provide the same counters, but they just provide information from either the logical or physical disk perspective. Of particular interest is Avg. Disk Queue Length, which is the average number of both read and write requests that are queued for a particular disk.

You may want to try the exercise from the "Log Growths" section earlier to see if you can stress the Avg. Disk Queue Length in your test system. For more details about these performance counters and storage stress tools, please refer to Chapter 11.

SQL Compilations/Sec and Recompilations/Sec

Under the SQLServer:SQL Statistics object, these performance counters can help you monitor the compilations and recompilations happening in your system. Compilation refers to the query optimization process in which the query optimizer produces an efficient execution plan for a query to be executed.

A query is optimized only once, and since query optimization is an expensive operation, the resulting execution plan is expected to be kept in memory and reused as many times as possible. This is especially true for reusable code such as stored procedures. For this reason, a large number of compilations or recompilations may indicate a problem and should be researched. It may be the case that you have an ad hoc workload or a large number of ad hoc queries, causing a large number of optimizations. An ad hoc workload typically submits different queries that are used only once, each one requiring an optimization and potentially using plan cache memory for a plan that may not be required again. Although in this case you cannot minimize the number of optimizations, you can reduce the memory used by the plan cache by enabling the "optimize for ad hoc workloads" configuration option, as described in Chapter 3. If changing the application is allowed, you can try to promote reusing code using stored procedures.

A recompile is a new optimization of a query in which usually there is already an execution plan. Recompiles can happen for a large number of reasons including change of schema in objects like adding a column or an index, change in the session-related SET options, statistics being updated, or even explicitly requesting a recompile in the code (e.g., using the RECOMPILE hint). There are also multiple reasons why a plan may be removed from the plan cache, including memory pressure, some instance or database configuration changes, or the issue of a statement directly impacting the plan cache like

DBCC FREEPROCCACHE. In those cases, since the plan was purged, performing a new query optimization is considered a new compilation, not a recompile.

Reusing plans is one of the best ways to help in the performance of a system, and, if you follow just a few recommendations like using stored procedures, this is something that SQL Server can do automatically. Even though reusing plans works perfectly almost all the time, you need to be aware of a few cases when it could be a problem. A typical scenario is when running parameter-sensitive queries in which reusing the wrong plan could be catastrophic for the performance of your system.

You can get more information about compiles, recompiles, and plan caching by referring to Chapter 1. In addition, I would recommend you reading the Microsoft white paper "Plan Caching in SQL Server 2008," available at https://technet.microsoft.com/en-us/library/ee343986 (v=sql.100).aspx.

Memory Grants

In SQLServer:Memory Manager, Memory Grants Outstanding and Memory Grants Pending return the number of processes that have successfully acquired or are waiting for a memory grant, respectively. You could get additional wait information using the Memory Grant queue waits on the SQLServer:Wait Statistics object including average wait time in milliseconds, cumulative wait time per second, waits in progress, and waits started per second. Memory and memory grants and their impact on system performance were covered in Chapter 1.

Processes Blocked

Under the SQLServer:General Statistics object, process blocked returns the number of processes currently blocked. Additional information about blocking including waits and troubleshooting information can be found in Chapter 5.

Log Flush Counters

SQL Server has to flush to disk the log records in the log buffer after a transaction is committed, persisting this information in the transaction log file. Under SQLServer:Databases, SQL Server has four performance counters that can help you determine if flushing log records to disk is a performance bottleneck in your system. Again, their definitions are straightforward as you can see in the following list:

Log Flushes/sec	Number of log flushes per second
Log Flush Waits/sec	Number of commits per second waiting for the log flush
Log Flush Wait Time	Total wait time to flush the log, measured in milliseconds
Log Flush Write Time (ms)	Time required, measured in milliseconds, to perform writes of log flushes that were completed in the last second

Checkpoint Pages/Sec

Also under the SQLServer:Buffer Manager object, the Checkpoint pages/sec
performance counter monitors the number of pages flushed to disk per second either
by a checkpoint or any other operation that requires all dirty pages to be flushed to disk.
A checkpoint is a database engine operation in which the modified pages in memory
buffer pool (also called dirty pages) and any required transaction log information are
written to disk.

Memory Manager

The SQLServer:Memory Manager object includes a variety of memory-related counters
that can be helpful to monitor the memory used by connections, the database cache,
locks, log pool, query optimization, or the memory granted to executing processes (for
hash, sort, and create index operations). Some other counters have general information
about the memory in the system including the following:

> Free Memory (KB): Indicates the amount of committed memory
> the server is currently not using

> Target Server Memory (KB): Specifies the ideal amount of memory
> the server can consume

> Total Server Memory (KB): Indicates the amount of memory the
> server is currently consuming

sys.dm_os_performance_counters

The sys.dm_os_performance_counters DMV contains a subset of the same performance counters and information that you can access from Windows, for example, using Performance Monitor, as explained earlier. However, this DMV only includes the SQL Server–related counters. The DMV returns a large number of rows that also depends on the number of available instances for some counters. For example, in SQLServer:Databases, there is an entry per counter_name per instance_name column, which in this case is for each database. In other words, having 60 counters and 10 databases would make 600 entries alone.

A small sample output of this DMV is shown in Table 8-1.

Table 8-1. *Sample Output*

object_name	counter_name	instance_name	cntr_value	cntr_type
SQLServer:Buffer Manager	Buffer cache hit ratio		1133	537003264
SQLServer:Buffer Manager	Buffer cache hit ratio base		1175	1073939712
SQLServer:Buffer Manager	Page lookups/sec		162331031	272696576
SQLServer:Buffer Manager	Free list stalls/sec		0	272696576
SQLServer:Buffer Manager	Database pages		285880	65792
SQLServer:Buffer Manager	Target pages		16138240	65792
SQLServer:Buffer Manager	Integral Controller Slope		127	65792
SQLServer:Buffer Manager	Lazy writes/sec		24010	272696576

In addition, the data is exposed in raw form, and additional processing may need to be performed for the data to be useful. For more information, see the article "Interpreting the counter values from *sys.dm_os_performance_counters*" at https://blogs.msdn.microsoft.com/psssql/2013/09/23/interpreting-the-counter-values-from-sys-dm_os_performance_counters.

According to the article, the values of the cntr_value columns should be interpreted according to the cntr_type column. For example, buffer cache hit ratio has a cntr_type value of 537003264, which according to the article corresponds to the PERF_LARGE_RAW_FRACTION value shown in Table 8-2.

Table 8-2. *Sample Output*

Decimal	Hexadecimal	Counter Type Define
1073939712	0x40030500	PERF_LARGE_RAW_BASE
537003264	0x20020500	PERF_LARGE_RAW_FRACTION
1073874176	0x40020500	PERF_AVERAGE_BULK
272696576	0x10410500	PERF_COUNTER_BULK_COUNT
65792	0x00010100	PERF_COUNTER_LARGE_RAWCOUNT

A PERF_LARGE_RAW_FRACTION counter type represents a fraction of its corresponding PERF_LARGE_RAW_BASE counter value, also shown in Table 8-2 with the value 1073939712. For our example, PERF_LARGE_RAW_BASE represents the buffer cache hit ratio base, also listed in the previous DMV sample output. Then we can use the following formula:

Buffer cache hit ratio % = 100 * Buffer cache hit ratio / Buffer cache hit ratio base

In our case, using the values of the previous DMV output, we have 100 * 1133 / 1175 or 96.43%. For more details about other counters, please refer to the mentioned article.

Dynamic Management Views and Functions

We have covered a large number of DMVs in other chapters of this book. This section will include some additional DMVs critical for performance troubleshooting. You can find the entire list of documented DMVs and DMFs at https://msdn.microsoft.com/en-us/library/ms188754.aspx.

sys.dm_io_virtual_file_stats

The sys.dm_io_virtual_file_stats DMF provides a rich amount of I/O information for each data and log file in a database, including not only I/O activity data but also wait latency information. The statistics returned are metrics accumulated since the SQL Server instance was started or since the time a database or data file changed its status from offline to online. This DMF replaces the old fn_virtualfilestats function.

The I/O activity returned by this DMF alone may not have much meaning as it depends on the number of days the SQL Server instance (or database or file) has been online, but it can be helpful when compared to other files on the same instance. Once you find that a database file may have excessive I/O activity, you may need to correlate with some other performance information to take action. Many times you can alleviate these problems by tuning and optimizing your queries (e.g., providing the right indexes, looking to improve the execution plan, verifying statistics, etc.). Some other times, depending on your results, placing the database files on a different volume may help as well, for example, spreading the I/Os of a busy volume into additional volumes. Trying to correlate I/O activity with the sys.dm_db_index_usage_stats can also provide valuable information.

The sys.dm_io_virtual_file_stats DMF has two optional parameters, database ID and file ID, which can be used as shown in the following example:

```
SELECT * FROM sys.dm_io_virtual_file_stats(DB_ID('AdventureWorks2017'),
NULL)
```

Calling this DMF without parameters will list all the files in all the databases, as shown in the following example:

```
SELECT DB_NAME(mf.database_id), physical_name, fs.*
FROM sys.dm_io_virtual_file_stats(NULL, NULL) fs
JOIN sys.master_files mf
ON mf.database_id = fs.database_id
AND mf.file_id = fs.file_id
```

A sample partial output is shown in Table 8-3.

Table 8-3. *Sample Output*

database_name	num_of _bytes_read	io_stall _read_ms	num_of _bytes_written	io_stall _write_ms
tempdb	18735104	5642	2605056	999
tempdb	1015808	186	2162688	281
tempdb	2260992	803	1507328	201
tempdb	2121728	322	1613824	1388
tempdb	2301952	420	1662976	714
AdventureWorks2017	275603456	147988	43155456	9587
AdventureWorks2017	185999360	12248	202964992	258568
AdventureWorksDW2017	113778688	35233	74670080	3129
AdventureWorksDW2017	1130496	2322	47136768	14632

All columns provide important I/O information. Just to list the most critical ones:

num_of_reads: Number of reads made on the database file.

num_of_bytes_read: Total number of bytes read on the database file.

io_stall_read_ms: Total time that the users waited for reads made on the database file. Measured in milliseconds.

num_of_writes: Number of writes made on the database file.

num_of_bytes_written: Total number of bytes written to the database file.

io_stall_write_ms: Total time that users waited for writes to be completed on the database file. Measured in milliseconds.

io_stall: Total time that users waited for I/O to be completed on the database file. It is basically io_stall_read_ms plus io_stall_ write_ms. Measured in milliseconds.

size_on_disk_bytes: Number of bytes used on the disk for the database file.

sys.dm_os_volume_stats

The sys.dm_os_volume_stats DMF returns information about the volumes in the system, based on the provided database ID and file ID. Unlike the other functions in this book, parameters must be provided. Some of the information returned includes volume mount point; logical volume name; file system type such as NTFS, FAT, or RAW; volume total size in bytes; available free space; whether the volume supports operating system compression; alternate streams or sparse files; and finally if the volume is read-only and compressed.

An example requesting volume information for the file_id 1 on AdventureWorks:

```
SELECT * FROM sys.dm_os_volume_stats (DB_ID('AdventureWorks2017'), 1)
```

Note   A mount point is a method to add volumes to a file system without the need of a drive letter and can be created in a directory on an NTFS file system. Mount points were introduced with Windows Server 2000.

---

sys.dm_db_index_usage_stats

The sys.dm_db_index_usage_stats DMV returns information about the operations performed on tables and indexes of a database including the number of seeks, scans, bookmark lookups, and updates by both user queries and system queries. It also reports the last time each of these operations was performed. The information is reported per index and table (i.e., a clustered index or heap). User activity is the queries submitted by users and applications. System queries are internally generated queries such as the operations required to perform statistics update.

This DMV could be used in conjunction with the sys.dm_io_virtual_file_stats DMV to drill down which objects in a database may have excessive I/O activity. However, it works in a different way as sys.dm_io_virtual_file_stats, as it does not show bytes or waits but mostly shows the activity from the query processing point of view. Keep in mind that this DMV returns information for the entire instance so you may want to select results for a specific database only, like in the following code:

```
SELECT OBJECT_NAME(object_id), * FROM sys.dm_db_index_usage_stats
WHERE database_id = DB_ID()
ORDER BY object_id, index_id
```

You can optionally join this DMV to sys.indexes for additional index details. Here is a basic query example:

```
SELECT OBJECT_NAME(s.object_id) AS object_name, i.name, s.*
FROM sys.dm_db_index_usage_stats s JOIN sys.indexes i
ON s.object_id = i.object_id AND s.index_id = i.index_id
WHERE database_id = DB_ID()
ORDER BY object_id, index_id
```

A basic sample output is shown in Table 8-4.

Table 8-4. *Sample Output*

Name	index_id	user_seeks	user_scans	user_lookups	user_updates
PK_ProductReview _ProductReviewID	1	1	0	0	0
PK_Document _DocumentNode	1	1	0	0	0
PK_SalesOrderDetail _SalesOrderID _SalesOrderDetailID	1	0	46	14	0
IX_SalesOrderDetail _ProductID	8	14	8	0	0
PK_SalesOrderHeader _SalesOrderID	1	0	8	4	3

sys.dm_exec_query_stats

The sys.dm_exec_query_stats DMV returns query performance information for cached query plans in SQL Server. Although the information in this DMV is extremely helpful, I also strongly recommend you enable the Query Store (or the Data Collector, if you are in an older SQL Server version) to collect better quality query performance data.

As mentioned in Chapter 6, the Query Store provides some additional benefits to using this DMV including the following:

    a. Using the sys.dm_exec_query_stats DMV provides a view of only the plans currently in the plan cache. Only the current version of a plan exists, and even this version can be removed from the plan cache at any time. The Query Store persists all the history of plans for every query.

    b. Not every plan gets cached and therefore exposed by the sys.dm_exec_query_stats DMV. All the plans and query information are stored by the Query Store, even those of incomplete queries.

Having said that, the sys.dm_exec_query_stats DMV has a lot of benefits as it can be queried without any performance impact. This is a huge improvement over older versions of SQL Server where getting similar information would require running an expensive SQL Trace session along with complex methods to process and aggregate data.

The DMV tracks performance information such as worker time (CPU time), physical reads, logical writes, logical reads, Common Language Runtime (CLR), elapsed time, and rows returned. For each one of these indicators, total, last, minimum, and maximum statistics are returned. The section about performance counters earlier in this chapter includes a typical example using the sys.dm_exec_query_stats DMV to obtain the most expensive queries in the system by CPU, which can be easily updated to list expensive queries by other available metrics such as logical reads or physical reads. Starting with SQL Server 2016, this DMV includes additional performance information related to the degree of parallelism, amount of reserved memory grant, amount of ideal memory grant, reserved parallel threads, and used parallel threads.

sys.dm_db_index_physical_stats

This DMV allows you to get the fragmentation information of your tables and indexes. Fragmentation could exist in three flavors: page, logical, and extent fragmentation. Page fragmentation occurs when data pages are not totally full. On the other side, logical and extent fragmentation appears when the pages of an object are not physically in order. Logical fragmentation occurs when pages are not physically in order according to the index logical order. Extent fragmentation is a similar concept in which the extents of a heap are not physically in order.

Fragmentation could be a performance problem only for table and index scan operations, for example, while performing page read-ahead operations. A workload of mostly index lookups would not be affected by fragmentation (at least logical or extent fragmentation). Two columns on the sys.dm_db_index_physical_stats, avg_page_space_used_in_percent and avg_fragmentation_in_percent, reflect the fragmentation level of the table or index.

The column avg_page_space_used_in_percent indicates the average percentage of space used in data pages, which basically indicates page fullness. Page fullness can usually be controlled by configuring an adequate fill factor value, which specifies the percentage of space to be filled with data for data pages, and can be configured at different levels ranging from the server to the object level. For example, a fill factor of 90 means the page is 90% full, leaving only the remaining 10% for new rows. An optimal value would depend on the application and database usage. The server default configuration fill factor value, 0 (which, by the way, is exactly the same as 100), means that pages are filled to capacity and work perfectly fine when rows are usually added at the end of a table, such as when using an IDENTITY constraint. This default value would also be optimal for disk space usage as the page is full and scans will be efficient as well (meaning there is no need to scan partially empty pages performing additional I/O operations). But full pages may not be optimal for random insert data operations where page splits will be required creating a performance problem in addition to fragmentation.

A value less than 100% may be adequate for cases requiring random insert data operations. This could be achieved by adjusting the fill factor configuration according to the particular insert data requirements of the application. A page split occurs when SQL Server has no room in a page for either additional rows or to update an existing row whose new larger size does not fit in the page anymore. The split operation basically creates a new page in which about half of the rows of the original page are moved to the new page.

Page splits are an expensive operation and lead to fragmentation as they end with two pages about only 50% full. Page splits should be avoided or minimized and can be monitored using the SQLServer:Access Methods Page Splits/sec performance counter or the page_split extended event. As covered in Chapter 9, a performance recommendation for an index is to have an ever-increasing value to minimize these problems.

The column avg_fragmentation_in_percent refers to the percentage of logical fragmentation for indexes or extent fragmentation for heaps. Logical fragmentation refers to the percentage of out-of-order pages in the leaf pages of an index, where pages are not physically in order according to the index logical order. Extent fragmentation is a similar concept for heaps in which the extents of a heap are not physically in order.

Fixing page fragmentation in a database would require adjusting the fill factor configuration level if your application needs to insert rows on existing pages. Logical or extent fragmentation can be fixed by rebuilding or reorganizing the index or table. You would usually only need to update the fill factor once. Rebuilding or reorganizing the index or table, on the other hand, may need to be performed on a periodic basis, usually in a database maintenance job. When to decide to rebuild or reorganize an index would depend on your database, but usually a safe starting point is to reorganize the index when the fragmentation goes from 10 to 40% and to rebuild the index when the fragmentation is greater than 40%. A heap by definition does not include a clustered index, but you can also defragment it by creating a clustered index on it and then dropping it. Creating a clustered index on the heap will redistribute the data in an optimal way, without any fragmentation, and later dropping it will just remove the metadata definition of the index, leaving the data the same.

The following code will return the indexes that may require defragmentation in the current database by looking at the avg_fragmentation_in_percent column with fragmentation greater than 10%:

```
SELECT *
FROM sys.dm_db_index_physical_stats (DB_ID(), NULL, NULL , NULL, 'LIMITED')
WHERE avg_fragmentation_in_percent > 10
```

You can then write a script to make the choice to either run ALTER INDEX REORGANIZE or ALTER INDEX REBUILD, based on the percentage, as shown in the following pseudocode:

```
IF avg_fragmentation_in_percent < 30.0
SET @command = 'ALTER INDEX ' + ... + ' REORGANIZE'
IF avg_fragmentation_in_percent >= 30.0
SET @command = 'ALTER INDEX ' + ... + ' REBUILD'
EXEC (@command)
```

The `sys.dm_db_index_physical_stats` documentation at `https://msdn.microsoft.com/en-us/library/ms188917.aspx` includes the basic code to do this, which you can adapt for your specific needs.

Note: I strongly recommend using Ola Hallengren's SQL Server maintenance solution for backups, integrity checks, and index and statistics maintenance. This maintenance solution is free and can be downloaded from `https://ola.hallengren.com/`.

sys.dm_exec_query_optimizer_info

The `sys.dm_exec_query_optimizer_info` DMV returns information about the optimizations performed by the query optimizer. You can use this information to obtain query optimization information regarding your system or a specific workload. Currently, the DMV returns 39 rows listing great information such as the total number of optimizations, average elapsed time per optimization, average estimated cost per optimization, and details about optimizations such as trivial plans, timeouts, memory problems during optimization, or the number of optimizations related to inserts, deletes, updates, merges, subqueries, hints, view references, remote queries, and indexed views. This can give you great info about the optimizations happening in your system. Some of the entries of this DMV are undocumented.

A short sample output is shown in Table 8-5.

Table 8-5. *Sample Output*

counter	occurrence	value
timeout	495	1
memory limit exceeded	0	NULL
insert stmt	12836	1
delete stmt	93	1
update stmt	12	1
merge stmt	0	NULL
contains subquery	7161	1
unnest failed	11783	1

sys.dm_os_sys_info

The sys.dm_os_sys_info DMV returns information about the system where SQL Server is running, including both information about the server and SQL Server instance. Starting with SQL Server 2016, it includes a large list of columns, including information such as the number of logical processors, total amount of physical memory on the server, quantum in milliseconds for a nonpreemptive task, maximum number of workers, number of user schedulers configured in the SQL Server process, total number of schedulers, date and time when the SQL Server instance was last started, and whether SQL Server is running in a virtual machine or NUMA configuration.

For example, my test system returns the sample shown in Table 8-6. (The result is only one row. Only a few columns are included in the following list.)

Table 8-6. *Sample Output*

Column	Value
cpu_count	4
hyperthread_ratio	4
physical_memory_kb	8266712
virtual_memory_kb	137438953344
os_quantum	4
max_workers_count	512
scheduler_count	4
scheduler_total_count	15
sqlserver_start_time	2016-06-17 07:49:24.397
affinity_type_desc	AUTO
virtual_machine_type_desc	NONE
softnuma_configuration_desc	OFF

sys.dm_os_windows_info

sys.dm_os_windows_info provides Windows information when SQL Server is running in this operating system. Microsoft Windows information such as operating system release, service pack level, Stock Keeping Unit (SKU), and Windows Locale Identifier (LCID) are returned by this DMV. To access similar information on a Linux system, you can use the sys.dm_os_host_info DMV.

Note   As mentioned in Chapter 2, starting with the SQL Server 2017 release, SQL Server can now run on Windows, Linux, and Docker containers.

---

sys.dm_os_host_info

The sys.dm_os_host_info returns operating system information and applies to both Windows and Linux. The column host_platform returns either Windows or Linux, and the host_distribution column returns a description of the operating system. All the other columns apply only to Windows and are also visible using the sys.dm_os_windows_info DMV described earlier.

SQL Trace/Extended Events

Along with performance counters and the data obtained directly from DMVs and DMFs, SQL Trace and extended events are the main tools to monitor SQL Server or obtain data to troubleshoot performance problems. Unlike performance counters, DMVs, and DMFs, though, collecting data from events is usually more expensive, and you will be collecting its data only as needed, for example, when troubleshooting a performance problem and filtering adequately. Although extended events were introduced with SQL Server 2008, as of SQL Server 2012, SQL Trace has been deprecated and it is planned to be removed in a future version of SQL Server. However, SQL Trace use, mostly by means of its client tool, SQL Profiler, is so widely spread that, at least in my opinion, I do not see it being removed from the product anytime soon.

Similar to performance counters, there are a huge number of events for both Extended Events and SQL Trace. For example, running the following code to return the existing Extended Event events would return 1846 for SQL Server 2019 RTM (compared to 1303 events returned in SQL Server 2016 RTM or 870 events in SQL Server 2014 RTM):

```
SELECT name, description
FROM sys.dm_xe_objects
WHERE object_type = 'event'
ORDER BY name
```

Although you will most likely be using scripts to work with extended events and run statements such as CREATE EVENT SESSION, ALTER EVENT SESSION, and DROP EVENT SESSION, you could get started easily by using its SQL Server Management Studio user interface. Such an interface can also help you to script the events and choices you select. The Extended Events user interface also allows you to select existing templates according to some common troubleshooting scenarios in pretty much the same way templates have been used in SQL Profiler since a long time ago. Custom templates can be created as well.

A discussion covering common events and how to use them would require a chapter on its own. In addition, we covered an example of using extended events to track waits for a specific process back in Chapter 5, so you may want to refer to it. But if you are troubleshooting a performance problem with no additional information, one of the top items to do is to see which expensive queries are running and to look for an optimization opportunity. The following list of events would help to collect such information that you can use to troubleshoot expensive queries:

> `sql_statement_completed`: Indicates that a SQL statement has been completed. Its SQL Trace counterpart is `SQL:StmtCompleted`.

> `sp_statement_completed`: Occurs when a SQL statement inside a stored procedure has been completed. Its SQL Trace counterpart is `SP:StmtCompleted`.

> `module_end`: Occurs when the execution of a module has been completed. Its SQL Trace counterpart is `SP:Completed`.

> `sql_batch_completed`: Indicates that a batch has been completed. Its SQL Trace counterpart is `SQL:BatchCompleted`.

> `rpc_completed`: Indicates that a remote procedure call has been completed. Its SQL Trace counterpart is `RPC:Completed`.

These events would look for completed SQL statements only. Unfortunately, there is no way to use events to find performance information about statements that were not able to finish, but you can get such information with the new Query Store feature, as covered in Chapter 6. In some cases, incomplete statements could be a performance problem so troubleshooting those can be required and important.

You can find the documented SQL Trace events at `https://msdn.microsoft.com/en-us/library/ms175481.aspx`.

Note   Although at the time of writing I don't see the entire Extended Events documentation published online, you can use the SQL Server Management Studio user interface to quickly search events by typing either their full or partial names. Selecting a specific event can also show its description along with the description of its event fields.

SQL Server Data Collector

The SQL Server Data Collector, a feature introduced with SQL Server 2008, is a great tool for collecting system data and troubleshooting performance problems. It is definitely the most underused SQL Server tool and one I have used extensively in the past. Collecting system data is essential to troubleshoot performance problems as it is very common that while researching a problem when there are no symptoms, the information may not be available anymore.

Among the information collected are the following:

a. Disk usage: Includes disk usage information for both data and transaction log files

b. Query statistics: Includes query performance information

c. Server activity: Includes a large list of performance counters and server activity information such as waits, schedulers, virtual file statistics, and data from some other DMVs

These three items correspond to the three collection sets defined when you enable the Data Collector. You can get specific details about the data collected on each collection set by looking at their properties. For example, in SQL Server Management Studio, expand the Management folder, select Data Collection and then System Data Collection Sets, right-click any of the collection sets, and select properties.

As an example, the Server Activity collection set properties is shown in Figure 8-4, which includes two collection items. You can inspect the T-SQL code used to collect data on the first collection item, called "Server Activity–DMV Snapshots," which obtains the data from multiple DMVs. The second collection item in the list, called "Server Activity–Performance Counters," shows the defined performance counters. It contains a large list of performance counters, and, as mentioned earlier in this chapter, you could fine-tune this list by including additional performance counters. A very small sample list of these performance counters is next:

> \Memory \% Committed Bytes In Use
>
> \Memory \Available Bytes
>
> \Memory \Cache Bytes
>
> \Memory \Cache Faults/sec

\Memory \Committed Bytes

\Memory \Free & Zero Page List Bytes

\Memory \Modified Page List Bytes

\Memory \Pages/sec

\Memory \Page Reads/sec

\Memory \Page Writes/sec

...

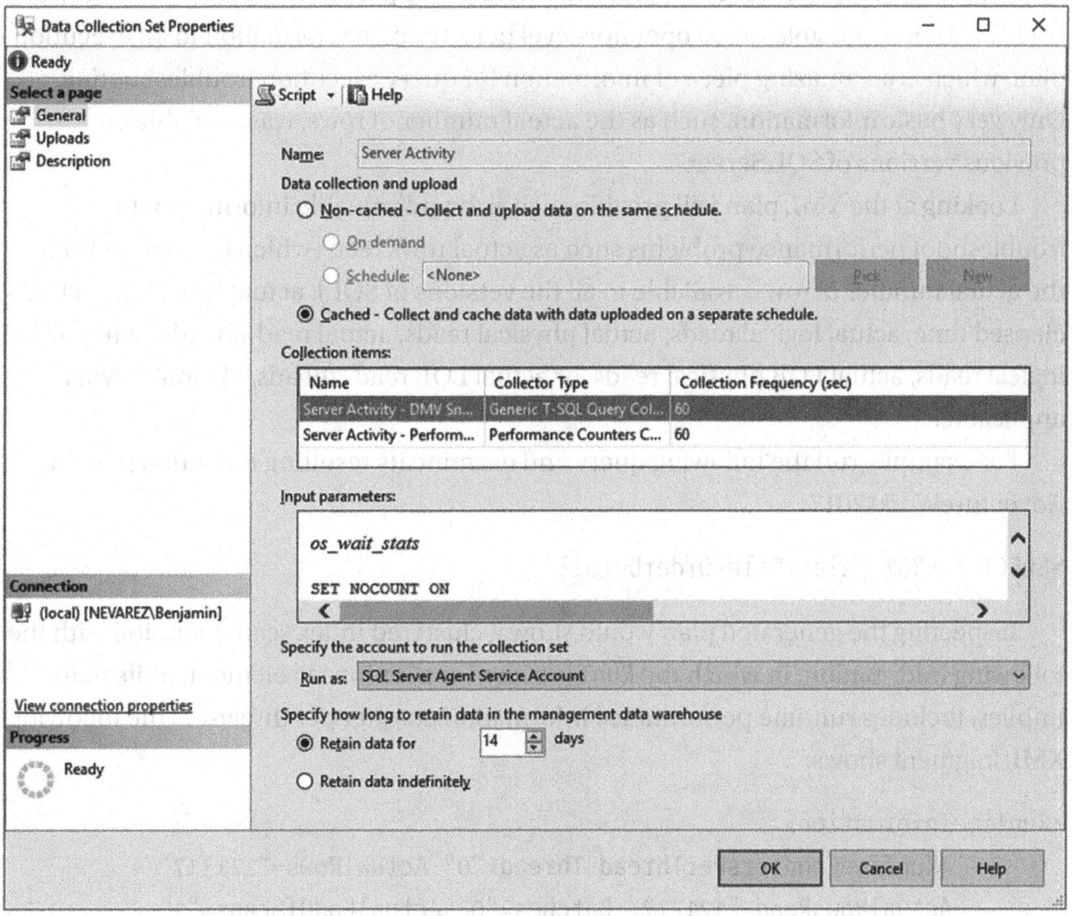

Figure 8-4. *Server Activity collection set properties*

The data collected by this tool is persisted in a database, and you can define the retention policies depending on your needs. Finally, the Data Collector contains reports that you can use to see the collected information in a nice graphical way. You could also create your own reports or write customized queries to obtain data directly from the Data Collector database. For more details about the Data Collector, please refer to the SQL Server documentation.

Operator-Level Performance Statistics

Introduced with SQL Server 2016, and later included as part of SQL Server 2014 Service Pack 2, it is now possible to see operator-level performance information in an execution plan, which is an amazing piece of information for query execution troubleshooting. Only very basic information, such as the actual number of rows, was available on previous versions of SQL Server.

Looking at the XML plan will provide such rich and valuable information to troubleshoot performance problems such as actual rows read (which is different from the actual number of rows, available in all the versions of SQL), actual CPU time, actual elapsed time, actual logical reads, actual physical reads, actual read-aheads, actual LOB logical reads, actual LOB physical reads, or actual LOB read-aheads, obviously when applicable.

For example, run the following query and examine its resulting execution plan in AdventureWorks2017:

```
SELECT * FROM Sales.SalesOrderDetail
```

Inspecting the generated plan would show a clustered index scan operation with the following information, in which the RunTimeCountersPerThread element, as its name implies, includes runtime performance information counter per thread, as the following XML fragment shows:

```
<RunTimeInformation>
        <RunTimeCountersPerThread Thread="0" ActualRows="121317"
        ActualRowsRead="121317" Batches="0" ActualEndOfScans="1"
        ActualExecutions="1" ActualExecutionMode="Row"
        ActualElapsedms="396"
        ActualCPUms="44" ActualScans="1" ActualLogicalReads="1266"
```

```
    ActualPhysicalReads="3" ActualReadAheads="1376"
    ActualLobLogicalReads="0"
    ActualLobPhysicalReads="0" ActualLobReadAheads="0" />
</RunTimeInformation>
```

Although this performance information is by thread, for simplicity, the previous example includes a serial plan and only thread 0 is shown. A parallel plan will show the same level of detail by thread. For example, in my test system with four logical processors, I can see five entries for RunTimeCountersPerThread, one for thread 0, which is the coordinator or main thread, plus four entries for each of the actual threads performing the actual clustered index scan operation.

You can look at this information by requesting the actual execution plan. As we know, getting an actual execution plan from SQL Server Management Studio is straightforward and not an expensive operation to do. Getting an actual execution plan from queries executed by applications in a production environment could be more expensive as it would require capturing the required events. As an alternative, a new extended event, query_thread_profile, can be used to get the same information. This event is triggered at the end of the query execution by each operator and thread used in the plan. Additionally, you could use the node_id attribute in the event to correlate it with the respective operator in the plan.

Trace Flags on Plans

Introduced with SQL Server 2014 Service Pack 2 and SQL Server 2016 Service Pack 1, execution plans now show information about enabled trace flags. This includes the instance level, session level, and query level trace flags enabled both at optimization time and execution time (if an actual execution plan is requested). Both session and query levels show as session in the plan.

Note   Query level trace flags are indicated using the QUERYTRACEON query hint, and although this hint has been available for several versions of SQL Server, has only recently been documented, and has been supported for only a limited number of trace flags, as shown on https://support.microsoft.com/en-us/kb/2801413.

By using this new feature, you can see if a specific behavior has been introduced by means of a trace flag, which impacts the choice of an execution plan or may impact the query performance in some other way. This feature will be especially helpful when sharing execution plans where you do not have direct access to the server that produced them.

Summary

This chapter covered performance troubleshooting by monitoring or collecting data from a SQL Server instance. It also demonstrated how proactively collecting and persisting this data for later analysis could be extremely beneficial to understand how a specific system works, to create a baseline, and to understand when performance is deviating from a desirable or expected behavior.

Performance problems could arise for multiple reasons, some of those even benign, for example, a website increasing the number of customers and sales. Consequently, proactively monitoring and understanding performance trends is essential to anticipate and react to those changes. Although it is impossible to have a comprehensive list, this chapter covered the most critical performance counters, dynamic management objects, and events, along with some of the tools used to display and collect such data. Some other performance counters, dynamic management objects, and events have been introduced in other chapters of the book as well as related to the topic at hand.

CHAPTER 9

Indexing

Indexing is, without a doubt, one of the best ways to improve the performance of your queries and applications, and this book would not be complete without covering this topic. This chapter explains how indexes work, how you can define the right indexes for your application, and how you can use some of the tools available in SQL Server to help you make the best possible decisions about your indexes. These tools include the missing indexes feature and the Database Engine Tuning Advisor, also called the DTA.

This chapter will also show you why the lack of indexes or even poorly designed indexes can negatively impact your query execution performance. After all, having a proper index can be the difference between having to scan an entire table and just reading a couple of pages to find the required data. Indexing may sound like a trivial task, and, in fact, it is common to see beginner database professionals who usually just blindly create indexes on columns without a proper analysis or background about the database, schema, or queries, hoping the created indexes will just magically improve the performance of a database.

Although a large part of this chapter focuses on using tools to design indexes, it is always emphasized that no recommendations from such tools should be applied without proper analysis and performance testing, as many times they are blindly implemented. In other words, it is up to the SQL Server professional to decide whether the recommended indexes make sense and to verify they really improve the performance of your queries. For this reason, the chapter starts by covering indexes, what they are, and in which situations they might be a good choice.

In order for you to properly design indexes, you need to know how indexes work and in which situations they can be useful, in addition to understanding your workload and queries. Tools like the DTA can figure this out very well. If you feed them a proper workload and queries, they can help you and do most of the job. But it is finally up to you to decide if the provided recommendations are in fact a good choice for your queries.

© Benjamin Nevarez 2021
B. Nevarez, *High Performance SQL Server*, https://doi.org/10.1007/978-1-4842-6491-1_9

Do I recommend using the DTA all the time? Yes. Even for experienced database professionals, it is always interesting to see what the DTA recommends. After all, the DTA uses the query optimizer estimations to select the best indexing choices, which makes a lot of sense as it is also the query optimizer that decides if your index is useful or not when the query is finally executed. In addition, this tool can analyze thousands of choices in about the same time you just stare at a query trying to understand what the query does. But then again keep in mind that estimations are just that, estimations.

Finally, this chapter focuses on traditional tables and indexes, such as clustered indexes, nonclustered indexes, and filtered indexes, which are either heaps or b-tree structures. Newer technologies such as In-Memory OLTP, also known as Hekaton, or columnstore indexes include new types of indexes that can greatly improve the performance of your databases. These new technologies are covered in detail in Chapter 7, which is dedicated to SQL Server in-memory features. There are some other types of less commonly used indexes like XML, spatial, or full-text indexes that are only needed for more special cases and will not be covered here.

How SQL Server Uses Indexes

It is usually difficult to anticipate all the required indexes during database design so, in many cases, new indexes are always added after the application has been put in production. Indexes are also being added as new business functionality or new code— for example, queries or stored procedures—are being introduced to the database. Although not intended to be a query tuning and optimization lesson, this chapter focuses mostly on the tools SQL Server has to make your job easier. Having said that, a good understanding of how SQL Server works is always important. In this section, I will show you how SQL Server uses indexes and how it can help you with the performance of your queries.

Creating the right indexes could range from a very simple to an overwhelming task. I've seen many beginner SQL Server professionals who just say, well, my query WHERE clause uses column col1 so I just have to create an index on col1. Right, it might help. But in production scenarios, the choices are usually many and more complicated, and creating the right indexes could be time-consuming. In addition to understanding how indexes work, before designing indexes for your database, you should have the following knowledge or at least consider some or all of the following points:

a. Understand the database schema and workload, like OLTP, Reporting, Data Warehouse, or a mix of some of those. I am not sure if a pure OLTP workload really exists; every OLTP database I have ever seen includes some other non-OLTP queries as well.

b. Understand your queries and especially which ones are your critical queries and which are most frequently executed.

c. Understand the query predicates where an index can be used (e.g., an equality, nonequality, or complex expressions, more on this later).

d. Understand whether to use clustered indexes or heaps on your table design.

e. Understand whether to use clustered or nonclustered indexes.

f. Understand whether you need single-column or multicolumn indexes and what the order of the columns could be.

g. Understand what the query predicates are that may benefit from an index and what their selectivity is.

h. Understand whether you need unique or filtered indexes.

i. Understand whether you need included columns in addition to the index keys.

j. Understand whether you need to change the default fill factor value.

k. Understand whether you need to consider partitioning or filegroup placement.

Note   Selectivity is a measure of the number of rows that are returned by a predicate. A predicate returning a small number of rows is said to be highly selective.

Having said that, the syntax for the CREATE INDEX statement has a large number of choices as you can see in the documentation at https://msdn.microsoft.com/en-us/library/ms188783.aspx. Some options such as ASC (ascending) or DESC (descending) are rarely needed as ascending is the default when you create an index, and the database engine can navigate such indexes in either direction. You will need to explicitly use these options, however, if you need to transverse two or more columns and at least one of them is accessed in the opposite direction. As an example, if you have an index on both columns `col1` and `col2`, it could be used on a query using `ORDER BY col1, col2` but not on `ORDER BY col1, col2 DESC`. If helping such a query is important, you could define the index as `col1, col2 DESC` so it matches the requested query order and a potentially expensive sort operation can be avoided.

As suggested in the introduction to this chapter, although indexes have several uses, definitely the most important is navigation, that is, to find one or more rows as quickly and efficiently as possible. This is traditionally accomplished using b-tree structures. Index searches use random disk I/Os and are extremely effective for a small or limited number of rows, so they are essential for OLTP workloads. However, each random disk I/O usually requires reading a few database pages, so as the number of rows increases, it became more and more expensive. The reason this cost is high is because it requires traversing the b-tree structure from the root to the leaves, potentially reading a few database pages, and, although each page usually contains many rows, most of the time only one is needed.

For this reason, when SQL Server is required to process a large number of rows, the query optimizer will most likely choose instead to perform sequential disk I/Os, such as a table scan or an index scan. Some query processing operations, such as sorting and hashing, heavily used in reporting and Data Warehouse workloads, will definitely benefit from this sequential disk I/O as well. This is the case, for example, of star join queries or queries using aggregations.

Another interesting behavior is that random disk I/O cost greatly depends on the number of rows being accessed, which is totally different from sequential disk I/O in which the cost is usually the same disregarding the number of requested rows. For example, a table scan cost is the same if we request only 5% of the rows or the entire table. Random disk I/O cost, however, increases dramatically if we request only a few rows or if we request a few hundred or thousand rows, switching quickly from an extremely efficient operation to a very expensive one. In addition, random disk I/Os are potentially performed twice per search when the selected index does not cover the query as very likely the base table also has to be accessed as well. Finally, SQL Server could use more than one nonclustered index at a time if this helps the performance of the query. This operation is called index intersection, and, as usual, making this choice will be a cost-based decision.

Where to Use Indexes

The SQL Server query optimizer uses indexes in some of the following ways:

    a.   To find rows according to a filter predicate or a join predicate.

    b.   To deliver rows in a specific order.

    c.   If the index covers the query, meaning it includes all the required columns, the main table does not need to be accessed at all.

Let us take a look at those choices in more detail. SQL Server can use an index on expressions such as the following:

```
col1 = 12
col2 = 'California'
col3 > 30
col4 IN (7, 23, 38)
col5 BETWEEN 23 AND 38
```

SQL Server may not be able to match an index on more complicated expressions such as the following:

```
col6 = ABS(col1)
col7 = (col1 * 3.1416) / col2
```

As we will show later, equality vs. nonequality predicates greatly impact the selection of an index. Complex expressions are an interesting query processor limitation too. You may be surprised to learn that the query optimizer is not able to resolve some of these expressions. This means that not only the query optimizer cannot choose an index to find the rows that qualify for this expression, but it also cannot estimate the number of rows returned by the predicate. This estimation, called cardinality estimation, is usually provided by statistics, and it is essential for the query optimization process. Obviously, SQL Server will always return the correct data even with a bad cardinality estimation; it is just that getting the data may not be very efficient in these cases.

For example, the following query will create an efficient execution plan using an index seek as the SalesOrderDetail table has an index on the ProductID column:

```
USE AdventureWorks2017
GO
SELECT * FROM Sales.SalesOrderDetail
WHERE ProductID = 898
```

However, if we try the following query adding a function, we will instead get the most expensive plan shown in Figure 9-1, which has to perform a table scan, reading all the rows on the table and introducing a filter operator later in the process to return the correct data:

```
SELECT * FROM Sales.SalesOrderDetail
WHERE ABS(ProductID) = 898
```

Figure 9-1. *Plan ignoring a nonclustered index*

Computed columns may be able to help in both cases—to have a better cardinality estimation and to create and use an index. They help by providing more information to the query optimizer as statistics are now automatically created when needed. You could also create an index on a computed column if it can help to find rows quickly.

Although sometimes used by the SQL Server community, the term "sarg" (search argument) is not really used in the official documentation or the database research community so I would not use it here. Sarg refers to predicates that can be converted into an index operation, but it is an old term that originated from the old Sybase code and documentation and should no longer be applied to SQL Server. In *The Guru's Guide to SQL Server Architecture and Internals*, Ken Henderson says, "The query optimizer in all recent versions of SQL Server is far more sophisticated in terms of its ability to use an index to speed up a query than it was in older versions of the product" (Addison-Wesley, 2004). Since the query optimizer's ability to use indexes is no longer constrained to simple expressions, the term "sarg" is no longer relevant.

Although I have yet to see a pure OLTP system, index requirements vary depending on how a system goes from OLTP to Reporting or Data Warehouse. OLTP is more about finding a row or a very small number of rows quickly, so nonclustered indexes are essential for this type of workload. On the other hand, OLTP systems have a large number of updates, so limiting the number of indexes is important too. Reporting and Data Warehouse workloads focus on processing large amounts of data, and although you can use traditional indexes to help with their queries, as covered in Chapter 7, columnstore indexes are a more appropriate choice.

The main reason you create an index is to help with filter and join predicates, so SQL Server can find the rows requested on those predicates as quickly as possible. Filter predicates are specified on queries using the WHERE clause, usually in equality comparisons, where join predicates are specified when two tables are joined. Queries using the WHERE clause with greater than, less than, or BETWEEN comparisons are usually referred to as range queries, and they can also benefit from an index, especially if the index covers the query. Sometimes, you can define a clustered index to help on those range queries, but since only one such index is possible per table, a second choice could be to create a nonclustered covering index. It is not likely that a noncovering nonclustered index will be chosen for a range scan operation by the query optimizer if the number of lookups is high.

Returning the rows in order is another important use of indexes, and this can happen in several cases, like when you request data in some specific order (e.g., using an ORDER BY operation) or when the query optimizer finds it useful for some operators that can benefit from ordered data, like a merge join or a stream aggregate. Such an index can avoid expensive sort operations or some other less efficient query processing strategy.

In summary, index seeks are helpful but usually only for a relatively small number of rows. Using an index for range scans is helpful for any number of rows as long as the index covers the query. This is the reason why range scans are very effective on clustered indexes as by definition they cover all the columns on a table.

Index Usage Validation

It is extremely important after you create your indexes to verify their execution plans to make sure the index is not only used by your query but used in the expected way. For example, you may create an index for a specific query, and although the index is chosen in the execution plan, it may be used to perform an index scan instead of the desired index seek operation. It may not be as drastic, but you might also define a multicolumn index, and although you see an index seek, a seek predicate is used only for the first column. Obviously, the performance metrics are the main indicator of the success of your indexing strategy. If your query was originally taking one minute to execute, and if after creating the required indexes, it runs in one or two seconds, you may decide it is good enough.

It is worth clarifying that just because the query optimizer selects an index, it does not mean you will get good performance. As shown later, navigating an index b-tree is an expensive operation, and it is only worth it when searching for a few rows or a relatively small number of rows. As usual on query optimization decisions, there is a tipping point where the cost increases in a way that using other access methods or operations, such as scanning a table, could be more efficient. The fact that an index does not cover all the columns required by the query makes the cost even worst, as potentially you need to navigate a b-tree structure twice, one for the nonclustered index and a second one for the main table, usually a clustered index. Such an operation is called a key lookup. The main table could also be a heap where there is no b-tree, but a similar operation, a RID lookup, will be required too.

Now, having said that, the query optimizer is designed to make the correct decision in these cases, but sometimes problems may occur, maybe because of some bad cardinality estimations or other limitations of the query processor. In addition, some reusable code, like stored procedures, may create such a problem when some queries are sensitive to parameters, especially in cases with uneven data distribution. In this case, the query optimizer will originally create the optimal plan when the stored procedure is executed for the first time. As mentioned in Chapter 1, the query optimizer accomplishes this by using the first provided parameter or parameters to make the decision about the operations to perform to execute such query. A problem may appear later for such queries when running a second instance with different parameters in which the previously created plan may no longer be a good choice.

Finally, just because there is a WHERE clause in a query predicate, it does not mean that a new index has to be created or has to be used by the query optimizer if it already exists. In the end, this is a cost-based decision, and in some cases other navigation choices may be more appropriate and less expensive. Typical cases of this are query predicates that are not selective enough or the index may not cover the query. There could be several reasons why an index is not chosen by the query optimizer, even assuming the index was created correctly.

a. Cost: Maybe using the index is a good idea for the current value or parameter but not for some other values. This problem happens with data with uneven distribution. Examples of these cases are shown later in this chapter.

b. Complex expressions: Maybe because you are using a function or a complex expression that, at least on the current version of SQL Server, the query optimizer is not able to fully understand.

c. Not useful: Maybe the index is not useful at all. You could research if an index is not being used and may decide to delete it. Index usage is recorded in the `sys.dm_db_index_usage_stats` DMV, which is covered in Chapter 8.

d. Bad cardinality estimations or some other query processor limitations.

If, after analyzing these choices, you suspect that an index could in fact be useful and for some reason the query optimizer is not selecting it, you could research such query behavior by using a hint to force index selection. I usually don't recommend using hints as they break the declarative specification of queries, restrict the choices the query optimizer has, and make maintenance of the query more difficult as hints are basically a new dependency. For example, if a query hint uses a specific index, dropping the index will make the query fail.

Index Maintenance

We definitely don't want to create indexes for every single query in the system. Indexes could be recommended to help on the performance of critical or frequently used queries only, as having too many indexes can introduce a new performance problem. Since every index would require maintenance, either automatically by the database engine with every insert, update, or delete operation or by the database administrator when scheduling jobs to remove fragmentation or update statistics, you should limit the number of indexes you create per table. In addition, indexes use valuable storage and potentially more memory resources.

The number of indexes to create on a table would also depend on whether you have an OLTP system where data is changing all the time or a Data Warehouse where data only changes on a periodic basis (e.g., using ETL jobs). Index characteristics are also different for both workloads where the first one could be to help single lookups and the second to help on data aggregations. In summary, some of the issues of having too many indexes are the following:

a. Performance of update operations such as `INSERT`, `UPDATE`, `DELETE`, `MERGE`, and others may be negatively impacted.

b. Maintenance jobs for index rebuild or index reorganization operations (to eliminate or minimize index fragmentation) or statistics update may take longer, use more resources, and expand the database maintenance window.

c. More disk space storage and potentially more memory will be required.

For more details about fragmentation, you can refer to Chapter 8, where we also discuss the `sys.dm_db_index_physical_stats` DMV.

Heaps

A heap is not an index or a b-tree structure per se, but it is also important to cover it here as any table has to be configured either as a heap or as a clustered index. A heap is a data structure where rows are stored in no specific order. Although choosing between a heap and a clustered order sometimes can be a topic of debate and will depend on your database and workload, usually a well-designed clustered index offers the advantage of offering an order that can be used for range scans or return sorted data. Having said that, a heap can also be used in some other cases like in a small table or tables where a proposed candidate clustering key could be larger than the heap row identifier or RID. A RID is only eight bytes long and serves the row locator for rows in a heap. Small tables may not only be configured as heaps, but they may not require nonclustered indexes at all, as in some cases scanning the entire table could be less expensive than navigating any alternate b-tree index structure.

Although most of the time it is recommended to use clustered indexes as they offer the benefit of accessing data in order, there are some other benefits of using heaps, especially with small tables or to avoid issues like page splits and minimize fragmentation. For a great discussion about choosing clustered indexes vs. heaps, see the article "Clustered Indexes and Heaps" located at `https://technet.microsoft.com/en-us/library/cc917672.aspx`.

Clustered Indexes

Usually, a table will have, or more precisely be, a clustered index. A few of the exceptions were listed previously in the "Heaps" section. Mentioned earlier was when a proposed clustered index key is restrictively large while a heap RID uses only eight bytes. Something similar in size to this eight-byte heap RID could be achieved by using an identity property, which could be either the int or bigint data types, which use four and eight bytes, respectively. That is, you could start using an int data type, and later upgrade to a bigint, if required. If you already know up front you will need a bigint, you should start with it to avoid a conversion maintenance later in production use.

Since a heap does not provide any order and requires a nonclustered index to find specific rows, a clustered index has the advantage of providing that benefit already, but since only one clustered key or order is available, it would have to be chosen wisely. The best choice of a clustered key is one that can help with range queries where the index can quickly find the first row in a range and follow the logical, and hopefully physical, index order to find the remaining rows. Range queries are queries that filter predicates using greater than or less than operators such as >, >=, <, or <= or the BETWEEN clause. Clustered indexes also help on JOIN predicates, for example, when defining master-detail tables and foreign key constraints. They greatly benefit ORDER BY and GROUP BY queries if these are based on the table clustering key.

Best practices throughout the years have shown that clustered index keys are recommended to be unique, narrow, static, and ever-increasing, especially for performance and disk-space-used considerations. As a side note, those four recommendations are not a problem on a heap as an RID follows those four properties. A RID is relatively narrow as it uses only eight bytes. Let us review the unique, narrow, static, and ever-increasing properties, recommended for a clustered index key:

a.   Unique: Clustered index key is recommended to be unique. If it is not, a four-byte uniqueifier will be added to make sure it is unique.

b.   Narrow: Clustering key is recommended to be as narrow as possible as it saves disk storage and memory usage. A very important consideration in this point is that every nonclustered index row will also store this clustering key, again impacting storage and memory usage. A clustering key could be one or more columns so it is recommended to be as few columns as possible or one column and a short key.

c. Static: I would say this should be a requirement for a clustering key. A volatile clustering key, which may change or it is constantly changing, can be a huge performance problem as rows have to be moved from one page to another and create page splits and fragmentation.

d. Ever-increasing: It is recommended to use an ever-increasing value like the one provided by an IDENTITY property. This helps to add new rows always in new pages at the end of the index, avoiding page splits and fragmentation. However, in very intensive workloads with high concurrency, scenarios may create contention as all the new rows are inserted always at the same and last page. This problem is commonly known as "last page insert contention" and may impact heaps as well.

Note   If the "last page insert contention" problem is a serious bottleneck in your application, you definitely should consider using memory-optimized tables and In-Memory OLTP. For details about this SQL Server feature, see Chapter 7. Fragmentation and page splits are covered in more detail in Chapter 8.

Finally, defining a primary key will by default also create a clustered index using either T-SQL or SQL Server Management Studio. In order to change this behavior (e.g., to instead create a nonclustered index), it needs to be required explicitly.

Nonclustered Indexes

Nonclustered indexes are the traditional secondary indexes used by SQL Server and can be created on the main clustered index or a heap. As such, they contain only one or a few columns of the base table as index keys. They can optionally contain one or more columns, not as keys, but as additional data to cover a query, using the INCLUDE clause.

Nonclustered indexes are essential for exact match queries, which are used to find one or a few rows using equality comparisons. Like clustered indexes, they could be extremely useful for range queries but only if the index covers the query. Range queries could be helpful when using a noncovering index only for a very limited number of rows as the main table would in that case have to be accessed anyway, and, as mentioned earlier, random disk I/Os become very expensive as the number of rows increases. Nonclustered indexes can benefit ORDER BY and GROUP BY queries as well, again assuming they cover the query.

As mentioned earlier, if you want to cover a column that is not required for searching purposes, it can be added to the index using the INCLUDE clause. For example, if column col1 is included, it can be returned by a query, but you cannot use it to search in a filter predicate such as col1 = 12. I've seen in the documentation advice that an INCLUDE column can help you to avoid the index limitation of 16 key columns or key size of 900 bytes, but if you are getting even close to those limits, you should rethink your index design. As mentioned earlier, it does not exactly play the same role as such columns cannot be used in a search predicate. A reminder that a nonclustered index also covers the clustered index keys, and like those, we should keep nonclustered indexes as small as possible.

Finally, be aware that the term "nonclustered index" is also used with In-Memory OLTP and columnstore index technologies, so it is usually a good practice to always call the indexes in these new technologies memory-optimized nonclustered indexes and nonclustered columnstore indexes.

Note   The recommended properties for a clustered index (unique, narrow, static, and ever-increasing) either do not apply for nonclustered indexes or are less relevant.

Filtered Indexes

Filtered indexes were introduced with SQL Server 2008 and can be very helpful in situations where subsets of data can be eliminated from the query results. Typical scenarios for filtered indexes are data with sparse columns, data with large number of NULL values, or columns with heterogeneous data. Filtered indexes require a WHERE clause with a filter predicate indicating the rows to include in the index.

Note   Sparse columns, also introduced with SQL Server 2008, are columns that have an optimized storage for NULL values and are used in cases when a large number of the values in the column are NULL.

Working with Indexes

Let's take a quick tour creating a few indexes for some basic scenarios, reviewing some of the concepts explained in this chapter and looking to the missing indexes feature along the way, showcasing some of its benefits and limitations. Create a new database called "test" and run the following code to populate it with some data. Keep in mind that the missing indexes feature is not an index tuning tool and, as discussed, has a number of limitations. It helps as it is always available and can provide feedback even without requesting it. If you need an index tuning tool, you should use the DTA.

```
SELECT *
INTO dbo.SalesOrderDetail
FROM AdventureWorks2017.Sales.SalesOrderDetail
GO
SELECT *
INTO dbo.SalesOrderHeader
FROM AdventureWorks2017.Sales.SalesOrderHeader
```

At this moment, we are ready to run some queries on the test database. Let's try a few simple ones while looking at the produced execution plans. We will immediately see a couple of limitations of the missing indexes feature, the first one being that it cannot be used to recommend clustered indexes. The following query would be a great example for such a tool to recommend a clustered index as it would be helpful to perform a range scan by first finding the row with SalesOrderID 50000 and navigating the index throughout SalesOrderID 70000:

```
SELECT * FROM SalesOrderHeader
WHERE SalesOrderID BETWEEN 50000 AND 70000
```

We don't see any missing index recommendation on the graphical execution plan. There is, however, a second limitation that may be blocking providing any recommendation. The produced plan is a trivial plan, and the missing indexes feature does not work with a trivial plan either. Missing index information is provided by the query optimizer during a full optimization, and since a trivial plan skips this optimization, no missing index information is provided. There are several ways to avoid a trivial plan although, in fact, you would rarely see this problem on your real-life databases, as even some minor changes make the query require a full optimization.

A simple way to avoid a trivial plan is to use an undocumented trace flag to force a full optimization. This is trace flag 8757, and, as an undocumented trace flag, it is not supported and should not be used in a production environment.

Trying the following query will create a full optimized plan, but the limitation with clustered indexes remains, and we still got no recommendation. By the way, the DTA, as covered later, would recommend a clustered index on the SalesOrderID column for this range query.

```
SELECT * FROM SalesOrderHeader
WHERE SalesOrderID BETWEEN 50000 AND 70000
OPTION (QUERYTRACEON 8757)
```

Many times the decision to create a clustered index and which keys to use for such index is performed during database or table design. Let's manually create clustered indexes for both tables.

```
CREATE CLUSTERED INDEX PK_SalesOrderHeader ON
SalesOrderHeader(SalesOrderID)
GO
CREATE CLUSTERED INDEX PK_SalesOrderDetail
ON SalesOrderDetail(SalesOrderID, SalesOrderDetailID)
```

A foreign key constraint on this master-detail table would be a natural choice here. I may not go that far to cover an entire exercise but will just discuss the basic steps to see how the tools work. Let's continue the exercise with a very simple query:

```
SELECT * FROM SalesOrderDetail
WHERE ProductID = 898
```

This time, we get a clustered index scan, technically a table scan, with no missing index recommendations yet, as shown in Figure 9-2.

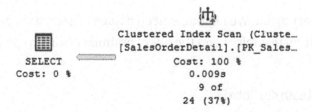

Figure 9-2. *Plan with no missing index recommendation*

Even with the clustered index, the trivial plan limitation remains. Let's try the trace flag 8757 again to disable a trivial optimization:

```
SELECT * FROM SalesOrderDetail
WHERE ProductID = 898
OPTION (QUERYTRACEON 8757)
```

You can now verify, by looking at the execution plan, that the optimization level is full, but we still get the same plan, as expected, as nothing has really changed. But this time we get a missing index recommendation. This is the code generated:

```
CREATE NONCLUSTERED INDEX [<Name of Missing Index, sysname,>]
ON [dbo].[SalesOrderDetail] ([ProductID])
INCLUDE
([SalesOrderID],[SalesOrderDetailID],[CarrierTrackingNumber],[OrderQty],
[SpecialOfferID],
[UnitPrice],[UnitPriceDiscount],[LineTotal],[rowguid],[ModifiedDate])
```

Note   To show this code in SQL Server Management Studio, right-click the green-colored Missing Index message at the top of the execution plan and select Missing Index Details. A new query window will be opened with the listed code.

For a query returning 9 rows out of 121,317, this recommendation seems like a good idea. But, although creating an index on ProductID seems to go in the right direction, including all the remaining columns of the table in the index seems overkill. Basically, it will duplicate the space required for the table. A better choice may be to just create the index on ProductID, with no included columns, as shown next:

```
CREATE NONCLUSTERED INDEX IX_ProductID
ON SalesOrderDetail (ProductID)
```

Let's run the query again. We no longer need a trace flag since we now have an index, and it will create alternate choices and the query optimizer will have to perform a full optimization.

```
SELECT * FROM SalesOrderDetail
WHERE ProductID = 898
```

We now get a full optimization with the plan shown in Figure 9-3.

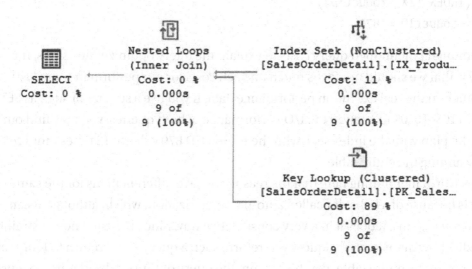

Figure 9-3. *Plan using an index seek operation*

This plan is looking a lot better now that we have the index seek that we wanted to see to fully utilize an index. In this particular case, there is no missing index recommendation as it seems that the optimum index is already available and used. But we have something else, a key lookup. A key lookup is needed because we are requesting all the columns of the table, and the index alone does not cover them all. As explained earlier, a key lookup (or its equivalent on a heap, a RID lookup) is an expensive operation that only makes sense for a relatively small number of rows. There is no percentage to give as an example, but it is very low and depends on the query optimizer estimates. Let's now run the following same query with a different ProductID value:

```
SELECT * FROM SalesOrderDetail
WHERE ProductID = 870
```

This time, it returned 4688 rows, but it went back to a table scan as the query optimizer estimated that using an index seek and a key lookup for such a large number of rows could be more expensive than scanning the entire table. You can verify both costs by looking at the plans, but you will have to force the use of an index for ProductID 870. The table scan will cost 1.25303 units, and forcing the index using the following query will cost 5.27841, a big difference. You can force the index seek using the following INDEX hint and verify both costs in the generated execution plans:

```
SELECT * FROM SalesOrderDetail
WITH (INDEX (IX_ProductID))
WHERE ProductID = 870
```

Although I mentioned query costs to explain the query optimizer decisions, the reality is that we should not focus much on such costs for our performance analysis but rather on the real execution performance data. If you use a statement such as SET STATISTICS IO ON to analyze the I/O performance of both queries, you may find out that using the plan with the index seek with the ProductID 870 will use 12 times more I/Os than scanning the entire table.

It is worth mentioning here that the reason we have different plans for the same query is because of a behavior called auto-parameterization, which, although it can help to reuse plans, it does it in a very conservative way. Since there are no constraints to predict how many rows the query will return, such a query could return 0, 1, or many rows or even the entire table. For this reason, the query optimizer decides not to reuse the previous plan and creates a new one, tailored to the new value. If we were using stored procedures, where reusing plans is mostly encouraged, the existing plan will be reused. You may be asking which of the two plans will be reused. Obviously, it is the one created for the first optimization.

In summary, index seeks and key lookups are extremely efficient for a small number of rows but become very expensive as the number of rows increases. Obviously, this does not mean that you should avoid them. In fact, there is no bad query operator, and each one could be the best choice in the right circumstances. Sometimes, I see developers trying to get rid of key lookups entirely, and that is not the right approach. There has to be a balance, especially when you cannot create indexes for every query.

Let's suppose we change the query slightly to the following:

```
SELECT SalesOrderID, SalesOrderDetailID, ProductID FROM SalesOrderDetail
WHERE ProductID = 870
```

This time, we get a new plan with just an index seek and no key lookup, as shown in Figure 9-4.

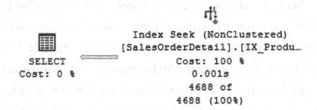

Figure 9-4. *Plan without a key lookup*

So why has the key lookup gone? Every nonclustered index includes the table clustering key, so in this case both SalesOrderID and SalesOrderDetailID are available without having to access the base table. Let's add one more column:

```
SELECT SalesOrderID, SalesOrderDetailID, ProductID, UnitPrice FROM
SalesOrderDetail
WHERE ProductID = 870
```

Because the index does not include the UnitPrice column, it no longer covers the query, and we go back to the clustered index scan. But this time we get a new index recommendation. Most SQL Server versions would show the following index definition:

```
CREATE NONCLUSTERED INDEX [<Name of Missing Index, sysname,>]
ON [dbo].[SalesOrderDetail] ([ProductID])
INCLUDE ([SalesOrderID],[SalesOrderDetailID],[UnitPrice])
```

In this case, it looks like a good recommendation. However, we don't want to include SalesOrderID and SalesOrderDetailID as they are already contained on the nonclustered index, as we mentioned earlier. Even if we do add them, they will not be duplicated, but it is clearer not to do it in the index definition. This column duplication on the index definition is fixed in SQL Server 2019 which only includes the UnitPrice column.

Let's drop the existing index and create a new one with the recommendation:

```
DROP INDEX SalesOrderDetail.IX_ProductID
GO
CREATE NONCLUSTERED INDEX IX_ProductID
ON SalesOrderDetail (ProductID)
INCLUDE (UnitPrice)
```

Running our last SELECT statement again will get the best possible plan using an index seek and similar to the one in Figure 9-4. Assuming that the query is worth it (e.g., it is used multiple times), you can create the index with that included column. It is your decision when to use INCLUDE as doing so too frequently will require data duplication. After the index is created, we have the optimal index for the query, either with parameter 898 or 870 or, in fact, any other parameter. In both cases, we have only the index seek without the need for a key lookup.

We have just covered filter predicates and will cover join predicates shortly, but let's first see some other good uses of the index we have just created. This index can provide some other benefits like returning its data in order (e.g., on a query using ORDER BY or when the query processor needs to add some operations like a merge join) and aggregations. Let's drop the index:

```
DROP INDEX SalesOrderDetail.IX_ProductID
```

Run the following query:

```
SELECT SalesOrderID, SalesOrderDetailID, ProductID FROM SalesOrderDetail
ORDER BY ProductID
```

As you can see in Figure 9-5, an expensive sort operation has to be added to provide the required order.

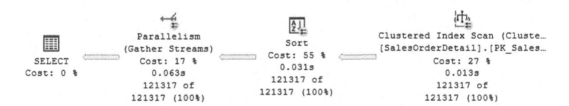

Figure 9-5. *Plan with a sort operation*

Create the index again:

```
CREATE NONCLUSTERED INDEX IX_ProductID
ON SalesOrderDetail (ProductID)
```

Running the query again will create a very simple plan using only the created index with no need for a sort operation. This is shown in Figure 9-6.

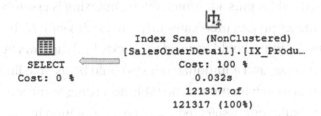

Figure 9-6. *Plan using an index to get sorted data*

No sort operation is required in this case as the data is already sorted. Just an index scan is needed, as we need all the rows. The Ordered property of the operation, if you look at the execution plan, will show True, meaning that it is taking advantage of the fact that the data is already ordered.

The index will also be used for the following query, aggregating data by ProductID, which otherwise would require a table scan and a hash aggregation. The resulting plan would just scan the nonclustered index and would do a simple aggregation called stream aggregation, taking advantage of the fact that the data is already sorted. The Ordered property is again True on the index scan operator.

```
SELECT ProductID, COUNT(*) FROM SalesOrderDetail
GROUP BY ProductID
```

In summary, this section showed how to use an index to do the following:

a. Quickly find data on a filter predicate (using the WHILE clause)

b. Return data in order (using the ORDER BY clause)

c. Aggregate data (using the GROUP BY clause)

What would be a good index recommendation for a join predicate? Although the query optimizer can take several different decisions about indexes for joins, usually the database administrator can focus on two main choices: joining the entire tables or joining the tables plus additional filters.

a. Joining the entire tables: In this case, since the entire tables are scanned anyway, indexes are less relevant and might not be used.

b. Joining both tables plus additional filters: Indexing is essential here as indexes on join predicates help on queries with high selectivity. An index could be used to quickly find the rows by a filter predicate, and additional indexes could be used to find the rows that match on the second table according to the join predicate. Again, query selectivity and cost estimation impact the query optimizer decision.

For example, running the following query will create the plan shown in Figure 9-7:

```
SELECT * FROM SalesOrderDetail d
JOIN SalesOrderHeader h
ON d.SalesOrderID = h.SalesOrderID
WHERE ProductID = 898
```

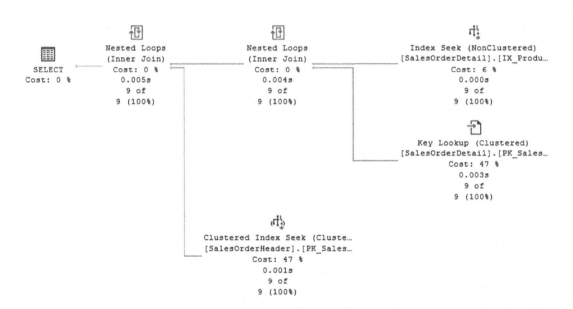

Figure 9-7. *Plan optimized for joining two tables with a high selective predicate*

This is a very efficient plan. The IX_ProductID index is used to efficiently find the nine rows for the ProductID 898, and nine additional key lookups are needed to obtain the remaining columns from the same table. Once we get the nine rows on SalesOrderDetail, we can use an index (in this case, the clustered index) to efficiently find the nine matching rows on the master table, SalesOrderHeader, assuming they exist.

However, changing to a less selective predicate would produce a totally different plan. (See Figure 9-8.)

```
SELECT * FROM SalesOrderDetail d
JOIN SalesOrderHeader h
ON d.SalesOrderID = h.SalesOrderID
WHERE ProductID = 870
```

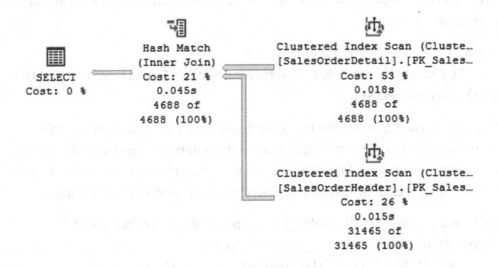

Figure 9-8. *Plan joining two tables for a predicate with low selectivity*

The plan now uses two table scans, as shown in Figure 9-8, but remember it is more likely that you will be using stored procedures to reuse plans. Consequently, in this case, one of these plans would be reused for all the instances of the provided parameter. This is also a scenario where two or more indexes could have been recommended, but you may have noticed that the missing indexes feature only recommends one index at a time for a specific query execution. This is also true if you would inspect the XML version of the execution plan or the missing indexes DMV.

Next, I'll show you a query using the INDEX query hint. As mentioned earlier, if you drop such an index, the query will fail. Keep in mind that it is a possible scenario as many times the maintenance of indexes is separated to the maintenance of code. If you are using INDEX hints, you should document them or research where an index may be used before it is removed. For example, earlier we tried the following query to force the use of the ProductID when the query optimizer was not selecting it:

```
SELECT * FROM SalesOrderDetail
WITH (INDEX (IX_ProductID))
WHERE ProductID = 870
```

Drop the index we created for the ProductID column:

```
DROP INDEX SalesOrderDetail.IX_ProductID
```

Trying to run the previous SELECT statement will now fail and instead will return the following error message:

```
Msg 308, Level 16, State 1, Line 1
Index 'IX_ProductID' on table 'SalesOrderDetail' (specified in the FROM
clause) does not exist.
```

Finally, let's take a look at the index depth property, which shows the number of levels of an index and can also roughly tell you the number of pages an index uses to find a specific row. You could use the sys.dm_db_index_physical_stats DMV as shown next. Let's run this exercise this time against the AdventureWorks2017 database:

```
SELECT name, index_depth, index_level, page_count, record_count
FROM sys.dm_db_index_physical_stats(DB_ID (),
        OBJECT_ID ('Sales.SalesOrderDetail'), null, null, null) s
JOIN sys.indexes i
ON s.index_id = i.index_id
WHERE name in ('IX_SalesOrderDetail_ProductID',
        'PK_SalesOrderDetail_SalesOrderID_SalesOrderDetailID')
```

You can also use the IndexDepth property of the INDEXPROPERTY function to get the same results:

```
SELECT INDEXPROPERTY(OBJECT_ID('Sales.SalesOrderDetail'),
        'IX_SalesOrderDetail_ProductID', 'IndexDepth')
SELECT INDEXPROPERTY(OBJECT_ID('Sales.SalesOrderDetail'),
        'PK_SalesOrderDetail_SalesOrderID_SalesOrderDetailID', 'IndexDepth')
```

In both cases, we will have a depth of 3 for the clustered index PK_SalesOrderDetail_SalesOrderID_SalesOrderDetailID and 2 for the nonclustered index IX_SalesOrderDetail_ProductID. In a similar way, you can measure the number of pages used by a query using the following statement:

```
SET STATISTICS IO ON
```

If you run the following statement, which uses a clustered index seek navigating the index b-tree, you could see three logical reads if you look at the Messages tab:

```
SELECT * FROM Sales.SalesOrderDetail
WHERE SalesOrderID = 43659 AND SalesOrderDetailID = 1
```

In a similar exercise, to see the logical pages used by an index seek of the listed nonclustered index like in the following query, you would see two logical reads:

```
SELECT ProductID FROM Sales.SalesOrderDetail
WHERE ProductID = 898
```

The Missing Indexes Feature

We have already seen the missing indexes feature in action. Let's use this section to summarize what the missing indexes feature is and also take a look at the missing indexes DMVs. Basically, the missing indexes feature is a database engine behavior enabled by default as a result of the query optimizer analyzing which indexes would benefit the current query being optimized. During this process, the query optimizer estimates if an index would benefit the performance of the query if it existed and provides this information in the execution plan. In addition, SQL Server is keeping this information on the missing indexes DMVs. But, then again, remember this is an estimation and has some of the following limitations, some of which were demonstrated earlier:

a. It does not work for a trivial plan.

b. It does not recommend clustered indexes or filtered indexes.

c. The missing indexes DMVs can collect information only up to about 500 index groups.

d. Data on the DMVs is not persisted.

e. It is not an index tuning tool.

Looking at the missing index information in the XML plan can be complicated. Fortunately, SQL Server Management Studio can help you assemble the `CREATE INDEX` statements for the recommended indexes, as shown earlier.

In summary, the missing indexes DMVs are the following:

sys.dm_db_missing_index_group_stats: Returns summary information regarding missing index groups

sys.dm_db_missing_index_groups: Returns information regarding a specific group of missing indexes

sys.dm_db_missing_index_details: Returns detailed information regarding a missing index

sys.dm_db_missing_index_columns: Returns information regarding the database table columns that are missing an index

To give you a quick tour on how to use the missing indexes DMVs, let's follow this exercise. Create a new test database and run these statements again to have some data to play with:

```
SELECT *
INTO dbo.SalesOrderDetail
FROM AdventureWorks2017.Sales.SalesOrderDetail
GO
SELECT *
INTO dbo.SalesOrderHeader
FROM AdventureWorks2017.Sales.SalesOrderHeader
```

Since by using such a simple table and schema we can hit once again the trivial plan limitation, let's use the undocumented trace flag 8758 one more time. (Remember never to use this trace flag in a production environment.)

```
SELECT * FROM SalesOrderDetail
WHERE ProductID = 898
OPTION (QUERYTRACEON 8757)
```

Your execution plan shows a recommendation as indicated earlier in this chapter. But this time we will take a look from the data collected on the missing indexes DMVs. Run the following query:

```
SELECT g.*, statement, column_id, column_name, column_usage
FROM sys.dm_db_missing_index_details AS d
CROSS APPLY sys.dm_db_missing_index_columns(d.index_handle)
```

```
INNER JOIN sys.dm_db_missing_index_groups AS g
        ON g.index_handle = d.index_handle
WHERE d.database_id = DB_ID()
ORDER BY g.index_group_handle, g.index_handle, column_id
```

Notice we are filtering on the current database, so we would want to run this query connected to the test database. A lot of information may be returned for other databases in your instance without such a filter. Missing index information in index groups will be returned, and, since we just created the test database, there is only one index group now. The information for this index group is the same information that we can see in the graphical or XML plan. An abbreviated output to fit the page that shows the column information for the existing index group is next. The column_usage column will show how the column is used by the query and may contain the values EQUALITY, INEQUALITY, and INCLUDE. This can help you to build the CREATE INDEX statement for the recommended index, but remember, SQL Server Management Studio can do that for you too.

Statement	column_id	column_name	column_usage
[test].[dbo].[SalesOrderDetail]	1	SalesOrderID	INCLUDE
[test].[dbo].[SalesOrderDetail]	2	SalesOrderDetailID	INCLUDE
[test].[dbo].[SalesOrderDetail]	3	CarrierTrackingNumber	INCLUDE
[test].[dbo].[SalesOrderDetail]	4	OrderQty	INCLUDE
[test].[dbo].[SalesOrderDetail]	5	ProductID	EQUALITY
[test].[dbo].[SalesOrderDetail]	6	SpecialOfferID	INCLUDE

The following query will use the sys.dm_db_missing_index_group_stats DMV to return additional performance information about the missing indexes:

```
SELECT d.*, s.*
FROM sys.dm_db_missing_index_group_stats AS s
INNER JOIN sys.dm_db_missing_index_groups AS g
    ON s.group_handle = g.index_group_handle
INNER JOIN sys.dm_db_missing_index_details AS d
    ON g.index_handle = d.index_handle
WHERE d.database_id = DB_ID()
```

Among this information, we have the `column avg_user_impact`, which is also shown on SQL Server Management Studio as Impact and in this case has the value 99.31. `avg_ user_impact` is the average percentage benefit that user queries will gain if the missing index group were implemented. This value is based on the query cost, and as such it does not represent any specific unit.

Run the next query:

```
SELECT * FROM SalesOrderDetail
WHERE OrderQty = 1
OPTION (QUERYTRACEON 8757)
```

Running the previous queries to display information about the missing indexes DMVs will show a second `index_group_handle` with details about creating an index for the `OrderQty` column and include several other columns of the table. The second `SELECT` query in this exercise will show an `avg_user_impact` of 96.97, along with other performance information. SQL Server will continue to accumulate this information until the limit of 500 missing index groups is reached.

Finally, when you consider the limitations of the missing indexes feature, keep in mind that this information is always available. It does not have any performance impact, and you don't have to do any additional effort to obtain it. Even if you don't plan to apply any of its recommendations, consider it as a warning that maybe it is time to review your index strategy, at least for the current execution plan you are working with.

Note   There is a documented SQL Server startup option that can be used to disable the missing indexes feature, but I am not aware of collecting this data being a problem or anyone ever needing to use it.

The Database Engine Tuning Advisor

The Database Engine Tuning Advisor (DTA) has been available since SQL Server 2005. Its predecessor, the Index Tuning Wizard, was introduced with SQL Server 7.0 when its database engine included a rearchitected query processor.

The DTA works by using the cost estimated by the query optimizer. This DTA architecture decision makes a lot of sense as it is actually the query optimizer that makes the decision whether or not to use the index during the query optimization process.

Now, you may be asking how on earth can the query optimizer estimate the cost of an index which does not exist yet. The reality is that the query optimizer never directly uses the index data during query optimization but only its statistics. Statistics contain information about the data distribution of a column or columns. For the DTA, to create an index temporarily would be very expensive and time-consuming, and it would require disk space and other resources, something probably not desirable on production or even some other environments. But the DTA can temporarily create statistics for the candidate indexes. Those index statistics are created temporarily for the DTA session and are called hypothetical indexes. Although you can create such indexes using the undocumented `CREATE INDEX WITH STATISTICS_ONLY` statement, it does not make much sense as they are only useful during a DTA session. For example, although you can create those indexes yourself, they will be ignored by the query optimizer.

You can see if an index is a hypothetical index by looking at the `is_hypothetical` column of the `sys.indexes` catalog. Since these indexes are automatically deleted as soon as they are no longer needed during a DTA session, it is possible that some of them may survive if, for example, the DTA crashes before the index can be deleted. It is always safe to delete those hypothetical indexes if no DTA session is using them.

You can get more interesting details about how the DTA and the Index Tuning Wizard were originally architected by looking at the academic papers by Surajit Chaudhuri and Vivek Narasayya "An Efficient, Cost-Driven Index Selection Tool for Microsoft SQL Server" at `www.microsoft.com/en-us/research/publication/an-efficient-cost-driven-index-selection-tool-for-microsoft-sql-server/` and "Self-Tuning Database Systems: A Decade of Progress" at `www.microsoft.com/en-us/research/publication/self-tuning-database-systems-a-decade-of-progress/`.

The DTA can analyze workloads from several different sources: a file containing queries, a file or table containing a SQL trace, or, starting with SQL Server 2012, directly from the plan cache. Introduced with SQL Server Management Studio 16.2, you can also use the Query Store to select a workload to tune. As suggested in Chapter 6, the difference between using the Query Store and the plan cache is that the former contains a longer history of queries, while the plan cache only contains a subset of recently executed queries. We will try some of these workload sources in a moment.

In addition to recommending clustered, nonclustered, and filtered indexes and statistics along the way, the DTA also has the choice to recommend indexed views, partitioning, and columnstore indexes. Using the trace workload option requires to capture a trace using the Tuning template available with SQL Profiler or manually using the events defined on that template.

We tried a simple exercise earlier in this chapter relying on both our knowledge on how indexes work and the missing indexes feature and getting feedback from execution plans. Now let's feed the same queries to the DTA and see what recommendations we get. To make sure you start fresh, you can either delete the current tables on the test database or delete the entire database and create it again. Then run these statements to populate such tables:

```
SELECT *
INTO dbo.SalesOrderDetail
FROM AdventureWorks2017.Sales.SalesOrderDetail
GO
SELECT *
INTO dbo.SalesOrderHeader
FROM AdventureWorks2017.Sales.SalesOrderHeader
```

Create the file with the queries to tune. Copy the following queries and save them on a file in the file system:

```
SELECT * FROM SalesOrderHeader
WHERE SalesOrderID BETWEEN 50000 AND 70000
GO
SELECT * FROM SalesOrderDetail
WHERE ProductID = 898
GO
SELECT * FROM SalesOrderDetail
WHERE ProductID = 870
GO
SELECT SalesOrderID, SalesOrderDetailID, ProductID FROM SalesOrderDetail
WHERE ProductID = 870
GO
SELECT SalesOrderID, SalesOrderDetailID, ProductID, UnitPrice FROM
SalesOrderDetail
WHERE ProductID = 870
GO
SELECT SalesOrderID, SalesOrderDetailID, ProductID FROM SalesOrderDetail
ORDER BY ProductID
GO
```

```
SELECT ProductID, COUNT(*) FROM SalesOrderDetail
GROUP BY ProductID
GO
SELECT * FROM SalesOrderDetail d
JOIN SalesOrderHeader h
ON d.SalesOrderID = h.SalesOrderID
WHERE ProductID = 898
GO
SELECT * FROM SalesOrderDetail d
JOIN SalesOrderHeader h
ON d.SalesOrderID = h.SalesOrderID
WHERE ProductID = 870
GO
```

Open the DTA and create a new session. On the session General tab, provide a session name or use the default name provided. Specify the test database both as the database to tune and database for workload analysis. Select the file containing the queries to tune using the Workload and File choices. Selected choices are shown in Figure 9-9.

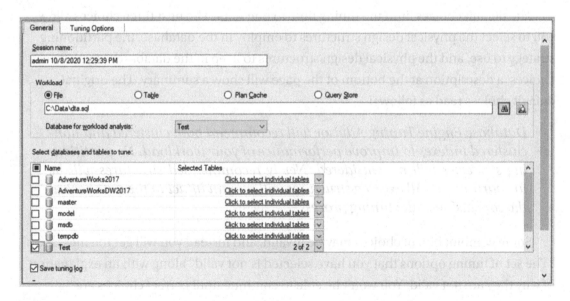

Figure 9-9. *DTA General tab*

Session Tuning Options has very important choices. For this exercise, we will use the original defaults, which are shown in Figure 9-10. I will explain the most important ones later.

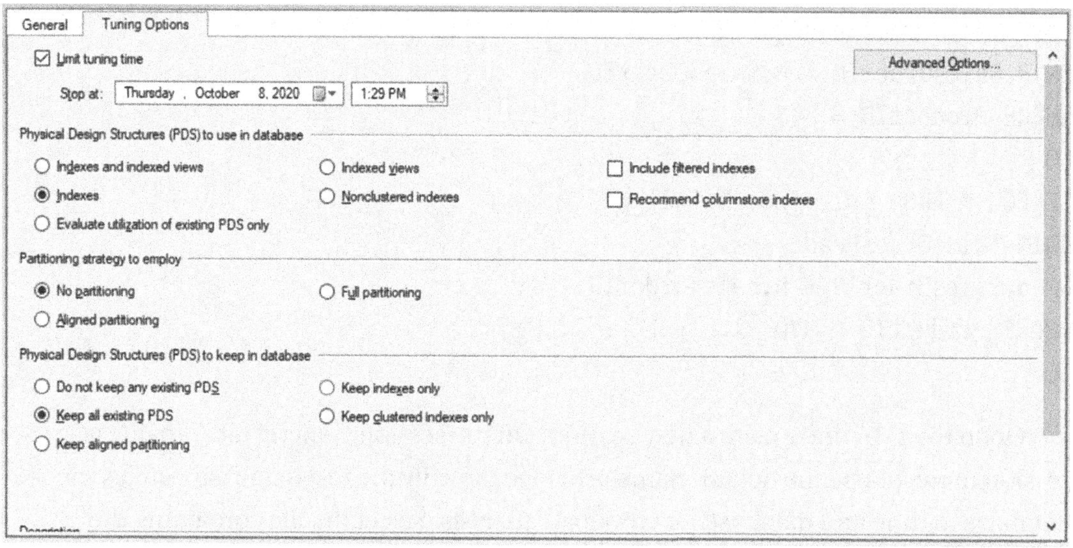

Figure 9-10. *DTA Tuning Options tab*

The default choices limit the tuning time to one hour. The next three choices allow you to select the physical design structures to employ in the database, the partitioning strategy to use, and the physical design structures to keep in the database. As you select choices, a description at the bottom of the page will show a summary. The original default choices read as follows:

> *Database Engine Tuning Advisor will recommend both clustered and non-clustered indexes to improve performance of your workload. No partitioning strategies will be considered. Newly recommended structures will be un-partitioned. All existing structures will remain intact in the database at the conclusion of the tuning process.*

Some combination of choices may be invalid, and instead you will get the message "The set of tuning options that you have selected is not valid" along with an explanation of why they are not valid. You won't be able to continue until correct choices are supplied.

Note   The DTA remembers the tuning options you select, and these will be considered the new default for any future session until changed again.

Click Start Analysis from the toolbar. Although the time scheduled is up to one hour, the analysis for this exercise should be completed in just a few minutes. The Progress tab will be displayed, or you can select it to see the progress of the tuning process. After the analysis is completed, you can look at the recommendations by using the Recommendations tab or take a look at the tuning summary and reports using the Reports tab. Part of the Recommendations tab, which is too large to fit in this book, is shown in Figure 9-11.

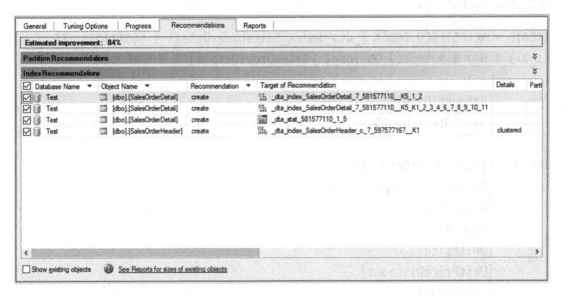

Figure 9-11. *DTA Recommendations tab*

The Recommendations tab shows information such as the recommended objects to be created or dropped along with the required code to perform such operation. The `Target of Recommendation` column shows the objects to be, in this case, created where statistics start with `_dta_stat`, indexes start with `_dta_index`, and views with `_dta_mv` prefixes. The last column of the Recommendations tab shows the `Definition` column, which is clickable and would show the code to create the recommended objects. This is the code for the four recommended objects in this exercise. (Code is shown as provided, so it does not follow the style and format as the rest of the book.)

```
CREATE STATISTICS [_dta_stat_565577053_1_5] ON [dbo].[SalesOrderDetail]
([SalesOrderID], [ProductID])

CREATE NONCLUSTERED INDEX [_dta_index_SalesOrderDetail_9_565577053__K5_1_2]
ON [dbo].[SalesOrderDetail]
(
        [ProductID] ASC
)
INCLUDE ([SalesOrderID],
        [SalesOrderDetailID]) WITH (SORT_IN_TEMPDB = OFF, DROP_EXISTING =
        OFF, ONLINE = OFF) ON [PRIMARY]

SET ANSI_PADDING ON

CREATE NONCLUSTERED INDEX [_dta_index_SalesOrderDetail_9_565577053__K5_
K1_2_3_4_6_7_8_9_10_11] ON [dbo].[SalesOrderDetail]
(
        [ProductID] ASC,
        [SalesOrderID] ASC
)
INCLUDE ([SalesOrderDetailID],
        [CarrierTrackingNumber],
        [OrderQty],
        [SpecialOfferID],
        [UnitPrice],
        [UnitPriceDiscount],
        [LineTotal],
        [rowguid],

[ModifiedDate]) WITH (SORT_IN_TEMPDB = OFF, DROP_EXISTING = OFF, ONLINE =
OFF) ON [PRIMARY]

CREATE CLUSTERED INDEX [_dta_index_SalesOrderHeader_c_9_581577110__K1] ON
[dbo].[SalesOrderHeader]
(
        [SalesOrderID] ASC
)WITH (SORT_IN_TEMPDB = OFF, DROP_EXISTING = OFF, ONLINE = OFF) ON
[PRIMARY]
```

344

Let's do a quick analysis of the recommendations. We see a slight variation in the recommendations compared to what we got in the earlier exercise with missing indexes mostly due to the fact that we knew the `SalesOrderHeader` and `SalesOrderDetail` are master-detail tables, and we decided to create clustered indexes on it up front. As we discussed, the missing indexes feature does not have the capability to suggest clustered indexes. This exercise showed that, by just using the defaults, we got recommendations on clustered indexes, nonclustered indexes, and statistics.

As expected, the recommended clustered index on the `SalesOrderHeader table` is the result of our supplied range query (the one with the WHERE SalesOrderID BETWEEN 50000 AND 70000 predicate). We also got recommended a couple of nonclustered indexes and a multicolumn statistics object. These recommendations could be a good choice, but it does not match our previous exercise as we manually created a clustered index on `SalesOrderDetail`, which was part of the original design for these master-detail tables. There is no recommended clustered index for `SalesOrderDetail` as we didn't supply any range query either. Obviously, the DTA cannot recommend on something it does not know, so it is important to feed them all the important queries. It is also interesting to note that the DTA recommended a multicolumn statistic on SalesOrderID and ProductID. Multicolumn statistics are never created automatically by SQL Server.

As you can see, even for this simple exercise, it may take you some time to analyze, evaluate, and verify the provided recommendations on a test environment, but this is something that we definitely have to do before deploying it to a production instance. I cannot emphasize enough that we don't want to implement these recommendations blindly.

The Reports tab shows a large amount of interesting information about the tuning process including a summary with the tuning information plus 15 different reports. All the information presented in the DTA is stored in the `msdb` database, so you may want to take a look at it if you have some special needs. The information is stored on the DTA_ tables and will be kept there until you delete the DTA session.

Finally, as covered earlier, two very useful DTA features introduced in the latest releases of the product are that you can now use the plan cache and the Query Store as the source for the workload to analyze, so you don't need to collect any data at all. This makes a lot of sense as it is very likely that your most expensive queries can be found there, as we showed you with the `sys.dm_exec_query_stats` DMV in Chapter 8 or the Query Store in Chapter 6.

Let's take a look at these features with the following exercise. To simulate a real workload in the plan cache, you can run our test queries in SQL Server Management Studio preceded by the DBCC FREEPROCCACHE statement, which is used to clear the existing plan cache, as shown next:

```
DBCC FREEPROCCACHE
GO
SELECT * FROM SalesOrderHeader
WHERE SalesOrderID BETWEEN 50000 AND 70000
GO
SELECT * FROM SalesOrderDetail
WHERE ProductID = 898
GO
SELECT * FROM SalesOrderDetail
WHERE ProductID = 870
GO
SELECT SalesOrderID, SalesOrderDetailID, ProductID FROM SalesOrderDetail
WHERE ProductID = 870
GO
SELECT SalesOrderID, SalesOrderDetailID, ProductID, UnitPrice FROM
SalesOrderDetail
WHERE ProductID = 870
GO
SELECT SalesOrderID, SalesOrderDetailID, ProductID FROM SalesOrderDetail
ORDER BY ProductID
GO
SELECT ProductID, COUNT(*) FROM SalesOrderDetail
GROUP BY ProductID
GO
SELECT * FROM SalesOrderDetail d
JOIN SalesOrderHeader h
ON d.SalesOrderID = h.SalesOrderID
WHERE ProductID = 898
GO
SELECT * FROM SalesOrderDetail d
JOIN SalesOrderHeader h
```

```
ON d.SalesOrderID = h.SalesOrderID
WHERE ProductID = 870
GO
```

After the queries are executed, most likely they will be in the plan cache, and then you can create a DTA session selecting Plan Cache as a workload. When you are tuning the plan cache, you are not explicitly submitting queries. Therefore, it is more important to look at the reports at the end of your tuning session (e.g., the Statement detail report) to learn about what kinds of queries were tuned. You can find these on the Reports tab as indicated earlier. In my case, I got the same recommendations as with the file exercise earlier, but just a reminder that when you are tuning the plan cache, you may have less control about which queries to tune.

Curious to see how the DTA decides which queries from the plan cache to tune? You can just take a look at the queries the DTA submits to the database engine by using either SQL trace or extended events. This is what I got on my test, which shows the DTA submits the following query to find out the 1000 most expensive queries based on duration:

```
select top 1000 isnull(st.objectid,0),
        isnull(st.dbid,0), avg(cp.execution_count), st.text
from sys.dm_exec_query_stats cp
cross apply sys.dm_exec_sql_text(cp.plan_handle) st
where cp.creation_time < N'2016-08-08 03:47:06.273' and st.dbid in (9)
group by st.text,st.objectid,st.dbid
order by sum(total_elapsed_time) desc
```

You can follow exactly the same exercise to instead use the Query Store; just make sure this component is enabled and configured. For details on how to do this, you can refer to Chapter 6.

Summary

This chapter covered how SQL Server uses indexes and why they are critical for the performance of your database applications. Indexes are of paramount importance for OLTP workloads as they allow you to quickly find one or a small number of rows in a potentially large table. Although using such indexes improves the performance of lookups by using expensive random IOs, their use is limited to a small number of rows. Indexes can also provide some other benefits, such as providing ordered data without having to perform expensive sort operations or covering a query, providing all the required columns without having to use the main table, eliminating the need for more database pages and logical reads.

The chapter also provided emphasis on using SQL Server tools to help create indexes such as the missing indexes feature and the more sophisticated Database Engine Tuning Advisor. Finally, maintenance considerations for indexes were explained as well. Just because indexes are useful does not mean you should have many as both the database engine and user maintenance operations are required to keep the indexes updated and defragmented.

CHAPTER 10

Intelligent Query Processing

This chapter provides an overview to intelligent query processing, a collection of features designed to improve the performance of your queries. Intelligent query processing was introduced with SQL Server 2017 with three original features under the umbrella of adaptive query processing. The term intelligent query processing, however, was not used until the SQL Server 2019 release, which included five more features. As an introductory chapter, I am not covering these features exhaustively so you can refer to the SQL Server documentation for more details.

The intelligent query processing features provide performance enhancements with no application changes needed or no effort required. These features are enabled by default using at least the database compatibility level of the SQL Server version where they were introduced. Figure 10-1, taken from the SQL Server documentation, shows all the current intelligent query processing features.

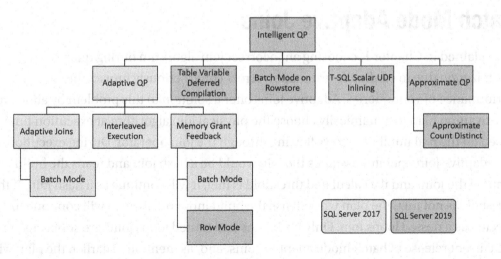

Figure 10-1. *Intelligent query processing features*

© Benjamin Nevarez 2021
B. Nevarez, *High Performance SQL Server*, https://doi.org/10.1007/978-1-4842-6491-1_10

As you can notice in Figure 10-1, intelligent query processing may also be grouped in families of features. For example, the adaptive query processing family includes features like adaptive joins, interleaved execution, and memory grant feedback. Approximate query processing includes for now just one feature, approximate count distinct. More intelligent query processing features are planned to be included in future versions of SQL Server.

Adaptive query processing includes a new generation of query processing features that enable the query optimizer to make runtime adjustments to execution plans and optimizer statistics. This allows the query optimizer to discover new information that can lead to better query performance. Adaptive query processing offers some improvements to the traditional query optimization process. In the normal query optimization process, if a bad cardinality estimation contributed to a suboptimal execution plan, no additional changes or optimizations were allowed to such plan, and it was used to execute the query anyway.

Figure 10-1 also shows the version when each of these features was introduced. This means that SQL Server 2017 only contains the features in blue, while SQL Server 2019 contains all the features listed. To enable any of these features, you would have to use the compatibility level of the version the feature was released, as seen in Figure 10-1, or a later compatibility level. For example, this could be compatibility level 140 for SQL Server 2017 and compatibility level 150 for SQL Server 2019. An example on how to set compatibility level for a database is next:

```
ALTER DATABASE AdventureWorks2017 SET COMPATIBILITY_LEVEL = 150
```

Batch Mode Adaptive Joins

As explained in Chapter 1, choosing an incorrect join algorithm during query optimization due to cardinality estimation errors could seriously impact the performance of your queries. Adaptive joins offer a solution to this problem by allowing an execution plan to dynamically choose the physical join algorithm at execution time based on the real number of rows flowing through the join operator. During execution, the adaptive join operator assumes the join would be a hash join and reads the build input of the join, and if a calculated threshold is met, it will continue as a hash join. If the threshold is not met, the plan will still use the build input but instead will continue to execute as a nested loops join. Only hash joins and nested loops joins are supported in the current release of batch mode adaptive joins, and, as mentioned earlier, the plan will initially assume the physical join is a hash join.

Batch mode adaptive joins, as the name of the feature suggests, are limited to queries using batch mode operators. In SQL Server 2017, this means it is basically limited to operations with columnstore indexes. In the latest release, however, it also includes operations using batch mode for rowstores, a new feature also discussed later in this chapter.

Finally, there might be cases when you may need to disable this or any of the other features covered in this chapter. This could be the case when you encounter a performance regression. To disable batch mode adaptive joins for the entire database level without changing the database compatibility level, you can use the following statement for SQL Server 2017:

```
ALTER DATABASE SCOPED CONFIGURATION
SET DISABLE_BATCH_MODE_ADAPTIVE_JOINS = ON
```

The following statement does the same for SQL Server 2019:

```
ALTER DATABASE SCOPED CONFIGURATION
SET BATCH_MODE_ADAPTIVE_JOINS = OFF
```

If you need to reenable this feature, you can reverse the values ON and OFF accordingly.

You can also apply the USE HINT clause if you need to disable batch mode adaptive joins for a specific query but keeping the feature enabled for the rest of the database queries as shown next:

```
SELECT * ...
OPTION (USE HINT('DISABLE_BATCH_MODE_ADAPTIVE_JOINS'))
```

Let us try an example of this feature by creating a columnstore index on the SalesOrderHeader table:

```
CREATE NONCLUSTERED COLUMNSTORE INDEX CIX_SalesOrderID
ON Sales.SalesOrderHeader(TaxAmt)
```

Next is our example query:

```
SELECT SUM(soh.TaxAmt)
FROM Sales.SalesOrderHeader soh
JOIN Sales.SalesOrderDetail sod ON soh.SalesOrderID = sod.SalesOrderID
```

Running the previous query in SQL Server 2019 will produce the plan in Figure 10-2. If you are using SQL Server 2017, you will need to use the Live Query Statistics feature to see the same information.

Note: The Live Query Statistics feature was introduced with SQL Server 2016 and allows you to visualize the number of rows processed on each executed branch.

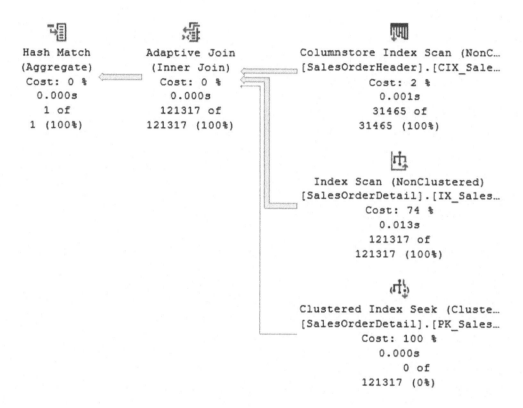

Figure 10-2. *Adaptive join query plan*

The most important part of the plan in Figure 10-2 is the new adaptive join operator which, different than a regular physical join, has three inputs. The first or top branch is the build input, in this case a columnstore index scan operator. The second or middle branch is the input that would be used if the hash join is selected. As you can notice, the plan shows that 121317 of 121317 rows were processed, meaning the branch was selected. The third and bottom branch is the input that would be used if the nested loops join is selected. Again, you could see in Figure 10-2, since 0 of 121317 rows were processed, the branch was not selected.

You can also inspect the value defining the threshold the plan uses to make this decision. If you take a look at the properties of the adaptive join operator, the Adaptive Threshold Rows property will show the value 1398.57. Any number of rows equal or larger than this threshold will make the plan to continue as a hash join. A smaller number will switch the join to a nested loops join.

Finally, drop the created index:

```
DROP INDEX Sales.SalesOrderHeader.CIX_SalesOrderID
```

Memory Grant Feedback

SQL Server uses the buffer cache pages to keep the data used by your queries. Some other operations such as sorting and hashing, however, may require significant amounts of additional memory but cannot use the plan cache and instead require a memory grant. A memory grant is required to store the rows to be sorted or to store the hash tables used by the hash join and hash aggregate operators, and it is only required for the duration of the query. In some very rare cases, parallel plans with multiple range scans may also require a memory grant.

The amount of memory required by a query is estimated by the query optimizer when the plan is generated. Although this process usually correctly estimates the required memory, in some cases, some of the following performance problems may occur:

a) A plan underestimating the required memory could lead to additional query processing or spilling data to disk.

b) Plans overestimating the required memory may waste valuable resources and may lead to other queries having to wait for their own requested memory.

The memory grant feedback was designed to help with these situations by recalculating the memory required by a query and updating it in the cached query plan. The memory grant feedback may get information from tempdb spill events or from the actual amount of memory really utilized. Although this improved estimate may not help in the first execution of the query, it can be used to improve the performance on following executions. The memory grant feedback is in fact a learning process, and, as the name suggests, it actually gets feedback from real runtime information. The memory grant feedback comes in two flavors, batch mode, which was introduced with SQL Server 2017, and row mode, which was introduced with SQL Server 2019.

The memory grant feedback will be automatically disabled for parameter-sensitive queries. As explained in Chapter 1, in some cases when we have skewed or uneven data distribution, reusing a plan created with one parameter may not be adequate for the same query with a different parameter. It may take several repeated runs for this feature to be disabled in the case of parameter-sensitive queries as it may take time to find out that the query has a variation on memory requirements. You can monitor when the feature was disabled by monitoring the memory_grant_feedback_loop_disabled extended event.

Since the memory grant feedback information is stored in the execution plan, this posts a few limitations. For example, a query using OPTION (RECOMPILE) or RECOMPILE at the procedure level would never cache a plan. A plan can also be removed from the plan cache and by doing that also losing its feedback information. In these cases, the memory grant feedback feature cannot be used. For more details about recompilation and the plan cache, please refer to Chapter 1.

As with all the features covered in this chapter, you can disable them at the database level if you encounter any performance problem. Since you may still want to keep some other benefits of using a particular database compatibility level, you can use the ALTER DATABASE SCOPED CONFIGURATION statement to enable a particular database configuration setting at the individual database level. To disable the memory grant feedback feature in SQL Server 2017, you can use the following statement within the context of the applicable database:

```
ALTER DATABASE SCOPED CONFIGURATION
SET DISABLE_BATCH_MODE_MEMORY_GRANT_FEEDBACK = ON
```

The following statement does the same for SQL Server 2019:

```
ALTER DATABASE SCOPED CONFIGURATION
SET BATCH_MODE_MEMORY_GRANT_FEEDBACK = OFF
```

You can enable back by switching the values ON and OFF on the previous statements.

If you only need to disable this feature at the query level, instead of a database level, you can use the USE HINT as shown next:

```
SELECT * ....
OPTION (USE HINT('DISABLE_BATCH_MODE_MEMORY_GRANT_FEEDBACK'))
```

Row mode memory grant feedback works in a similar way to the batch mode version, but it is only available with SQL Server 2019. To enable this feature, you would need to set the compatibility level to 150. If you need to disable it while still keeping the database compatibility level, you can use the following statement:

```
ALTER DATABASE SCOPED CONFIGURATION
SET ROW_MODE_MEMORY_GRANT_FEEDBACK = OFF
```

You can just change to an ON value if you want to enable this feature back. Same as with batch memory grant feedback, you can disable this feature just at a query level. This can be useful if you are having a performance regression on a single query.

```
SELECT * ....
OPTION (USE HINT('DISABLE_BATCH_MODE_MEMORY_GRANT_FEEDBACK'))
```

Interleaved Execution

As I mentioned earlier in this chapter, traditional query optimization produces an execution plan, and independently if the cardinality estimates happen to be accurate or not, the plan is executed anyway. Usually, we only know about bad cardinality estimations after query execution, especially after a bad query performance problem. Interleaved execution is a new feature designed to help with some of those bad cardinality estimation problems.

A historic problem with multistatement table-valued functions is that traditionally they have a fixed cardinality estimate. This guesstimate is 100 rows for SQL Server 2014 and later, and just 1 row for any earlier versions. This fixed cardinality estimate can lead to the query optimizer making bad decisions when the real number of rows to be processed is higher than the mentioned estimated guess. In these cases, a nonoptimal execution plan may be created leading to query performance problems.

Starting with SQL Server 2017, interleaved execution enables query plans to adapt based on a revised cardinality estimation. In this process, SQL Server can optimize part of a query, pause the current query optimization, execute the partial plan, capture accurate cardinality estimates, and resume the optimization for the remaining parts of the query. Capturing accurate cardinality information helps the query optimizer to make better decisions for the remaining part of the query. The benefits would be bigger depending on how wide the difference between the actual and estimated number of rows is and how many downstream operations in the plan consume those rows. For the current release, interleaved execution works only with multistatement table-valued functions, but more constructs are planned to be added in the future.

You could use the interleaved_exec_status extended event to find out if interleaved execution is occurring. In the same way, you can use the interleaved_exec_stats_update extended event to verify if cardinality estimates were updated by the interleaved execution feature.

Same as the other features in this chapter, any new feature in any complex piece of software like a database engine may cause a regression for some queries. Because of this, you may decide to disable this feature at the database level and probably turn on only at the query level. To disable interleaved execution at the database level, use the following statement for SQL Server 2017:

```
ALTER DATABASE SCOPED CONFIGURATION
SET DISABLE_INTERLEAVED_EXECUTION_TVF = ON
```

If you are in the latest version of SQL Server, you can use

```
ALTER DATABASE SCOPED CONFIGURATION
SET INTERLEAVED_EXECUTION_TVF = ON
```

To disable at the query level, use the following hint:

```
SELECT * ...
OPTION (USE HINT('DISABLE_INTERLEAVED_EXECUTION_TVF'))
```

Finally, let us see an example of how interleaved execution works. Create the following function:

```
CREATE FUNCTION dbo.ufn_SalesOrderDetail(@year int)
RETURNS @SalesOrderDetail TABLE
(
 [SalesOrderID] [int] NOT NULL,
 [SalesOrderDetailID] [int] NOT NULL,
 [CarrierTrackingNumber] [nvarchar](25) NULL,
 [OrderQty] [smallint] NOT NULL,
 [ProductID] [int] NOT NULL,
 [SpecialOfferID] [int] NOT NULL,
 [UnitPrice] [money] NOT NULL,
 [UnitPriceDiscount] [money] NOT NULL,
 [LineTotal] money NOT NULL,
 [rowguid] [uniqueidentifier] ROWGUIDCOL NOT NULL,
 [ModifiedDate] [datetime] NOT NULL)
AS
BEGIN
 INSERT @SalesOrderDetail
 SELECT * FROM Sales.SalesOrderDetail
 WHERE YEAR(ModifiedDate) = @year
 RETURN
END
```

First, I would like to show you a plan before interleaved execution was introduced. As mentioned, there are several ways to disable this feature such as changing the database compatibility level, using a database scoped configuration option, or using a query hint. Let us try the last choice.

```
SELECT * FROM dbo.ufn_SalesOrderDetail(2014) o
JOIN Sales.SalesOrderHeader h ON o.SalesOrderID = h.SalesOrderID
OPTION (USE HINT('DISABLE_INTERLEAVED_EXECUTION_TVF'))
```

This query would create the plan in Figure 10-3.

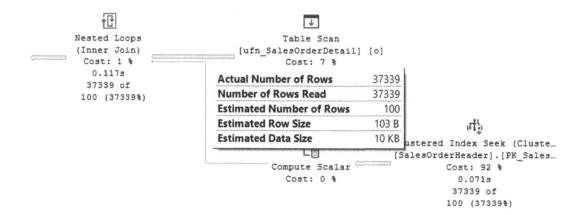

Figure 10-3. *Plan without interleaved execution*

You may notice that the expected estimated number of rows of 100 makes the query optimizer believe a nested loops join may be the most appropriate physical operator for such low number of rows. Now run the query without any hint:

```
SELECT * FROM dbo.ufn_SalesOrderDetail(2014) o
JOIN Sales.SalesOrderHeader h ON o.SalesOrderID = h.SalesOrderID
```

This time, we get the plan in Figure 10-4.

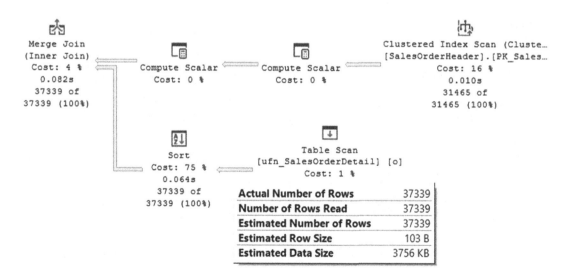

Figure 10-4. *Plan with interleaved execution*

You can now see that the estimated number of rows is the same as the actual number of rows, and the query optimizer is making a different decision regarding the plan. This time, the plan uses both sort and merge join operations to process the same data which may be more appropriate for such a large number of rows.

Batch Mode on Rowstore

The batch mode on rowstores feature was introduced with SQL Server 2019. Batch mode for columnstore has been available several versions back, starting when columnstore indexes were introduced back in SQL Server 2012. As covered in Chapter 7, batch mode processing is a vector-based execution method designed to improve the query performance by processing multiple rows at a time instead of using the traditional operators that process a row at a time.

The query optimizer can use batch mode on rowstores on bitmap filters, on-disk heaps, and b-tree indexes, which basically means on-disk clustered and nonclustered indexes. The feature also supports all existing batch mode–enabled operators available for columnstores. Batch mode on rowstores can help in cases when you do not want to create a columnstore index or one cannot be created because you also need a feature not supported by columnstore indexes. A current limitation of batch mode on rowstores, however, is that it is not available for In-Memory OLTP tables or queries that fetch or filter a large object (LOB) column.

Even when batch mode is available for rowstores, this feature is still only beneficial for queries that process a larger number of rows, for example, analytical or business intelligence queries. As suggested in Chapter 1, the decision to use batch mode is, like anything else in the query optimizer, a cost-based decision. This cost estimation will show if using batch rowstore is beneficial for the performance of the query. Some of the minimal requirements by the optimizer to ever consider batch mode are the size of the tables, the operators used, and the estimated cardinalities in the input query. You can validate if your plan is using batch mode by checking the Actual Execution Mode property at the operator level. You can find more detail about batch mode by looking at the "Columnstore Indexes" section in Chapter 7.

To use batch mode on rowstore, you only need to change the compatibility mode to SQL Server 2019 or 150. To disable batch mode on rowstore at the database level without changing the database compatibility level, you can use

```
ALTER DATABASE SCOPED CONFIGURATION
SET BATCH_MODE_ON_ROWSTORE = OFF
```

To reenable this feature, just change the value to ON.

To disable this feature at a query level, assuming you found a performance regression, you can try the USE HINT as shown next:

```
SELECT * ...
OPTION(USE HINT('DISALLOW_BATCH_MODE'))
```

There is also a hint to enable batch mode when it is disabled via a database scoped configuration. In this case, you can try

```
SELECT *
OPTION(USE HINT('ALLOW_BATCH_MODE'))
```

Table Variable Deferred Compilation

Probably the main reason table variables are not extensively used is that, similar to multistatement table-valued functions mentioned earlier, SQL Server does not provide optimizer statistics that can be used to generate an optimal execution plan. As mentioned earlier, table variables and multistatement table-valued user-defined functions have no support for statistics, so the query optimizer will use a fixed estimate of 100 rows for the recent versions of SQL Server or just 1 row for versions before SQL Server 2014.

Starting with SQL Server 2019, table variables will behave in a similar way as the interleaved execution feature mentioned earlier, in which SQL Server will execute the table variable code, and so it will know the real cardinality estimate or real number of rows. Deferred compilation will then use such accurate estimate to produce a better performing execution plan. Finally, keep in mind that although this behavior may look now very similar to temporary tables, even for SQL Server 2019, table variables still do not have statistics.

As before, if you need to disable at the database level, you can use

```
ALTER DATABASE SCOPED CONFIGURATION
SET DEFERRED_COMPILATION_TV = OFF
```

You can use ON to revert back. Similar to our earlier cases, you can use the USE HINT as in

```
SELECT * ...
OPTION (USE HINT('DISABLE_DEFERRED_COMPILATION_TV'))
```

Scalar UDF Inlining

A scalar user-defined function (UDF) is a UDF which returns a single data value. Scalar UDFs have traditionally been a performance problem for SQL Server as they do not follow the set-oriented model that SQL Server uses. Instead, they follow a less effective iterative mode. For example, when a UDF is used in a query with multiple rows, the code is processed one row at a time. Costing, as you saw in Chapter 1, which is used to cost operators and make a better decision for building an execution plan, is not available on UDFs. Intra-query parallelism is not available on queries using UDFs either.

Scalar UDF inlining, a new feature with SQL Server 2019, automatically transforms scalar UDFs into relational expressions embedding them in the SQL Server query. This greatly improves the performance of queries using scalar UDFs as they now use a set-oriented model instead of using the traditional iterative model.

Similar to the previous features discussed in this chapter, you can use the following statement if you need to disable scalar UDF inlining at the database level:

```
ALTER DATABASE SCOPED CONFIGURATION
SET TSQL_SCALAR_UDF_INLINING = OFF
```

In the same way, you can reenable the feature using the ON value.

The hint needed to disable this feature at the query level is shown next:

```
SELECT * ...
OPTION (USE HINT('DISABLE_TSQL_SCALAR_UDF_INLINING'))
```

Approximate Count Distinct

Different than all of the intelligent processing features covered in this chapter, APPROX_COUNT_DISTINCT is a new SQL Server function, and as such it does not require a database compatibility level mode to use it. The APPROX_COUNT_DISTINCT function is an alternative to using COUNT(DISTINCT) and returns the approximate number of unique non-null values in a group by evaluating an expression for each row in a group. This function is designed to provide aggregations across very large amounts of data where responsiveness is more critical than absolute precision.

The APPROX_COUNT_DISTINCT function is based on the HyperLogLog algorithm whose purpose is to calculate an approximation of the number of distinct elements in a set, and its SQL Server implementation guarantees up to a 2% error rate within a 97% probability. You can find more details about this algorithm by looking at `https://en.wikipedia.org/wiki/HyperLogLog`.

Let me show you an example using the AdventureWorksDW2017 database. Keep in mind that since we do not have a very large table, we may not be able to notice any performance difference. Run the following statements while requesting actual execution plans:

```
SELECT COUNT(DISTINCT(UnitCost))
FROM FactProductInventory
SELECT APPROX_COUNT_DISTINCT(UnitCost)
FROM FactProductInventory
```

You could see that the generated execution plans are very different. As expected while manipulating large amounts of data, the COUNT(DISTINCT) query contains a hash aggregation operator, as you can see in Figure 10-5. The plan for the APPROX_COUNT_DISTINCT function, which you can see in Figure 10-6, does not include a hash aggregation operator and, as such, requires less memory, and there is no need for a memory grant. The results on my test system are 89,161 and 92,430, in which the first value is the exact number of distinct values and the latter is the approximation.

Figure 10-5. *Partial plan for COUNT(DISTINCT)*

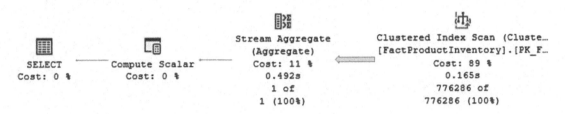

Figure 10-6. *Plan for APPROX_COUNT_DISTINCT*

Finally, as suggested earlier, there is no need to enable or disable this feature. You could just decide if COUNT(DISTINCT) or APPROX_COUNT_DISTINCT is better for your application needs.

Summary

SQL Server 2017 introduced several query processing features under the umbrella of adaptive query processing. The SQL Server 2019 release expanded the number of features giving them a new name, intelligent query processing. Intelligent query processing features provide performance enhancements with no application changes needed and no effort or very minimal effort. Microsoft has said more intelligent processing enhancements will be released in future versions of the product.

This was an introductory chapter on intelligent query processing, so covering these features in detail is outside the scope of this book. For more details, you may want to refer to the SQL Server documentation.

CHAPTER 11

SQL Server Storage

This chapter covers storage from the SQL Server point of view, and although other factors such as availability and recoverability play a very important role in selecting and configuring storage, we focus mostly on performance. Disk is traditionally the slowest component in a database system, so tuning storage for performance is essential and usually comes in two high-level areas: directly tuning the storage and tuning the components to make efficient use of the storage. The first area refers to tuning and configuring the storage hardware itself, while the second one relates to tuning the other components of the system to make optimal use of the storage and includes items such as proper SQL Server configuration and creating the right indexes.

All the topics presented so far in this book mostly involve the SQL Server database professional, including such roles as database developer, database administrator, and database architect. But implementing a high performance application in production always involves several other roles and sometimes teams in a corporation. Nothing is truer as it relates to storage.

I still remember the old days when I used to sit with my Windows administrator and configure the drives for our servers using RAID 1, 5, or 10. As storage—especially enterprise-level storage—becomes more and more sophisticated, tuning and administering it will usually fall outside the scope of the SQL Server database professional and very likely even onto a different team.

Whatever the separation of responsibilities in a corporation is, storage does not have to be a black box for the SQL Server professional. As a result, it is very important to understand how the storage works and properly communicate to the storage team the database requirements. Performance is not only the initial configuration but also continuous monitoring and troubleshooting, so this should also be an iterative process. In fact, the same is true as it relates to good communication with the teams that own the remaining parts of the application whether it is the operating system, application servers, web servers, or the hardware itself.

© Benjamin Nevarez 2021
B. Nevarez, *High Performance SQL Server*, https://doi.org/10.1007/978-1-4842-6491-1_11

In hardware trends, as we noticed in Chapter 7, relational databases were originally architected based on the hardware available in the 1970s. Memory size was limited, and relational databases were built around the fact that they were not able to fit in memory, reading data from disk only as needed and creating buffer managers to keep the most used data in memory. Although processor and memory speeds, along with memory and disk sizes, have increased dramatically, the disk access speed has not kept up at the same rate, making a big gap between the disk access time and processor and memory processing times. Limited by moving mechanical components, disk has been traditionally the slowest component in a database system (or as the late Jim Gray sometimes described it, "disk is the new tape").

New trends like larger amounts of data, high-availability requirements, and virtualization put additional requirements on a database system. I still remember the days when a few dozen GB size was considered a large database, but database sizes now are measured in terabytes, and even sizes in petabytes are common. Data is now also required to be available 24/7 (ironically, I originally wrote this during a major Delta Air Lines outage that stopped their business operations for days). Data availability or, even worse, data loss can seriously impact a business. Virtualization and cloud services are another important trend as more and more high performance and mission-critical applications are being migrated to services like Amazon AWS or Microsoft Azure.

Fortunately, there are also new technologies to help with these new trends and new demanding requirements. As the cost of flash-based storage continues to decline, flash drives are expected to gradually replace spindle-based magnetic disk in data centers, becoming the de facto enterprise standard for primary storage. But since relational database engines still use the same architecture defined back in the 1970s, it is being suggested that new query processing algorithms should be developed to take advantage of this faster storage. In addition, as many databases can now fit in memory, new technologies such as in-memory databases are being developed and implemented. SQL Server incorporates those technologies, and they are covered in Chapter 7.

As hinted earlier, the second part on optimizing storage is within your database. Many times, what seems to be a storage problem or an issue with storage struggling to keep up with the required performance can be fixed within SQL Server. We cover many of those techniques in the rest of the book. For example, when storage is not able to keep up with your workload, the problem could be fixed by creating the right indexes, by properly configuring SQL Server and tempdb, or by taking benefit of new in-memory technologies such as In-Memory OLTP or columnstore indexes. With flash drives replacing spindle-based magnetic disks, a myth quickly arose suggesting that optimizing database and code was no longer important. Nothing could be farther from the truth.

Finally, when selecting and reviewing a storage solution, in addition to performance, some other important factors such as reliability and availability are considered as well. Redundancy choices such as RAID (redundant array of independent disks) or high-availability and disaster recovery solutions, such as Windows failover clustering or SQL Server Always On availability groups, are usually implemented in mission-critical applications.

Storage Types

Although it is outside the scope of this book to cover details about the storage commonly used in SQL Server, I would say it usually falls in the following main categories, any of which could use traditional spindle-based magnetic disks, flash disk storage, or hybrid, except where otherwise specified:

   a. Storage area networks (SAN): A dedicated network that provides access to consolidated storage. The most common storage for mission-critical applications.

   b. Peripheral Component Interconnect Express (PCIe)–based solid-state drives (SSDs): This is flash disk storage connected throughout this bus standard.

   c. Internal storage: Traditional storage on server bays using drives such as Serial Attached SCSI (SAS) or Serial AT Attachment (SATA).

   d. Direct-attached storage (DAS): Storage directly attached to a server as opposed to internal storage or storage accessed over the network. DAS could be SAS/SATA drives usually connected to a server using a host bus adapter (HBA).

   e. File shares/servers: File servers that can be used for SQL Server databases such as Server Message Block (SMB) file server. An SMB file share can also be used for Windows failover clustering installations. For more details, see `https://msdn.microsoft.com/en-us/library/hh759341.aspx`.

Although I have used these types of storage for SQL Server implementations, most of the mission-critical or high performance applications I have seen in my career use some kind of SAN storage. SAN storage comes in a lot of varieties ranging from the traditional spindle-based magnetic disk to all-flash disk storage or hybrid. SAN storage solutions also provide additional features similar to those available in SQL Server such as snapshots, replication, and compression, although in some cases those features can complement those available on SQL Server. In other cases, they may perform the same functions and compete for resources when enabled, so be sure to review with your storage administrator what those choices are and which ones may be beneficial to implement. Once again, working closely with your storage administrator is essential to define the database and storage architecture of your application.

There are some other advantages of using SAN storage such as providing the shared storage required for traditional failover clustering. A SAN allows the nodes of a SQL Server cluster to access the same storage volume and move the storage between nodes. Only one node can access the volume at a time though.

Finally, some other high-availability or disaster recovery solutions such as Always On availability groups, whose popularity increases every day, or the currently deprecated database mirroring technology can work with any kind of storage. Both availability groups and database mirroring work in a similar way by replicating the data at the database level in either a synchronous or an asynchronous way. Database mirroring only supports a single secondary, while availability groups can have multiple replicas or secondaries (but only in SQL Server Enterprise edition). A flavor of availability groups, called basic availability groups, can be used on SQL Server Standard edition to implement failover environment solution for a single database.

Flash-Based Storage

As the cost of flash-based storage continues to decline, flash drives are expected to gradually replace spindle-based magnetic disks in data centers, becoming the de facto enterprise standard for primary storage. Flash storage has been available for a while. But as has happened with other popular technologies, widespread adoption may be initially slow as sometimes the technology is either initially prohibitively expensive or it may take time to mature.

Spindle-based electromechanical magnetic disks contain spinning disks and movable read and write heads, compared to flash, which is a nonvolatile semiconductor technology and has no moving mechanical components. Flash storage is many times faster than magnetic disks for random I/O reads, although the performance improvement is more modest for sequential reads and especially for writes. Their performance and price comparisons depend on the kind of flash drive, which can range from consumer levels like TLC (triple-level cell) or MLC (consumer multilevel cell) to enterprise storage such as EMLC (enterprise multilevel cell) or SLC (single-level cell), although submillisecond latency has been reported in the best cases.

Because of these performance characteristics, flash can be an excellent choice for applications with a high number of random I/O read requests such as the ones using OLTP databases. Data warehouse workloads with large sequential reads will have less benefit. Another limitation of flash is that it has a finite number of possible writes, called program-erase cycles, which may introduce errors and failures impacting the storage life. Once again, the probability of error depends on the type of flash, decreasing from consumer to enterprise levels.

Finally, when flash drives originally became available, their speed helped to start some myths indicating that query optimization would no longer be required when using this storage (e.g., no need to worry about index tuning, fragmentation, or other optimizations). I even remember hearing these statements directly from vendors. The reality is that even when flash improves the disk performance access, especially for random I/Os, all those optimizations and configurations are still required and highly recommended. This is especially true if you have a bottleneck somewhere else, as the flash drive performance will not shine until such a bottleneck is fixed.

Database Configuration

Understanding your I/O workload and how your database uses disk is essential for an efficient design focused on performance. Be sure to do this research and provide the required information to the storage administrator so disk can be configured accordingly. Sometimes, an I/O workload may be hard to estimate in advance. It is easy to say that an OLTP database will use only random disk I/Os, but I have yet to see a pure OLTP workload. It is very common for OLTP systems to have some reporting queries, queries running aggregations, or even business-related batch processing jobs. In addition, OLTP systems also require database maintenance activities such as database backups, database integrity checks, index rebuild and reorganization, statistics update, and so on, which require sequential disk I/O reads. On the other hand, reporting workloads and Data Warehouse databases will have mostly sequential I/Os, with mostly reads, in addition to periodic ETL jobs updating data in the database. Finally, as covered in Chapter 7, with the introduction of updatable nonclustered columnstore indexes, it is now possible to have analytical workloads on OLTP systems as well, creating a workload with random and sequential I/Os combined.

Database Files

Database file placement is still important. Traditionally, a best practice has been to separate data, transaction log and `tempdb` files, into different volumes. Although in some cases SAN storage abstraction might make this not strictly necessary, it is still a good practice as separation also helps with maintenance and administration purposes. Like `tempdb`, as covered in Chapter 4, having multiple data files for a database can benefit performance and manageability instead of having a single huge data file for the entire database, especially when you can separate them into different drives to avoid contention. You can research I/O usage information per file if needed, using the `sys.dm_io_virtual_file_stats` DMV, as covered in Chapter 8. As with `tempdb`, data files should be initially configured of equal size to take benefit of the proportional fill algorithm.

The vast majority of the times, only one transaction log file is required per database, being perhaps the only possible exception when a second file is needed being when a volume becomes unexpectedly full and you need to use space from a different volume. A transaction log file benefits from sequential reads so, if you have multiple databases, you may consider separating each database transaction log file on their own volume. Having transaction log files for multiple databases on the same volume may change the sequential to random reads as activity may be happening for all databases simultaneously.

Correctly sizing your database files and configuring autogrowth settings are also important, as usually SQL Server defaults are not appropriate. The values to use would depend on your database size and needs, and, as mentioned earlier in this book, it is recommended to assign the maximum file size depending on the allocated drives in order to avoid expensive autogrowth operations and possible fragmentation. Remember that instant file initialization can help on data files but is not yet available on transaction log files. Researching the maximum size the transaction log file can grow and having that size is a best practice for performance. Don't ever shrink this file unless you are sure it is not going to grow again. Growing file size operations are very slow, especially in transaction log files, and may also introduce a specific kind of fragmentation, as covered later in this section.

As an example, if you assigned a 512 GB volume to a database including size for future growth, allocate all the possible disk space from the beginning, perhaps just leaving enough space as required by your disk-monitoring tools (so you do not get those disk full or disk almost full notifications). Obviously, this becomes a little bit more complicated if more than one database shares the volume so keeping database growth trends and statistics can help you make those decisions.

Setting the maximum size on database files, even with a large percentage of empty space, does not affect the size of your backups, although it will impact copies of the database used for availability groups, log shipping, or database mirroring configurations. Copies of the databases to other environments such as QA and development will be impacted as well, although they can be shrunk upon restore to save some disk space.

Fragmentation

Fragmentation is a problem that can occur in clustered and nonclustered indexes and heaps and may hurt performance for workloads doing scans or sequential I/Os. Operations performing random disk I/Os are not impacted by fragmentation. Fragmentation may also limit the efficiency of read-ahead operations as it relies on contiguous pages on disk. The read-ahead mechanism used by SQL Server anticipates the data pages needed to fulfill a query request by bringing the pages into the buffer pool before they are actually used by the query. A read-ahead operation can read up to 64 contiguous pages or 512 KB. Monitoring and dealing with fragmentation is also important on flash-based storage.

Fragmentation can be fixed by periodically running index reorganize and index rebuild maintenance jobs and configuring indexes with an appropriate fill factor. These topics are covered in Chapter 9. Fragmentation is also possible on transaction log files, and it is covered next.

Virtual Log Files

The SQL Server transaction log file is divided into virtual log files (VLFs), and it can become internally fragmented when a large number of these VLFs are created. Such file fragmentation can impact the performance of the transaction log operations and increase the database recovery time. An adequate number of VLFs would depend on the size of the transaction log file, and although there is no specific recommended value, it definitely should not be in the hundreds or thousands.

When a transaction log file is originally created, it will have an initial number of VLFs, which is usually adequate. But every time an autogrowth operation occurs or the size is manually expanded, SQL Server adds several VLFs, usually 4, 8, or 16, depending on the added size. Performing multiple grow operations over time can create hundreds or thousands of VLFs. To display the number of VLFs in your transaction log file, run the following statement, which will return a row for every VLF file:

DBCC LOGINFO

A typical summarized output is next.

RecoveryUnitId	FileId	FileSize	StartOffset	FSeqNo	Status	Parity	CreateLSN
0	2	458752	8192	70	2	64	0
0	2	458752	466944	71	2	64	0
0	2	458752	925696	72	2	128	0
0	2	712704	1384448	73	2	128	0

Note   For more details about the algorithm used to determine how many VLFs are added for create, grow, and autogrowth operations, you can refer to the following article: www.sqlskills.com/blogs/paul/important-change-vlf-creation-algorithm-sql-server-2014/.

Compression

Compression is another SQL Server feature to consider to improve I/O performance and storage usage although at the price of additional CPU resources. SQL Server offers several types of compression. Row and page compression for regular tables was introduced with SQL Server 2008, and it is a feature that has to be explicitly enabled at several levels: heap, clustered index, nonclustered index, and indexed views. It can also be configured at the partition level when partitioning is being used. On the other hand, columnstore indexes always use compression, and this feature is not user configurable. Finally, compression can also be enabled on database backups.

SAN and some other storage solutions may offer compression capabilities as well, so coordinate with your storage administrator to understand which choices are available before making a decision, especially since enabling compression in both places may possibly use additional resources probably without additional benefits.

Finally, delayed durability, a feature introduced with SQL Server 2014, may help you in some very specific scenarios where you want to improve the performance of the transaction by delaying log buffer flushes to disk but with the very important caveat that you may lose transactions in case of a system failure. Even when data loss is only possible in a system failure, this may not be acceptable, especially when there are a large number of applications expecting guaranteed durable transactions. Delayed durability can be specified by an administrator at the database level using the ALTER DATABASE SET DELAYED_DURABILITY statement or within Hekaton natively compiled stored procedures using the DELAYED_DURABILITY clause. The ALTER DATABASE SET DELAYED_ DURABILITY statement also allows delayed durability to be enabled at the transaction level, in which case it must be explicitly declared at every required transaction. For more details, please refer to the SQL Server documentation.

Metrics and Performance

In this section, I'll show you the main metrics used to measure storage performance and which tools you can use to see such information, whether it is from Windows or SQL Server. The main metrics are as follows:

    a.   IOPS (input/output operations per second): It is the number of input/output operations per second.

b. Latency: Also called response time, it is the time required to complete a single input/output operation. Latency is usually measured in milliseconds, with flash-based storage now achieving single input/output operations in a fraction of a millisecond.

c. Throughput or bandwidth: It is the amount of data transferred in some specific time, for example, megabytes per second.

These three metrics—IOPS, latency, and bandwidth—are closely related. Since latency is the time to complete a single input/output operation, by using latency, we could estimate how many operations could be completed per second (IOPS). For example, if you have a latency of 1 millisecond, you can roughly process 1000 operations per second, or 1000 IOPS. In the same way, the throughput can show the amount of data transferred per second.

In Chapter 8, we covered how the `LogicalDisk` and `PhysicalDisk` objects provide a large variety of counters that can help you to monitor I/O operations in your system. `LogicalDisk` and `PhysicalDisk` provide the same counters, but they just provide information from either the logical or physical disk perspective. By looking at the most useful performance counters, you could easily correlate which ones measure IOPS, latency, or bandwidth.

The following performance counters measure latency:

Avg. Disk sec/Transfer: Avg. Disk sec/Transfer is the time, in seconds, of the average disk transfer.

Avg. Disk sec/Read: Avg. Disk sec/Read is the average time, in seconds, of a read of data from the disk.

Avg. Disk sec/Write: Avg. Disk sec/Write is the average time, in seconds, of a write of data to the disk.

The following performance counters measure throughput:

Disk Bytes/sec: Disk Bytes/sec is the rate at which bytes are transferred to or from the disk during write or read operations.

Disk Read Bytes/sec: Disk Read Bytes/sec is the rate at which bytes are transferred from the disk during read operations.

Disk Write Bytes/sec: Disk Write Bytes/sec is the rate at which bytes are transferred to the disk during write operations.

The following performance counters measure IOPS:

> Disk Transfers/sec: Disk Transfers/sec is the rate of read and write operations on the disk.

> Disk Reads/sec: Disk Reads/sec is the rate of read operations on the disk.

> Disk Writes/sec: Disk Writes/sec is the rate of write operations on the disk.

Finally, an important performance counter, Avg. Disk Queue Length, shows the average number of both read and write requests that are queued for a particular disk.

There are several tools that you can use to measure the storage performance, which can be helpful to create a baseline or troubleshoot performance problems, either before or after the database is implemented in production. Such tools range from Performance Monitor, a tool very familiar to database professionals, which is covered in Chapter 8, along with some important performance counters, to other Windows tools like Resource Monitor or some utilities like Diskspd or SQLIOSim. Some very popular utilities used in the past, such as sqlio or SQLIOStress, have been replaced. Diskspd or SQLIOSim should be used instead. In this section, I'll take a high-level overview of such tools.

Resource Monitor

Resource Monitor is a Windows utility that can be used to obtain information about the use of hardware such as processor, memory, disk, and network and software such as file handles and modules and resources in real time. For a quick tour on how to see file performance information in real time, let's create an exercise to stress the system doing the same exercise we did in Chapter 8. Create a new database using SQL Server default options and run the following statement:

```
CREATE TABLE t1 (id int IDENTITY(1,1), name char(8000))
```

Add data to stress the transaction log file:

```
BEGIN
INSERT INTO t1 VALUES ('Hello')
INSERT INTO t1 VALUES ('Hello')
INSERT INTO t1 VALUES ('Hello')
```

```
INSERT INTO t1 VALUES ('Hello')
INSERT INTO t1 VALUES ('Hello')
INSERT INTO t1 VALUES ('Hello')
INSERT INTO t1 VALUES ('Hello')
INSERT INTO t1 VALUES ('Hello')
INSERT INTO t1 VALUES ('Hello')
INSERT INTO t1 VALUES ('Hello')
END
GO 30000
```

On Resource Monitor, select Disk and Sort by Write (B/sec), and you will see the effect of the stress test on the database files, both data and transaction log files, as shown in Figure 11-1.

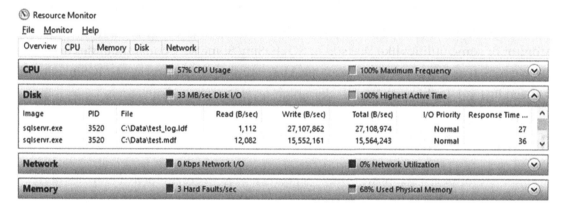

Figure 11-1. *Windows Resource Monitor showing disk information*

Diskspd

The Diskspd or Diskspeed utility is a command-line storage testing tool that replaces sqlio, a popular tool SQL Server professionals have been using for years but is no longer available to download. Diskspd's main focus is performance testing, although accuracy is an important part as well as the tool verifies that the data was correctly read and written. Different from SQLIOSim, which uses a minimal number of parameters and automatically tests all common SQL Server storage access patterns, Diskspd knows nothing about SQL Server storage usage, and it is up to you to use the right parameters to simulate a proper test.

Diskspd can be used on all kinds of storage, such as local disks, LUNs on a SAN, or SMB file shares, and, like SQLIOSim, does not require a SQL Server installation. Diskspd can be downloaded at `https://gallery.technet.microsoft.com/DiskSpd-a-robust-storage-6cd2f223`, and, since it is currently open sourced, its C++ source code is provided as well at `https://github.com/microsoft/diskspd`.

If you have ever used sqlio before, Diskspd should be very simple and straightforward to use as it works in a very similar way. If you are new to any of these utilities, it may take a while to learn how to use it to simulate specific SQL Server I/O patterns.

Diskspd includes its own documentation, which is available with the software download, and in addition includes documentation about guidance on using Diskspd to simulate SQL Server workloads. The document, called "Using DiskSpd in SQL Server environments," contains information about the typical read and write patterns used in SQL Server for different operations like normal activity, checkpoints, lazy writer, bulk insert, backup, restore, DBCC CHECKDB, index rebuilds, read-aheads on data files, or normal activity on log files. For example, the normal activity in SQL Server reads and writes from 8 KB up to 128 KB of data, read-ahead uses up to 512 KB, or a checkpoint can write from 64 KB up to 128 KB. The document also includes information about the number of threads used and if the I/O pattern is random or sequential. You can use this tool to help simulate those SQL Server I/O patterns in Diskspd. Please refer to the document for additional details.

Let's create an exercise opening a command prompt window running as administrator and execute the following:

diskspd -c1024M -d120 -r -w0 -t8 -o8 -b8K -L test.dat

The meaning of the chosen parameters is the following:

-c1024M: Creates a 1,024 MB file

-d120: Duration of the test, in this case 120 seconds

-r: Random I/O

-w0: Percentage of write requests, 0, in this case because it is a read-only workload

-t8: Number of threads

-o8: Number of outstanding I/O requests per thread

-b8K: Block size

-L: Measures latency statistics

test.dat: File to create for test

Optionally, you can use the output parameter to have more control of the outputted data instead of just looking at it in the command prompt window. After the test is completed, information similar to the following will be shown. The first section will show a summary of the parameters used. The second will show a per-processor CPU utilization summary, as shown next:

```
CPU | Usage |  User  | Kernel |  Idle
-------------------------------------------
   0|  21.38%|  14.66%|   6.72%|  78.62%
   1|  22.47%|  15.53%|   6.94%|  77.53%
   2|  19.36%|  14.52%|   4.84%|  80.64%
   3|  23.29%|  17.40%|   5.90%|  76.71%
-------------------------------------------
avg.|  21.63%|  15.53%|   6.10%|  78.37%
```

The following three sections show read I/Os, write I/Os, and total I/Os. Since I requested only reads, write I/Os will show 0, and read I/Os and total I/Os will be the same. A small sample is next:

```
Read IO
thread | bytes     | I/Os | MB/s | I/O per s | AvgLat  | LatStdDev | file
-----------------------------------------------------------------------------
    0 | 16072704 | 1962 | 0.13 | 16.35    | 489.401 | 267.067  | test.dat (1024MB)
    1 | 15753216 | 1923 | 0.13 | 16.02    | 498.270 | 282.754  | test.dat (1024MB)
    2 | 15998976 | 1953 | 0.13 | 16.27    | 491.140 | 266.429  | test.dat (1024MB)
    3 | 15687680 | 1915 | 0.12 | 15.96    | 501.054 | 279.055  | test.dat (1024MB)
    4 | 15982592 | 1951 | 0.13 | 16.26    | 491.862 | 271.641  | test.dat (1024MB)
    5 | 16105472 | 1966 | 0.13 | 16.38    | 488.446 | 271.681  | test.dat (1024MB)
    6 | 15613952 | 1906 | 0.12 | 15.88    | 503.282 | 275.617  | test.dat (1024MB)
    7 | 15769600 | 1925 | 0.13 | 16.04    | 498.274 | 266.536  | test.dat (1024MB)
-----------------------------------------------------------------------------
total:  126984192 | 15501 | 1.01 | 129.17   | 495.157 | 272.671
```

The last section of the report shows latency, as requested by the L parameter, again in this case only reads:

```
%-ile | Read (ms) | Write (ms) | Total (ms)
------------------------------------------------
  min |     0.007 |       N/A  |      0.007
 25th |   313.126 |       N/A  |    313.126
...
  max |  1816.870 |       N/A  |   1816.870
```

Note   Additionally, you could use the CrystalDiskMark utility, which has a graphical user interface but runs Diskspd on the background.

SQLIOSim

Different from Diskspd, SQLIOSim is designed to directly simulate SQL Server I/O patterns and is more focused on checking for correctness and corruption problems. SQLIOSim is used to perform reliability and integrity tests on your storage system, and it does so by simulating SQL Server read, write, checkpoint, backup, sort, and read-ahead activities. You can do some similar testing with Diskspd, but you have to understand the I/O pattern and define the required command-line statements.

SQLIOSim replaces SQLIOStress, and it has been included with SQL Server since version 2008, which you can locate in the Binn folder (e.g., on a default installation at C:\ Program Files\Microsoft SQL Server\MSSQL15.MSSQLSERVER\MSSQL\Binn). It can also be downloaded from https://support.microsoft.com/en-us/kb/231619. This tool complements Diskspd as it provides different tests, so you don't have to decide between one or the other and instead use both if you are testing your storage infrastructure.

Although both Diskspd and SQLIOSim are command-line utilities, SQLIOSim also has a graphical interface that makes it a lot easier to use. By specifying some minimum parameters, the utility will perform all the required tests and may take a considerable amount of time to complete. An example executing SQLIOSim can be seen in Figure 11-2.

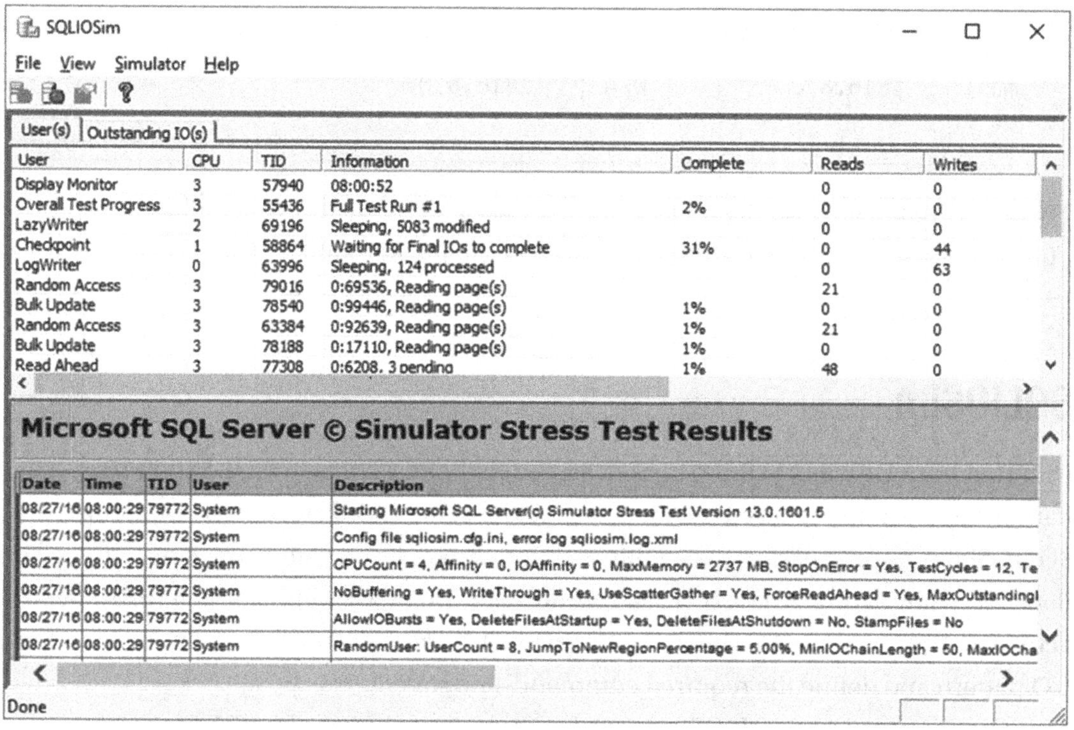

Figure 11-2. SQLIOSim stress test running

SQLIOSim stress test is designed for testing storage before a production implementation, so do not run this test in a live production environment. Running this test on shared storage may impact other storage connected systems or users, even if your volumes or LUNs are not used by anyone else. Communicate with your storage administrator before running such stress test.

DMVs/DMFs

Several DMVs and DMFs can be used to show storage usage and information and are covered in Chapter 8, including the sys.dm_io_virtual_file_stats DMF, the sys.dm_os_volume_stats DMF, the sys.dm_db_index_physical_stats DMV, and the sys.dm_db_index_usage_stats DMV.

The sys.dm_io_virtual_file_stats DMF provides a rich amount of I/O information for each data and log file in a database, including not only I/O activity data but also wait latency information. The sys.dm_os_volume_stats DMF returns information about the volumes in the system, based on the provided database ID and file ID. The sys.dm_db_index_physical_stats DMV allows you to get the fragmentation information of your tables and indexes. The sys.dm_db_index_usage_stats DMV returns information about the operations performed on tables and indexes of a database including the number of seeks, scans, bookmark lookups, and updates by both user queries and system queries. Please refer to that chapter for more details and additional DMVs.

In addition, for tuning purposes, sometimes you would want to know which queries are using the most I/O resources. Those queries can be collected if you have enabled the Query Store, as covered in Chapter 6. In addition, you can use the sys.dm_exec_query_stats DMV to list such queries based on the query statistics available in the plan cache. Also covered in Chapter 8, you could use this DMV to list the most expensive queries based on I/O resources such as logical reads, physical reads, or logical writes. Finally, query I/O information can also be available by using the SET STATISTICS IO statement.

Volume Configuration

Windows allocation unit size and disk partition alignment are two topics that are usually ignored while configuring storage. Although the Windows allocation unit size default when formatting an NTFS volume is 4 KB, Microsoft has long been recommending to use a 64 KB size when formatting an NTFS volume that will be used for SQL Server data files and transaction log files.

Disk partition alignment remains an important consideration, especially for older versions of Windows. Partition misalignment refers to a problem present on Windows 2003 and older in which the very first block of data written to a partition was 63K in size.

But since Windows would instead work with blocks of an even size such as 4K or 64K of data, such disk operations would require spanning two sectors, creating a performance problem.

Preexisting partitions attached to Windows Server 2008 or later may still have this problem as partitions are not automatically aligned when servers are upgraded to Windows Server 2008 and, as a result, must be rebuilt for optimal performance. Even when disk partition alignment is not a problem with newer Windows versions, the correct configuration could be validated as well. To validate the correct partition alignment or fix a partition alignment problem, see the article at `https://support.microsoft.com/en-us/kb/929491`. For more details about disk partition alignment, see the Microsoft white paper "Disk Partition Alignment Best Practices for SQL Server" at `https://technet.microsoft.com/en-us/library/dd758814(v=SQL.100).aspx`.

RAID Levels

As covered earlier in this chapter, SQL Server storage solutions usually implement some flavor of RAID (redundant array of independent disks), so let's use this section to discuss some of these most popular configurations, including RAID levels 0, 1, 5, 6, and 10. RAID is also possible at the software level, but it has limitations and performance penalties compared to using hardware RAID controllers. RAID employs techniques such as mirroring, striping, and parity error detection.

Again, keep in mind that even if you have some enterprise-level storage and you only need to request disk space to your storage administrator, you still need to understand which RAID configuration flavor such volumes may have and maybe even request a configuration according to your needs.

RAID 0

RAID 0, or striping, refers to the process in which data is spread across two or more drives. Striping alone offers no data redundancy so one drive failure means you will lose your data. RAID 0 has no extra storage cost because all the drive capacity is used. Since there is no redundancy, it should not be used for data or transaction log files but may have a use elsewhere, such as for temporary storage for backups before they are copied to a permanent location. A RAID 0 configuration is shown in Figure 11-3.

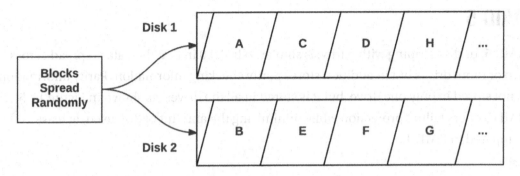

Figure 11-3. *RAID 0*

RAID 1

RAID 1, or mirroring, writes the same data on two or more drives at the same time. Obviously, the cost of this implementation is, at least, 50% of the storage used. RAID 1 can recover from a driver failure as the data is on at least a second copy. In such cases, the failed drive should be replaced as soon as possible so the RAID controller can copy the drive data again, as data will be at risk until the failed drive is completely rebuilt. You can have data loss only if the second drive fails before the failing mirrored one is rebuilt.

A typical use for RAID 1 is to mirror the local operating system drive of a server, which also usually hosts the SQL Server installation software. RAID 1 is shown in Figure 11-4.

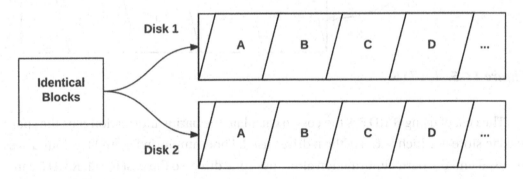

Figure 11-4. *RAID 1*

RAID 5

RAID 5, or disk striping with parity, is similar to RAID 0 in that the data is spread across two or more drives but in addition stores parity checking information. Parity information is not stored in only one drive, but it is stored in all the drives, as shown in Figure 11-5. RAID 5 offers failure protection while minimizing the amount of disk used, at least compared to RAID 1.

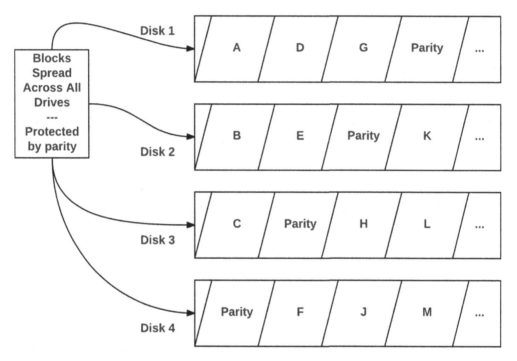

Figure 11-5. *RAID 5*

The cost of using RAID 5 is the cost to calculate the parity information plus the space used to store it, which is 1/n of the n drives used. For example, in Figure 11-5, four drives are used and the parity information alone uses one drive, so the cost is 1/4. RAID 5 can recover from one drive failure, but it cannot recover from two or more drive failures. The minimum number of drives in a RAID 5 configuration is three.

RAID 6

RAID 6, or disk striping with double parity, is similar to RAID 5, but it adds another level of parity information, basically extending RAID 5 by adding another parity block. If RAID 5 protects against a single disk failure, RAID 6 can tolerate losing two disks.

The cost of using RAID 6 is the cost to calculate the parity information plus the space used to store it, which is 2/n of n drives used. For example, in Figure 11-6, five drives are used while the parity uses two drives, so the cost is 2/5.

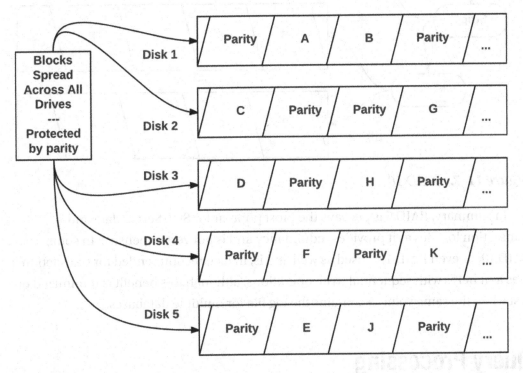

Figure 11-6. *RAID 6*

RAID 10

RAID 10, or RAID 0+1 or mirroring and striping, is a combination of the basic RAID levels RAID 0 and RAID 1, so this configuration uses mirroring and striping and no parity information. Similar to RAID 1, the cost of this implementation is 50% of the storage used. In RAID 10, the data is first mirrored and then striped, as shown in Figure 11-7. A variation of this configuration is RAID 01 or RAID 0+1 in which the data is first striped and then mirrored.

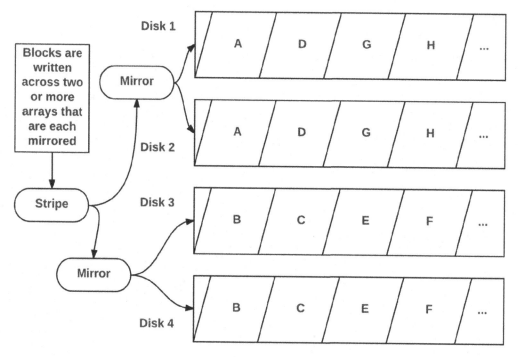

Figure 11-7. *RAID 10*

In summary, RAID 5 is perhaps the most popular for SQL Server data and transaction log files as it provides redundancy and is not very expensive. In some cases, RAID 10, or even RAID 1, is used as well and is, in fact, recommended for transaction log files as it helps with sequential write operations, although this benefit is minimized or lost when the same volume contains the log file for multiple databases.

Query Processing

Query optimization and processing are a critical part of the storage usage. As we have noted before in this book, a decent query optimizer should create a plan that filters out data as early as possible to improve the query performance. If this filtering can be done at the storage engine level, the query would be very efficient as no additional processing is required for rows that are not needed. Unfortunately, for several reasons, sometimes a query has to scan an entire table and process all the rows throughout multiple query operations, just to filter out the required rows at the end, having a very expensive process. A typical example was shown in Chapter 9 where the query processor was able to create a very efficient plan for the following query:

```
SELECT * FROM Sales.SalesOrderDetail
WHERE ProductID = 898
```

But as soon as the filter predicate changed to WHERE ABS(ProductID) = 898, the query processor was no longer able to understand it, requiring instead a very expensive table scan. Having said that, typically having the right indexes is one of the best ways to help with query performance but not the only one. As you saw with this example, even with a perfect index, due to a query processor limitation, SQL Server was not able to use it. This is where additional query tuning and optimization may help to further improve the performance of your databases.

It is worth reminding here that a query optimizer limitation in no way means you may get incorrect data as it is more related to how efficiently you get the data.

Finally, recent database research is focusing on the impact of flash-based storage on database and query processing algorithms. In "Query Processing Techniques for Solid State Drives," which you can find at http://nms.csail.mit.edu/~stavros/pubs/SSD_sigmod09.pdf, Goetz Graefe et. al show how using new data structures and algorithms can take advantage of flash storage to improve the database performance as current relational database engines were developed based on traditional disk usage. In addition, in "Do Query Optimizers Need to be SSD-aware?," which you can read at www.adms-conf.org/p44-PELLEY.pdf, Steven Pelley et. al analyze if the cost estimation model of query optimizers should be updated to account for the increased speed on random I/O operations on solid-state disks.

Summary

This chapter covered storage from SQL Server's point of view and showed how storage usage can be optimized at several levels, going from the storage hardware itself all the way into database design and configuration and query tuning and optimization. Storage trends were covered as well, including how flash-based storage is becoming the de facto enterprise standard for primary storage as its cost continues to decline.

Finally, focus has been given to minimizing the storage usage by database requests by using techniques shown in several chapters of the book, for example, creating the right indexes, as covered in Chapter 9; by properly configuring SQL Server and tempdb, as covered in Chapters 3 and 4; or by taking benefit of new in-memory technologies such as In-Memory OLTP or columnstore indexes, explained in Chapter 7.

Index

© Benjamin Nevarez 2021
B. Nevarez, *High Performance SQL Server*, https://doi.org/10.1007/978-1-4842-6491-1

W, X, Y, Z

Printed in the United States
By Bookmasters